Entrepreneurship

David A. Kirby

Entrepreneurship

David A. Kirby
Professor of Entrepreneurship, University of Surrey, England
Adjunct Professor of Entrepreneurship, University of South
Australia

Mc Graw Hill Education

London   Boston   Burr Ridge, IL   Dubuque, IA   Madison, WI   New York
San Francisco   St Louis   Bangkok   Bogotá   Caracas   Kuala Lumpur   Lisbon
Madrid   Mexico City   Milan   Montreal   New Delhi   Santiago   Seoul

Entrepreneurship
David A. Kirby
ISBN 0077098587

 **Education**

Published by McGraw-Hill Education
Shoppenhangers Road
Maidenhead
Berkshire SL6 2QL
Telephone: 44 (0) 1628 502 500
Fax: 44 (0) 1628 770 224
Website: www.mcgraw-hill.co.uk

British Library Cataloguing in Publication Data
A catalogue record for this book is available from the British Library

Library of Congress Cataloguing in Publication Data
The Library of Congress data for this book has been applied for from the Library of Congress

Acquisitions Editor: Tracey Alcock
Associate Development Editor: Catriona Watson
Editorial Assistant: Nicola Wimpory
Senior Marketing Manager: Petra Skytte
Production Editor: Eleanor Hayes
New Media Developer: Doug Greenwood

Text design by Claire Brodmann
Cover design by Senate Design
Printed and bound by Bell & Bain Ltd., Glasgow

The **McGraw·Hill** Companies

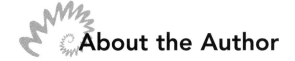# About the Author

David A. Kirby is Professor of Entrepreneurship at the University of Surrey in England and Adjunct Professor of Entrepreneurship at the University of South Australia. He has worked in six universities in the United Kingdom as well as overseas. He is a former Senior Vice President and Director of the International Council for Small Business and, in recognition of his training and consultancy work with small and medium-sized enterprises, has been elected to a Fellowship of the Institute of Business Advisers. In 1986, his graduate entrepreneurship programme, Graduate Enterprise in Wales, received the recognition of the Royal Society of Arts under its Education for Capability Programme, being recognized for 'the way it has developed the personal competence and confidence of its participants and for the way such a high proportion of those participants have turned their academic knowledge and skills into successful products and businesses of their own'. Subsequently, he was elected to a Fellowship of the Society for his contribution to that programme. He is currently a member of a working party of the UK Council for Excellence in Leadership and Management, which is examining the role of business schools in the creation of leaders and managers for the twenty-first century, and, at the University of Surrey, he has responsibility for entrepreneurship activity, under the Higher Education Innovation Fund. He has published 15 books and research monographs, and more than 115 articles in learned journals.

# Dedication

This text is dedicated to Sheila, a natural entrepreneur, Kristoffer, a nascent entrepreneur, and my late parents, who were responsible for any entrepreneurial tendencies I may display.

Brief Table of Contents

Section 1   Entrepreneurship and the Environment   7

Section 2   Entrepreneurship and the Person   105

Section 3   Entrepreneurship and the Organization   207

Detailed Table of Contents

Section 1 Entrepreneurship and the Environment 7

List of Figures

List of Tables

 # Preface

In the Introduction to his book *The Portable MBA in Entrepreneurship*, Bygrave (1994: ix) makes the following point:

> I am in INSEAD in France on sabbatical leave from Babson College. As I write this introduction, it is a glorious spring day. The nearby Fontainebleau forest is teeming with life. Everything is budding and sprouting. Fresh green shoots are everywhere. Nature is busily renewing herself, unaware that the economy lies deep in winter, frozen in an economic recession. Unemployment, already too high, is on the rise. In Europe entrepreneurial springtime, with its green shoots of economic growth, seems a long way off. What a contrast with the United States. . . . Entrepreneurship is what America does best. No other advanced industrial nation comes close.

Within six years, all this had changed. Writing in the journal *Fortune* on 19 June 2000, for example, Justin Fox suggested: 'It is a new era in the Old World. Entrepreneurs have become stars, equity investing has become celebrated (if not universally practiced).'

It is against this background of change that this text has been written. While it does not seek to explain the creation (or rather re-creation) of an entrepreneurship culture in the economies of Europe and elsewhere, it does attempt to explore the reasons for the current emphasis on entrepreneurship, and how it can be promoted and developed.

The starting premise is that the world, as Peters (1987) and others have recognized, is in an era of unprecedented change, a 'world turned upside down'. This is not new. Change has always been a part of social and economic evolution. Previously, however, change was, as Handy (1990: 5) has observed:

> . . . more of the same only better. That was incremental change and to be welcomed. Today, we know that in many areas of life we cannot guarantee more of the same, be it work or money, peace or freedom, health or happiness, and cannot even predict with confidence what will be happening in our own lives.

Under such circumstances—Drucker's (1989) 'new realities'—society needs not only to accommodate change but to be capable of anticipating and, more importantly perhaps, initiating it.

At the same time, there is a somewhat paradoxical set of trends occurring within the world economy. While globalization and the interdependence of markets have been recognized increasingly in recent years, it has also become apparent that we can no longer rely upon 'they'. Whether 'they' are the wealthy nations of the world, the state or large firms, we cannot rely on them to provide us with our wealth, our jobs, our homes, our healthcare, etc. Increasingly, we are having to rely on ourselves. So, we are having to empower individuals, communities, organizations and even nations in a way that, previously, has been unrecognized. We are all interdependent, but increasingly we are being required to take ownership of our own destinies—for the benefit of ourselves, our families, our colleagues, our fellow countrymen and world citizenry. Within individuals, communities, organizations and societies we need to develop a greater sense of enterprise and self-help. We need people who see opportunity, create and build, initiate and achieve. As a consequence it is possible to agree with Kanter (1984: 354) that:

> Today, more than ever, because of profound transformations in the economic and social environment . . . it should be a national priority to release and support the skills of men and women who can envision and push innovations.

These are the characteristics of the entrepreneur. While there is no uniform, single definition of the term entrepreneurship, and, in all probability, there is no such thing as 'The Entrepreneur', it is held here that:

> Entrepreneurship is the ability to create and build something from practically nothing. It is initiating, doing, achieving and building . . . rather than just watching, analysing and describing. . . . It is the knack of sensing an opportunity where others see chaos, contradiction and confusion . . . (Timmons, 1989: 1)

In the UK this need for people who can envision opportunities and make them happen has been recognized by the National Committee of Inquiry into Higher Education (1997: 201), which urged higher education institutions to '. . . consider the scope for encouraging entrepreneurship through innovative approaches to programme design'.

This text is a response to that challenge. I trust that in your quest to become an entrepreneur you will find it not only interesting and stimulating, but also helpful.

Professor David A. Kirby

 ## Reading

Bygrave, W.D. (1994) *The Portable MBA in Entrepreneurship*. Chichester: John Wiley.

Drucker, P.F. (1989) *The New Realities*. London: Heinemann.

Handy, C. (1990) The Age of Unreason. Random Century.

Kanter, R. (1984) *The Change Masters: Corporate Entrepreneurs at Work*. London: Unwin.

National Committee of Inquiry into Higher Education (1997) *Higher Education in the Learning Society: Report of the National Committee*. London: HMSO.

Peters, T. (1987) *Thriving on Chaos: Handbook for a Management Revolution*. London: Pan Books.

Timmons, J.A. (1989) *The Entrepreneurial Mind*, Andover MA: Brick House Publishing.

Acknowledgements

The production of any text is inevitably the work of a number of people and I would like to acknowledge the support I have received in producing this work. In particular, I would like to thank my publishers, McGraw-Hill, for giving me this opportunity, and especially Melissa, Tracey and Catriona for ensuring that the work reached fruition. Though embedded in theory, much of the text is based on personal experience and I would like to thank all those with whom I have worked over the years, especially—though not exclusively by any means—my 'students'. I have learned a lot from them. In particular, I would like to thank, also, the late Lord Morris of Castlemorris who, as Principal of the University of Wales College, Lampeter, created the enterprising environment in which I could experiment, innovate and make mistakes without fear of reprisal. My colleagues and staff at Middlesex University Business School during the period 1996–99 cannot go without mention; I obtained considerable insights from working with them, particularly into intrapreneurship and change management. I wish continued success to those who remain. *Nil desperandum.* I wish to thank Dr Roet and Class Publishing for allowing me to reproduce Dr Roet's Cartoon from his book *Positive Action for Health and Wellbeing* (2001). Picture A on p. 154 is 'My Wife and My Mother-in-Law' by W. E. Hill, published in *Puck* Magazine, 1915. Picture B on p. 154 is unattributed.

Last, but not least, I would like to acknowledge the support of Sheila and my family: Alison, David and Kristoffer. When I have not been at my desk at the university, inevitably I have been working on this text at my desk in the study. To ensure completion, it is they who have had to make a sacrifice. For me it has been fun. I would like to thank them, therefore, for their unending support, sacrifice and good humour. I trust they will feel that the end product has been worth it.

My thanks go, also, to the following reviewers for their comments at various stages in the text's development: Dr Alistair Anderson, University of Aberdeen; Professor Graham Beaver, University of Nottingham; Alan Benson, University of Hull; Colin Bottomley, University of Strathclyde; Jan Brown, Liverpool Hope; Dr David Johnson, University of Durham; Dr Jonathan Levie, University of Strathclyde; Phil Morgan, Oxford Brookes University; Frank Martin, University of Stirling; Dean Patton, De Montfort University; Dr Peter Rosa, University of Stirling; Gilly Wiscarson, Oxford Brookes University.

We have endeavoured to clear all permissions for material reproduced in this book. However, if you are aware of any outstanding permissions, please do not hesitate to contact us.

Guided Tour

Learning Outcomes

The Learning Outcomes identify the key concepts you should understand and be able to apply when you have completed the chapter.

Introduction

Each chapter opens with an Introduction, which sets the scene for the reader and introduces them to the issues that will be addressed in the chapter.

Pause for Thought

This feature aims to get the reader to think about the topic under consideration and, in particular, relate it to his/her own experiences before moving on through the chapter.

Case Examples

Case Examples are integrated throughout each chapter to illustrate the main themes of the chapter, allowing the reader to visualize entrepreneurship in practice.

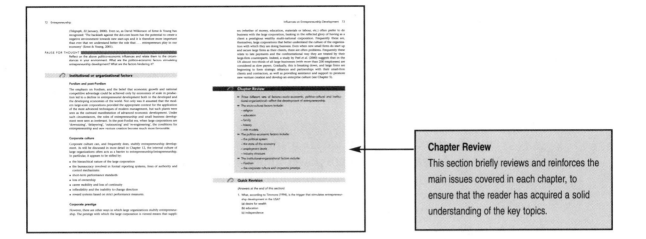

Chapter Review

This section briefly reviews and reinforces the main issues covered in each chapter, to ensure that the reader has acquired a solid understanding of the key topics.

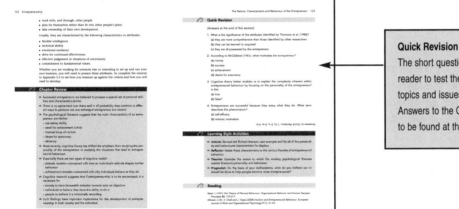

Quick Revision

The short questions in this section enable the reader to test their understanding of the main topics and issues discussed in the chapter. Answers to the Quick Revision questions are to be found at the end of the section.

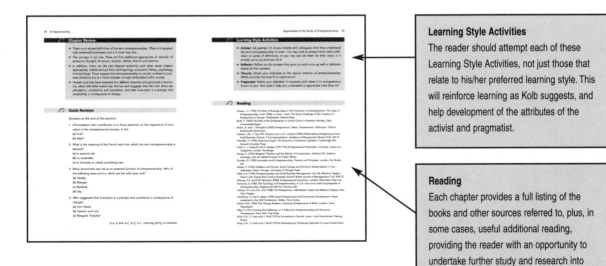

Learning Style Activities

The reader should attempt each of these Learning Style Activities, not just those that relate to his/her preferred learning style. This will reinforce learning as Kolb suggests, and help development of the attributes of the activist and pragmatist.

Reading

Each chapter provides a full listing of the books and other sources referred to, plus, in some cases, useful additional reading, providing the reader with an opportunity to undertake further study and research into topics of interest.

 # The Living Spirit

Our deepest fear is not that we are inadequate.
Our deepest fear is that we are powerful beyond measure.
It is our light, not our darkness, that most frightens us.
We ask ourselves,
Who am I to be brilliant, gorgeous, talented and fabulous?
Actually who are you not to be?
You are a child of God
Your playing small doesn't save the world.
There's nothing enlightened about shrinking the world so far that
    other people won't feel insecure around you.
We were born to make manifest the glory of God that is within us.
It's not just in some of us, it's in everyone.
And as we let our light shine, we unconsciously give other people
    permission to do the same.
As we are liberated from our own fear,
Our presence automatically liberates others.

Nelson Mandela
Inaugural Presidential Address, 1994

# Introduction

For some time, very considerable attention has been paid to the role of higher education in the creation of graduate entrepreneurs (Hills, 1986; Scott and Twomey, 1988). As Brockhaus (2001: xiv) recognizes, one of the first courses was offered at Harvard Business School in 1947 and Drucker taught another at New York University in 1953. Since then, numerous courses have been developed not just in the USA but globally (Vesper and Gartner, 1998). Within the field, however, there has remained considerable debate over whether universities in general and business schools in particular can contribute to this objective. To some, entrepreneurs are born not bred, while to others: '. . . to teach individuals to become not only more enterprising but businessmen as well . . . is an undertaking that in both time and scope is beyond the capabilities of an academic business school . . .' (Johannisson, 1991: 79).

Interestingly, research on entrepreneurship undertaken by the UK Small Business Research Trust (1988) indicates that only 13 per cent of the surveyed sample believed that entrepreneurial skills could not be acquired by a process of learning. Hence, the basis of this text is that universities and business schools can develop entrepreneurs but that, as Chia (1996: 410–11) has suggested, 'a radical change in intellectual and educational priorities is needed'.

Indeed, it would seem that, all too frequently, 'education in the sense of a formal academic training dulls the cutting edge of commerce' (Bartlett, 1988: 26). Even in the United States of America, that hotbed of entrepreneurship, courses designed to introduce students to the principles of business and management have appeared, according to Solomon (1989), to 'teach students how to become proficient employees instead of successful business persons'.

Since these statements were made, numerous entrepreneurship programmes have been introduced in many parts of the world (Interman, 1991; Vesper and Gartner, 1998). Often they do little, however, to develop the entrepreneurial tendencies that are being sought. The reason for this, it is contested, is that such programmes educate 'about' entrepreneurship and enterprise rather than 'for' entrepreneurship. They fail to develop in their students the skills, attributes and behaviours of the successful entrepreneur. For example, the comprehensive *Interman Directory* lists three types of entrepreneurship programme:

- entrepreneurship orientation and awareness programmes which focus on general information *about* entrepreneurship and encourage participants to think in terms of entrepreneurship as a career

- new enterprise creation programmes designed to develop competences which lead to self-employment, economic self-sufficiency or employment generation

- programmes which focus on small business survival and growth.

It is not possible in this Introduction to analyse each of the 205 programmes listed in the Interman report, but clearly it would seem from the descriptors that the emphasis in these programmes is on learning *about* entrepreneurship and how to manage a small business, rather than acquiring the particular set of attributes, skills and behaviours that can be equated with entrepreneurship.

In his highly acclaimed *Portable MBA in Entrepreneurship*, Bygrave (1994) purports to provide the reader with an insight into: 'how top business schools are preparing students to meet the challenges of the entrepreneurial-driven business climate of the 1990s and beyond'.

In 14 chapters and 450 pages, the student learns about the entrepreneurial process, opportunity recognition, entry strategies, market opportunities and marketing, creating a successful business plan, financial projections, venture capital, debt and other forms of financing, external assistance for start-ups and small businesses, legal and tax issues, intellectual property, franchising, harvesting and entrepreneurship economics. If this is how the top business schools are preparing their students 'to meet the challenges of the entrepreneurial business climate of the 1990s and beyond', it seems hardly surprising that, as Burns and Dewhurst (1989: 4) have observed, many students 'come to business school harbouring a deep-seated desire to set up their own business. Sadly few do so.'

Clearly, it is important that business entrepreneurs understand the principles and processes involved in managing a commercial organization successfully. But knowing about 'debt and other forms of financing', for example, or even being able to 'create a successful business plan' and make 'financial projections' will not, *per se*, equip the student 'to meet the challenges of the entrepreneurial business climate of the 1990s and beyond'. This is only one, relatively minor, element in the equation.

The successful entrepreneur has a set of personal skills, attributes and behaviours that go beyond the purely commercial. It is these attributes, this way of thinking and behaving, that needs to be developed in our students if their entrepreneurial capabilities are to be enhanced. This means that both the content of courses and the process of learning need to change. As Rae (1997: 199), has suggested, 'the skills traditionally taught in business schools are essential but not sufficient to make a successful entrepreneur'.

While students still need to develop their business skills and understanding, more attention needs to be paid to the development of their entrepreneurial skills, attributes and behaviours. Thus, the challenge is to develop a system of learning (and assessment) that complements the traditional, and develops in its students the skills, attributes and behaviours characteristic of the enterprising or entrepreneurial individual (Kirby, 1992). If universities in general, and business schools in particular, are to succeed in developing entrepreneurs, this is the challenge facing them. How can the education system be changed so that, rather than constraining, it releases and develops the enterprising tendencies of our young people?

Developing entrepreneurs in the classroom is about developing the enterprising environments and approaches to learning in which entrepreneurial aptitudes and capabilities can flourish, alongside business acumen and understanding. As Chia (1996: 426) argues:

❝❞ The unique contribution university business schools can make to the business community is not through the vocationalising of business/management education programmes. Rather it is through adopting a deliberate educational strategy which privileges the 'weakening' of thought processes so as to encourage and stimulate the entrepreneurial imagination.

At the same time, it must not be assumed that entrepreneurship education is solely about encouraging 'students' to set up and run their own small businesses. While there is some evidence that experience in a small firm can help the development of more enterprising individuals (Kirby and Mullen, 1989), entrepreneurship should not be equated solely with new venture creation, small business management, owner-management and self-employment as so often it is (Gibb, 1996). This is to over-simplify the concept. The term is much broader than these concepts would suggest. Not all owner-managers are entrepreneurs, nor are all small businesses entrepreneurial, and not all large businesses are un-enterprising. Increasingly, entrepreneurs are to be found in large organizations, as well as in the public and voluntary sectors (Kirby *et al.*, 1991). As Kao (1997: 237–8) has recognized, the concept is about 'making a change' and 'even those who relate entrepreneurship with business undertakings have noted that only those who innovate and develop new combinations are entrepreneurs'.

Thus, this text is not about small or new businesses *per se*. Rather it is about developing more entrepreneurial economies, people and organizations. Hence it is divided into three sections: Entrepreneurship and the Environment, Entrepreneurship and the Person, and Entrepreneurship and the Organization. In Section 1, attention is focused on the various theories of entrepreneurship (Chapter 1), and the role entrepreneurs play in the economy and society (Chapter 2). This is followed by a consideration of the factors influencing entrepreneurship development (Chapter 3) and the support needed, somewhat paradoxically, to create an enterprise culture (Chapter 4). The focus shifts, in Section 2, from the macro consideration of the environment to the micro consideration of the person. Initially, attention is focused on the characteristics and behaviour of the entrepreneur (Chapter 5) before going on to consider two of the fundamental entrepreneurial characteristics—creativity and the ability to innovate (Chapter 6), and leadership and the ability to motivate (Chapter 7)—and how these might be developed. The section concludes with a review of the characteristics of the entrepreneurial manager (Chapter 8), and a consideration of his/her ability to create and manage teams, and resolve conflict. This leads, in Section 3, to an examination of the entrepreneurship and the organization, which starts with a consideration of the nature of the entrepreneurial new venture (Chapter 9) before going on to review the business plan, and its role in determining the feasibility of a venture and in raising finance (Chapter 10). While few new businesses grow, the issue of growth is considered in Chapter 11, where attention is focused on the problem of retaining entrepreneurship. Finally, in Chapter 12, the focus is on developing (or re-developing) entrepreneurship in large organizations.

Throughout, the emphasis is on applying theory to practice. The reader will be asked to reflect on what has been learned and to relate it to the 'real world'. The term 'entrepreneur' is derived from the French verb *entreprendre* (to undertake). The entrepreneur is, then, an 'undertaker'—someone who undertakes to make things happen, and does. In the process of developing entrepreneurial tendencies, therefore, it is important to shift the emphasis away from passive to active learning. If the dependency culture is to be broken, students need to take ownership of their own learning and to reduce their dependency on their tutor. Clearly this is not easy to do in a textbook. However, the emphasis throughout is on reading and doing. In part this is intended to reinforce the learning, in part to encourage students to question, to develop an enquiring mind and to become more action-oriented.

According to Kolb (1984), there is a learning cycle that starts with active experimentation and leads through concrete experience and reflective observation to abstract conceptualization (see Fig. A). Traditionally, education systems around the world have concentrated on reflection and theory, as will be considered in Chapter 6, and perhaps it is for this reason that so many entrepreneurs have not succeeded academically. Entrepreneurs, as will be shown, are much more concerned with concrete experience and testing in new situations.

Although all stages of the cycle are necessary for learning, Honey and Mumford (1986) have suggested that individuals tend to be more comfortable with some stages of the loop than with others. This has led them to suggest that there are preferred learning styles based on Kolb's learning cycle. These are termed the 'activist learning styles' and comprise the reflector, the theorist and the pragmatist. According to Cameron (1999: 55–6) activists are 'open minded and love new experiences, get bored easily, are highly sociable, love group decisions and bring welcome energy to a task', while pragmatists 'love new ideas provided you can put them into practice. You will hate open-ended discussion and love problems and the search for a better way of doing things.'

As will be shown, these are precisely the sort of attributes possessed by entrepreneurs and the ways that entrepreneurs learn (Gibb, 1996). Hence, the text attempts to move the reader through Kolb's learning cycle in order to reinforce

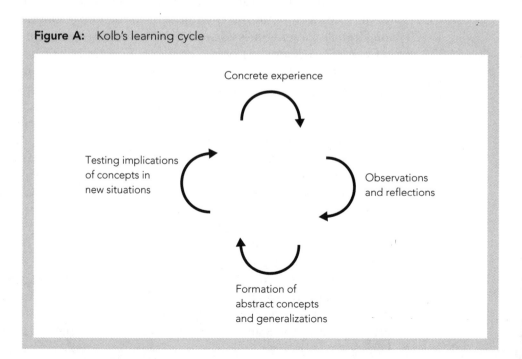

Figure A: Kolb's learning cycle

Concrete experience

Testing implications of concepts in new situations

Observations and reflections

Formation of abstract concepts and generalizations

the learning process. However, irrespective of whether these are the reader's preferred learning styles, efforts are made throughout the text to encourage 'learning by doing' in the belief that not only will the reader become a more effective learner, by developing some of the strengths of his/her non-preferred styles, but he/she will acquire some of the attributes, values and behaviour patterns of the activist and pragmatist.

At the end of each chapter, therefore, there are a series of Learning Style Activities. The reader should attempt each of these, not just those that relate to his/her preferred learning style. This will reinforce the learning as Kolb suggests, and assist development of the attributes of the activist and pragmatist. Throughout each chapter, also, the reader is encouraged to Pause for Thought—to think about the topic under consideration and, in particular, relate it to his/her own experiences before moving on. This is very important and clearly an integral link in Kolb's learning cycle. However, it is also important since not only does it help the reader relate the learning to concrete experience, it encourages self-discovery and, hopefully, self-confidence and self-assurance, coupled with the realization that, quite frequently, the answers are within us.

If you wish to determine your preferred learning style, you can do so by completing Honey and Mumford's Learning Styles Questionnaire at **www.psi-press.co.uk/LSS-I/LSS_Admin.htm**. However, you can get a rough idea now by considering which of the following replies is most characteristic of your own response to a new learning situation.

1. I'm game, let's get started. (**Activist**)

2. I need to think about it first. (**Reflector**)

3. Hm, what are the basic assumptions? (**Theorist**)

4. What's the purpose of it? (**Pragmatist**)

Reading

Bartlett, A.F. (1988) *Profile of the Entrepreneur or Machiavellian Management*. Leatherhead: Ashford Press.

Brockhaus, R.H. (2001) Foreword, in Brockhaus, R.H., G.E. Hills, H. Klandt and H.P. Welsch (eds) *Entrepreneurship Education: A Global View*. Aldershot, Hants: Ashgate Publishing.

Burns, P. and J. Dewhurst (1989) *Small Business and Entrepreneurship*. Basingstoke: Macmillan.

Bygrave, W.D. (1994) *The Portable MBA in Entrepreneurship*. Chichester: John Wiley.

Cameron, S. (1999) *The Business Student's Handbook: Developing Transferable Skills*. London: Pitman.

Chia, R. (1996) Teaching Paradigm Shifting in Management Education: University Business Schools and the Entrepreneurial Imagination. *Journal of Management Studies* **33** (4), 409–28.

Gibb, A.A. (1996) Entrepreneurship and Small Business Management: Can We Afford to Neglect Them in the Twenty-First Century Business School? *British Journal of Management* **7** (4), 309–22.

Hills, G.E. (1986) Entrepreneurship Behavioural Intentions and Student Independence, Characteristics and Experience, in Ronstadt, R. *et al.* (eds) *Frontiers of Entrepreneurship Research: Proceedings of the Sixth Annual Babson College Entrepreneurship Research Conference*. Babson College, Babson Park MA, 173–6.

Honey, P. and A. Mumford (1986) *The Manual of Learning Styles*. Peter Honey.

Interman (1991) *Profiles of Entrepreneurship Development Programmes*. Geneva: International Labour Office.

Johannisson, B. (1991) University Training for Entrepreneurship: Swedish Approaches. *Entrepreneurship and Regional Development* **3** (1), 67–82.

Kao, R.W. (1997) *An Entrepreneurial Approach to Corporate Management*, London: Prentice Hall.

Kirby, D.A. (1992) Developing Graduate Entrepreneurs: The UK Graduate Enterprise Programme. *Entrepreneurship, Innovation and Change* **1** (2), 165–75.

Kirby, D.A. and D. Mullen (1989) Developing Enterprising Undergraduates. *Journal of European Industrial Training* **14** (2), 27–32.

Kirby, D.A., P. Livett and J. Rindl (1991) *Innovations in Service*. Luton: Local Government Training Board.

Kolb, D.A. (1984) *Experiential Learning*. Englewood-Cliffs NJ: Prentice Hall.

Rae, D.M. (1997) Teaching Entrepreneurship in Asia: Impact of a Pedagogical Innovation. *Entrepreneurship, Innovation and Change* **6** (3), 193–227.

Scott, M.G. and D.F. Twomey (1988) The Long-term Supply of Entrepreneurs: Students' Career Aspirations in Relation to Entrepreneurship. *Journal of Small Business Management* **26** (4), 5–13.

Small Business Research Trust (1988) *Entrepreneurship*. Milton Keynes: Open University.

Solomon, G. (1989) Youth: Tomorrow's Entrepreneurs. *ICSB Bulletin* **xxvi** (5), 1–2.

Vesper, K. and W. Gartner (1998) *University Entrepreneurship Programmes Worldwide*. Los Angeles: University of Southern California.

Section 1

Entrepreneurship and the Environment

Chapter 1

Approaches to the Study of Entrepreneurship

Learning Outcomes

On completion of this chapter, the reader will:

- appreciate the complexity of the concept of entrepreneurship
- recognize the different schools of entrepreneurial thought
- be aware of the different approaches to entrepreneurship in the social sciences
- understand that entrepreneurship is not confined either to business or to small and medium-sized enterprises
- have begun to formulate a definition of his/her own.

Introduction

In recent years, there has been considerable and growing interest in entrepreneurs and entrepreneurship. According to Alvarez (1996: 192): 'entrepreneurship fervour in the 1980s became a worldwide movement, spreading across countries regardless of level of development or even of their basic mentality or value orientation towards business activities'. There are several reasons for this, which will be examined later (in Chapter 2). For the present, it needs to be recognized that while there is this contemporary interest in the topic, it is not new. Since the middle of the eighteenth century at least, scholars have deliberated on it, and its role in economy and society. Hence the purpose of this chapter is to consider what entrepreneurship is and to explore the various theories that have been developed out of the different approaches to the subject. This should provide not only an insight into the topic, but will also set the scene for subsequent analysis.

✺ Defining the term 'entrepreneurship'

Despite its apparent importance, there is no agreed definition of either what constitutes an entrepreneur or entrepreneurship. Indeed, according to Chell *et al.* (1991: 1), 'the problem of identification of an entrepreneur has been confounded by the fact that there is still no standard, universally accepted definition of entrepreneurship'. Often the term entrepreneurship is equated with new venture creation and small business management (Gibb, 1996), and the concepts of owner-management and self-employment. While people like Bill Gates or Richard Branson (both founders of new businesses) are clearly entrepreneurs, the term is much broader than these concepts would suggest. Not all owner-managers can be regarded as entrepreneurs, nor are all small businesses entrepreneurial. Carland *et al.* (1984: 358) have recognized this point and suggest that there is a clear distinction between the entrepreneur and the entrepreneurial venture, and the small business owner and the small business venture. They suggest that:

❝❞ An entrepreneur is an individual who establishes and manages a business for the principal purposes of profit and growth. The entrepreneur is characterised principally by innovative behaviour and will employ strategic management practices in the business.

An entrepreneurial venture is one that engages in at least one of Schumpeter's four categories of behaviour: that is, the principal goals of an entrepreneurial venture are profitability and growth and the business is characterised by innovative strategic practices.

In contrast, they propose that:

❝❞ A small business owner is an individual who establishes and manages a business for the principal purpose of furthering personal goals. The business must be a primary source of income and will consume the majority of one's time and resources. The owner perceives the business as an extension of his or her personality, intricately bound with family needs and desires.

A small business venture is any business that is independently owned and operated, not dominant in its field, and does not engage in any new marketing or innovative practices.

While it is possible to agree with them that there is this distinction between entrepreneurship and small business ownership and management, it must be recognized also that entrepreneurship is not confined solely to new ventures or that entrepreneurs only work for themselves in their own businesses. Many large organizations are entrepreneurial, as Carland *et al.* imply but do not articulate, and many entrepreneurs are to be found, increasingly, in such organizations. Frequently they are employed in the private sector but, given the pervasiveness of the concept, may be found in the public and not for profit sectors too (Kirby *et al.*, 1991a; 1991b). More will be said about this in Chapter 2; suffice it now to point out that these realizations have led to the view that entrepreneurship is not about the act of founding or owning a (usually small) business, but about a pattern of behaviour or a set of behavioural characteristics. For example, Harwood (1982: 98) has suggested that an entrepreneur is someone who 'takes initiative, assumes considerable autonomy in the organisation and management of resources, shares in the asset risk, shares in an uncertain monetary profit, and innovates in more than a marginal way'. In contrast, Meredith *et al.* (1982: 3) see entrepreneurs as 'people who have the ability to see and evaluate business opportunities; to gather the necessary resources to take advantage of them; and to initiate appropriate action to ensure success'.

Certainly entrepreneurs take initiative, assume autonomy and innovate. In the process they inevitably take risks. Doing anything that is new or different involves uncertainty or risk. However, they also have the ability to see and assess opportunities and, importantly, initiate the appropriate actions to ensure success. Indeed, it is probably this last factor that distinguishes them from the inventor. They make things happen.

Thus it is possible to agree with Timmons (1989: 1), as mentioned in the Preface, that entrepreneurship is:

> . . . the ability to create and build something from practically nothing. It is initiating, doing, achieving, and building an enterprise or organisation, rather than just watching, analysing or describing one. It is the knack for sensing an opportunity where others see chaos, contradiction and confusion . . .

However, this is only one of many such behavioural definitions. For example, Wickham (1998: 34) proposes an equally appealing definition, suggesting that entrepreneurship is about: 'creating and managing vision and communicating that vision to other people. It is about demonstrating leadership, motivating people and being effective in getting people to accept change.'

As will be considered later (in Chapter 7), this is certainly something that entrepreneurs tend to do, but they also have the ability to make sense out of chaos and to see opportunity. Thus, there is no precise, agreed definition, though it would appear that it is possible to identify entrepreneurs in society. Like the Heffalump in the Winnie the Pooh stories, however, it seems that:

> He has been hunted by many individuals using various trapping devices, but no one so far has succeeded in capturing him. All who claim to have caught sight of him report that he is enormous, but disagree on his particulars.
>
> *(Quoted in Kilby, 1971)*

This is not at all surprising if the argument of Lessem (1986) is accepted. Lessem suggests that there is, in fact, no such thing as an entrepreneur—no single individual who displays, in equal degree, the full range of entrepreneurial attributes. Rather, he contends, there are different types of entrepreneur, each with a different personality type and set of attributes and behaviours. More attention will be paid to Lessem's work in Chapter 5, but for the present attention is focused on the various hunters and their approaches—to the theories of entrepreneurship and its role in economy and society.

PAUSE FOR THOUGHT

Consider the above definitions. What are their strengths and weaknesses? What would be your definition of 'entrepreneurship'?

Economic contributions

Economists have identified and debated the role of the entrepreneur for centuries, and several schools of thought have emerged. Two approaches can be identified: that of the early, or classical, economists and that of the neo-classical economists.

Classical economics

This refers to the economic contribution made before the latter part of the nineteenth century. Often it is referred to as 'political economy' rather than straight economics. Several approaches can be identified, and these can be categorized according to country of origin.

The American School

This emerged through the work of Amasa Walker (1799–1875), who saw the role of the entrepreneur as a creator of wealth. Subsequently his son, Francis A. Walker (1840–97), suggested that successful entrepreneurs have foresight, a facility for organization, and administration, energy and leadership qualities. He identified four types of entrepreneur:

1. 'the rare, gifted person'—has foresight, is firm and resolute and is able to motivate and lead others

2. 'those with high-ordered talent'—have a natural mastery, are wise, prompt and resolute

3. 'those that do reasonably well in business'—are diligent rather than people with genius and flair

4. 'the ne'er-do-wells'—those who have misidentified their vocation.

Additionally, he believed that profit is the return to the entrepreneur for his/her skill, ability or talent.

In contrast, Hawley (1843–1929) saw profit as the reward to the entrepreneur for assuming risk and, as a result of his work, the concepts of risk and uncertainty attracted considerable attention. For Hawley and his followers, all business transactions were carried out in a condition of uncertainty, and people who engaged in business transactions were, therefore, entrepreneurs. For others, however, risk-bearing was not seen to be an entrepreneurial activity.

The Austrian School

This originated with the work of Carl Menger (1840–1921) who suggested that entrepreneurial activity is about obtaining information in order to make decisions that give rise to economic change. Throughout the process, Menger recognizes, the entrepreneur faces uncertainty with regard to the quantity and quality of the goods to be produced. He contends, however, that risk bearing is not an essential function of the entrepreneur.

The British School

Initially, the British School, epitomized by the writings of Adam Smith (1723–90) and David Ricardo (1772–1823), conflated the function of the entrepreneur with that of the capitalist. Profits were seen as the reward for risking capital, not for anticipating the future and directing the business accordingly. Entrepreneurs invested in their own businesses according to the demand for their products and were rewarded accordingly. This concept was taken further in the writings of Jeremy Bentham (1748–1832) who proposed the concept of *laissez-faire*, arguing that there are three key factors that impinge on production:

1. inclination (the will to produce wealth)
2. technical knowledge (the knowledge of how to produce wealth)
3. capital power (the ability to produce wealth).

He argued that governments could do little through legislation to affect these three factors, thereby advocating the *laissez-faire* approach. However, although he did not address the issue of the nature of the entrepreneur directly, by inference he suggested that entrepreneurs possess the inclination, technical knowledge and capital power to create wealth.

The French School

As mentioned in the Introduction, the term entrepreneur comes from the French verb *entreprendre* (to undertake). It is not surprising, therefore, that the first economist believed to have recognized the role of the entrepreneur was Richard Cantillon who, in an essay published posthumously in 1755, suggested that the entrepreneur engages in exchanges for profit and is someone who exercises business judgement in the face of uncertainty. For Cantillon, there was a distinction between the capitalist and the entrepreneur. In his view, the entrepreneur was a risk-taker unable to calculate the risks involved in making decisions but not an innovator, in that he was expected to estimate demand but not to create it.

Subsequently, successive French economists developed the concept further. Between 1730 and 1792, Baudeau espoused the concept of the entrepreneur as innovator, arguing that entrepreneurs invent and apply new techniques in order to reduce costs and raise profits. To achieve this, he recognized that certain qualities—ability and intelligence—were needed.

Meanwhile, Jean-Baptiste Say (1767–1832) helped popularize Cantillon's theory. Like Cantillon he distinguished between the entrepreneur and the capitalist but, unlike him, did not see risk or uncertainty as being central to the function of the entrepreneur. Rather, for him, the entrepreneur was a manager who was required to estimate or forecast demand. However, he did not see him as a force for change in a dynamic economy.

The German School

Traditionally the German School focused on how the entrepreneur is compensated for his/her activity. For example, von Thunen (1785–1850) distinguished between the return to the entrepreneur and the return to the capitalist by emphasizing a residual, which is the return for entrepreneurial risk: uninsurable risk. He went on to distinguish further between the manager and the entrepreneur, suggesting that unlike the manager, the entrepreneur takes the problems of the firm home. For von Thunen the entrepreneur is both risk-taker and innovator. His/her return is thus the reward for uninsurable risk-taking and entrepreneurial ingenuity as problem-solver and innovator.

The issue of risk was developed further by Mangoldt (1824–58) who distinguished between producing goods to order or for market. This enabled him to focus on the nature of production and the degree of risk. Where goods are produced to order, clearly the risk entailed is reduced. He also suggested that the longer the time to final sale, the greater the uncertainty, and vice versa, implying that the greater the uncertainty, the greater the entrepreneurialism.

PAUSE FOR THOUGHT

Consider the different schools of thought. Identify their strengths and weaknesses. From them, try to define the nature, role and characteristics of the entrepreneur.

Neo-classical economics

As Glancey and McQuaid (2000: 43) point out, 'the central principle of neo-classical economics is that the economy can be modelled as a system in which equilibrium is attainable'. It relates not to command economies where governments decide on resource allocation, but to free or mixed market economies where market forces operate. In such economies, there is believed to be little scope for entrepreneurship when the system is in equilibrium and, in the early equilibrium models, the entrepreneur was seen as a manager or co-ordinator of the three main factors of production: land, labour and capital. He/she is a superintendent of the production process, who is responsible for determining the profit-maximizing level of output for a given set of consumer preferences.

However, in the partial equilibrium model developed by Marshall (1842–1924) a distinction is made between those who develop new and improved methods of business and who are unable to avoid taking risks, and those who 'follow beaten tracks' and are given 'wages of superintendence'.

To Marshall, business development requires more than 'superintendence', it requires:

- knowledge of the trade
- technical knowledge
- the ability to forecast
- the ability to identify opportunities
- cautious judgement
- leadership capability
- the desire to improve performance.

Additionally, he considered that the job of managing a profitable enterprise comprises two important elements: the mental strain of organizing and devising new methods, and anxiety and risk. He saw profits as the payment for such services and not merely for the job of superintending the business. Also, he believed that new small firms survive and grow through the process of natural selection. Those with the best ideas learn and improve, though there comes a point in time when a firm's ability to do this declines.

The concept of risk was advanced through the work of Knight (1921) who was probably the first neo-classical economist to identify a specific entrepreneurial function in a general equilibrium system, other than one of superintendence. He distinguished between insurable and uninsurable risk, and proposed a theory of profit that related non-insurable uncertainty to rapid economic change and differences in entrepreneurial ability. He argued that in situations of risk it was possible to estimate the likely probability of an event, whereas in cases of uncertainty this was not possible. This theory of uncertainty helps establish the boundary between the manager and the entrepreneur. According to the theory, a manager becomes an entrepreneur when the exercise of his/her judgement is liable to error and he/she assumes the responsibility for its correctness. Thus he suggests that entrepreneurs possess the ability to direct others in conditions of uncertainty, which requires:

- knowledge and judgement
- foresight
- superior managerial ability
- confidence.

According to this theory, entrepreneurial income comprises two parts: a wage/rent for his/her abilities, and payment for uncertainty bearing. Accordingly entrepreneurs can be found in any type of organization and large organizations are seen as pools of entrepreneurs. The best entrepreneurs, Knight suggests, get to the top of such organizations through ability and active competition. Additionally, he assumes that the choice between self-employment and paid employment is determined by the relative income that can be earned from each activity. It is assumed that individuals will choose self-employment if they can earn more from it than from paid employment. Hence, when wage rates fall, more people are attracted into self-employment than when they are high.

According to von Mises (1881–1972), all economic decisions involve making choices and coping with future uncertainties. He put forward the view that human action both influences, and is influenced by, the future. The entrepreneur, for von Mises, is a decision-taker whose behaviour both influences the future and is influenced by his vision of it. He viewed uncertainty in a similar way to Knight and contended that profitability is a consequence of such entrepreneurial behaviour. However, he saw making decisions about innovative practices as only one of the decision-making activities of the entrepreneur.

An important deviation from the general equilibrium model of neo-classical economics was provided by Schumpeter (1883–1950), a Moravian economist educated in Vienna and Germany. According to Glancey and McQuaid (2000), he saw the entrepreneur as someone who implements 'new combinations of means of production', an innovator. In his theory of economic development, the entrepreneur's role is to disturb the status quo (the general equilibrium) through innovation. Innovation may take various forms:

- the creation of a new product
- alterations to the quality of an existing product
- development of a new process of production

- opening up a new market
- capturing a new source of supply
- developing a new organization or industry.

According to Schumpeter, entrepreneurship is the source of change. Innovation creates new activities and markets. Under such circumstances, profit is a surplus or residual that arises due to an innovative act that results in lower costs or higher prices. The size of the surplus is directly attributable to the entrepreneur's productivity, and the surplus (profit) is both the price and the payment for the services rendered by the entrepreneur. It is not the reward for risk.

If Schumpeter is correct and entrepreneurship disturbs the equilibrium state, then according to neo-classical economics, a new equilibrium will need to be found. Glancey and McQuaid (2000) suggest that this is achieved through an adjustment in the number of entrepreneurs.

Other social science contributions

Swedberg (2000) provides a valuable review of research into aspects of entrepreneurship of social scientists other than economists, though he excludes two of the more prolific disciplines: business and management, and geography. Possibly this is because they are both inter-disciplinary subjects and it is difficult to determine the parent discipline. However, geographers have made a significant contribution to the development of the subject, particularly in terms of the contribution of small firms (and entrepreneurship) to local regional development (see Chapter 2). Otherwise, as Swedberg observes, there is no cohesive theoretical doctrine in the social sciences, as there is in economics, which means that the literature, though sprawling and hard to survey, is 'very lively and multi-faceted' and 'much closer to reality'. While the former is certainly true, the latter is debatable. Whatever, it is possible to identify a range of contributions.

Anthropology

Comparatively little work has been conducted in this field since the overview provided by Owens (1978). Even so, the contributions of anthropologists—such as Geertz (1963) in Indonesia, and Barth (1963) in Norway and Africa—reputedly provide some of the finest work on the subject. According to Barth, entrepreneurship is about connecting two spheres in society between which there exists a difference in value, and transferring value between them. His theory places emphasis on entrepreneurship as opportunity recognition, and stresses that it may involve challenging some of the basic values in a community.

Economic history

In all probability, the number of studies within the field of economic history 'exceeds what all the other social sciences have produced together' (Swedberg, 2000: 34). Much of it emanates from the work of the multi-disciplinary Research Center for Entrepreneurial History that operated out of Harvard University from

1948 to 1958. The focus of much of this was not the entrepreneur but the enterprise, and the issue of relationships both within the enterprise, and between the enterprise and its environment. In probably the most significant such contribution, Chandler's (1990) history of the industrial corporation, relatively scant attention is paid, in fact, to the entrepreneurial founders. Rather, the corporations are seen as the drivers of economic growth and entrepreneurship during the twentieth century. Similarly in North's (1990) study of institutions, institutional change and economic performance, the entrepreneur is only mentioned in passing. However, North sees him/her as the agent of change.

Psychology

As will be shown in Chapter 5, there has been a very considerable contribution to the study of entrepreneurship by psychologists. Much of it has focused on the personality of the entrepreneur and his/her behavioural characteristics, suggesting that the entrepreneur is a risk-taker and social deviant, with a high need for achievement, internal locus of control and autonomy. Such approaches, which will be discussed in more detail in Chapter 5, are now somewhat discredited. More recent psychological research has shifted away from studying the personality of the entrepreneur to studying the situations that lead to entrepreneurial behaviour. This cognitive approach to entrepreneurship suggests that individuals will activate their entrepreneurial potential if they have a specific ability, there are environmental possibilities and there is support. Hence it suggests that entrepreneurship can be developed in both individuals and society, which is the basic rationale for the various support measures introduced to promote entrepreneurship and small business development (as discussed in Chapter 4).

Sociology

Probably the greatest sociological contribution to the study of entrepreneurship was made by Weber (1864–1920) through his studies of charisma and the Protestant (work) ethic. In the former he argued that the charismatic leader is constrained neither by tradition nor law and that his/her appeal is the very fact that he/she undertakes to break the constraints imposed by established customs and roles in order to bring about change. Thus the charismatic leader is an innovator whom others want to follow. He recognized, though, that in capitalist exchange economies, the influence of charismatic leadership is somewhat constrained as change is due to the activities of enterprises and their pursuit of profit in the market.

In the latter work on the Protestant ethic, he identified the positive change that took place in public attitudes towards entrepreneurship after the Reformation in the western world and proposed that Protestantism had helped bring this about. According to Weber, Calvinists became noted for their moralistic dedication to work and their willingness to deny immediate gratification in order to invest effort and wealth in the long-term improvement of their worldly condition. It was such attitudes that made Protestant Europe the locus for the development of the modern capitalist economy. Once such attitudes had become accepted, not only did it become legitimate to make money, but society became imbued with a new, more disciplined and methodical, approach to work. For example, the British industrialist and former Euro MP, Sir Frederick Catherwood, believes that:

❝❞ It is the duty of the Christian to use his abilities to the limit of his physical and mental ability. He cannot relax as soon as he has got enough money, or as soon as he has mastered his job. He has a duty to train himself and develop his abilities. . . . When he has mastered one job, he should go on to another. He should not be content to administer, but should try to improve and innovate. He should not stop until it is quite clear he has reached his ceiling.

(Quoted in the Rt Rev David Sheppard's 1984 Dimbleby Lecture, *The Other Britain*)

Weber also addressed the concept of bureaucracy and, in his later works, counterposed the entrepreneur with the bureaucrat. Bureaucracy, he argued, becomes more prevalent, both within the firm and the state, as society becomes more rationalized. Because the entrepreneur is used to assuming responsibility and making his/her own decisions, he/she is not prepared to obey orders or follow procedures. Hence he/she is the only person who can check the progress of bureaucracy, which Weber regarded with considerable apprehension.

Following on from Weber, Lipset (2000) has argued that cultural values affect entrepreneurship and economic development. To illustrate this he points to the difference between the Latin and North American cultures. Whereas the former is influenced by early Iberian culture, which downgraded manual labour, commerce and industry, the latter was influenced more by the Protestant ethic of post-Reformation Europe, with its puritan values and emphasis on work and money-making as a vocation in God's honour. Thus a scholarly humanities education and landed property became the mark of success in Latin America. In contrast, engineering and science became the foundations of the American education system, with fortunes made in business as the mark of success. In all probability, such thinking has led to investigations of the different rates of entrepreneurship in the various sectors of society, such as the study of ethnicity and entrepreneurship, and why different cultural groups appear to possess different propensities for entrepreneurship. (More will be said about this in Chapter 2.)

Following this theme of the propensity for entrepreneurship in the different sectors of society, Merton (1968) has suggested that there is an inadvertent link between entrepreneurship and crime. It is argued that in those societies where there is a strong emphasis on economic success and few means through which the average person can achieve it, there is often an increase in deviancy and crime. This has been witnessed in Thatcherite and post-Thatcherite Britain, where efforts have been made, also, to create an entrepreneurial culture (Chapter 4).

Intrapreneurship, or corporate entrepreneurship, has also attracted the attention of sociologists, and scholars such as Kanter (1984) have written extensively about the conditions under which an entrepreneurial culture can be created (or re-created) in large organizations (this is the subject of Chapter 12). Meanwhile there are other sociologists who have argued that entrepreneurs can exist in spheres of society other than the economy.

Non-business entrepreneurship

Social entrepreneurship

Throughout history, people have had social as well as economic needs and, as Glancey and McQuaid (2000: 159) have recognized, 'the changing causes and nature of social problems requires much innovative thinking and entrepreneurial action', particularly in an era when, as Bolton and Thompson (2000: 122) point out, a 'nation's welfare system does not, cannot or will not' meet such needs. Under such circumstances, innovative solutions are regularly required, which may involve:

- generating and acting on new ideas
- providing new services in a new way
- creating new organizations or ways of delivering services.

A CASE EXAMPLE

Anne-Marie Huber

Anne-Marie Huber is a journalist, activist, publicist and Nobel Peace Prize winner. She is also the founder of Justgiving.com. She was born in Belgium and in 1991 joined Médecins san Frontières (MSF), a French-based humanitarian organization that specializes in delivering medical aid free from bureaucratic and political interference. In 1993 she came to Britain, where she had previously worked as a journalist on the *Birmingham Post*, to head MSF's British operation, and recruit doctors with expertise in tropical medicine. Unlike the International Red Cross, which had to obtain political clearance before it could commence operating, MSF was not constrained by political bureaucracy, but had little in the way of money or resources. Under such circumstances, according to Huber, they had to 'convince people we were serious players, even if we had no money at all'. Accordingly she began to promote the organization, using consumer marketing techniques to raise its profile and boost its brand image. Aware of the power of the press, she also instilled an awareness of the importance of press relations into the organization. Under her direction, the UK operation became the key press and fund-raising centre for the organization. In 1999, much to the chagrin of some of the other longer-established aid organizations, MSF was awarded the Nobel Peace Prize.

Having experienced the difficulties of raising money for MSF and been in Rwanda during and after the genocide, she has now moved on to set up the online charitable fund-raising organization, Justgiving.com. Funded by a group of private individuals and Vesta Capital, the site exploits the British tax system to help the charitable sector save an estimated £1 billion unnecessarily paid to the Inland Revenue. According to Huber:

> . . . just over £6bn of the £23bn donated to charity in the UK comes from individuals. Only about a quarter of this is tax efficient and the rest is net income, taxed money. People don't realise that charities can reclaim the tax they have already paid on their contribution. We're here to make that happen.

Justgiving.com enables people to donate money to charity online. It is linked to the websites of various charities so that anybody wanting to make a donation can do so with a credit card. All of the donations are aggregated and Justgiving.com reclaims the tax from the Inland Revenue on behalf of the charities. It earns its revenue through a 4–5 per cent commission on each donation, depending on whether the donor has come through its own site or that of one of the 41 charities it serves. This, according to Huber, 'is the lowest achievable rate for a payment that relies on credit cards and follows the Charities Aid Foundation's guidelines'. To see it through to breakeven in 2002, Justgiving.com itself needs a fresh injection of funding; however, the objective of the business is not to make lots of money for its founders and backers, but to help the charity sector get online and 'get them raising funds from people who would never dream of answering direct mail'.

A CASE EXAMPLE

Margaret Sanger, the premiere feminist?

Margaret Sanger was born into an Irish working-class New York family in 1879. She was one of 11 children who, after seeing her own mother deprived of her health, sexuality and ability to care by 18 pregnancies, witnessed similar experiences among the working-class women of New York in her role as a midwife. At that time it was a criminal offence even to send information on contraception through the post, yet the wealthy of New York were able to gain access to such information (and products).

In 1914, spurred by such experiences and the injustice of it all, she launched *The Woman Rebel*, a monthly feminist magazine that advocated birth control. As a consequence she was indicted for inciting violence and promoting obscenity. Undeterred, she continued to defy both Church and state, and in 1916 opened the first US family planning clinic in Brooklyn NY. For this she was jailed for 30 days; the centre, however, continued to dispense 'woman-controlled' forms of birth control, and she continued to push back the legal and social boundaries of the time by initiating sex counselling.

In 1921, she founded the American Birth Control League which, in 1942, became the Planned Parenthood Federation of America. Following the organization of the first international population conference, her work began to spread and gain international recognition, and the organizations she helped establish still flourish. Even so, legal change was slow and it was not until 1965 that the US Supreme Court repealed a Connecticut Law that prohibited the use of contraception by married couples. The law prohibiting unmarried couples from engaging in contraception was not repealed until 1973, seven years after her death in 1966 at the age of 87. According to the head of the New York branch of Planned Parenthood—her grandson, Alexander Sanger—Margaret 'made people accept that women had the right to control their own destinies'. She achieved this by leading by example, and through the network of friends and colleagues she inspired through her charismatic, somewhat quixotic, personality. Although having two husbands and many lovers, she had only three children and never abandoned her focus on women's freedom and its larger implications for social justice. As Gloria Steinem (co-founder of *Ms* magazine) has observed, 'she lived as if she and everyone else had the right to control her or his own life. By word and deed, she pioneered the most radical, humane and transforming political movement of the [twentieth] century.'

These are precisely the skills of the entrepreneur, and Leadbeater (1997) has suggested that social entrepreneurs differ from the traditional entrepreneur identified in the economic literature only in that they do not have profit as their main aim. Instead they concentrate on social rather than commercial outputs. This is contested by Johnstone and Basso (1999) who, from their study of the role of social entrepreneurs in community development, conclude that there are both similarities and differences. They argue that social entrepreneurs differ from traditional entrepreneurs not only in terms of their motives with respect to profit and personal wealth, but also with respect to their time-frames, being more concerned with long-term capacity-building than with short-term outcomes. Equally they are different in terms of their 'scavenger-like' use of resources, recognizing that most communities have under-utilized resources that need to be harnessed for the good of society. Whatever, there is an increasing interest in this form of entrepreneurship and readers may wish to consult two important websites: that of the School for Social Entrepreneurs in the UK (**www.sse.org.uk**) and the National Center for Social Entrepreneurs in the USA (**www.socialentrepreneurs.org**). Both have been established to promote and develop social entrepreneurship. The former is itself an interesting case of social entrepreneurship. Essentially it is the brainchild of the late Michael Young (Lord Young of Dartington). Young was the co-author of a number of significant sociological texts, including the seminal *Family and Kinship in East London* (Penguin Books, 1957) with Peter Willmott. He worked closely with Aneurin Bevan, the Minister for Health in the Labour Government of 1945–51 and during this period became convinced that successful social innovation was more likely to come from individuals than from the state. In 1997, he founded the School for Social Entrepreneurs with funding from the HSBC Holdings plc, the National Lottery Charities Board and the Esmee Fairbairn Charitable Trust. It is one of up to 40 new initiatives with which Young has been associated, including the Consumer Association and what is now known as the Economic and Social Research Council. The objective of the School for Social Entrepreneurs, which is located in east London, is 'to nurture talent outside the commercial sector'. To achieve this objective, it works with local organizations throughout the UK to establish a network of social entrepreneurship programmes. The local organizations are supported by the school through a package of services, including advice and consultancy.

Civic entrepreneurship

As Drucker (1985: 201) has recognized, 'Public service institutions . . . need to be entrepreneurial and innovative fully as much as any business does.' Throughout the western world, and increasingly in eastern bloc countries too, governments have begun to recognize the need for change in the way public services are resourced, organized and managed. Invariably this process of change from a largely bureaucratic supply-led organization to a more responsive, customer-oriented organization is not easy. While further consideration will be paid to this topic in Chapter 12, suffice it to say here that, as research on local government in Britain by Kirby *et al.* (1991a; 1991b) has demonstrated, this requires leaders at all levels in the organization whose responsibility it is to create a culture for change in order to dismantle 'dysfunctional old truths and to prepare people and organisations to deal with—to love, to develop affection for—change *per se*, as innovations are proposed, tested, rejected, modified and adopted' (Peters, 1987: 388). Such leaders are entrepreneurs or, more accurately perhaps, *intra*preneurs working to change the organizations in which they are engaged. They have responsibility not only for developing a vision for the organization, and for ensuring it is understood, communicated and shared, but also for ensuring that all staff are involved and empowered to take new initiatives aimed at ensuring that service delivery best meets the needs of the consuming public.

A CASE EXAMPLE

Margaret Thatcher, a feminine premier

Baroness Thatcher of Kesteven was born Margaret Hilda Roberts in 1925. The daughter of a Grantham grocer, she read chemistry at Oxford University. On leaving Oxford she worked as a research chemist before marrying Denis Thatcher, a wealthy businessman. This enabled her to read for the Bar and to specialize in taxation law. Fascinated by politics, she stood for Parliament in 1954, but it was not until

1959 that she won the relatively 'safe' Conservative seat of Finchley North in north London. By 1961 she had become joint Parliamentary Secretary to the Ministry of Pensions and Insurance and, by 1970, the Secretary of State for Education and Science. In 1975, after the Conservative Party had lost two elections in 1974, she succeeded Edward Heath as party leader. At the 1975 Conservative Party Conference in Blackpool she outlined her vision, which was:

> . . . a Man's right to work as he will, to spend what he earns, to own property, to have the state as a servant and not a master. . . . They are the essence of a free country, and on that freedom all our other freedoms depend.

In 1979, the Conservative Party was elected to government and, for the next 11 years, the 'Iron Lady', as she was known, 'ruled' Britain as Prime Minister and was a dominant figure in world politics. Both loved and loathed, she 'challenged and changed the definition of what was politically feasible not only in Britain, but around the world' (Davies, 1993). Initially, she focused her attention on Britain's trades unions, which had dominated British political life before 1979. Their power was seriously curtailed. Next she turned to Britain's ailing state-owned enterprises. No matter how inefficient they had been, hitherto the country's nationalized industries had been sacrosanct. She set about privatizing them. By the end of the 1980s, the governments of more than 50 countries had followed her example and established privatization programmes, floating loss-making public companies on the stock markets and, in most cases, transforming them into successful enterprises. Having reduced the level of government 'interference' in the economy, she turned her attention to social policy, extending her 'Thatcherite Revolution' to education, healthcare and housing. As a result, public expenditure was cut, enabling personal taxes to be reduced. However, it was not just in Britain that Thatcher exerted her influence. The then President of the United States of America, Ronald Reagan, was one of her most ardent admirers. He adopted many of her policies and strategies, and together they encouraged Mikhail Gorbachev, then President of the Soviet Union, to pursue his policies of *perestroika* and *glasnost*. This not only brought an end to Soviet communism, but also to socialism in Europe.

It has been said of her that, as a result of her actions, 'all the forces that had made the twentieth century such a violent disappointment to idealists—totalitarianism, the gigantic state, the crushing of individual choice and initiative—were publicly and spontaneously defeated'. They were replaced by the values she espoused—often in the face of considerable opposition—free markets and free minds. She believed passionately and devoutly that 'any set of social and economic arrangements which is not founded on the acceptance of individual responsibility will do nothing but harm. We are responsible for our own actions. We cannot blame society . . .' (speech to the leaders of the Church of Scotland, 21 May 1988).

In large measure, this was the key to her achievement. She had conviction and was prepared to fight for her beliefs. To her, courage, loyalty and perseverance were cardinal virtues, which she possessed in the highest degree. Additionally, she had an interest in ideas, could get to the heart of an issue and could make tough decisions. However, her autocratic style alienated many former colleagues and in 1990 the lady who, by her own admission, 'was not for turning', was ousted from the leadership of her party. For a further two years she remained a Member of Parliament, pulling the reins from the back benches. In 1992, at the age of 64, she 'retired' to the House of Lords as Baroness Thatcher of Kesteven. However, she remained active until March 2002, when she was advised to retire from public life on health grounds.

Case example exercise

Evaluate the characteristics of the women in the three cases included in this chapter (Margaret Sanger, Anne-Marie Huber and Margaret Thatcher). Identify any similarities and consider the attributes they display. On the basis of this evaluation, determine whether, in your view, they may be regarded as entrepreneurs. Justify the case you make.

A taxonomy of entrepreneurial theory

Against this very diverse theoretical background, Herbert and Link (1988) have developed a useful taxonomy, which identifies 12 themes. According to these, the entrepreneur is:

1. the person who assumes the risk associated with uncertainty
2. the person who supplies financial capital
3. an innovator
4. a decision-maker
5. a leader
6. a manager or superintendent
7. an organizer and co-ordinator
8. the owner of an enterprise
9. an employer of factors of production
10. a contractor
11. an arbitrageur
12. an allocator of resources.

From these 12 themes, they are able to identify three major intellectual traditions with their roots in the work of Cantillon, namely:

- the Chicago tradition
- the German tradition
- the Austrian tradition.

According to Herbert and Link, all three share various themes (perception, uncertainty and innovation), and emphasize the function of the entrepreneur, which is as a dynamic force to restore equilibrium in a market economy. They do not focus on his/her personality, however they do address the issue of 'uncertainty' and suggest that it is a consequence of change, whereas innovation is a precept of change. From their perspective it is immaterial whether entrepreneurs initiate change or simply respond to it. For them, both actions require perception, courage and action. Failure in any one of these renders the entrepreneur ineffective.

PAUSE FOR THOUGHT

Review the theories of entrepreneurship we have looked at in this chapter and develop a definition of it. Relate your definition to the taxonomy of Herbert and Link.

Chapter Review

➡ There is no agreed definition of the term entrepreneurship. Often it is equated with new/small businesses, but it is more than this.

➡ The concept is not new. There are five traditional approaches or 'schools' of economic thought: American, Austrian, British, French and German.

➡ In addition, there are the neo-classical economic and other social science approaches, mainly derived from anthropology, economic history, psychology and sociology. These suggest that entrepreneurship is not just confined to business situations but is a much broader concept embedded within society.

➡ Herbert and Link have reviewed the different theories and produced a taxonomy, which identifies twelve key themes and suggests that the main three are perception, uncertainty and innovation, and that innovation is a precept and uncertainty a consequence of change.

Quick Revision

(Answers at the end of this section)

1. Schumpeter's main contribution is to focus attention on the importance of innovation in the entrepreneurial process. Is this:
   (a) true?
   (b) false?

2. What is the meaning of the French verb from which the term entrepreneurship is derived?
   (a) to assume risk
   (b) to undertake
   (c) to innovate or create something new

3. Many economists see risk as an essential function of entrepreneurship. Who of the following does not (i.e. which are the odd ones out)?
   (a) Hawley
   (b) Menger
   (c) Marshall
   (d) Say

4. Who suggested that innovation is a precept and uncertainty a consequence of change?
   (a) Tom Peters
   (b) Herbert and Link
   (c) Margaret Thatcher

Answers to Quick Revision: 1–a; 2–b; 3–b and d; 4–b

Learning Style Activities

→ **Activist:** Ask perhaps 12 of your friends and colleagues what they understand the term entrepreneurship to mean. You may wish to present them with a definition or series of definitions, or you may just ask them for their views. It is entirely up to you how you do it.

→ **Reflector:** Reflect on the answers they give you and come up with a definition based on their answers.

→ **Theorist:** Relate your definition to the various theories of entrepreneurship. Which provides the best fit or explanation?

→ **Pragmatist:** Refine your definition if necessary and relate it to entrepreneurs known to you. How does it help you understand or appreciate what they do?

Reading

Alvarez, J.L. (1996) The Role of Business Ideas in the Promotion of Unemployment: The Case of Entrepreneurship in the 1980s, in Gual, J. (ed.) *The Social Challenge of the Creation of Employment in Europe*. Cheltenham: Edward Elgar.

Barth, F. (1963) *The Role of the Entrepreneur in Social Choice in Northern Norway*. Oslo: Universitetsforlaget.

Bolton, B. and J. Thompson (2000) *Entrepreneurs, Talent, Temperament, Technique*. Oxford: Butterworth-Heinemann.

Carland, J.W., F. Hoy, W.R. Boulton and J.A.C. Carland (1984) Differentiating Entrepreneurs from Small Business Owners: A Conceptualisation, *Academy of Management Review* **9** (2), 354–9.

Chandler, A. (1990) *Scale and Scope: The Dynamics of Industrial Capitalism*. Cambridge MA: Harvard University Press.

Chell, E., J. Haworth and S. Brealey (1991) *The Entrepreneurial Personality: Concepts, Cases and Categories*. London: Routledge.

Davies, S. (1993) *Margaret Thatcher and the Rebirth of Conservatism*. Ashland OH: Ashland University, John M. Ashland Center for Public Affairs.

Drucker, P.F. (1985) *Innovation and Entrepreneurship: Practice and Principles*. London: Pan Books Ltd.

Geertz, C. (1963) *Peddlers and Princes: Social Change and Economic Modernisation in Two Indonesian Towns*. Chicago: University of Chicago Press.

Gibb, A.A. (1996) Entrepreneurship and Small Business Management: Can We Afford to Neglect Them in the Twenty-First Century Business School? *British Journal of Management* **7** (4), 309–22.

Glancey, K.S. and R.W. McQuaid (2000) *Entrepreneurial Economics*. London: Macmillan Press Ltd.

Harwood, E. (1982) The Sociology of Entrepreneurship, in C.A. Kent *et al*. (eds) *Encyclopedia of Entrepreneurship*. Englewood-Cliffs NJ: Prentice-Hall.

Herbert, R.F. and A.N. Link (1988) *The Entrepreneur—Mainstream Views and Radical Critiques*. New York: Praeger.

Johnstone, H. and G. Basso (1999) Social Entrepreneurs and Community Development. Paper presented to the ASB Conference, Halifax, Nova Scotia.

Kanter, R.M. (1984) *The Change Masters: Corporate Entrepreneurs at Work*. London: Urwin Paperbacks.

Kilby, P. (1971) Hunting the Heffalump, in P. Kilby (ed.) *Entrepreneurship and Economic Development*. New York: Free Press.

Kirby, D.A., P. Livett and J. Rindl (1991a) *Innovations in Service*. Luton: Local Government Training Board.

Kirby, D.A., P. Livett and J. Rindl (1991b) Developing an Enterprise Approach to Local Government:

Innovative Methods of Service Delivery in the Public Sector in England. *Proceedings of the ENDEC World Conference on Entrepreneurship and Innovative Change.* Singapore: Nanyang Technological University.

Knight, F.H. (1921) *Risk, Uncertainty and Profit.* New York: Houghton Mifflin.

Leadbeater, C. (1997) *The Rise of the Social Entrepreneur.* London: Demos.

Lessem, R. (1986) *Enterprise Development.* Aldershot: Gower.

Lipset, S.M. (2000) Values and Entrepreneurship in the Americas, in R. Swedberg (ed.) *Entrepreneurship: The Social Science View.* Oxford: Oxford University Press.

Meredith, G.G., R.E. Nelson and P.A. Neck (1982) *The Practice of Entrepreneurship.* Geneva: International Labour Office.

Merton, R.K. (1968) *Social Theory and Social Structure.* New York: Free Press.

North, D. (1990) *Institutions, Institutional Change and Economic Performance.* Cambridge: Cambridge University Press.

Owens, R. (1978) The Anthropological Study of Entrepreneurship. *Eastern Anthropologist* **31**, 65–80.

Peters, T. (1987) *Thriving on Chaos: Handbook for a Management Revolution.* London: Pan Books.

Swedberg, R. (2000) *Entrepreneurship: The Social Science View.* Oxford: Oxford University Press.

Timmons, J.A. (1989) *The Entrepreneurial Mind.* Andover MA: Brick House Publishing.

Wickham, P.A. (1998) *Strategic Entrepreneurship: A Decision-Making Approach to New Venture Creation and Management.* London: Pitman Publishing.

Chapter **2**

The Role of Entrepreneurship in the Economy and Society

Learning Outcomes

On completion of this chapter, the reader will:

- appreciate the role of entrepreneurship in society and the economy, including the role of cultural entrepreneurship
- understand the reasons for the emphasis that is placed on entrepreneurship, in particular the role of entrepreneurship in
  - innovation and change
  - new venture creation
  - job creation
  - business growth
- have gained some insight into the factors affecting entrepreneurial performance in economy and society.

Introduction

As pointed out in Chapter 1, entrepreneurship is frequently equated with new venture creation and small business management. There are sound economic reasons for this. As Baumol (1987) points out, most neo-classical economists recognize the three primary economic factors of production as raw material, labour and capital. All products (both goods and services) are a mixture of these three components. Value is created by combining them in such a way as to satisfy human needs. However, the components do not combine by themselves. They have to be brought together by individuals, usually working together and undertaking different tasks. Since the days of the Industrial Revolution, the co-ordination of

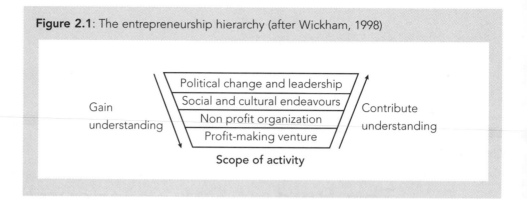

Figure 2.1: The entrepreneurship hierarchy (after Wickham, 1998)

these tasks has traditionally taken place in organizations. Under such circumstances some economists regard entrepreneurship as a kind of fourth factor, which acts on the other three to combine them in productive ways. Thus the role of the entrepreneur is to:

- find new combinations of economic factors to meet human needs (to innovate)
- organize the resources effectively and profitably (to create new organizations)
- create wealth by adding value (to generate employment).

However, entrepreneurs operate within both an economic and societal context, as Chapter 1 has demonstrated. Not only do they make the economic system more competitive, they also drive changes in the structure of society. Accordingly, Wickham (1998) has proposed that there is, in fact, a hierarchy of entrepreneurial activities operating in different social areas. At the core or base is what is conventionally understood to be entrepreneurship, namely the profit-making business venture; at the next level there is the management of not for profit organizations, such as charities and public-sector institutions; above this there might be social and cultural activities, such as sporting and artistic ventures; while at the top are activities aimed at creating wholesale social change, such as political activity (see Fig. 2.1).

Where does entrepreneurship occur?

While the concept of a strict hierarchy, with its suggestion of superiority, is somewhat debatable, there is little doubt that entrepreneurship is not confined to the world of business, and entrepreneurs can be found in all walks of life. As Bolton and Thompson (2000: 96) have recognized, entrepreneurial opportunities:

66 99   . . . can be found 'everywhere'. Some are genuinely new; others are innovatory improvements on a theme. Some are limited growth ideas; others can be used to build global businesses. They only succeed if they are different in some meaningful way and executed effectively. There is, then, an infinite set of possibilities for people with the talent and temperament to become successful entrepreneurs to choose from.

This concept that entrepreneurship is about innovation and change has led Wickham (1998: 34) to suggest that it is concerned with 'creating and managing vision and communicating that vision to other people. It is about demonstrating leadership, motivating people and being effective in getting people to accept change.'

If this is the case, entrepreneurship is not restricted to new or small ventures, to private-sector organizations or to profit-making enterprises. Rather, it is a way of life that permeates society to a greater or lesser extent. However, in a business studies context, it is normally associated with profit-making activities and is perceived to serve five main functions, namely: innovation and change; new venture creation; business growth; job generation; and regional development. Before proceeding to examine each of these in some detail, perhaps it is appropriate to digress slightly to consider one form of entrepreneurship mentioned by Wickham that was not discussed in Chapter 1: cultural or aesthetic entrepreneurship. Here the main driver is not wealth creation or business capability but creativity. However, many successful businesses have been, and are, created by such people. In the process, the more successful make money out of their talent and become extremely wealthy, but monetary wealth is not their main motivation. Rather, it is the desire to 'produce original, imaginative and innovatory work—often, but not always, sustained for many years—which influences others' (Bolton and Thompson, 2000: 148). Frequently their creativity is 'extreme' and they possess a determination to succeed that overcomes initial scepticism, opposition and criticism. They believe in themselves and their creative genius, and get satisfaction out of it, often not caring what others think. Not infrequently they are self-taught.

Their contribution to the economy and society, therefore, is not to wealth creation *per se* but to the enrichment of life, by challenging convention and by opening up ways of thinking and behaving that previously did not exist. As Jensen (1999) has recognized, such entrepreneurs contribute to what may be called 'the dream society'. This is based not on the rational thinking that so typifies the 'information society', but on emotion. This could be important as in an era of very rapid change, it seems inevitable that emotion, intuition and instinct will replace reasoning and logic as the premiere thought processes driving societal development.

A CASE EXAMPLE

Cultural entrepreneurship: The Beatles

The Beatles are probably the most celebrated popular music group of all time. Certainly, they had a most profound effect on modern popular music and, some would argue, contemporary society. In the early years, however, they were derided, while record companies refused to sign them. The group was formed by John Lennon and Paul McCartney out of Lennon's original group The Quarry Men. The two met at Woolton Parish Church in Liverpool in July 1957 and, in February 1958, Paul introduced George Harrison to the group. In the early years, at least, Lennon and McCartney were quite close. They shared many feelings and desires including an obsessive fondness for the guitar and a desire for fame. During these early years, the now famous Lennon and McCartney writing collaboration began. Although they were not all that successful at home in Liverpool, in 1960 their manager booked them into nightclubs in Hamburg. Here they gained a reputation for their wild and audacious rock performances, and attracted considerable attention, including that of the German police who deported them back to Liverpool.

Among those attracted to The Beatles was Astrid Kirchherr, a professional photographer. As a result, they now had a portfolio of photographs to show the record companies what they looked like. However, on returning to Liverpool, they did not play for about six weeks and, when they did, were not well received. They soon returned to Hamburg, but quickly tired of the city and returned to Liverpool once more, although without their bass guitarist, Stuart Sutcliffe, who had fallen in love with Astrid and been awarded a scholarship to study art in Hamburg. Paul took over his role.

Back in Liverpool, they had a better reception this time, not least because there was a groundswell of popularity for what had become known as Mersey Beat or the Mersey Sound, the music of the various Liverpool bands. Soon The Beatles were to become the leading Mersey group. In part this was helped by Brian Epstein who was to become their manager. Epstein ran his father's music store, North End Music Store, or NEMS, in Liverpool. One day, apparently, someone came into the store and asked for a record by The Beatles. The record could not be found and Epstein claimed he had not heard of them, though they had featured in the magazine *Mersey Beat*, which was sold in the store. Epstein discovered they played regularly at The Cavern nightclub in Liverpool and, on 9 November 1960, he went to see them perform. He was captivated by their music and, after the show, met them and was fascinated further by their charm and sense of humour. After this meeting, McCartney is reputed to have taken Epstein to one side and told him that while he believed the band could go right to the top, whatever happened *he* was going to make it; McCartney was determined to succeed. He was an unforgiving perfectionist with an unshakeable conviction that he knew what was right for the band.

After this initial meeting, Epstein became a regular at the club and eventually decided he wanted to manage them. In response to his initial approach, the group enquired whether they would have to change their music, to which Epstein answered 'No'. They agreed to his proposal and, on 3 December 1960, one of the most successful partnerships in the history of modern music was formed. Whilst not changing their music, Epstein did change their appearance and behaviour, however. He bought them suits and told them to stop eating, fighting, swearing and smoking on stage. As their manager, Epstein used his contacts in the industry to try to get them a recording contract. Although several record companies agreed to audition them, out of respect for Epstein, none was prepared to offer them a contract. As a last resort, Epstein went to Parlophone, a minor offshoot label of EMI. There he met George (now Sir George) Martin and the rest, as they say, is history.

Martin reluctantly gave them an audition, though Epstein told the group it was a recording contract so they would not be as nervous as they had been previously. Martin saw what everyone else, other than the record companies, had recognized—that special spark and charm of The Beatles. There was one aspect of the group that Martin was not happy with, however: the drummer, Pete Best. He was too quiet for Martin's liking and he suggested that a new drummer was needed. John, Paul and George told him about a drummer they had met in Hamburg, Richard Starkey (Ringo Starr). However, Martin refused to let them have him, preferring another drummer, Andy White. John and Paul continued writing and after having some success with 'Love Me Do/PS I Love You' (which reached No. 17 in the British charts) thought they had a great song with their new composition 'Please Please Me'. Martin disagreed. He believed that a song he had discovered, 'How Do You Do It', should be their next single. The band disagreed, and refused to record it unless he allowed them to perform their own number 'Please Please Me' with Ringo on drums. They recorded both and after they had finished recording 'Please Please Me', Martin called through the studio intercom to tell them they had their first number one. He was right, and from then on they dominated the charts with 27 consecutive number one hits.

Despite some dubious behaviour, they rarely faltered in anything they did. They expanded their writing and sound, and developed a phenomenal international following. By October 1963, the British press were writing about 'Beatlemania' and, in February 1964, when they visited America for the first time, they were met at the airport by 3000 screaming fans and 100 journalists. In June 1967 some 400 million people around the world are reported to have watched them performing live their record 'All You Need Is Love', possibly confirming John Lennon's somewhat irreverent claim in March 1966 that they were 'more popular than Jesus now'. In 1974, the group broke up and, on 8 December 1980, John Lennon was killed outside his New York apartment. However, their music remains; they continue to sell more albums and merchandise than ever before. They were, and remain, a phenomenon, largely because of their charisma and their innovativeness, and the way they defied the way things were done. They created great music that reflected their era but remains relevant today. It was their message of peace and love, and their innovative sound that transformed the world and continues to influence popular music today. By 2001, Paul (now Sir Paul) McCartney was reputed to be the 37th richest person in Britain, with a personal fortune estimated to be in the order of £640 million, while the late George Harrison had a £105 million fortune and was ranked 293rd.

Case example exercise

Review this case example, and your learning from Chapter 1, including your own definition of entrepreneurship. On the basis of this review, consider who, in the above case, was the entrepreneur? Was it Brian Epstein, or one or all of The Beatles? Consider the concept of the entrepreneurial team.

The reasons for entrepreneurship

According to Gibb (1996), there are essentially three main reasons for the contemporary interest in entrepreneurship. These are:

- job creation and economic development
- strategic adjustment/realignment
- deregulation, and the privatization of public utilities and state-owned enterprises.

Clearly these are indeed 'reasons'; however, they are also the manifestations of a much more profound and fundamental set of reasons. According to Peters (1987) and others, society is entering an era of unprecedented uncertainty, a 'world turned upside down'. But that is nothing new—change has always been a part of social and economic evolution. What *is* new, as we saw in the Preface, is the nature of contemporary change. As Handy (1990: 5) has observed change used to be:

> . . . more of the same only better. That was incremental change and to be welcomed. Today we know that in many areas of life we cannot guarantee more of the same, be it work or money, peace or freedom, health or happiness, and cannot even predict with confidence what will be happening in our own lives . . .

Under such circumstances—Drucker's 'new realities' (1989)—it is necessary not only to accommodate change but to be capable of anticipating and, more importantly perhaps, initiating it. At the same time, and again as was mentioned in the Preface, there is a somewhat paradoxical set of trends occurring within the world economy. While globalization and the interdependence of markets have been recognized increasingly in recent years, it has also become apparent that we can no longer rely on 'they'; whether 'they' are the wealthy nations of the world, the state or large firms, we cannot rely upon them to provide us with our wealth, our jobs, our homes, our healthcare, etc. Increasingly, we are having to rely on ourselves. So, we are having to empower individuals, communities, organizations and even nations in a way that, previously, has been unrecognized. We are all interdependent, but increasingly we are being required to take ownership of our own destinies—for the benefit of ourselves, our families, our colleagues, our fellow countrymen and world citizenry. Within individuals, communities, organizations and societies we need to develop a greater sense of enterprise and self-help. We need people who see opportunity, create and build, initiate and achieve. As a consequence it is possible to agree with Kanter (1984: 354) that 'Today, more than ever, because of profound transformations in the economic and social environment . . . it should be a national priority to release and support the skills of men and women who can envision and push innovations.'

Innovation and change

As shown already, innovation is a crucial part of the entrepreneurial process and a major reason for the emphasis on it in contemporary society. According to Drucker (1997: 17) 'innovation is the specific tool of entrepreneurs, the means by which they exploit change as an opportunity for a different business or a different service'.

In *Job Creation in America: How Our Small Companies Put the Most People to Work*, Birch (1987) presents an exceptionally clear analysis of the contribution of entrepreneurs to the development and growth of the US economy, tracing the relative contributions of three major classes of company, namely:

- elephants—the typical large, slow-growth companies that are unresponsive to changes in the economy
- mice—small, 'Mom and Pop', no-growth firms that reproduce rapidly at a rate of over a million a year in the USA
- gazelles—new ventures that grow rapidly and are based on significant innovation.

This latter group represented only 5 per cent of new ventures in the USA between 1984 and 1987, but produced 87 per cent of the new jobs.

Further, according to research undertaken in the 1980s and 1990s by such bodies as the US Department of Commerce and the National Science Foundation, small entrepreneurial firms were responsible in the USA for:

- half of all innovation post-World War II and 95 per cent of all radical innovation
- twice as many innovations per R&D dollar spent than the larger firms
- 24 times as many innovations per R&D dollar than the 'megafirms' with more than 10,000 employees.

While such findings are particularly impressive, and have influenced government thinking globally, it should be remembered that:

- the vast majority of small firms and new ventures are not at all innovative, as Birch has recognized
- as Deakins (1999: 159) has observed, in most countries 'innovative entrepreneurs face tremendous barriers to development'.

At the same time, it needs to be remembered that, in a business sense, innovation can mean a lot more than just developing a new product or a new technology—

it encompasses any new way of doing something so that value is created. Apart from meaning a new product or service, this can also include:

- a new way of delivering an existing product or service
- new ways of informing the consumer about a product and promoting it to them
- new ways of organizing labour and capital in order to produce the product or service, or even
- new approaches to managing relationships with consumers and other organizations.

Clearly, the recent proliferation of e-commerce (dot.com) companies is important here, as are some of the innovative changes that are taking place in the management of the public sectors of most developed and transition economies. However, particularly against a decline in the traditional manufacturing base, most developed economies have become interested in what are known as the 'sunrise' industries: the high-technology sectors, including the biotechnology, computer software and electronics industries. Indeed, small firms in such sectors have been perceived as the source of innovation, economic growth and regeneration throughout the world (Berry, 1998; Eisenhardt and Forbes, 1984). In order to flourish, however, such enterprises require, according to Galbraith (1985), a complex infrastructure that comprises universities, government research laboratories and mature firms. While such an infrastructure provides a source of entrepreneurs and ideas, it also provides technical assistance to the new, small enterprise and, as Roberts (1991) has observed in the case of Boston, results in both a high number of technological spinouts and a high success rate. It is for this reason that there has been such international enthusiasm for the creation of university science parks—an attempt to create an environment, similar to Silicon Valley in California or Route 128 in Boston, Massachusetts, where the gazelles can graze and flourish.

Opinions on the success of science parks vary, however. While the work of Monck *et al.* (1988) has suggested that they play an important role in stimulating development, Massey *et al.* (1992) have questioned whether they can play an important role in local economic development, and Westhead and Storey (1994) have concluded that it is the educational attainment of the founders that is the key factor in determining the success of technological new ventures, not the environment: 'Technologies are advancing so rapidly that only those with a deep understanding of technology are able to ensure its commercial exploitation' (Storey, 1994: 272). In contrast, Cooper (2000: 236–7) points to the fact that technical entrepreneurs differ in their educational, employment and skills base, and stresses the importance of the founder's occupational work background since 'the founder gains important sectoral and market knowledge and his/her occupation influences the extent of commercial and business expertise which he/she acquires'.

A CASE EXAMPLE

Amaze: a university spinout

Amaze started life in 1995 producing CD-Roms for customers such as IBM and ICL. It was founded by Stuart Melhuish a 28-year-old graduate of Liverpool John Moores University. In the late 1980s he had been President of the Student Union at the university and on relinquishing this appointment, the then Vice Chancellor, Professor Peter Toyne, recruited him to set up a marketing department. According to Melhuish, Toyne 'gave me an enormous amount of freedom as long as we were delivering results'. When, in the mid-1990s, British universities began to develop spinout businesses, Melhuish developed a training product for cytologists that eventually won a European Multimedia Award, ahead of Microsoft's *Encarta* encyclopaedia. 'With this product we realized,' says Melhuish, 'we had something very special. We had realized that the greatest potential for a product was if the user could be put in control of the environment—almost to get inside the computer and let the environment reorganize itself around them. We saw that that would increase the level of engagement with the information.'

Amaze was formed out of this innovation. By 1997, it was decided that the company would be sold as it had become too big for the university. The management team decided to buy it. Shortly afterwards they realized that buying a company with a CD-Rom product capacity was not the most sensible of decisions. Some of the company's 30 staff were made redundant, and it restructured and refocused, this time on the Internet. 'We put our noses to the grindstone,' says Melhuish. 'It took us 18 months to really get things going and start to win customers.' However, by 2000, Amaze had managed to raise US$12 million in funding and had acquired a 30-strong German agency, Y2K medien. It had also strengthened its management team so that it included senior executives from companies like Arthur Andersen, Microsoft and Oracle. According to Melhuish, the intention is that Amaze will not be just another large company delivering Internet services, so it is only looking for customers who share that vision.

New venture creation

Entrepreneurs are creative individuals who are keen to take ownership of their own destinies. Accordingly, many create and own new ventures. This does not mean that all entrepreneurs do this or that all new ventures are owned and/or managed by entrepreneurs. Often, new ventures are not owned, in fact, by the entrepreneur, but by venture capital companies or institutional investors. This does not make the entrepreneur any less effective; rather it could be an indication to the contrary—that he/she possesses the entrepreneurial attributes that have enabled him/her to present the venture in such a way as to attract the support of investors. Similarly, many firms are giving their employees the opportunity, through share option schemes, to own part of their firms. While this may have the effect of making them more entrepreneurial, it does not make them entrepreneurs.

Again, the creation of a new venture need not indicate the presence of entrepreneurship. Throughout the 1970s, 1980s and 1990s, large corporations have been 'downsizing' either by:

- 'spinning out' whole departments of their organizations to create new freestanding ventures, or
- making employees (including senior and middle management) redundant.

Many new ventures have been created in this way and this process has become known as 'forced entrepreneurship'. Similarly, many people are forced to create new ventures as an alternative to unemployment. This is particularly true in periods of economic recession and in countries where high unemployment prevails, but it is also the case in societies where discrimination (on the grounds of either gender or race, for example) is high. Whatever the causes, while some new ventures may be run by entrepreneurs, many are not. Largely as a consequence, many new ventures fail.

The failure rate of new small firms is not clear. Firms that close or are not traceable need not necessarily have failed; and not only are there no really accurate data relating to failure, but it is difficult to trace firms that have ceased to trade. However, in the UK in 1997, some 182,600 new ventures were registered for VAT purposes, representing 39 registrations for every 10,000 people over the age of 16. In contrast, there were 164,500 de-registrations, or 35 for every 10,000 people. While not all of the de-registrations would have been new ventures, and these figures do not represent those new firms below the VAT threshold, it is estimated that 38 per cent of all new businesses fail within the first year and 57 per cent by the end of year two.

There is no definitive reason as to why new ventures fail, but according to Scarborough and Zimmerer (2000) the most common causes of failure are:

- managerial incompetence
- lack of experience
- poor financial control
- lack of strategic management
- inappropriate location
- lack of inventory control
- inability to make the entrepreneurial transition.

If this is the case, in all probability the root causes of failure are managerial incompetence and lack of experience, since all of the other factors essentially result from these two. Interestingly, the work of Brough (1970) appears to confirm this. From his study of the causes of failure among firms that were compulsorily wound up in 1965, he discovered that the Official Receiver regarded mismanagement as the overwhelming cause. In contrast, the directors of these firms cited insufficient working capital, insufficient capital overall and bad debts, while the owners pointed to factors beyond their control, such as the weather, ill-health, etc. Some 20 years later, the situation seemed to have changed somewhat. Repeating the exercise for voluntary liquidations in 1973, 1978 and 1983, Hall and Young (1991) and Hall (1992) found little divergence of opinion between the owners and the Official Receiver, who seemed agreed that the main causes of failure were under-capitalization and the shortage of working capital.

Whatever the rate and cause of failure, in most western countries the rate of new firm creation is high, though it varies sectorally, spatially and temporally. With the growth of the service sector, particularly in the developed economies of the western world, it is inevitable that the greatest concentrations of new firm formations in recent years have been in the service sector, but there are marked variations. In the UK the growth of small service-sector firms has been studied by

Keeble *et al.* (1992: 43) who point out that this growth 'has been most dramatic in professionally-based, information-intensive business service sectors such as computer services, management consultancy and professional, scientific and technical services rather than support services employing manual workers such as contract cleaning or road haulage'. In the transition from a skill-intensive to a knowledge-intensive economy (Stonier, 1983), such a development is to be expected and it is no surprise, therefore, to see the very considerable growth in the UK of the number of new small management (Keeble *et al.*, 1992) and technical (Jones-Evans and Kirby, 1993) consultancies, for example. It is equally no surprise to discover that such a development is not unique to the UK (Kirby *et al.*, 1996).

While the rate of new firm creation is high in most economies, there are marked spatial variations. In Europe, for example, research by Van der Horst (1992) reveals that firm formation rates in the UK are higher than in the rest of Europe, other than Denmark where special circumstances prevail. Indeed, the UK rates are almost five times as high as those in The Netherlands, the lowest-ranking country. There are no apparent (economic) explanations for this. Similarly, considerable variations are known to exist *within* countries. Keeble *et al.* (1993) have shown that in the UK, for example, new firm formation rates were in the order of three times greater in some areas rather than others. The greatest concentrations were found to be in areas of relative prosperity with a service-based economy. More generally, it would seem that the greatest proportion of new firms is to be found:

- around the largest and most diversified city regions (where there is a sizeable market)
- in rural areas (where, inevitably, the base levels are relatively low).

In contrast, the lowest rates of new firm formation are in the oldest, most specialized urban-industrial regions (where demand is weakest and the need is greatest). Three theories are traditionally used to explain these differences. First, structural theory argues that differences in technology, rates of market growth, capital requirements, etc., result in different propensities for new firm formation. Second, socio-cultural theory posits that the rate of new firm formation is determined by the socio-economic mix and demographic characteristics of the population and the regional tradition for entrepreneurship. Finally, economic theory suggests that small firms are most likely to grow in those environments where infrastructural conditions are available and most conducive to development. These include premises, venture capital, market demand, educational support, training and consultancy, and research and development. Whichever theory is correct, it would appear that those areas most in need of economic development/regeneration are those least likely to generate new firms or successful small businesses (Johnstone, 1996; Johnstone and Kirby, 1999).

While the rate of new firm formation varies sectorally and spatially, it also varies over time. Traditionally it has been believed that new firm formation is highest in periods of economic recession—people are 'pushed' into self-employment as an alternative to unemployment. Certainly this was true in the United Kingdom in the 1930s, the period of the Great Depression. However, research by

Keeble *et al.* (1993) suggests that this was not the case in the 1980s. During that decade in the UK, unemployment was falling and new firm formation rates were rising, suggesting that new businesses were being created in response to the improving market conditions and opportunities. This ignores the influence of government policy and the major efforts during the decade not only to raise awareness of the opportunities that self-employment affords but to encourage business start-ups (see Chapter 3). Inevitably, with the increase in self-employment over the decade the unemployment rate would fall. Thus it is generally held that there is a positive correlation between the rate of new firm formation and the level of unemployment in an economy. Though the weight of evidence supports this view, it is not conclusive, and the work of Bartlett (1993) on co-operatives suggests that in Italy the higher rates of co-operative formation are associated with improved economic conditions, whilst in Spain they seem to be a defence against unemployment.

PAUSE FOR THOUGHT

Consider the number and types of new business in your environment. How many of them fail? Why do they fail?

A CASE EXAMPLE

Boo.com: a new venture 'failure'

Wednesday 17 May 2000 was the day of reckoning for the highest-profile Internet retailer in Europe, net-based fashion merchant Boo.com. Having failed to secure a £20 million new financing package, all but 30 of the 250 staff employed in the company's head office in Carnaby Street in London were sent home, the offices were closed, the website was no longer taking orders and the liquidators were called in. This was just 18 months after the firm had been founded by the former Swedish model Kasja Leander and her business partner, the former poetry critic, Ernst Malmsten.

The company had started life as a global net retailer of designer clothes, and with the help of American bank JP Morgan, had raised some £80 million of funding, tempting such international investors as the Benetton family and Goldman Sachs. However, the firm experienced problems from the outset. First the website was delayed for five months, then there were technical problems with some of the 3D animations, which meant that by the time Boo.com opened for business it had already spent a third of its marketing budget. After the first three months of trading its turnover was only £460,000, and although sales increased they were not sufficient to support the 450 staff

employed in six offices worldwide, and a third of these had to be made redundant.

It was shortly after this that the restructuring plan was announced. This called for a further £20 million investment, the closure of all overseas offices and the laying off of another 100 staff. The rejection of the plan by investors left the company with no option but to agree to the appointment of the liquidators, KPMG, which sold Boo's technology assets to the Internet software and services group Brighton Station for £250,000, and its brand and website to the American Internet fashion retailer Fashionmail for an undisclosed sum.

Case example exercise

There are a number of explanations for Boo's failure, as outlined below.

● The inexperience of the founders: although Kasja Leander had been the co-founder of bookus.com, a Swedish online bookstore, she and Malmsten had little business experience and they failed to appoint an experienced financial director for months. When they did, he stayed for only two months. His resignation was felt to be the end of the firm's credibility with investors.

- Too rapid growth: the company's plans were too ambitious. It insisted on creating a global business at once, planning to launch in 18 countries. This led to it over-investing.
- Inappropriate development strategy: the company did not appreciate that the Internet allowed it to serve a global market from one or two locations. It did not require six offices worldwide.
- Failure to plan and poor financial control: one investor is reputed to have said, 'Every week they kept asking for money. It was just a never-ending story.'

Review the case and consider whether these are adequate explanations for Boo's failure. Are there other possible explanations? Evaluate each explanation, and any others you might identify, and try to determine which was the most critical from your perspective.

Job creation

Clearly the creation of new ventures creates employment opportunities for both the entrepreneur and others. However, prior to the 1980s, the analysis of self-employment received only scant attention from the economics profession. Set against a background of declining numbers, 'full' employment and the massification of organizations in the search for economies of scale, this was hardly surprising. However, the work of Birch (1979) in America revealed that new and small firms were a source of new job generation. With unemployment increasing and large firms downsizing, both governments and academics around the world developed an interest in self-employment and the employment generation opportunities provided by new and small businesses.

In Britain, for example, the total number of self-employed people increased over the period 1981 to 1997 by slightly in excess of 1 million, from 2.2 million in 1981 to 3.25 million in 1997, a 47.5 per cent increase. In the period 1981–90 the number of self-employed people actually increased by 59 per cent. By 1991, approximately 12 per cent of the total workforce was self-employed, compared with 9 per cent in 1981. The numbers entering self-employment appear to vary by gender, age, marital status, ethnic origin and education level. We will now look at each of these factors in turn.

Gender

Traditionally, males have made up a significantly greater proportion of the self-employed sector than females. In Britain little more than 26 per cent of those self-employed are females while in the United States the proportion of female-owned businesses is only in the order of 33 per cent of the total. However, in both countries female self-employment has grown rapidly in recent years and is continuing to do so. According to Carter and Allen (1997) the share of female-owned businesses in the total US business population increased by 550 per cent between 1972 and 1987, and a further 125 per cent between 1987 and 1992. Similarly, in Britain between 1979 and 1997, the number of self-employed women increased by 163 per cent, while the number of self-employed men rose by only 67 per cent over the same period. Not surprisingly, therefore, there has emerged a very considerable literature (Allen and Truman, 1993; Carter, 2000) on the characteristics of female entrepreneurs and, in particular, the problems they encounter. Much of this has focused on the sectors in which they are concentrated—essentially the service sectors, which have been the main growth sectors for new and small firms.

Age

Self-employment appears to become increasingly inviting nearer middle age when the potential entrepreneur can afford the start-up costs of a new venture, redundancy/early retirement is most likely to occur, and the entrepreneur has the experience to identify opportunities or ways of doing things better. Indeed, a recent survey of 600 of Britain's most successful entrepreneurs (Ernst & Young, 2001) reveals them to have an average age of 45 and while this has long been the case, David Wilkinson, Head of Entrepreneurial Services for Ernst & Young, has made the point that:

> If you get caught up in the hype, it's easy to imagine that entrepreneurs are all twenty-somethings, but men and women who have worked in industry for years are often best placed to spot an opportunity or identify ways of doing things better. You don't necessarily need youth on your side to have the spark and drive to build a successful entrepreneurial business. Most entrepreneurial success is achieved by hard graft and determination and is measured by results over time—and rarely happens over night.

However, this does not mean that young people cannot set up successful new small businesses, as Charlie Muirhead has demonstrated (see Chapter 5).

Marital status

Self-employment is much less likely for single people than it is for people in other categories (married, widowed, divorced or separated). In part, this reflects the fact that people below the age of 25 are less likely to be married than those in the older age categories. However, it does seem that marriage provides the support necessary to establish a successful new venture, and spouses are often partners in such enterprises.

Ethnic origin

In most high-level advanced economies, there has been a significant increase in self-employment among ethnic minorities over the past 20 years (Ram and Barrett, 2000). In Britain, about 7 per cent of the self-employed are from minority ethnic groups, while such groups make up about 4.5 per cent of those in employment. Self-employment levels in Britain are much higher among the Asian population, for example, than among those of West Indian origin. Even so, about 86 per cent of Asians still work for someone else. By contrast, those people of Mediterranean background (people from Cyprus, Malta and Gibraltar) are over twice as likely to be self-employed as those of Asian background, and over four times as likely as whites. The explanations for this are varied. To some (Basu, 1995) it results from cultural difference, with certain community groups being perceived as 'naturally entrepreneurial'. To others (Jones et al., 1992) it is a result of discrimination in society, forcing people from ethnic minorities to seek opportunities through self-employment. Interestingly, Stanworth and Curran (1976) in an early discourse cite the entrepreneurial proclivity of the Jews and suggest that this has been acquired at least partly in response to the discrimination they have experienced in society over perhaps 2000 years. Thus ethnicity does appear to influence the rate of self-employment, though ethnic differences need to be taken into consideration, and it remains unclear why such variations should exist.

Education level

According to Curran and Burrows (1989) the self-employed in Britain appear to have a lower level of educational attainment than wage-earners. However, this contrasts with the later findings of both Daly (1991) and Meager (1991), who discovered that the self-employed appear to have a higher level of educational achievement than employees, and the higher the level of the qualification the higher the likelihood of the individual being self-employed. According to Meager (1991), the differences in the findings result from the fact that Curran and Burrows (1989) excluded the 'professional self-employed' from their data set. Whatever, it would seem that the educational level of the self-employed is increasing and, as has been mentioned already, educational attainment is likely to be of increasing importance in a knowledge-based society and economy in which 'there are going to be more offices than factories . . . more schools, universities and colleges than construction yards . . . factories will have polished floors and white-coated workers . . . rather than concrete areas for foundries, steel-making and cars' (Handy, 1985: 6).

Apart from creating jobs for the entrepreneurs themselves, new and small firms create employment for others. Clearly circumstances vary, but from the work of Birch (1979), it would seem that in the United States between 1969 and 1976, something like half of all gross job gains were created by new ventures and, of these, half were produced by independent entrepreneurs. Such findings were hard to believe as they contradicted the assumptions of most businesses and governments, which believed that large firms were essential to a healthy economy.

Largely as a result of the Birch study, small firms were regarded, during the 1980s, by most governments, as the panacea for unemployment. In the United States during the period 1980–86, for example, 34 million jobs were lost from established enterprises but 44.7 million were created, 32 million through new venture creation. A similar situation prevailed in the European Community where nearly every member-state experienced large firm job losses but employment generation through the small firm sector. In the UK alone, over 1 million additional jobs were created during the 1980s by firms employing fewer than 20 people. Since then, new and small businesses have continued to contribute to the job creation process in the UK. Between 1995 and 1999, new businesses created 2.3 million jobs and the vast majority (85 per cent) of these were provided by micro, small or medium-sized enterprises. Additionally, existing small and medium-sized (SME) enterprises created more than half the jobs gained from expansion over the same period, even though one in three jobs provided by the SME sector in 1995 had been lost by 1999.

However, there have been criticisms of Birch's work (Storey, 1994) and Armington and Odle (1982), for example, have reworked his data but have been unable to replicate his results. Indeed, research undertaken in the UK (Hakim, 1989a) using Labour Force Survey Statistics has revealed that the contribution to employment generation by new small firms is not as great as perhaps it might have been thought initially. Out of a small business population in excess of 3 million, approximately two-thirds (68 per cent) are without employees and under 26 per cent employ fewer than nine persons. Additionally, it has been discovered (Hakim, 1989b) that fewer than three-quarters of one-person micro-businesses in Britain do not plan to take on any further staff, as is the case with the majority of those with one or two employees. Overall, half of the small firms with fewer than 50 employees would seem to have no intention whatsoever of expanding their business.

Over the years, there has been considerable academic debate over the contribution of small firms to job generation. While the rates of job creation reported by Birch may be somewhat over-optimistic, Storey (1994) has concluded that they do create jobs at a faster rate than large firms and that they are more consistent, since they are less influenced by changes in the macro economy.

PAUSE FOR THOUGHT

Examine the situation in your environment. What proportion of the firms are small businesses? What is the rate of new firm creation? Who starts them? How many people do they employ?

Business growth

According to the UK Committee of Inquiry on Small Firms (1971: 343) 'small firms provide the means of entry into business for new entrepreneurial talent and the seedbed from which new large companies will grow to challenge and stimulate the established leaders'. While very little research has been undertaken to support or refute this statement, there is evidence in retailing, for example, that lends credence to it (Kirby, 1986). However, it is known that very few new small businesses do grow. And, as has been shown, many do not survive either. Of those that do, only a very small number actually grow, and Storey (1993) has suggested that three groups of small firms can be identified: the 'failures', the 'trundlers' and the 'flyers'. The 'flyers' are the growth firms, or Birch's 'gazelles', while the 'trundlers' are his 'mice'. Like the gazelles, the flyers are in a minority and it would appear that only '4 per cent of those businesses which start would be expected to create 50 per cent of employment generated' (Storey, 1994: 115).

There are numerous reasons why new ventures should not grow and Barber et al. (1989) have suggested that the literature on the barriers to growth can be classified under three headings: 'Management and Motivation', 'Sources and Market Opportunities' and 'Structure'. However, more recent work by the Cambridge Small Business Research Centre (1992) points to financial constraints, the level of demand in the economy and the nature of competition, suggesting that external factors are more significant barriers to growth than are the internal factors, such as managerial skills or the availability of skilled labour.

While the barriers to growth are known, the precise catalysts for growth are not. Considerable descriptive research has been carried out into this area and it is known, for example, that growth firms are younger and smaller (2–20 employees) than non-growth firms. They are more likely to be limited companies (rather than sole traders or partnerships) and tend to be located in accessible rural areas (rather than urban areas or inaccessible rural areas). Equally, they are likely to be owned by individuals who share equity with external individuals or organizations, and who are prepared to devolve decisions to non-owning managers, to occupy particular niches or segments where they can exploit any quality advantages they may have, and to be innovative. However, understanding of the factors that lead to growth remains weak, though Storey (1994: 137) has suggested that:

" " "   . . . the motivation for establishing the business appears to be of some importance, with individuals who are 'pushed', possibly through unemployment, into establishing businesses being less likely to found a rapidly growing firm than those attracted by a market opportunity. The evidence also suggests that individuals with higher levels of education are more likely to found rapidly growing firms, as are those with some prior managerial experience. More rapidly growing firms are more likely to be founded by groups, rather than single individuals. Finally, middle-aged owners are most likely to found rapidly growing firms.

If this is the case, then it reinforces the argument that perhaps the primary reason for failure is the quality of management and the inexperience of the founder. What motivates growth, however, is unclear, other than the personal attitudes, behaviour and drive of the founding entrepreneur and, as appropriate, his/her team.

Clearly, the fact that so few new ventures grow restricts the contribution they make to the job generation and economic recovery processes. Equally it minimizes the seedbed effect and has led to the suggestion that perhaps a more selective approach should be taken to new venture creation, whereby the 'winners' are picked out at birth for special attention and nurturing. More will be said about this in Chapter 4. For the present, suffice it to say that this is not easy and that if management is crucial to both survival and growth, as it would seem, it is probable that with appropriate managerial support many more businesses could make a more significant contribution. Rather than attempting to pick out the seeds that are worthy of more favoured attention, perhaps the conditions for growth need to be improved. Attention will be paid to this in Chapter 4.

A CASE EXAMPLE

The Spar Foodliner at Treherbert: trundler or flyer?

The Spar Foodliner at Treherbert in South Wales is a 2200 sq ft (202.4 sq m) grocery store. It was opened as a family business in 1972 at a time when independent retail grocery stores were in decline in Britain. This trend has continued but the Foodliner has gone from strength to strength, despite increased competition from the multiple retailers. The current owner-manager is Michael Pritchard, who took over from his father in 1983. In 1975, at the age of 18, Michael spent a year with Spar Hamburg, studying business and learning German. On returning to the UK in 1976, he undertook a two-year course in Supermarket Operations at the College of the Distributive Trades in London, from where he obtained a Diploma in Supermarket Retailing, a Certificate in Meat Pricing and the Royal Society Diploma in Hygiene. Subsequently, from 1978 to 1980, he studied for an HND in Business Studies (specializing in Distribution) before joining the family business. In 1983, at the age of 25, he took over full management control and, despite having a young family, became a member of the Spar Guild Committee.

Within 10 years, despite a recession and an increasingly competitive environment, Michael had steered the already successful business to a position of pre-eminence as one of Britain's most successful small independent grocery businesses. By September 1992, the Foodliner had won the prestigious Independent Grocer of the Year Award and had been named runner-up in the Best Independent Retailer Award organized by Booker plc. In the previous five years (1987–92) it had seen its turnover increase by 62 per cent, while its gross profitability had risen by 2.3 per cent, from 19.0 to 21.3 per cent, over the same period.

To a very large extent the success of the store, which employed 4 full-time and 23 part-time staff, was down to the vision and drive of its owner-manager, Michael Pritchard. The business was located at the northern end of the Rhondda Valley in South Wales. This is in the heart of the former South Wales coal-mining region. With the closure of the mines, the population of the region had been in decline for some time and, between 1981 and 1991, it had been reduced by 5.2 per cent. Unemployment in the region was around 13.5 per cent and while home ownership was higher than the national average, car ownership was lower with 45 per cent of households not owning a car. With most of the younger people of the region seeking work opportunities elsewhere, the local population was ageing and approximately 21 per cent were at or above retirement age. Competition in the immediate locality was strong. There were five independent grocery outlets, numerous greengrocery businesses, general stores and off-licences, a large supermarket belonging to a national chain 1 mile away and a national discount store 7 miles away.

Pritchard analysed his market, and identified the opportunities and threats it provided. He adopted a focused strategy targeting those potential customers at the lower end of the income scale, many of whom were relatively immobile with limited facilities for food storage in the home, making it difficult to purchase in bulk. He had realized that to succeed in this market he must not only meet the needs/wants of the customer, but also keep costs as low as possible, at the same time ensuring that customer satisfaction levels were maintained. Accordingly he had set about meeting these objectives. First, he had introduced electronic scanning tills to monitor sales, profitability and stock levels on the 2450 lines stocked. This ensured that while minimum stock levels were maintained, the store was never out of high-demand items. Additionally, he introduced a 16-camera closed circuit television system to minimize shrinkage levels, and a computerized refrigeration temperature recording system to ensure compliance with hygiene regulations. All refrigeration units were equipped with blinds and sava-watt controls to minimize energy costs. As a further check on costs Michael monitored the business plan on a monthly basis, checking the projected expenditures against the actual. Any significant deviations were noted and, as appropriate, immediate remedial action was taken.

He had recognized that cost-control was not sufficient. He needed to grow the business. Apart from national Spar advertising, the store began printing its own promotional leaflets; 6000 were produced and distributed each month, each with a redemption coupon, enabling Pritchard to assess their impact. Perhaps more importantly, he began to integrate the store into the local community, arranging promotional events, providing sponsorship for local causes and initiating fund-raising activities. All of these activities drew attention to the store (and, frequently, the community) but were relatively inexpensive and generated considerable 'goodwill'. Pritchard's charity events became well known. Not to be outdone by the multiples, he even operated a twice-weekly free bus service intended to help the large number of elderly, less mobile customers shop at the store.

Pritchard recognized that his staff were his most important asset and that if he was to be successful, they needed to be loyal and highly motivated. The key to this, he believed, was a sound recruitment strategy and ongoing training, coupled with close monitoring and control systems as well as both fiscal and non-fiscal incentives. When he was away from the business, it would operate as well as, if not better than, when he was there, and he would ensure that the staff were aware that he knew this, and were rewarded.

Despite all of the problems facing such businesses, the store was clearly successful. As an adjudicator for one of the awards observed, 'the store represents all that is best in independent retailing. It performs an indispensable service to the local community. The staff are well trained and enthusiastic. Shopping at the Pritchards' store, in short, is a pleasurable experience.'

Case example exercise

Evaluate the case of the Spar Foodliner at Treherbert in the context of the literature on business growth. Place it in the classifications of Birch and Storey, and justify your placing. Explain why it has been so successful.

Chapter Review

➡ Most economists recognize three primary economic factors: raw material, labour and capital. Many see entrepreneurship as the fourth, acting on the other three to combine them in productive ways.

➡ Entrepreneurs operate within both an economic and a societal context, not only making the economic system more competitive, but driving changes in society.

➡ Although entrepreneurship is not restricted to profit-making enterprises, in a business studies context it is normally associated with new venture creation, job creation, and innovation and change.

➡ Not all new ventures are entrepreneurial. Many fail and very few grow. As many as 57 per cent fail within the first two years.

➡ New ventures are seen as a means of reducing unemployment, and research suggests that as many as half of gross job gains may be created by new ventures.

➡ Firms can be grouped into three categories: elephants, mice and gazelles. The latter account for about 5 per cent of all new ventures and a large percentage of a country's innovation.

Quick Revision

(Answers at the end of this section)

1. According to Wickham (1998), there is a hierarchy of entrepreneurial activity with the management of not for profit activities on the highest level in the hierarchy. Is this:
   (a) true
   (b) false?

2. Does the term 'forced entrepreneurship' mean that people are forced to become self-employed because of:
   (a) high levels of unemployment
   (b) discrimination
   (c) redundancy
   (d) social pressure?

3. How many new ventures are estimated to fail within two years of their formation?
   (a) 38 per cent
   (b) 57 per cent
   (c) 75 per cent

4. Which factors appear to affect the rate of self-employment?
   (a) gender
   (b) age

   (c) ethnic origin

   (d) education level

5. According to the work of Storey (1994), what proportion of all new ventures might be expected to create 50 per cent of the employment generated?

   (a) 4 per cent

   (b) 10 per cent

   (c) 20 per cent

Answers to Quick Revision: 1–b; 2–a; 3–b; 4–a, b, c and d; 5–a

Learning Style Activities

➡ **Activist:** Visit either the UK Department of Trade and Industry website (**www.dti.gov.uk**), or any more appropriate site, and obtain the most up-to-date statistics on small firms in the economy.

➡ **Reflector:** Think about the data you have collected. What does it tell you about the role of entrepreneurship in the economy and society?

➡ **Theorist:** Relate your findings to the various theories about the role of entrepreneurship in the economy and society. How do your findings corroborate or refute the findings from earlier research?

➡ **Pragmatist:** How useful are the theories in helping you understand the role of entrepreneurship in the economy and society? Do they need to be revised? Was the data adequate? Is further data needed?

Reading

Allen, S. and C. Truman (1993) *Women in Business: Perspectives on Women Entrepreneurs*. London: Routledge.

Armington, C. and M. Odle (1982) Small Business—How Many Jobs? *The Brookings Review*, Winter **1** (2) 14–17.

Barber, J., J.S. Metcalfe and M. Porteous (1989) *Barriers to Growth in Small Firms*. London: Routledge.

Bartlett, W. (1993) Employment in Small Firms: Are Co-operatives Different? Evidence from Southern Europe, in Atkinson, J. and D.J. Storey (eds) *Employment, Small Firms and the Labour Market*. London: Routledge.

Basu, A. (1995) Asian Small Businesses in Britain: An Exploration of Entrepreneurial Activity. Paper presented at the Second International Journal of Entrepreneurial Behaviour and Research Conference, Malvern, 18–20 July.

Baumol, W.J. (1987) Entrepreneurship in Economic Theory. *American Economic Review: Papers and Proceedings* **58**, 64–71.

Berry, M. (1998) Strategic Planning in Small High Tech Companies. *Technovation* **31** (3), 455–66.

Birch, D. (1979) *The Job Generation Process*. Massachusetts: MIT Program on Neighbourhood and Regional Change.

Birch, D.L. (1987) *Job Creation in America: How our Smallest Companies put the Most People to Work*. New York: Free Press.

Bolton, B. and J. Thompson (2000) *Entrepreneurs: Talent, Temperament, Technique*. Oxford: Butterworth-Heinemann.

Brooksbank, D. (2000) Self-employment and Small Firms, in Carter, S. and D. Jones-Evans (eds) *Enterprise and Small Business: Principles, Practice and Policy*. Harlow: Prentice Hall.

Brough, R. (1970) Business Failures in England and Wales. *Business Ratios*, 8–11.

Cambridge Small Business Research Centre (1992) *The State of British Enterprise*. University of Cambridge: Department of Applied Economics.

Carter, S. (2000) Gender and Enterprise, in Carter, S. and D. Jones-Evans (eds) *Enterprise and the Small Business: Principles, Practice and Policy*. Harlow: Prentice Hall.

Carter, S. and K.R. Allen (1997) Size Determinants of Women-Owned Businesses: Choice or Barriers to Resources? *Entrepreneurship and Regional Development* **9** (3), 211–20.

Committee of Inquiry on Small Firms (1971) *Small Firms* (Cmnd 4811). London: HMSO.

Cooper, S. (2000) Technical Entrepreneurship, in Carter, S. and D. Jones-Evans (eds) *Enterprise and Small Business: Principles, Practice and Policy*. Harlow: Prentice Hall.

Curran, J. and R. Burrows (1989) National Profiles of the Self-employed. *Employment Gazette*, July, 376–85.

Daly, M. (1991) The 1980s: A Decade of Growth in Enterprise. *Employment Gazette*, March, 109–34.

Deakins, D. (1999) *Entrepreneurship and Small Firms*. London: McGraw-Hill Publishing Company.

Drucker, P.F. (1989) *The New Realities*. London: Heinemann.

Drucker, P.F. (1997) *Innovation and Entrepreneurship*. Oxford: Butterworth-Heinemann.

Eisenhardt, K.M. and N. Forbes (1984) Technical Entrepreneurship: An International Perspective. *The Columbia Journal of World Business* **19** (4), Winter, 31–8.

Ernst & Young (2001) *Entrepreneur of the Year: Report 2001*. London: Ernst & Young.

Galbraith, C.S. (1985) High Technology Location and Development—the Case of Orange County. *California Management Review* **28** (1), 98–109.

Gibb, A.A. (1996) Entrepreneurship and Small Business Management: Can We Afford to Neglect Them in the Twenty-First Century Business School? *British Journal of Management* **7** (4), 309–22.

Hakim, C. (1989a) New Recruits to Self-Employment in the 1980s. *Employment Gazette*, June, 286–97.

Hakim, C. (1989b) Identifying Fast Growth Small Firms. *Employment Gazette*, January, 29–41.

Hall, G. (1992) Reasons for Insolvency Amongst Small Firms—A Review and Fresh Evidence. *Small Business Economics* **4** (3), 237–50.

Hall, G. and B. Young (1991) Factors Associated with Insolvency Amongst Small Firms. *International Small Business Journal* **9** (2), 54–63.

Handy, C. (1985) *The Future of Work*. Oxford: Basil Blackwell.

Handy, C. (1990) *The Age of Unreason*. Random Century.

Jensen, R. (1999) *The Dream Society*. Maidenhead: McGraw-Hill.

Johnstone, H.J. (1996) *Small Firms and Local Economic Recovery: The Case of Britain's Depleted Communities*. Unpublished PhD thesis, University of Durham, England.

Johnstone, H. and D.A. Kirby (1999) Limits on the Prospects for Small Firm Led Employment Growth: Regional Development and the Small Firm. Paper Presented at the 44th ICSB World Conference on Entrepreneurship, June.

Jones, T., D. McEvoy and G. Barrett (1992) *Small Business Initiative: Ethic Minority Business Component*. Swindon: ESRC.

Jones-Evans, D. and D.A. Kirby (1993) Technical Entrepreneurs in the Service Sector: The Growth of Small Technical Consultancies in the United Kingdom, in Chittenden, F., M. Robertson and D. Watkins (eds) *Small Firms: Recession and Recovery*. London: Paul Chapman Publishing Ltd.

Kanter, R.M. (1984) *The Change Masters: Corporate Entrepreneurs at Work*. London: Unwin.

Keeble, D., J. Bryson and P. Wood (1992) Entrepreneurship and Flexibility in Business Services: The Rise of Small Management Consultancy and Market Research Firms in the UK, in Caley, K., E. Chell, F. Chittenden and C. Mason (eds) *Small Enterprise Development: Policy and Practice in Action*. London: Paul Chapman Publishing Ltd.

Keeble, D., S. Walker and M. Robson (1993) *New Firm Formation and Small Business Growth: Spatial and Temporal Variations and Determinants in the United Kingdom*. London: Employment Department Research Series, No. 15, September.

Kirby, D.A. (1986) The Small Retailer, in Curran, J., J. Stanworth and D. Watkins (eds) *The Survival of the Small Firm: The Economics of Survival and Entrepreneurship.* Aldershot: Gower.

Kirby, D.A., D. Jones-Evans, P. Futo, S. Kwiatkowski and J. Schwalbach (1996) Technical Consultancy in Hungary, Poland and the UK: A Comparative Study of an Emerging Form of Entrepreneurship. *Entrepreneurship Theory and Practice* **20** (4), 9–24.

Massey, D., P. Quintas and D. Wield (1992) *High Tech Fantasies: Science Parks in Society, Science and Space.* London: Routledge.

Meager, N. (1991) Self-employment in the United Kingdom. *IMS Report* No. 205. Institute of Manpower Studies.

Monck, C.S.P., R.B. Porter, P.R. Quintas, D.J. Storey and P. Wynarczyk (1988) *Science Parks and the Growth of High Technology Firms.* London: Croom Helm.

Peters, T. (1987) *Thriving on Chaos: Handbook for a Management Revolution.* London: Pan Books.

Ram, M. and G. Barrett (2000) Ethnicity and Enterprise, in Carter, S. and D. Jones-Evans (eds) *Enterprise and the Small Business: Principles, Practice and Policy.* Harlow: Prentice Hall.

Roberts, E.B. (1991) *Entrepreneurs in High Technology: Lessons from MIT and Beyond.* New York: Oxford University Press.

Scarborough, N.M. and T.W. Zimmerer (2000) *Effective Small Business Management: An Entrepreneurial Approach.* Upper Saddle River NJ: Prentice Hall.

Stanworth, M.J.K. and J. Curran (1976) Growth and the Small Firm—An Alternative View. *Journal of Management Studies* **13**, 95–110.

Stonier, T. (1983) *The Wealth of Information: A Profile of the Post-Industrial Economy.* London: Methuen.

Storey, D.J. (1993) *Should we Abandon Support to Start Up Businesses?* Coventry: Warwick University SME Centre. Working Paper 11.

Storey, D.J. (1994) *Understanding The Small Business Sector.* London: Routledge.

Van der Horst, R. (1992) *The Volatility of the Small Business Sector in The Netherlands.* Paper presented to the International Conference on Small Business, OECD, Montreal, Canada, 24–27 May.

Westhead, P. and D.J. Storey (1994) *An Assessment of Firms Located on and off Science Parks in the UK.* London: HMSO.

Wickham, P.A. (1998) *Strategic Entrepreneurship: A Decision-making Approach to New Venture Creation and Management.* London: Pitman Publishing.

Chapter 3

Influences on Entrepreneurship Development

Learning Outcomes

On completion of this chapter, the reader will:

- appreciate the nature and importance of an enterprise culture and the difficulties associated with its definition
- understand that although entrepreneurship occurs naturally in society, it can be fostered or hindered by both macro and micro factors
- appreciate the importance of such socio-cultural factors as religion, education and history, and the presence or absence of role models on the development of an enterprise culture
- be aware of the significance of such politico-economic factors as the state of the economy, employment levels and the industry structure
- see that institutional or organizational factors constitute the main micro factors
- recognize that the key institutional or organizational influences are Fordism, the corporate culture and corporate prestige.

Introduction

Clearly, entrepreneurship development is driven by the motivations of individuals seeking to satisfy their own personal goals. However, while the key to initiating the process of entrepreneurship lies within the individual members of society, its development is affected by the degree to which the spirit of enterprise exists, or can be stimulated. The question then arises, what are the factors that stimulate or prevent individuals from behaving in an entrepreneurial manner? According to Timmons (1994: 9) the trigger in the USA is:

66 99   . . . a culture that prizes entrepreneurship, an imperative to educate our population so that our entrepreneurial potential is second to none; and a government that generously supports pure and applied science, fosters entrepreneurship with enlightened policies, and enables schools to produce the best educated students in the world.

Essentially, this quotation by Timmons identifies the key factors: an entrepreneurship culture and a political economy that promotes enterprise. Before any analysis can be made it is necessary, however, to consider the concept of the enterprise culture.

The enterprise culture

Since the late 1970s, there has been considerable academic and political debate in both Britain and the USA about the concept of an enterprise culture. As Chapter 1 has shown, the concept of entrepreneurship had been considered for some time prior to that date but it was not until the late 1970s that the debate about what constituted an enterprise culture really came to the fore. Probably the catalyst, certainly in Britain, was the advent of a Conservative government in 1979 under the leadership of Margaret Thatcher. Prior to that date the role of government, whether Conservative or Labour, had been interventionist. With the advent of 'Thatcherism', the 'rightful role of the state was seen to be to provide a facilitative framework within which companies could grow unfettered by either government or trade union interference' (Scase, 2000: 35). However, impetus was also provided by the publication in 1979 of Birch's findings in America on the importance of small firms in job generation, as discussed in Chapter 2. In a post-Fordist era, when companies, globally, were downsizing, politicians throughout the world became interested in the job generation characteristics of small and medium-sized enterprises. Hence the enterprise culture became synonymous with small firms or, as Southern (2000: 81) has suggested, it became 'the metaphor for the small firm'. In reality, the concept is much broader than small and medium-sized enterprises or even new venture creation. In an economic context, these are one set of measurable outcomes of an enterprise culture. However, as the term 'entrepreneurship' is frequently equated with new and small businesses, so the concept of an enterprise culture is frequently equated with them also. As with entrepreneurship, there is no agreed definition of the concept of an enterprise culture. To some it equates with the concept of 'being business-like' or adopting a 'business-like' approach to the management of organizations, including such non-market-based activities as education (Ritchie, 1991b), policing (Hobbs, 1991), and health and social services (Kelly, 1991).

However, many businesses are neither enterprising nor entrepreneurial, and being business-like does not necessarily mean being enterprising. As Gibb (2000: 16) has suggested, 'separating enterprise and entrepreneurship in the personal behaviour sense from the notion of "being business-like" is wholly central to all policy-making approaches to entrepreneurship'. Thus it would seem that an enterprise culture is more than just a culture of business or a culture that promotes new and small enterprises. These may be the external manifestations of such a culture, but they are not the culture itself. Indeed, the concept might be conceived as requiring individuals, groups and organizations to take responsibility for their own destinies ('ownership'), whether in a business or non-business context. Rather than being dependent on others, it is about being dependent on oneself. In Timmons' terms (1989: 1), it is a proactive culture that is about 'initiating, doing, achieving', while according to the UK Department of Employment (1989: 3) the heart of any enterprise culture is the ability to 'innovate, recognise and create opportunities, work in a team, take risks and respond to challenges . . .'.

Under such circumstances, it is to be expected that there exists a wide range and diversity of entrepreneurial cultures, as Morrison (2000) has recognized. However, the one thing they appear to have in common is a positive social attitude towards personal enterprise that enables and supports entrepreneurial activity. As has been shown already (Chapter 1) entrepreneurial activity is not necessarily confined to business nor to new small firms. Thus an enterprise culture is not confined to either of these and may be seen to operate much more broadly, releasing and harvesting the enterprise in all sectors of society. At the same time, while it is generally assumed that an enterprise culture operates at a societal level, it can operate at an organizational level too, either reinforcing or challenging the values of society. Hence, when considering the culture of enterprise, and the factors that affect its development, it is possible to identify and consider three different but related sets of factors.

Socio-cultural factors

Although 'currently, the term "entrepreneurial culture" has become popular and widely accepted internationally', as Morrison (2000: 103) has observed, there is no such thing as a standard, identifiable and universal culture that stimulates entrepreneurship. Rather there exists a wide range of cultures that stimulate or stultify entrepreneurship to a greater or lesser extent. If the culture contains pro-entrepreneurial values, it serves as an incubator in the entrepreneurship initiation, as Johannisson (1987) has recognized. However, the converse can also hold true. In societies where entrepreneurship has become tainted, for example, it is not well received.

Fortunately culture is not static—it can change, if only slowly. Hence it has the potential to be modified. In her model of the key features associated with entrepreneurship initiation, Morrison (2000) identifies various inputs that influence culture, namely religion, education, family, history and role models. We will now look at each of these in turn.

Religion

According to Heelas and Morris (1992), neither Judaism nor Christianity are in opposition to the development of entrepreneurship. However, in the Bible, St Matthew (19; 23; 24) reports that Christ told his disciples:

" " Truly, I say unto you, it will be hard for a rich man to enter the kingdom of heaven. Again I tell you, it is easier for a camel to go through the eye of a needle than for a rich man to enter the kingdom of God.

Accordingly, in some Christian countries the religious leaders condemn wealth creation, equating it with corruption and, under such circumstances, Morris (2000) suggests, a culture is created that lacks a spirit of self-reliance, enterprise and innovation. Conversely, St Matthew (25: 14–30) also reports Christ's parable of the three servants:

" " For it will be as when a man going on a journey called his servants and entrusted them his property; to one he gave five talents, to another two, to another one, to each according to his ability. Then he went away. He who had received the five talents went at once and traded with them; and he made five talents more. So too, he who had the two talents made two talents more. But he who had received the one talent, went and dug in the ground and hid his master's money. Now after a long time the master of those servants came and settled accounts with them. And he who had received the five talents came forward, bringing five talents more, saying 'Master, you delivered to me five talents; here I have made five talents more.' His master said to him 'Well done, good and faithful servant; you have been faithful over a little, I will set you over much; enter into the joy of your master.' And he also who had the two talents came forward, saying 'Master, you delivered to me two talents; here I have made two talents more.' His master said to him 'Well done, good and faithful servant; you have been faithful over a little, I will set you over much; enter into the joy of your master.' He also who had received one talent came forward, saying 'Master, I knew you to be a hard man, reaping where you did not sow, and gathering where you did not winnow; so I was afraid and went and hid your talent in the ground. Here you have what is yours.' But his master answered him, 'You wicked and slothful servant! You knew that I reap where I have not sowed, and gather where I have not winnowed? Then you ought to have invested my money with the bankers, and at my coming I should have received what was my own with interest. So he took the talent from him, and gave it to him that had the ten talents. For to every one who has will more be given, and he will have abundance.'

From this, it is not difficult to see the link with the Protestant ethic considered in Chapter 1, especially when it is appreciated that according to the Christian doctrine man is created by God according to his own image. He has nothing from himself but owes everything to his creator with whom he shares responsibility for the preservation and consummation of the 'Creation' (Heaven and Earth). This fits easily into the concept of a Christian society that recognizes and celebrates diligence, personal drive, self-reliance and responsibility.

Equally, it fits with a religion that believes people are rewarded for their works ('The Lord will requite him for his deeds', 2 Timothy 4: 14; or 'whatsoever a man soweth, that shall he also reap', Galatians 6: 7), and particularly one that places a premium (1 Corinthians 13: 13) upon charity (liberality to the poor). Hence it is not surprising that religious leaders and devout Christians feature prominently in much of the recent trend towards social entrepreneurship, certainly in Britain. For example, Leadbeater (1997) reports on the work of two: the Rev Andrew Mawson, Minister at a United Reform Church in one of Britain's most depressed districts, Bromley-by-Bow; and Eric Blakebrough, a Baptist Minister in Kingston, South London. In 1984, Mawson persuaded his ageing congregation that the only way his church could respond to the mounting social crises of unemployment, illiteracy and ill-health in the neighbourhood was by putting its dilapidated facilities at the disposal of the local people. According to Leadbeater (1997: 12), 'out of nothing has emerged a thriving centre that combines health and welfare with work and enterprise, serving young and old, black and white, pulling together resources from the local and central state, the private sector and the church. Everything has been done to the highest possible standards. The centre is driven by a powerful ethic of creativity, excellence and achievement.' Similarly, from a club for young people, Eric Blakebrough has created 'one of the most innovative and effective drug treatment programmes in the country' (1997: 12), which is now run by his daughter, Adele, who has taken over both the ministry and the project. Next to the church, there is a hostel providing long-stay accommodation for 18 young people and in two adjacent houses there are a library, computer room, music and art workshops, and an education and enterprise centre. There are plans, also, for an intensive care unit and a cafeteria nearby.

Apart from their Christian beliefs and principles, these two social entrepreneurs take 'under-utilised and often discarded resources—people and buildings—and re-energise them by finding new ways to use them to satisfy unmet and often unrecognised needs' (1997: 14). In this way they create innovative ways of tackling some of the country's most depressing and intractable social problems.

However, not all religions are supportive of entrepreneurship. Kirby and Fan (1995) have examined Confucianism, for example. They discovered that when the entrepreneurial values identified by Timmons *et al.* (1985), Hornaday (1982) and Gibb (1990) are compared with the 59 traditional Chinese cultural values, it is found that there are a number of common values but also several that conflict with each other. The common values are:

- total commitment, determination and perseverance (Timmons, Hornaday, Gibb)
- diligence (Hornaday)
- integrity and reliability (Timmons)
- low need for status and power (Timmons)
- leadership (Gibb)
- team builder and hero maker (Timmons)
- ability to get along with people (Hornaday)
- emotional stability (Timmons)
- high intelligence and conceptual ability (Timmons)
- resourcefulness (Hornaday)
- moderate risk-taking (Gibb).

Conversely, the conflicting values were found to be:

- positive response to change (Hornaday)
- initiative (Hornaday, Timmons, Gibb)
- profit orientation (Hornaday)
- high belief in control of one's own life.

Perhaps of even greater significance, however, is the fact that three important entrepreneurial attributes (creativity, innovation and flexibility) are all missing from Chinese cultural values. This is not difficult to understand when it is appreciated that in Confucianism the key value is harmony and order. Taking initiative and innovating is disruptive to the existing order and regarded as a threat to social harmony. Only the person at the top of the hierarchy is supposed to take authority, though he is governed by a mandate from Heaven. Other members of society are expected to play a passive role and to conform. Equally, Confucianism belittles the importance of commercial activity and profit. The ideal man, under Confucianism, is not the successful entrepreneur but the scholar-bureaucrat—the person who rejects personal gain and profit. In the Chinese social hierarchy, the businessman is placed after workers, peasants, soldiers and students.

Thus it can be concluded that Confucian values are basically not supportive of entrepreneurship as it is understood and practised in the West. There are, however, many successful Chinese entrepreneurs. Does this imply that they have abandoned Confucianism and their traditional Chinese values or that the western theories of entrepreneurship need to be re-defined to accommodate eastern religious influences and philosophies? Alternatively, it could be that there are intervening factors that mitigate the religious factors, as Siu and Kirby (1995; 1999) have suggested. Without further research, it is difficult to say.

Education

In many societies the formal education system is recognized as a strong influence in the development of conformist, anti-entrepreneurial behaviour. As a consequence, many in society are at best ambivalent towards entrepreneurship as a result of their educational conditioning. At worst, students are unaware of it and its role in the economy and society, believing that the only alternative to employment in a large organization, whether in the private or the public sector, is unemployment. Indeed, writing in the 1980s, Handy (1985: 133) suggested that in Britain:

The education system today probably harms more people than it helps. This is not intentional. The teaching profession is, on the whole, both diligent and dedicated. It is the fault of the system, designed at other times for other purposes but now disabling rather than enabling to many who pass through.

The problem, as he recognized, was that the system was 'designed at other times for other purposes'. An educational system that placed, and continues to place, a premium on knowledge acquisition and retention, that restricts 'creativity, competence, capability and the ability to relate to others' (1985: 140) and that conditions young people to be dependent on others for employment opportunities (i.e. prepares them for work as employees in large organizations) is out of phase with the needs of society. Fundamental changes have taken, and are taking, place in the world economy, which suggest that 'the employment society is beyond its peak' (1985: xii) while society has entered an era of unprecedented uncertainty where predictability is a thing of the past (Peters, 1987). Under such circumstances, it is necessary both to 'grow new businesses which do things the others cannot do as well' (Handy, 1985: 177) and to develop in people the ability not only to cope with change but to initiate and manage it. As Peters (1987: xii) has observed, 'the winners of tomorrow will deal proactively with change'.

Thus in the traditional education system in the UK, 'the focus and process of much of education as it currently stands . . . may work against the nurturing of entrepreneurship' (Gibb, 1987: 35). The UK is not alone in this respect. Despite Timmons' assertion, in America, the bastion of entrepreneurship, students in the 1980s were 'clamouring for a chance at the free enterprise system', but 'most College curriculums prefer to teach students how to become proficient employees, instead of successful business persons' (Solomon, 1989: 1).

Since that time, much has been done to change the situation, not only in Britain (see Chapter 4) and America, but worldwide. There has been a proliferation of courses and programmes (Vesper and Gartner, 1998; Interman, 1991), and numerous textbooks and manuals about entrepreneurship in general and new venture creation in particular. These have been targeted at all levels of education and, as Gibb (2000) has shown, they have had different and frequently confused objectives. Often programmes have taught students *about* entrepreneurship but have not educated them *for* entrepreneurship by developing in them the attributes and behaviours of the entrepreneur (see Introduction and Chapter 5). On occasions they have developed in students a range of personal transferable skills but 'in general, transferable and "key" skills (such as communication, numeracy, literacy, IT knowledge and problem-solving) are arguably not "sufficient" for the pursuit of entrepreneurship or indeed entrepreneurial behaviour' (Gibb, 2000: 18). Probably as a consequence, the success of such initiatives has been questioned (MacDonald and Coffield, 1991; Ritchie, 1991b). Even so, numerous individuals (for example, Chia, 1996; Gibb, 1996) have continued to call for reforms to the UK education system and, in 1997, the UK National Committee of Inquiry into Higher Education, basing its evidence on a benchmarking exercise against entrepreneurial education in America in general and Babson College in particular, required universities to 'consider the scope for encouraging entrepreneurship through innovative approaches to programme design', for example. This has resulted in a further proliferation of initiatives, some of which will be discussed in Chapter 4, including the establishment of organizations to promote and champion entrepreneurship education amongst the student body. One such international initiative is the Chicago-based Collegiate Entrepreneur Organization (www.c-e-o.org), which intends 'to inform, support, and inspire college students to be entrepreneurial and seek opportunity through enterprise creation'. Over 100 universities belong to this body—mainly, but not exclusively, from the USA.

Family

A characteristic of entrepreneurship is that it tends to pervade family life. Not only does the family revolve around the firm, but research (Bannock, 1981; Stanworth *et al.*, 1989) reveals that the children of self-employed parents are more disposed to entrepreneurship than are those of employed parents, while many new ventures owe their success to the support of the family through the provision of funding and access to markets. This seems to be particularly true in minority ethnic businesses (Mitter, 1986), though even here there appear to be differences between, for example, the South Asian (Ward, 1991) and African-Caribbean

Dominic McVey

Approximately 10 people become millionaires in Britain every day. One of these is 16-year-old Dominic McVey of Leytonstone in east London. A millionaire by the age of 14, two years later he was the 49th richest person in Britain under the age of 30, one place ahead of Hollywood superstar Kate Winslet. With a personal fortune of £1.5 million from a business importing and selling micro-scooters from America, Dominic started buying and selling shares at the age of 10, using his father's credit card. Apparently he got interested in share dealing at the age of six or seven while travelling on his own to visit his father, the principal percussionist with the Royal Shakespeare Company, who was on tour in the Far East. 'I'd see all these men in suits in business class on the plane,' says Dominic, 'sitting in bigger seats and getting nicer food. I kept wondering why they were there when I was trying to watch the movie over hundreds of heads. My dad told me these men bought and sold shares.' So, back home, he bought the *Financial Times* and started reading the financial pages of the Sunday papers.

When he was 12, he used the money he had made on the stock market to buy five scooters, which he sold over the telephone in two days. He set up his business, Scooters UK, with the help of his mother who, for legal reasons, is the managing director of the company. When he went to the bank to set up an account, the small business manager 'thought it was a joke,' he says, so he went ahead and did it, just 'to prove a young kid is as capable of doing anything as anyone else'. Although the business has a £5 million turnover, it still operates from his bedroom. 'There's no point moving it anywhere else,' he says, 'it would be a waste of money.' However, he did not set up the business to make money. He still lives off £35 a week pocket money and re-invests a lot of his earnings back into the business. Currently he is looking to diversify and has been seeking new ideas in Japan with his father. He has identified a number of prospects, including an electronic toilet seat with a built-in bidet and a Japanese gambling game for use in clubs and pubs. When coupled with his determination to succeed this, perhaps, is his forte: his ability to see opportunities. As his mother says, 'when Dominic was very little he would drive me mad with all his ideas. He wouldn't stop asking questions. . . . You've got to have faith in your children. Whatever they pursue, you've got to be behind them 100 per cent.'

(Reeves and Ward, 1984) communities. Conversely, family attitudes can act as a barrier to entrepreneurship development, both by conditioning offspring to behave in an un-enterprising manner and by discouraging them from exploring the concept of self-employment either formally or informally. Clearly in a society where there are few entrepreneurs and few family businesses there are likely to be few family role models, and entrepreneurship development is unlikely to be encouraged.

History

Clearly, historical conditioning can impact 'upon the extent to which entrepreneurial characteristics exist within the population and the degree to which entrepreneurship is accepted as socially legitimate', as Morrison (2000: 108) has observed. In countries like the former socialist economies, there is no tradition for entrepreneurship and no role models. Thus in some, such as Slovenia, the transition to a free market economy has been slow. However, in others, such as Poland, the readjustment has been much quicker, possibly reflecting the more recent history of free enterprise in the country.

The same is true in the UK where, certainly in the nineteenth century and possibly even as early as the eighteenth, there was a significant tradition of entrepreneurship. In summary, it is possible to identify a series of phases in the UK economy over the past 200 years or more that may be seen to conform to waves (Kondratieff, 1935) or cycles (Schumpeter, 1939) of economic development, each lasting for a period of approximately 50 to 60 years. According to Massey (1988), the first phase began at the end of the eighteenth century and ended around the middle of the nineteenth. This was an era of innovation in the industrial base of the economy, especially in the steel and cotton industries, and in the utilization of steam as a source of power. The second phase, which ended around the turn of the century, was based upon innovations largely in rail transport, steam power and the production of coal and steel, and involved the massification of industry. The third phase, completed in the 1930s, involved innovations in electricity, chemicals, synthetic materials and the internal combustion engine, as well as further industrial massification. The fourth wave is believed to have started in the 1940s and was based on electrical and light engineering, petrochemicals and the motor industry. It involved the break-up of markets and the de-massification of industry in what has become known as a 'post-Fordist' economy. It came to an end in the late 1980s and can be regarded as a period of 'creative destruction' (Schumpeter, 1939). It has been superseded (Hall, 1985; Hall and Preston, 1988) by a fifth wave based on innovations in microelectronics, information and communication technologies and is concentrated around Cambridge and the M4 corridor—the 'Sunbelt' or Britain's equivalent to Boston's Route 128. It is this wave that the country is now in. Thus the present emphasis on entrepreneurship and small business development can be seen as developing out of the downswing in the cycle of economic development that characterized the fourth wave in Britain's recent historical development. It can be interpreted as a natural development in the evolution of a capitalist economy.

Role models

It is commonly held that role models are important in promoting the concept of entrepreneurship in society. According to Anderson (1995), the existence of role models in a society will have a positive effect on the development of entrepreneurship and vice versa. Hence in Scotland a deliberate attempt has been made to promote the achievements of new and successful entrepreneurs through the publication of *Local Heroes* (Scottish Enterprise, 1997), while in America many universities have Entrepreneurship Halls of Fame, through which they not only celebrate the achievements of entrepreneurs, but introduce them to their students. Competitions and awards are another way of celebrating and promoting the achievement of entrepreneurs. There are numerous of these, often run in association with national newspapers. (Details of the Entrepreneur of the Year Awards, sponsored by the Chartered Accountants firm Ernst & Young, are available at **www.ey.com.**)

Interestingly, Handy (1999: 12) profiles 29 entrepreneurs in his book *The New Alchemists*. In it he suggests that the purpose and scope of the book is that:

. . . others may see this selection of alchemists as models or even heroes, whose examples they might follow in their own lives. For these were, and still are, ordinary people who have gone on to do extraordinary things. It is often easier to learn from example than from precept or theory if we can personally identify with the examples.

For role models to have any effect, however, the population they are intended to influence needs to be able to relate to them. In order to emulate them, potential entrepreneurs need to be able to identify with them and relate to their experiences. Hence, it is important that if the enterprise culture is to be promoted throughout society and entrepreneurship is to be encouraged, particularly in those sectors where it is under-represented, role models in a western context should not all be male, middle-aged and white. Thus Handy's role models are of different ages, backgrounds, genders and nationalities. Similarly, Beveridge (2001) focuses her attention on 41 technological entrepreneurs that have 'spun out' of Cambridge University. As Bygrave observes in his foreword to the book *Cambridge Entrepreneurs*, it is required reading for would-be high-tech entrepreneurs and for anyone involved in the high-tech entrepreneurial process. In contrast, Wanogho (1997) focuses on the black female entrepreneur in Britain—a minority group that is believed to lack an entrepreneurial instinct and to be economically unproductive. Clearly the purpose of the book is to challenge these myths and to celebrate the achievements of the 21 black women featured in it. However, the book has a broader message:

> . . . we should all be proud of the Black women featured in this book, not just for having the courage to follow their dreams, but also for being role models for others within and outside the Black community. . . . The experiences of the businesswomen featured should serve as an inspiration to others. None of the women came from particularly wealthy families and only a handful went into higher education. They are ordinary women who, through sweat and toil, have achieved extraordinary success.

(Wanogho, 1997: 226)

The author herself is an interesting role model in her own right. Born in Nigeria, she received all her secondary and higher education in the UK, including an MBA from Middlesex University. For her MBA dissertation she carried out a study of the difficulties encountered by male and female black business owners in London, their achievements and successes. The book stems from that investigation and is one of a series of initiatives that Emete Wanogho is involved with to promote and assist women entrepreneurs through her three companies: EW International Ltd, Eteme Productions and Temony Management Consultancy.

PAUSE FOR THOUGHT
Consider the barriers and stimuli to entrepreneurship in your society. What factors encourage entrepreneurship development? What factors discourage it?

Politico-economic factors

Apart from the socio-cultural factors that stimulate or retard entrepreneurship development, there are a whole set that might be termed politico-economic factors. Perhaps the first of these is the political system itself, which can either promote or retard entrepreneurship directly through the way the economy is managed. Clearly in the command economies of the communist countries, entrepreneurship was not only discouraged, it was not accommodated. That is one extreme and there are varying degrees and types of direct state intervention that can affect the propensity for private enterprise development. However, there are other, less direct, ways in which entrepreneurship can be promoted or discouraged through the political system; these relate largely to style of government. In the more egalitarian and democratic countries (such as Australia and North America) entrepreneurial attitudes and behaviours tend to be encouraged by the non-interventionist policies of the state, whereas in countries where there is strong government and a sense of being 'ruled', either formally or informally, the tendency is 'to produce persons who are lacking in the personal attributes generally associated with entrepreneurs, in particular leadership, creativity, self-reliance and self-confidence' (Morrison, 2000: 107). As discussed in Chapter 1, many governments have adopted 'Thatcherism' and have attempted both to break this dependency culture and to stimulate entrepreneurship. The trend to privatize public utilities in the West (Dick, 1987) and to develop a more enterprising and business-like approach to the management of the public sector are manifestations of this. Moreover, as will be shown in Chapter 4, countries such as Britain have also attempted to stimulate an enterprise culture, somewhat paradoxically perhaps, through direct intervention and the provision of support to new small enterprises (Haskins *et al.*, 1986). The collapse of communism in central and eastern Europe might similarly be interpreted as evidence of such a development, especially when coupled with the various efforts that have been made to promote new, private-sector small businesses (Blawatt, 1995; Gibb and Haas, 1996; Ivy, 1996; 1997). According to Ivy (1996: 82), 'a carefully planned program of assisting new firm formation by small-scale entrepreneurs coupled with moderate privatisation may be the answer to private sector growth without adverse national or regional economic impacts'. The effects of such political intervention, however, have been mixed, as Morrison (2000) has recognized.

However, there are other factors that need to be taken into consideration: the state of the economy, employment levels, industry structure, homeworking and telecottaging, network/multi-level marketing, franchising, and the new dot.com businesses. We will now look at each of these in turn.

The state of the economy

Entrepreneurship becomes a prerequisite for economic development when economies are rapidly changing and development is uncertain. Attention has already been paid (in Chapter 2) to the significance of change in the modern global economy and, in particular, to the importance of having a populace and workforce that can not only cope with change, but can anticipate and initiate it. Under such conditions the flexibility of the entrepreneur, and his/her ability to cope with chaos and uncertainty, is at a premium. In conditions of little change and steady, predictable economic growth, entrepreneurship is less significant, perhaps, though clearly it is one of the roles and functions of the entrepreneur to disturb the status quo by seeing opportunities and innovating.

Traditionally, however, entrepreneurship and new venture creation has flourished when an economy has been in recession. Under such circumstances entrepreneurship represents a means by which the economy and the population can break out of the downward spiral of unemployment and low economic growth. When an economy flourishes, and there is full employment and high economic growth, the rate of entrepreneurship development tends to be somewhat lower. However, there are signs that this situation is changing. For example, the Singaporean economy, based as it is on small and medium-sized enterprises, has sustained a high level of economic growth even during the 1990s' meltdown of the Pacific Rim 'tiger economies', while places like Silicon Valley in California have seen entrepreneurship flourish on the back of a thriving and growing economy. Similarly, in England, the greatest number of new firm formations and the highest percentage of successful new ventures are to be found in the more prosperous regions of the country.

Equally, entrepreneurship is often only weakly developed in the least developed economies, possibly reflecting the influence of socio-cultural and political factors. At least this appears to be true in the sense of formal entrepreneurship (i.e. the entrepreneurship that manifests itself in the creation of new small businesses). South Africa is a classical example where this situation pertains, or did in the apartheid era. Traditionally it had been held that entrepreneurship was not a characteristic of the indigenous black population. According to research quoted by Neuland (1981), one in seven of the white population was purported to possess a drive for achievement, whereas among the black population it was only one in ninety-nine. If this was correct, then legislation was needed that, rather than further disadvantage the black communities, 'recognises the greater development needs of the Black population and gives them, if anything, preferential treatment' (Kirby, 1985: 46). As Phillips and Brice (1988) recognized, even when members of the black population did set up businesses, they were discriminated against by the politico-economic system and, when the discrimination was removed, many black business owners were 'understandably hesitant to compete "equally" [with whites] when, for years, they have been denied the opportunity to acquire skills, experience and the infrastructure necessary for effective competition' (1988: 55). However, anybody who has been to South Africa, certainly when the apartheid system was in place, will question the findings of research which suggest that the black population has less of a drive for achievement. Any individuals that could defy the Group Areas Act of 1950 and migrate to the 'illegal' black squatter communities that emerged in and around South African cities cannot be anything other than enterprising. Indeed, as one resident of Crossroads (the infamous squatter settlement outside Cape Town) responded when asked whether he intended to move to Guguletu (the official resettlement 'camp' for the residents of Crossroads), 'No, I am not going there. I am going to Sea Point' (the prestigious white residential area in Cape Town). While his response may have been somewhat tongue in cheek, the thought was there. This was a man making whips on a fire outside his Crossroads home, from offcuts of black plastic piping obtained free of charge (possibly stolen) from a nearby plastics factory.

Such enterprise is typical of the 'informal sector' not just of the South African economy, but of many developing and transition economies. Perhaps first identified by Hart (1971), there is no generally accepted definition of the informal sector and accordingly it has been variously defined (Sethuruman, 1977; Weeks, 1975). Typically it is characterized, as Maarsdorp (1983) has demonstrated, by the fact that it is not recorded in any official returns. Hence its contribution to the economy is difficult, if not impossible, to determine in any given country.

All commentators are agreed, however, that it is both important and significant, especially, but not exclusively, in some of the more impoverished economies of the world. In South Africa it is 'estimated to represent a portion of between 16 per cent and 40 per cent of current gross domestic product' (Morris and Pitt, 1995: 79) and for many it is an essential means of survival (Rauch, 1991). For example, Rogerson and Beavon (1982: 254) described the situation in the black township of Soweto during the apartheid era, where:

66 99   . . . against a backdrop of heightening levels of unemployment, the absence of state unemployment relief benefits for Blacks or an effective system of welfare to care for the aged, sick and disabled, a growing stream of Soweto residents are participating in the array of income-earning niches collectively styled as the 'informal sector'.

Most operations in such contexts are one-person or family businesses.

However, the informal sector is not confined to the developing and transition economies. It can be found in high-level economies too. Thus in all economies there is a hidden entrepreneurial activity. Much of it is legal activity operating 'illegally' outside the formal economy. Under such circumstances, it is the responsibility of society to harness that enterprise in order to reduce tax avoidance and, as appropriate, facilitate economic and social enhancement. Indeed, one of the objectives of the Enterprise Allowance Scheme (see Chapter 4) in Britain has been to encourage the formalization of those legal enterprise activities that have been operating unofficially, and illegally from a tax perspective, in the informal sector. Some of it, however, is illegal activity, such as the organized and often large-scale activities of the Mafia. While the activities of the Mafia are known to exist in contemporary society, and particularly in countries like Russia where mafiocracy (www.konanykhine.com/mafiocracy.htm) currently competes for control with communism and democracy, perhaps the activities of the Mafia are most closely associated with Chicago in the 1930s and the activities of the infamous Al Capone.

A CASE EXAMPLE

Al Capone

Born in Brooklyn, New York, in 1899, Al Capone became one of the leading Mafia 'Godfathers' of the time, building for himself a fearsome reputation as a ruthless gang leader. On 14 February 1929, though, in Florida, he is reputed to have organized the killing of seven members of a rival gang in what became known as the St Valentine's Day Massacre. After failing to appear before a Federal Grand Jury in 1929, he was sentenced to 11 years in prison in 1931 and fined US$50,000 with US$7692 court costs, not for violence or murder but for tax evasion amounting to some US$215,000. Like all of the Mafia gangs, Capone had a legitimate business, in his case cleaning and dyeing. However, his gang's main activity was the brewing, distilling and distribution of beer and liquor, which was banned under the country's prohibition laws. On 16 November 1939, Capone was released from prison having served only seven years of his sentence, but having paid all fines and back taxes. He retired to his estate on Palm Island near Miami in Florida and died on 25 January 1947 from a stroke and pneumonia.

Employment levels

Employment may affect the predisposition towards entrepreneurship in two ways. There is evidence to suggest that high levels of employment restrict entrepreneurship development (i.e. new firm formation) while high levels of unemployment encourage individuals to offer themselves for self-employment. However, unemployment, signalling a lack of buoyancy in the economy as it so often does, rarely provides the optimum circumstances for new venture creation. Indeed, Storey (1994: 128) has claimed that 'if the founder is unemployed prior to starting a business, that firm is unlikely to grow as rapidly as where the founder is employed'. This, he suggests, is because the unemployed 'have lower levels of skills (human capital) than individuals who are employed' (1994: 128). While this may have been the case in Britain in the 1980s and early 1990s, it is less likely to be true in the twenty-first century. With the continued advent of corporate downsizing, not only is such a contention somewhat dubious, but, as Kirby *et al.* (1996) have demonstrated, there are examples of successful new knowledge-based businesses being created as a direct result of 'forced' entrepreneurship, both in Britain and elsewhere.

Employment affects entrepreneurship in a number of other ways, however. For example, the changes in the pattern of employment have had a profound effect on the development of entrepreneurship. In the West, in particular, the demise of 'the job for life' and the onset of corporate downsizing/rightsizing have encouraged both individuals and governments to explore the opportunities afforded by entrepreneurship as a means of bringing more members of the population back into economic productivity. This is particularly important in an era when life-expectancy rates, and the costs and technology of healthcare are increasing, and governments are attempting to reduce the levels of personal taxation. Under such circumstances few governments are able to sustain high levels of unemployment, and entrepreneurship and self-employment are seen as the panacea. Indeed, commenting on the UK's Enterprise Allowance Scheme (see Chapter 4), Mills (1991: 93) has made the point that 'the rhetoric of the EAS claims to create an Enterprise Culture and encourage the growth of entrepreneurs in Britain. In practice it seems to have been a means of reducing the unemployment statistics.' There is little doubt that it was, for the reasons articulated already. In the process, however, it did raise awareness of the concept of self-employment and encourage the unemployed to explore it as an alternative to unemployment and increased dependency on the state. Thus it did contribute to the creation of a culture of enterprise by encouraging the unemployed to become more dependent on themselves and their own resources, if not any more creative and innovative. This way, it raised awareness of self-employment as an alternative to unemployment and the importance of new small firms to the economy.

Industry structure

Over the past 50 years or so there has been a very considerable shift in the structure of economies, with a movement out of manufacturing and into the service sector. While this is true of all economies, it is most noticeable in the developed economies (Daniels, 1993) where, on average, perhaps two-thirds of all employment is to be found in the service sector. Various theories have been put forward to explain this development, but essentially the debate focuses on whether the growth in services is independent of, or causally linked to, the decline in manufacturing. According to writers like Bell (1973), the growth of the service sector is part of a fundamental shift towards a post-industrial society. This involves a move away from blue-collar and towards white-collar employment as a result of the increased demand for services once basic demands have been met, and the consequent evolution of economies from agrarian to industrial and then to service activities. Alternatively, writers such as Bellon and Niosi (1988) argue that the changes do not signify the emergence of a new type of economy, but rather changes in an industry as it adjusts in an era of what is often referred to as 'late capitalism'. Thus they contend that the increases in service-sector employment are the result of manufacturers contracting out services to cut costs, increase flexibility and remain competitive. In all probability the two processes are not mutually exclusive and both are responsible, to some degree, for the resultant growth of the service sector in advanced-level economies.

Whatever the reasons for this shift in industrial structures from manufacturing industry to the service industries, there has been an increase not only in the number of smaller, more flexible medium-sized enterprises, but in new opportunities for potential entrepreneurs. In the UK, Keeble *et al.* (1991) and Jones-Evans and Kirby (1993) have pointed to the growth of small consultancy firms as part of this process, but the trend is much broader than the growth of the new knowledge-based industries and has embraced the whole of the service sector. Clearly, there is a trend in most advanced economies towards an economy based on information (Stonier, 1983) where access to knowledge is as important to economic development as access to raw materials has traditionally been. However, it is apparent, also, that while the knowledge-based industries (architecture, consultancy, design, education, financial services, publishing, research and development, etc.) are becoming the main wealth creators, around them is emerging a range of services, also dependent on skill and knowledge, associated with distribution, health and beauty, leisure, transport and communications, etc. (Kirby, 1995).

Thus there are two broad sets of services emerging: the new knowledge-based industries that are, perhaps, the core of a modern, post-industrial economy and those businesses that result from the wealth generated, in part, by the knowledge-based industries and that are based on turning into formal economic activities those functions that businesses and individuals previously did for themselves. Often the former are based on the new technologies, and can and do embrace the e-commerce revolution, but the latter are based on the more traditional knowledge and skills of the individual. Hence recent years have witnessed both a proliferation of new service-sector businesses that have taken a variety of forms, ranging from homeworking and telecottaging (Allen *et al.*, 1992; Stanworth and Stanworth, 1991), through network/multi-level marketing (Clothier, 1992) to franchising (Felstead, 1992; Price, 1997) and the new dot.com businesses.

Homeworking and telecottaging

Even in countries like Britain, which are reputed to have more reliable figures on homeworking than most other member states, it is difficult to assess the numbers involved. One of the reasons for this is the wide range of opportunities available. Hakim (1987) has identified five, which she calls Freelancers, Corporate Itinerants, Self-employed Itinerants, Personal Services/Own Account Workers and Traditional Homeworkers. However:

> 66 99   . . . technological changes and demographic trends are now leading to predictions that . . . a new army of millions of people currently working in large organisations will become home-based, computer-linked 'teleworkers', experiencing conditions akin to those experienced already by the many independently self-employed . . .
>
> *(Stanworth and Stanworth, 1991: 34)*

Also, several large organizations—among them Rank Xerox, the Department of Trade and Industry, and Texaco—are known to operate such schemes, while a company like the FI Group (see Chapter 4) was actually built by its founder, Steve Shirley, on the concept of women working from home (**www.figroup.co.uk**).

A CASE EXAMPLE

Color Me Beautiful

In Helen Fielding's novel *Bridget Jones's Diary* (Picador, 1996) the hapless Bridget records a conversation with her mother in the entry for Sunday 14 May. It reads:

> I'm taking you to have your colours done! And don't keep saying 'what', please, darling. Color Me Beautiful. I'm sick to death of you wandering round in all these dingy slurries and fogs . . . Mavis Enderby used to be all miserable in buffs and mosses, now she's had hers done she comes out in these wonderful shocking pinks and bottle greens and looks twenty years younger.

In reality, Color Me Beautiful (**www.cmb.co.uk**) is a UK image consultancy that gives advice to individuals, companies and politicians on how to present themselves. Founded in the UK in 1983, it operates through a network of approximately 1000 consultants covering 28 countries, including Russia and China. Color Me Beautiful trains the consultants and supplies them with product (coloured swatches, cosmetics, etc.). The consultants, who are all self-employed, pay £3000 for their training, and purchase from Color Me Beautiful any products they may use or sell. In return, they are permitted to use the Color Me Beautiful brand name in promoting their business and can benefit from the promotional activity that Color Me Beautiful engages in, through client referrals. Unlike network marketing organizations, however, the consultants are not expected to recruit other consultants to the organization and do not benefit from the sales of those members of the network they have recruited and 'manage'. Similarly the organization differs from franchising in that the consultants are not designated a defined geographical territory in which to operate, and pay no royalty fees to the parent organization.

The company was launched in 1983 by Mary Spillane, a 32-year-old graduate of Harvard's Kennedy School of Government, following the publication in the UK of Carole Jackson's best-selling book, *Color Me Beautiful*, in the same year. Mary secured a 25-year licence from Carole that gave her exclusive use of the name in the UK, Europe, the Middle East and Africa in return for a 10 per cent royalty on all UK sales. She started the venture from her kitchen in Battersea (London) with five consultants. Inevitably there were teething problems. Mary soon realized that she needed consultants who could not only sell the product (swatches of the coloured fabrics that most suited a woman's natural skin tone, eye and hair colourings) but who could advise British women on how to identify them. After 'Europeanizing' the wallets containing the swatches, making them better value for money, she started to recruit and train consultants, initially from among her network of friends and professional contacts. Assisted by her American partners, she provided the training, while the consultants funded it and generated the income for the business by marketing themselves and the Color Me Beautiful brand.

Through the sales of the book, interest in the concept continued to grow both in the UK and elsewhere. In 1985 Veronique Henderson, now a CMB director, joined to grow the business and it expanded into northern Europe, with distributors building consultancy networks in Germany, The Netherlands and Norway. Apart from diversifying into new geographical markets, the concept expanded to cover advice on style and body shape, and introduced its own range of cosmetics and scarves. Additionally it began to offer advice for men, including guidance on tailoring and personal grooming. By 1987, it had a network of 90 UK consultants. However, unlike in the USA, the UK consultants tended not to promote the CMB brand and a more proactive approach to marketing was adopted. Mary became more high profile in the business, writing books on the topic, and a marketing consultant (funded by the Department of Trade and Industry) was appointed. Additionally, the basic two-week training package, which cost approximately £2500, was expanded to include sessions on marketing and business administration.

In 1990, when the UK Parliament was first televised, Mary wrote to all of the MPs, advising them to consider the effect of their image on viewers and subsequent voting. Not only did this raise the profile of Color Me Beautiful, it resulted in both male and female MPs, from all parties, booking for personal consultations. By 1992, retailers were beginning to recognize the impact of colour coding and the company began to offer seminars targeted at the staff of retail companies, with the result that the corporate side of the business began to develop. Additionally, the business attracted as clients firms such as Andersen Consulting, Barclays Bank, British Airways, British Rail, British Telecom, Glaxo and IBM.

About this time, the contract was re-negotiated. Apart from concern over the original 25-year licence period, the business was becoming less and less dependent on the original concept of colour consulting and increasingly focused on image creation, something that had not been foreseen initial-

ly. Hence, under the revised agreement, ownership of the brand in the licence area was transferred to CMB Image Consultants who provided a royalty (of between 1 and 3 per cent) on sales to CMB USA. In return CMB USA paid a 3 per cent royalty to the UK company for any products or ideas it copied from it. Subsequent to this, retail interest in the UK increased further. Leading retail groups such as Burtons (see Chapter 12), Marks & Spencer, Next and Sears hired Color Me Beautiful consultants for sales training, customer promotions and design input, while a joint UK promotion with *Good Housekeeping* magazine in 1995/96 resulted in over 5000 women attending a consultation in six weeks. By 1997, Color Me Beautiful had joined forces with the specialist 'outsize' retailer, Evans, and had developed an in-store Color Me Beautiful consultation service at the company's premier retail store at Oxford Circus in London.

In 1999, Christopher Scarles, a former operations director with a firm selling beauty aids, bought the company and Mary left to spend more time developing her interests in business coaching. In the same year, Procter & Gamble asked Color Me Beautiful to help it launch a new product, and leading retail grocery chain Tesco invited CMB to join its Clubcard loyalty scheme. The business continued to develop and, by 2000, Color Me Beautiful was the most successful redemption programme on the Tesco Clubcard, accounting for 10.2 per cent of all redemptions. Meanwhile, a promotion in the *Daily Express* newspaper in February 2000 resulted in over 40,000 enquiries, while a further feature in the *Daily Mail* in September of the same year attracted some 20,000.

Since then there has been further collaboration with some of the country's leading retail companies. These have included fashion updates with such clothing retailers as Wallis and Evans, and joint promotional activities with Boots and WHSmith. Additionally CMB fronted a 30-venue roadshow intended to attract women drivers for the French car manufacturer Peugeot, while Emap/*Drapers Record* asked it to participate at the relaunch of its main trade exhibition: Premier Womenswear/Pure. In 2002, CMB launched its wedding programme.

Lorraine Greenspan (**stylecounsel@lineone.net**) is a CMB image consultant based in Portsmouth, offering colour analysis, style consultations, make-up lessons, personal shopping and wardrobe 'weeding'. She trained with the company, after working for Estée Lauder Cosmetics in a department store in Leeds and then for 10 years on cruise ships with Allders International Ships Ltd. When she gave up 'cruising', she was at a loss as to what to do. She got a job as a temp controller with a recruitment firm but left after a couple of years. She was looking for her 'niche'—that 'special something I was good at and would love doing'. In the mid-1980s she had seen a company similar to CMB and had thought at the time that she would love to do a job similar to that, but nobody in her family or circle of friends had ever run their own business before and she was not sure where to start. 'I was single,' she says, 'with a mortgage and needed a steady, reliable income.' However, having gone with her sister-in-law to an image consultant to have a colour analysis, she began looking around and was particularly impressed with CMB's website and promotional material. As she says, 'their training fees were also affordable and because CMB is not a franchise it meant that my initial outlay was not too high', which was important as she had been without any income for the previous eight months. Having done her training and set up her studio, she realized that people were not going to come to her unless she promoted herself. She bought the client base of another CMB consultant in her area, who was retiring, and set about promoting herself to them and more broadly. As a consequence, in her first year of trading, she saw 123 different clients and had a turnover in the order of £8000. As this was considerably less than she had expected, she took a part-time job to boost her income, which has created something of a tension as she wants to be at home more, marketing her business. As a result, she has had to work long hours and rarely has a complete day off. However, her plan for year two is to double her turnover and introduce a complete bridal service helping to co-ordinate everything. She believes this is possible as 'CMB are constantly trying to help and inspire us to increase our business and if I have ever asked for help they have been excellent.' Thereafter her intention is to become one of CMB's top 10 consultants within three years.

In contrast, Lesley Everett (**www.leconsultants. co.uk**) was trained with Color Me Beautiful in 1998 and has been acting as an image consultant ever since. Based in the Binfield area of Berkshire, Lesley left school at 18 and trained in skincare and make-up with the Swedish company Oriflame. At the time she saw this as a 'stop gap' and eventually found employment in the magistrates courts service in Lowestoft, where she began training as a lawyer. Although she had never seen a computer before, when a job came up as an IT manager for Suffolk Courts, she applied for it and was successful. After four years of doing this she was headhunted by the computer software company Unisys, where she was engaged as a customer support specialist with responsibility for training, pre-sales support, customer service, software maintenance and project management. Although she enjoyed the corporate life and the opportunity to learn to program, there was something missing. As she says: 'after five years or so I started to realize that I needed something a little more creative in my life, so I enrolled on various evening courses in beauty therapy, physiology, anatomy and massage, and some aromatherapy'. In 1993, when her son Max was born, she decided it was time to do what she really wanted and, in 1994, she set up in business as an independent IT consultant. However, after reading Carole Jackson's book, she trained with Color Me Beautiful and changed direction, becoming an image consultant, using her corporate contacts and experience to build up the corporate side of her enterprise. Now she has around 50 corporate clients and hundreds of private ones, and most of her life is spent working with individuals, teams and large audiences in the field of positive image creation. As a result of engaging an agent, she has developed a high media profile and regularly features on the television, on radio, and in business and consumer magazines. Increasingly she is moving into keynote speaking, as well as training, and is writing a book entitled *Walking Tall* (which, at the time of writing, was due to be published by McGraw-Hill in September 2002). Although her business has developed beyond the core activities of CMB, Lesley acknowledges its importance in getting her established. As she says:

> I think something like CMB is great. It gave me a wonderful opportunity to start my own business without the need for massive outlay and overheads. I knew I wanted to use it as a vehicle to develop my own corporate image business, which is exactly what I've done. They provide a great starting point and support for people . . .

Network/multi-level marketing

Although in a country like the UK no account is taken of it in official statistics (Brodie and Stanworth, 1998), direct selling via multi-level or network marketing has been one of the fastest-growing methods of self-employment in recent years. In part this has resulted from the success of a number of international (mainly American) companies, such as Amway International, that have helped overcome the mistrust that this method of operation has engendered. Often linked with the discredited system of pyramid selling, multi-level or network marketing is based on the principle of 'self-employed distributors being encouraged to build a sales organisation of persons like themselves by their own efforts' (Clothier, 1992: 259). They are rewarded financially on the basis of the total sales of the distributors within the organization developed by them and in this way are paid in propor-tion to their efforts with respect to both selling and 'sponsoring' (recruiting) others. Clearly the system has many attractions, not least the ability to start and build a business without any previous experience or skills, or any great capital investment (as the distributors work from home and stockholding is kept to the minimum of demonstration items). However, there is a downside to the system which, as Clothier (1992: 260) recognizes, relates to 'the over-enthusiastic, uneth-ical, and occasionally illegal activities of distributors'.

Franchising

Franchising is a further relatively low-cost means of setting up a new venture that has grown rapidly in recent years, both in Britain and internationally. In the UK, for example, the number of franchise systems was estimated to be 568 in 1998, a 40 per cent increase over the figure for 1994. Annual turnover was approximate-ly £7 billion (£36.6 billion if car dealerships, petrol retailing, the licensed trade and the soft drinks market are included) and something in the order of one-third of all retail sales were through franchised operations. However, while retailing is the largest sector of the franchise industry in the UK, it is by no means purely a retailing phenomenon (Kirby and Watson, 2000; Watson and Kirby, 2000). Essentially franchising is the arrangement whereby the owner of a product, process or service (the franchisor) allows someone else (the franchisee) the right to use it in exchange for some sort of payment or payments. It can take the form of granting the right to run railways, broadcast radio or television programmes, or sell products. The most common form of franchising occurs when a company allows a third party to operate a proven business system in a defined geographi-cal area using a common format for promoting, managing and administering the business. This is known as business format franchising.

Although systems vary according to the type of business, its objectives and the culture of the franchise company, the franchisor owns the business system but, in return for a fee, allows the franchisee to use it, and continues to support him/her with national promotion, training and administration as well as continuing prod-uct, service and system development in return for an annual fee, usually a per-centage of turnover. Prior to offering the business opportunity for sale, the fran-chisor should have piloted the concept to iron out all of the problems and ensure it works. Hence, the process should, in theory at least, be less risky than setting up an entirely new, independent small business and should result in fewer failures. As Stanworth and Kirby (1993: 333) have recognized, 'franchising offers a promising chemistry for combining the economies of scale enjoyed by the franchisor with the flexibility of the franchisee to exploit local market situations'. Under such circumstances, it is understandable that franchising has grown so rapidly, though there is evidence 'that points towards franchising being even more risky than conventional small business activity in the first four or five years for both franchisor and franchisee' (Stanworth *et al.*, 1998: 67).

While there is no definitive study of franchise failure rates, and the debate continues as to whether franchising is more or less of a risk than independent ownership, Stanworth and Purdy (2000: 199) have reported that, 'there is a striking similarity between the failure rates of young franchise systems and conventional small businesses at the same stage of development'. Certainly there are pitfalls for the unwary, and prospective franchisees need to ensure that the franchise systems they are buying into are proven and ethical. As the franchise industry is aware of

A CASE EXAMPLE

Amway

Amway (**www.amway.com**) is a US$5 billion network marketing business operating in 80 countries through 3 million independent business owners/distributors. It was founded in 1959 by two American entrepreneurs, Rich Devos and Jay Van Andel. After serving in the US Air Force in the 1940s they established various business ventures including a period as independent distributors for Nutrilite vitamins. During this time they realized that anyone willing to work hard could have a business of their own through this direct person-to-person method of marketing. In 1959 they created the Amway Sales and Marketing Plan, which offered anyone an opportunity to build a business of their own, marketing exceptional products (LOC Multipurpose Cleaner) through the network marketing method. In its first full year of business, Amway's sales were more than US$0.5 million. During the 1960s the business grew rapidly and, by the end of the decade, had expanded into Canada and was offering more than 200 products through some 10,000 independent distributors. The 1970s began with sales of more than US$100 million and, early in the decade, after a lengthy inquiry, which established that Amway was not a pyramid sales organization, it launched its second international affiliate in Australia. It then went on to open further affiliates in the UK, Hong Kong and Malaysia and, by 1980, sales had reached US$1 billion a year. The company continued to expand its product range and introduced the Amway Water Treatment System. At the beginning of the 1990s the two sons of Rich and Jay (Steve Van Andel and Dick Devos) succeeded their fathers as chairman and president respectively and, by 1997, sales had risen to US$7 billion. In the fiscal year ending 31 August 2000, the company had a turnover of US$5.1 billion, which it achieved via a network of more than 3 million independent business owners worldwide. In the UK, the Republic of Ireland and the Channel Islands, there were some 30,000 full- or part-time business associates. Enrolment is open to anyone of the age of 18 (20 in Jersey) or over, and no capital or prior experience is required. Potential associates have to be nominated by an existing associate and pay an enrolment fee of £80 (IR£89 in the Republic of Ireland and £77 in the Channel Islands). In return they receive a Business Opportunity Kit, containing sample products and business literature to help start the business. Additionally the company runs leadership programmes intended to help motivate associates and has an Amway Independent Business Owner Hall of Fame featuring its most successful associates. They earn their income through profit on the goods they sell (which averages at around 30 per cent) and a bonus based on the volume of sales generated by their own network (ranging from between 3 and 21 per cent of the total sales volume).

these difficulties, there is an International Franchise Association (IFA), with member associations representing individual countries (**www.british-franchise.org.uk**), which polices the sector. Thus a franchise system that belongs to the relevant country association is more likely to offer a sound business prospect than one that does not, though not all successful franchise systems are members of the IFA by any means. However, franchising is not suitable for everyone. Indeed, it would seem that the most entrepreneurial individuals do not make good franchisees (Fenwick and Strombom, 1998), and the prospective franchisee must ensure that he/she possesses the requisite attributes for success.

A CASE EXAMPLE

A tale of two franchises

Kall-Kwik is the leading print, copy and design franchise in the UK. It was founded in 1978 by Moshe Gerstenhaber who acquired the master licence for Europe from the American Kwik Copy Corporation. The first two franchises were opened in London, at Marble Arch and Pall Mall, and by 1999, when it was purchased by the Adare Printing Group plc, there were nearly 200 centres throughout Britain, and the business had a turnover of £70 million. Adrian and Ursula George are typical Kall-Kwik franchisees. Although they had no experience in the printing industry and lived in London, they purchased the Kall-Kwik franchise in Aberdeen in Scotland, 600 miles north of their London home. With effort, vision, the support of their franchisor and the advice of their fellow franchisees, turnover grew from £170,000 to £400,000 in just a couple of years. Adrian and Ursula now have a successful business, and Adrian's advice to anyone thinking about franchising is: 'The rewards are there if you work hard and accept the valuable support, but take it gradually and set realistic aims.'

In contrast, life was not so rosy for franchisees belonging to the Pierre Victoire franchise system. April 1988 saw the establishment of the company, a French bistro-style restaurant with a simple philosophy: good-quality food at affordable prices. The concept, which included basic decor that emphasized the quality of the food rather than the surroundings, was the brainchild of Pierre Levicky. He arrived in Scotland from his native France in the 1980s with less than £100 in his pocket. He opened his first restaurant, in Victoria Street, Edinburgh, and in 1992 the first franchise was opened. By 1998 this had increased to 86 and the company was looking to open more than 20 that year. Typically a Pierre Victoire franchisee would be required to pay an initial franchise fee of £17,500 (excluding VAT) and to invest a total of £60,000 to £90,000 in the venture, excluding working capital of £2000. In return, the company predicted a year one turnover of £450,000 and a projected profit of £57,000. By year three, this would have risen to £650,000 and £110,000 respectively. Unfortunately, in June 1998, the company went into voluntary liquidation with debts of over £6 million. As one customer is reported to have said on hearing the news, 'You would have thought that with good food at the right price they were on a winning formula, but I suppose you can never tell.' Certainly the market had become more competitive since the first outlet had opened and possibly the franchise had not responded to the changes in the market, but the main problem was probably that the company had expanded too rapidly. According to a spokesman for the franchise, 'If you are funding from cashflow and you have a slight downturn, you are suddenly left with a gaping hole in your finances. There was an insufficient capital base to justify this rate of expansion.'

Case example exercise

Evaluate the case studies of Color Me Beautiful, Amway, Kall-Kwik and Pierre Victoire. Consider the advantages and disadvantages of these forms of entrepreneurship for: (a) someone wishing to grow their own business; (b) someone wishing to become self-employed; and (c) the promotion of entrepreneurship in society.

The new dot.com businesses

Apart from such relatively traditional forms of doing business, new business opportunities have been created by advances in technology, particularly through the Internet, electronic mail and the World Wide Web. As a consequence of such developments, start-up businesses adopting the modern technology are born global. Simply by developing a website, new entrants can compete on a par with established businesses while the low cost of distribution on the Internet makes it viable for established businesses to serve whole new market segments. Thus what were formerly small niche businesses can be transformed into mass operators trawling the world for customers. Not surprisingly, under such circumstances, hundreds of new e-commerce businesses have been, and are being, established. In America in the five years up to March 2000, the Internet industry grew from one company, AmericaOnLine with a market value of US$1 billion, to more than 300 companies with a market capitalization totalling more than US$1 trillion.

By contrast, development in the UK has been slower, though in 1999 it was worth an estimated £2.8 billion. In September 1999, the Prime Minister, the Rt Hon Tony Blair, gave a speech in Cambridge during which he warned British businessmen that they risked going bankrupt if they did not embrace the commercial opportunity presented by the Internet. After that there emerged what can only be described as 'e-mania' with new dot.com businesses springing up rapidly across the country. Some of these new businesses were, themselves, high-tech businesses such as Orchestream (see Chapter 5), while others, such as Iglu.com (see Chapter 6), are more traditional businesses operating through the e-commerce medium.

However, the boom was short-lived. By March 2000, the senior Internet and e-commerce analyst at Merrill Lynch, Henry Blodget, was forecasting that 75 per cent of all the Internet companies would disappear in five years and 75 per cent would never make enough money to sell themselves. Within four months of this prediction, failures and redundancies among the dot.com companies were commonplace in America, though by July 2000 only the clothing retailer Boo.com had ceased trading in Britain (see Chapter 2).

As in most things, however, America was ahead of the rest of the world and, since then, the dot.com bubble has burst. Even so, it has done much to stimulate a spirit of enterprise, fuelled by such media headlines as 'Who wants to be an Internet millionaire? You too can get rich quick with your own dot.com business'

A CASE EXAMPLE

Amazon.com

Amazon.com was in 1999 the third-largest book retailer in the USA and the largest in the UK and Germany. Yet, it was less than five years old and, though it had not yet made a profit, was valued at US$11 billion. The business had been founded in 1994 by Jeff Bezos a graduate in computer science and electrical engineering from Princeton University who, at the age of 30, had given up a promising career in investment banking to participate in the dot.com boom. Armed with US$11 million that he had managed to secure from his network of contacts on Wall Street and venture capitalists on

America's west coast, he established the 'headquarters' of his operation in a 400 sq ft storeroom in Seattle, Washington, USA.

From the outset, Bezos did not want to replicate what existing bookstores did. Rather he wanted to remove the hassle of buying books and to demonstrate that buying online could result in an enhanced service to the customer. The company's staff were trained in dealing with customer queries and 20 per cent of them were dedicated to dealing with enquiries. Additionally, using the power of the Internet, he sought to get to know customers better and to offer a 'personalized' service. Apart from providing a catalogue of books on offer, the Amazon.com site offers book reviews from leading journals as well as from visitors to the site. Additionally, when customers look up a title, they are informed of two or three other titles purchased by others who have bought that book. Also, having purchased the book, customers receive regular e-mails about 'exceptional' books in the same or similar categories. Finally, because of the volume involved and the reduction in expensive overheads (such as premises), Amazon.com is able to offer texts at discount prices: 20 per cent off the price of a paperback edition and 30 per cent off a hardback.

Believing that economies of scale and scope are the key to success in such dot.com operations, Bezos has expanded the business rapidly through both buyouts and diversification. In 1998, he bought two Internet companies—PlanetAll and Junglee Corp—for a reported £259 million. PlanetAll was a provider of automated online services that enabled subscribers to update their address books, calendars and reminders on a minute-by-minute basis. It gave Amazon.com access to a client list of people who might want to send its merchandise as gifts, for example. In contrast, Junglee Corp made database systems that enabled customers to find any kind of merchandise on the Internet, sharing its revenues with the portals that subscribed to it. Its acquisition enabled Amazon to diversify its product range, which it did in June 1998 with its expansion into music, offering more than 125,000 CDs at discounts of up to 40 per cent. This was followed by diversification into the specialist children's and young people's market, offering a catalogue of more than 100,000 books for children and teenagers through Amazon.com Kids, together with all the traditional Amazon.com customer services. Finally, in order to improve service to local markets, it diversified geographically by purchasing Buying Bookpages in the UK—and setting up Amazon.co.uk—and Telebook in Germany, where it established Amazon.de.

When it went public in May 1997, its initial offering was three million shares at US$18 per share. By August the price had risen to US$28.75. Shortly after, the company negotiated a US$75 million credit facility from a bank consortium headed by Deutsche Morgan Grenfell and, by December 1998, Amazon was trading at US$284 a share. According to Jonathon Cohen of Merrill Lynch, this made Amazon 'probably the single most expensive publicly traded company in the history of US equity markets'. By June 1999, however, its share price had fallen to US$99, having lost US$125 million the previous year and amidst a growing belief that the real winners on the net will be firms that sell their own products directly to consumers.

Although sales continued to increase, net losses in the final quarter of 1999 were US$323 million and US$545 million on the same date in 2000. In February 2001 the company warned that sales would be more than 10 per cent lower than expected for the year. Even so, it predicted an operating profit for the fourth quarter, possibly reflecting the 1300 job cuts in the American operation, the closure of one of its warehouses and its diversification into toys, furniture and kitchen goods. According to the Wall Street analyst, Ravi Suria, however, this seemed unlikely. By February 2001 Amazon.com's shares had slumped to US$11.81 and Suria was predicting that the company would face the threat of a squeeze by creditors in the second half of the year, resulting in it running out of cash. According to Suria, 'in 1999 Amazon was a growth story. In 2000 it became a credit story and in 2001 it's a distress story. The party is over.'

Case example exercise

Review the above case of Amazon.com and find out as much additional information about the company as you can. What, in your view, are the lessons to be learned from Amazon about setting up a successful dot.com business? Are the problems facing new dot.com businesses similar to or different from those facing the more traditional business formats? Justify your answer.

(*Telegraph*, 22 January, 2000). Even so, as David Wilkinson of Ernst & Young has recognized: 'The backlash against the dot.com boom has the potential to create a negative environment towards new start-ups and it is therefore more important than ever that we understand better the role that . . . entrepreneurs play in our economy' (Ernst & Young, 2001).

PAUSE FOR THOUGHT

Reflect on the above politico-economic influences and relate them to the circumstances in your environment. What are the politico-economic factors stimulating entrepreneurship development? What are the factors hindering it?

Institutional or organizational factors

Fordism and post-Fordism

The emphasis on Fordism, and the belief that economic growth and national competitive advantage could be achieved only by economies of scale in production led to a decline in entrepreneurial development both in the developed and the developing economies of the world. Not only was it assumed that the modern large-scale corporations provided the appropriate context for the application of the most advanced techniques of modern management, but such plants were seen as the outward manifestation of advanced economic development. Under such circumstances, the roles of entrepreneurship and small business development were seen as irrelevant. In the post-Fordist era, when large corporations are 'downsizing', 'delayering', 'outsourcing' and 're-engineering', the conditions for entrepreneurship and new venture creation become much more favourable.

Corporate culture

Corporate culture can, and frequently does, stultify entrepreneurship development. As will be discussed in more detail in Chapter 12, the internal culture of large organizations often acts as a barrier to entrepreneurship/intrapreneurship. In particular, it appears to be stifled by:

- the hierarchical nature of the large corporation
- the bureaucracy involved in formal reporting systems, lines of authority and control mechanisms
- short-term performance standards
- loss of ownership
- career mobility and loss of continuity
- inflexibility and the inability to change direction
- reward systems based on strict performance measures.

Corporate prestige

However, there are other ways in which large organizations stultify entrepreneurship. The prestige with which the large corporation is viewed means that suppliers (whether of money, education, materials or labour, etc.) often prefer to do business with the large corporation, basking in the reflected glory of having as a client a prestigious wealthy multi-national corporation. Frequently these are, themselves, large corporations that better understand the culture of the organization with which they are doing business. Even when new small firms do start up and secure large firms as their clients, there are often problems. Frequently these relate to late payments and the confrontational way they are treated by their large-firm counterparts. Indeed, a study by Peel *et al.* (2000) suggests that in the UK almost two-thirds of all large businesses (with more than 200 employees) are considered as slow payers. Gradually, this is breaking down, and large firms are beginning to form strategic alliances and partnerships with their small-firm clients and contractors, as well as providing assistance and support to promote new venture creation and develop an enterprise culture (see Chapter 5).

Chapter Review

➡ Three different sets of factors—socio-economic, politico-cultural and institutional-organizational—affect the development of entrepreneurship.

➡ The socio-cultural factors include:

- religion

- education

- family

- history

- role models.

➡ The politico-economic factors include:

- the political system

- the state of the economy

- employment levels

- industry structure.

➡ The institutional-organizational factors include:

- Fordism

- the corporate culture and corporate prestige.

Quick Revision

(Answers at the end of this section)

1. What, according to Timmons (1994), is the trigger that stimulates entrepreneurship development in the USA?

   (a) desire for wealth

   (b) education

   (c) independence

2. Which of the following are not included in Morrison's five socio-cultural factors influencing the development of an enterprise culture?

(a) religion

(b) education

(c) family

(d) employment levels

(e) corporate culture

3. Traditionally entrepreneurship has flourished when an economy is in recession. Is this:

(a) true

(b) false?

4. How does corporate culture stultify entrepreneurship development?

(a) by emphasizing the benefits derived from economies of scale

(b) through the internal culture of the large organization

(c) by encouraging business with prestigious multi-national organizations

(d) by preventing small firms from entering the market

Answers to Quick Revision: 1–b; 2–d and e; 3–a; 4–b and c

Learning Style Activities

➡ **Activist:** Ask your friends, fellow students or work colleagues what they believe has most influenced their attitudes to entrepreneurship.

➡ **Reflector:** Reflect on their answers, and compare their responses to both your own experiences and the contents of this chapter.

➡ **Theorist:** On the basis of the empirical research you have just conducted, your own experience and the existing body of understanding, attempt to evolve a theory of the factors that stimulate entrepreneurship in the economy, society or the organization.

➡ **Pragmatist:** Make recommendations to your government or your employer about what needs to be done to create an enterprise culture.

Reading

Allen, S., C. Truman and C. Wolkowitz (1992) Home-Based Work: Self-Employment and Small Business, in P. Leighton and A. Felstead (eds) *The New Entrepreneurs: Self-Employment and Small Business in Europe*. London: Kogan Page Ltd.

Anderson, J. (1995) *Local Heroes*. Glasgow: Scottish Enterprise.

Bannock, G. (1981) *The Economics of Small Firms*. Oxford: Basil Blackwell.

Bell, D. (1973) *The Coming of Post-Industrial Society: A Venture in Social Forecasting*. New York: Basic Books.

Bellon, B. and J. Niosi (1988) *The Decline of the American Economy*. Montreal: Black Rose Books.

Beveridge, L. (2001) *Cambridge Entrepreneurs in the Business of Technology*. Cambridge: Granta Editions.

Blawatt, K.R. (1995) Entrepreneurship in Estonia: Profiles of Entrepreneurs. *Journal of Small Business Management* **33** (2), 74–9.

Brodie, S. and J. Stanworth (1998) Independent Contractors in Direct Selling: Self-employed but Missing from Official Records. *International Small Business Journal* **16** (3), 95–101.

Burrows, R. (1991) The Discourse of the Enterprise Culture and the Restructuring of Britain: A Polemical Contribution, in Curran, J. and R. Blackburn (eds) *Paths of Enterprise: The Future of the Small Business*, London: Routledge.

Chia, R. (1996) Teaching Paradigm Shift in Management Education: University Business Schools and the Entrepreneurial Imagination. *Journal of Management Studies* **33** (4), 409–28.

Clothier, P. (1992) *Multi-Level Marketing: A Practical Guide to Successful Network Selling*. London: Kogan Page.

Daniels, P.W. (1993) *Service Industries in the World Economy*. Oxford: Blackwell Publishers.

Department of Employment (1989) *Enterprise in Higher Education: Key Features of the Enterprise in Higher Education Proposals*. Sheffield: The Training Agency.

Dick, B.W. (1987) *Privatisation in the UK: The Free Market Versus State Control*. London: Longman.

Ernst & Young (2001) *Entrepreneur of the Year: Report 2001*. London: Ernst & Young.

Felstead, A. (1992) Franchising, Self-employment and the 'Enterprise Culture': A UK Perspective, in P. Leighton and A. Felstead (eds) *The New Entrepreneurs: Self-Employment and Small Business in Europe*. London: Kogan Page Ltd.

Fenwick, G. and M. Strombom (1998) The Determinants of Franchisee Performance: An Empirical Investigation. *International Small Business Journal* **16** (4), 28–45.

Gibb, A.A. (1987) Enterprise Culture—Its Meaning and Implication for Education and Training. *Journal of European Industrial Training* **2** (2), 3–37.

Gibb, A.A. (1990) Entrepreneurship and Intrapreneurship—Exploring the Differences, in Donckels, R. and A. Miettinen (eds) *New Findings and Perspectives in Entrepreneurship*. Aldershot: Gower.

Gibb, A.A. (1996) Entrepreneurship and Small Business Management: Can We Afford to Neglect Them in the Twenty-First Century Business School? *British Journal of Management* **7** (4), 309–22.

Gibb, A.A. (2000) SME Policy, Academic Research and the Growth of Ignorance: Mythical Concepts, Myths, Assumptions, Rituals and Confusions. *International Small Business Journal* **18** (3), 13–35.

Gibb, A.A. and Z. Haas (1996) Developing Local Support Services for Small Business Development in Central and Eastern Europe—The Donor Challenge. *Entrepreneurship and Regional Development* **8** (3), 197–216.

Hakim, C. (1987) Trends in the Flexible Workforce. *Department of Employment Gazette* **95**, 549–60.

Hall, P. (1985) The Geography of the Fifth Kondratieff Cycle, in Hall, P. and A. Markusen (eds) *Silicon Landscape*. London: Allen and Unwin.

Hall, P. and P. Preston (1988) *The Carrier Wave: New Information Technology and the Geography of Innovation, 1846–2003*. London: Unwin Hyman.

Handy, C. (1985) *The Future of Work: A Guide to a Changing Society*. Oxford: Basil Blackwell Ltd.

Handy, C. (1999) *The New Alchemist: How Visionary People Make Something Out of Nothing*. London: Hutchinson.

Hart, K. (1971) *Informal Income, Opportunities and the Structure of Urban Employment in Ghana*. Paper presented at a conference on Urban Employment in Africa. Brighton: University of Sussex, Institute of Development Studies.

Haskins, G., A.A. Gibb and A. Hubert (1986) *A Guide to Small Business Assistance in Europe*. Aldershot: Gower.

Hobbs, D. (1991) Business as a Master Metaphor: Working Class Entrepreneurship and Business-like Policing, in Burrows, R. (ed.) *Deciphering the Enterprise Culture*. London: Routledge.

Hornaday, J.A. (1982), quoted in R.W.Y. Kao (1990) Who is Entrepreneur?, in Donckels, R. and A. Miettinen (eds) *New Findings and Perspectives in Entrepreneurship*. Aldershot: Gower.

Interman (1991) *Profiles of Entrepreneurship Development Programmes*. Geneva: International Labour Office.

Ivy, R.L. (1996) Small Scale Entrepreneurs and Private Sector Development in the Slovak Republic. *Journal of Small Business Management* **34** (4), 77–83.

Ivy, R.L. (1997) Entrepreneurial Strategies and Problems in Post-Communist Europe: A Survey of SMEs in Slovakia. *Journal of Small Business Management*, 93–7.

Johannisson, B. (1987) Towards a Theory of Local Entrepreneurship, in R. Wyckham, I. Meredith and G. Bushe (eds) *The Spirit of Entrepreneurship*. Proceedings of 32nd ICSB World Conference, Vancouver.

Jones-Evans, D. and D.A. Kirby (1993) Technical Entrepreneurs in the Service Sector: The Growth of Small Technical Consultancies in the United Kingdom, in Chittenden, F., M. Robertson and D. Watkins (eds) *Small Firms: Recession and Recovery*. London: Paul Chapman Publishing Ltd.

Keeble, D., J. Bryson and P. Wood (1991) Small Firms, Business Services Growth and Regional Development in the UK—Some Empirical Findings. *Regional Studies* **25**, 439–57.

Kelly, A. (1991) The Enterprise Culture and the Welfare State: Restructuring the Management of the Health and Personal Social Services, in Burrows, R. (ed.) *Deciphering the Enterprise Culture*, London: Routledge.

Kirby, D.A. (1985) Small Firms in the Economy of South Africa. *International Small Business Journal* **4** (2), 36–48.

Kirby, D.A. (1995) The Development of the Service Sector, in Evans, L., P. Johnson and B. Thomas (eds) *The Northern Region Economy: Progress and Prospects in the North of England*. London: Mansell Publishing Ltd.

Kirby, D.A. and Y. Fan (1995) Chinese Cultural Values and Entrepreneurship: A Preliminary Consideration. *Journal of Enterprising Culture* **3** (3), 245–61.

Kirby, D.A. and A. Watson (2000) Franchising as a Small Business Development Strategy: A Qualitative Study of Operational and 'Failed' Franchisors in the UK. *Journal of Small Business and Enterprise Development* **6** (4), 341–9.

Kirby, D.A., D. Jones-Evans, P. Futo, S. Kwiatkowski and J. Schwalbach (1996) A Comparative Study of an Emerging Form of Entrepreneurship: Technical Consultants in Hungary, Poland and the UK. *Entrepreneurship, Theory and Practice* **20** (4), 9–23.

Kondratieff, N. (1935) The Long Waves of Economic Life. *Review Economic Studies* **17** (6).

Leadbeater, C. (1997) *The Rise of the Social Entrepreneur*. London: Demos.

Maarsdorp, G.G. (1983) Some Thoughts and Evidence on the Informal Sector. *Development Studies Southern Africa* **4** (4).

MacDonald, R and F. Coffield (1991) *Risky Business: Youth and the Enterprise Culture*. London: Falmer Press.

Massey, D. (1988) What's Happening to UK Manufacturing, in Allen, J. and D. Massey (eds) *The Economy in Question*. London: Sage.

Mills, V. (1991) Review of Some Economic and Psychological Considerations on the Effects of the EAS. *International Small Business Journal* **9** (4), 91–4.

Mitter, S. (1986) Industrial Restructuring and Manufacturing Homework. *Capital and Class* **27**, 37–80.

Morris, M.H. and L.F. Pitt (1995) Informal Sector Activity: Insights from a South African Township. *Journal of Small Business Management* **33** (1), 78–86.

Morrison, A. (2000) Initiating Entrepreneurship, in Carter, S. and D. Jones-Evans (eds) *Enterprise and Small Business: Principles, Practice and Policy*. Harlow: Prentice Hall.

Peel, M., N. Wilson and C. Howarth (2000) Late Payment and Credit Management in the Small Firm Sector: Some Empirical Evidence. *International Small Business Journal* **18** (2), 17–37.

Peters, T. (1987) *Thriving on Chaos: Handbook for a Management Revolution*. London: Pan Books.

Phillips, B. and H. Brice (1988) Black Business in South Africa: A Challenge to Enterprise. *International Small Business Journal* **6** (3), 42–58.

Price, S. (1997) *The Franchise Paradox: New Directions, Different Strategies*. London: Cassell.

Rauch, J.E. (1991) Modelling the Informal Sector Formally. *Journal of Development Economics* **35**, 33–47.

Reeves, F. and R. Ward (1984) West Indian Business in Britain, in Ward, R. and R. Jenkins (eds) *Ethnic Communities in Business*. Cambridge: Cambridge University Press.

Ritchie, J. (1991a) Enterprise Cultures: A Framework Analysis, in Burrows, R. (ed.) *Deciphering the Enterprise Culture*. London: Routledge.

Ritchie, J. (1991b) Chasing Shadows: Enterprise Culture as an Educational Phenomenon. *Journal of Education Policy* **6** (3), 315–25.

Rogerson, C.M. and K.S.O. Beavon (1982) Getting by in the 'Informal Sector' of Soweto. *Tijdschrift voor Economische en Sociale Geografie* **xxiii** (4).

Scase, R. (2000) The Enterprise Culture: The Socio-Economic Context of Small Firms, in Carter, S. and D. Jones-Evans (eds) *Enterprise and Small Business: Principles, Practice and Policy*. Harlow: Prentice Hall.

Schumpeter, J.A. (1939) *Business Cycles: A Theoretical, Historical and Statistical Analysis of the Capitalist Process*. London: McGraw-Hill.

Scottish Enterprise (1997) *Local Heroes*. Edinburgh: Insider Group.

Sethuruman, S.V. (1977) The Urban Informal Sector in Africa. *International Labour Review* **116** (3).

Siu, W.S. and D.A. Kirby (1995) Marketing in Chinese Small Business: Tentative Theory. *Journal of Enterprising Culture* **3** (3), 309.

Siu, W.S. and D.A. Kirby (1999) Small Firm Marketing: A Comparison of Eastern and Western Marketing Practices. *Asia Pacific Journal of Management* **16** (2), 259–74.

Smyth, J. (1999) Schooling and Enterprise Culture. *Journal of Educational Policy* **14** (4), 435–44.

Solomon, G. (1989) Youth: Tomorrow's Entrepreneurs. *ICSB Bulletin* **xxvi** (5), 1–2.

Southern, A. (2000) The Social and Cultural World of Enterprise, in Carter, S. and D. Jones-Evans (eds) *Enterprise and Small Business: Principles, Practice and Policy*. Harlow: Prentice Hall.

Stanworth, J. and D.A. Kirby (1993) Franchising and Franchise Entrepreneurship: Socio-economic Considerations in Development, in Hills, G.R., R. Laforge and D. Muzyka (eds) *Research at the Marketing/Entrepreneurship Interface*. Chicago: University of Illinois at Chicago.

Stanworth, J. and D. Purdy (2000) Franchising and Enterprise, in Carter, S. and D. Jones-Evans (eds) *Enterprise and Small Business: Principles, Practice and Policy*. Harlow: Prentice Hall.

Stanworth, J. and C. Stanworth (1991) Enterprise 2000: Workbase the Electronic Cottage?, in Curran, J. and R. Blackburn (eds) *Paths of Enterprise: The Future of the Small Business*, London: Routledge.

Stanworth, J., D. Purdy, S. Price and N. Zafiris (1998) Franchise Versus Conventional Small Business Failure Rates in the US and UK: More Similarities Than Differences. *International Small Business Journal* **16** (3), 56–69.

Stanworth, J., S. Blythe, B. Granger and C. Stanworth (1989) Who Becomes an Entrepreneur? *International Small Business Journal* **8** (1), 11–22.

Stonier, T. (1983) *The Wealth of Information: A Profile of the Post-industrial Economy*. London: Methuen.

Storey, D.J. (1994) *Understanding the Small Business Sector*. London: Routledge.

Timmons, J.A. (1989) *The Entrepreneurial Mind*. Andover MA: Brick House Publishing.

Timmons, J.A. (1994) *New Venture Creation*. Boston MA: Irwin.

Timmons, J.A., L.E. Smollen and A.L.M. Dingee (1985) *New Venture Creation*. Homewood IL: Irwin.

Vesper, K. and W. Gartner (1998) *Entrepreneurship Programs Worldwide*. Los Angeles: University of Southern California.

Wanogho, E. (1997) *Black Women Taking Charge*. London: EW International.

Ward, R. (1991) Economic Development and Ethnic Business, in Curran, J. and R.A. Blackburn (eds) *Paths of Enterprise: The Future of the Small Business*. London: Routledge.

Watson, A. and D.A. Kirby (2000) Explanations of the Decision to Franchise in a Non-traditional Franchise Sector: The Case of the UK Construction Industry. *Journal of Small Business and Enterprise Development* **7** (4), 343–51.

Weeks, J. (1975) Policies for Expanding Employment in the Informal Sector of Developing Countries. *International Labour Review* **111** (1).

Support for Entrepreneurship Development

Introduction

At a time when large firms appear no longer to be able to sustain the rate of growth capable of providing the levels of employment required, many countries have begun to recognize the importance of entrepreneurship and new venture creation, and the need to create (or re-create in certain cases) an enterprise culture. What they are attempting to do is break away from what has become known as the 'dependency culture'—the culture whereby a country's citizens become dependent on others (be it the state or large corporations) to provide for them. The environment they are attempting to create is what has been termed 'the enterprise culture'—the culture whereby both individuals and groups become empowered and take responsibility for, or ownership of, their own futures—that is, they become more self-reliant. If an enterprise culture is working, therefore, an economy might be expected to demonstrate:

- more new ventures, small firms and self-employment than previously
- more 'community' enterprises
- more management buyouts.

Possibly as a consequence of this, the term has become equated with new venture creation and small business management, as Gibb (2000) has recognized. However, it is much broader than this and it would seem that if a successful enterprise culture is to be created (or re-created, in countries like the UK), there needs to be, somewhat paradoxically, an extensive system of support. Creating that support network, at the same time as succeeding in breaking the dependency culture, is not easy.

In developing countries and the newly democratized transition economies of central and eastern Europe, the support system is often rudimentary or non-existent (Mugler, 2000). In contrast, in mature economies, like the United States and the United Kingdom, there is often a comprehensive and well-established system, though this need not necessarily be oriented to the needs of the new venture or the small business. Generally, however, support operates at the macro and the micro economic levels, as Glancey and McQuaid (2000) have recognized.

PAUSE FOR THOUGHT

Before considering the generic measures that can be taken to support entrepreneurship development, think specifically about the support available to new and small businesses in an area with which you are familiar.

Policies to support entrepreneurship

Macroeconomic policies

As has been shown, the success of the small firm sector in any economy is dependent to some extent on the prevailing economic conditions. Although entrepreneurs can probably cope with uncertainty better than most, and some are actually able to benefit from it, a stable macroeconomic environment is believed to be crucial to the development of entrepreneurship and a strong small business sector. Hence, the aim of much government policy is to create macroeconomic stability. To this end, low inflation is seen as important, as are low interest rates and stable exchange rates. In Europe, the single currency is intended to reduce the risks associated with transaction costs and fluctuations in the exchange rate.

Apart from economic stability, macroeconomic policies are frequently intended to reduce the level of bureaucracy facing new and small firms, with respect to taxation and compliance. As Glancey and McQuaid (2000: 177) have observed:

Simplifying and reducing the burden of taxation on new enterprises is claimed by many to reduce costs, encourage investment and increase incentives. A high level of taxation may act as a disincentive to entrepreneurs (or an incentive to move elsewhere) . . .

In recent years, therefore, the emphasis in the taxation systems of many countries has shifted from direct to indirect tax, with a corresponding reduction in the levels of personal taxation. This has resulted in relatively (if not absolutely) lower levels of public spending and/or increased levels of indirect taxation, such as Value Added Tax (VAT). Additionally, many countries have simplified taxation regulations and moved to a system of self-assessment in an attempt to reduce compliance costs for small firms. Indeed, it is an avowed objective of the European Parliament to reduce the burden of regulation on small firms and to simplify the financial environment in an attempt to create an environment more conducive to entrepreneurship.

As access to markets is important to the health of the small business sector, macroeconomic policies are often intended to create new market opportunities for small and medium-sized enterprises. In Japan, large firms are required by law to develop strategic alliances with local small and medium-sized enterprises, using them as suppliers and subcontractors. However, as the bureaucratic system is often one of the largest single sources of demand in an economy, it is more usual for governments to encourage their own departments and agencies to support small and medium-sized enterprises through their procurement strategies. This has long been the case in the USA, for example, where the Small Business Administration and other government departments have offered support to small and medium-sized enterprises seeking to secure government contracts, including a share of the defence budget. In Europe there has been a stronger tradition for governments to assist new and small firms in securing market opportunities overseas, through political alliances, trade missions and the provision of advice, information, etc.

Microeconomic policies

These are normally introduced to correct market failure and are intended to help new and existing small businesses acquire the opportunities, skills and resources they need to survive and grow. Often such policies are intended to strengthen economic competitiveness by creating a healthy, vibrant business sector. Generally they provide what is known as 'hard' and 'soft' support. Hard support refers to that which is tangible (money, buildings, equipment, etc.), while soft support is essentially intangible (education, know-how, etc.). Both can be provided nationally, regionally and locally, and can be targeted at all stages in the life cycle of the firm, though frequently they are intended to raise awareness of the opportunities for self-employment, stimulate the birth of new firms, and facilitate the survival and growth of small businesses. Equally, they can focus on different sectors of the economy.

In the contemporary knowledge-based economy, it is often the new technology sectors that are encouraged and promoted, but this is not always the case. In the developing economies, for example, support is frequently targeted at promoting business efficiency in the non-technological sectors, such as retailing. Indeed, this has been the case until relatively recently even in such high-level economies as Scandinavia (Gronmo *et al.*, 1980) and Japan (Kirby, 1984). For the present, such refinements will be ignored and attention will be focused on the primary 'hard' and 'soft' classification.

Hard support takes various forms. It includes the provision of finance and the physical infrastructure. Frequently, new and small firms experience difficulties raising finance. There are numerous reasons for this, including their lack of a previous 'track record', and as a consequence it is often difficult to find the relatively small amounts of funding needed for start-up and expansion. As will be shown in Chapter 10, funding for new and small firms normally comes from bodies such as banks, venture capital companies and private investors. Policies may be introduced to create new sources of funding for small firms or to improve the flow of funding through the existing channels. Hence in Europe and the USA, for example, there are government investment grants, loans and loan guarantee schemes, all intended to ease the flow of funding to the new and small firm sector.

While access to money is often difficult for new and small businesses, frequently it is equally difficult to find suitable premises. Not only are existing premises often too large for the new firm, they are frequently too expensive and/or only available on long leases. In many countries, therefore, governments have developed small factory or office units for rent, or offered subsidies to private property developers for developing such units. These have ranged from business incubator units to science parks, and are intended to create clusters of new and small businesses with similar needs and interests. In such environments, new and small firms can benefit from economies of proximity and association, as well as the provision of common support and advisory services. A specialist form of infrastructural support has been the Enterprise Zone. Modelled on Hong Kong, the enterprise zone is a 'tax-free' haven where government bureaucracy is kept to a minimum, particularly with respect to land use planning regulations.

Soft support is similarly varied. Perhaps training and advice/consultancy are the most widespread forms it takes. This includes helping prospective entrepreneurs and existing owner-managers acquire general business skills as well as specialist expertise in subjects such as accounting, taxation, legal issues, marketing and exporting. These may be provided through the education system or through specialist organizations in either the public or the private sector. Throughout Europe and the United States of America, the Chambers of Commerce have played an active role in this context. However, the rapid growth of small management consultancies specializing in the needs of small and medium-sized enterprises may be perceived as a reflection of the increased awareness of the importance of management know-how to the survival and growth of the small firm (see Chapter 2). It may also reflect, though, the efforts governments have made to encourage the supply of such expertise to the sector. Since small firms are often either unwilling or unable to pay for training and consultancy, governments have generally subsidized their provision, either in full or in part.

Not surprisingly, many governments have introduced policies to support innovation in technology. One set of policies is often targeted at the country's universities and government research departments, and is intended to encourage the commercialization of research. Another focuses on existing businesses and is intended to stimulate new product and process development through the provision of grants and awards. The third focuses on technology transfer, and the network of Business Innovation Centres—part-funded by the European Union—is witness to this sort of support, as is the growth in the number of small, private technical consultancies reported in Chapter 2. Frequently, these are manifestations of the new service sector that is emerging in the developed economies of the world in response to the decline of the manufacturing sector and the growth of the new knowledge industries (Kirby, 1995). Various policies have been introduced that have attempted to assist new and small firms to gain access to markets they might otherwise have difficulty penetrating. In Europe there is a network of Information Centres intended to help small firms increase trade and form links across Europe. It provides information on public contracts and potential partners, as well as other specialist matters such as taxation. Similarly, governments frequently provide assistance to encourage small firms to export and enter new overseas markets. Apart from training and consultancy, this often takes the form of market intelligence, trade fairs, missions, etc., as well as brokering services to assist SMEs in finding foreign partners for co-operative and joint ventures. In China, this is the role played, for example, by the Beijing-based Chinese Association of Small and Medium Enterprises for International Cooperation.

PAUSE FOR THOUGHT ████████████████████████████

Reflect on the above and compare it with the measures you identified previously. Are there any you identified that are not classified here? Are there any identified here that either you failed to identify or that are not provided in the area you considered?

The creation of a culture of enterprise in the UK

Since 1979, and the advent of the first Thatcher government, Britain has attempted to create an enterprise culture in its efforts to restructure the economy, cope with the problems of unemployment, and compete in an increasingly competitive and turbulent global environment. It has done this through a series of public- and private-sector support measures, though throughout the 1990s and beyond, the distinction has become increasingly blurred with a trend towards public/private-sector partnerships. As a consequence, Johnson *et al.* (2000) have identified four categories of support: public, semi-public, private and other. According to them, public support is that provided by national, regional and local government, while semi-public support is provided through bodies that are funded largely, though not exclusively, from the public purse. Other support often takes the form of that provided by not for profit organizations, though this point is not recognized by Johnson *et al.* The contribution of each of these key factors will be examined on the next few pages.

Public and semi-public support

Since the early 1980s there has evolved in the UK an infrastructure of public and semi-public support for small firms. Apart from the established institutions of further and higher education, which have evolved a role in the support of small and medium-sized enterprises, and the various agencies responsible for local and regional economic development, the two main network bodies have been the Training and Enterprise Councils (TECs) and Business Link. Both may be classed as semi-public bodies in that although they are private companies limited by guarantee, they are heavily dependent on public funding.

The now defunct TECs (known as Local Enterprise Companies, or LECs, in Scotland) were set up in 1990 as 'one-stop-shops' for the provision of manpower training and the promotion of enterprise. Approximately 10 per cent of their budget was devoted to the development of enterprise, their key activities being the delivery of national enterprise programmes and the small business training programmes previously provided centrally by such government agencies as the Manpower Services Commission and its successor the Training Agency. Indeed, one of the main purposes of the TECs was to ensure that training was provided in accordance with local rather than national needs. From the outset, however, the TECs met with only partial success. Take-up rates among the small business community were no higher than 20 per cent, possibly reflecting the perception that they were essentially bureaucratic government bodies staffed by civil servants (Down and Bresnen, 1997). However, there was also the problem that, initially at least, they were not embedded in the local community (Curran and Blackburn, 1994).

Partly because of the apparent limitations of the TECs, a national network of business advice centres was launched in 1992. Known as 'Business Link' in England, 'Business Shops' in Scotland and 'Business Connect' in Wales, the centres operate through a team of Personal Business Advisors (PBAs) who offer diagnostic assessments, information and referral to specialist counsellors. Traditionally the Link targeted growth companies with between 10 and 200 employees and, by the late 1990s, more than 80,000 businesses had availed themselves of the services on offer. However, although take-up has been strong, there have been concerns over the quality of the service provided with variations existing both between local offices and local advisers (Roche, 1997). Additionally, the need to generate income has meant that Business Link is often seen as competing with, rather than supporting, the private-sector network, which has created further hostility towards the concept (Summon, 1998).

Unlike the United States (1953), Germany (1960) and Japan (1963), the UK has not enacted legislation to promote and protect small firms, despite the policy recommendations of the Bolton Report of 1971. Nevertheless, the UK, like many other countries, has developed specific policy measures, both directly and indirectly, to promote and support entrepreneurship development. These include measures targeted at raising awareness, facilitating entry and facilitating growth. We will now look at each of these in turn.

Raising awareness

This ranges from measures channelled through the education system to young people to measures intended to encourage the unemployed to consider self-employment as an alternative to unemployment. Among the former are such school-based initiatives as Young Enterprise. Like its better-known partner, America's Junior Achievement programme, the Young Enterprise project is intended to develop pupil understanding of how to run a small business, at the same time developing what have been termed 'enterprise competences and aptitudes'. Similarly in higher education, numerous programmes have been introduced that are intended to raise awareness among students (of both business and non-business disciplines) of the importance of entrepreneurship and self-employment. In the 1980s, the Graduate Enterprise Programme (Kirby, 1992) allowed students to explore the opportunities of self-employment, while such initiatives as the Shell Technology Enterprise Programme (STEP) (Kirby and Mullen, 1989) and the Graduate Extension Programme provided them with the opportunity to develop their entrepreneurial capabilities through working in a small or medium-sized enterprise. While there is no evidence that such programmes encourage graduates either to secure employment in an SME or set up and run their own businesses (Westhead, 1997), there is evidence that they provided the host SMEs with the much-needed resource to carry out a project in their business, thereby helping them develop and grow (Kirby and Mullen, 1991; Westhead, 1997), 'smuggled' training into the firm and linked it with its local university.

However, such programmes were essentially vocationally oriented, the overall long-term objectives being to change attitudes and develop more enterprising individuals. These were objectives shared by the Enterprise Initiative in Higher Education (EHE). Launched in December 1987 by the Secretary of State for Employment, this £60 million project was hailed, wrongly, as an exercise in turning the country's universities into 'Enterprise Zones' producing 'Thatcherite entrepreneurs' (Crequer, 1988). Although there was some confusion over the precise aims of the exercise (Kirby, 1989), its actual aim was 'the development of qualities of enterprise amongst those seeking higher education qualifications'. In all probability it is here that the confusion arose as there was no precise definition of what these qualities were. For some it was the acquisition of business skills, whilst for others it was the acquisition of those personal transferable skills that characterize the enterprising or entrepreneurial person (see Chapter 5). Whatever, as Hawkins and Winter (1997) have observed, 'successive national evaluations of EHE have demonstrated that the initiative was a catalyst for change . . . learners are becoming better prepared for working life by developing lifelong learning and other key skills'.

Perhaps of more relevance in terms of entrepreneurship development have been the more recent Department of Trade and Industry initiatives intended to develop more entrepreneurial cultures with universities. These include the £60 million University Challenge initiative and the £25 million Science Enterprise Challenge. Launched in March 1999, the former is intended to assist 15 universities to provide local seed-funding to support the early commercialization of academic research, while the latter—which was launched in February 1999—is intended to create 12 world-class entrepreneurial centres in UK universities by bringing business and entrepreneurial skills into the science curriculum. As a consequence of such initiatives, there has been renewed interest in entrepreneurship in UK universities and particularly in the opportunities for new venture start-ups and spinouts (Hague and Oakley, 2000).

According to a press release published by the London-based Association of Business Schools in February 2001, four out of every ten British 16 and 17 year olds who are planning to study business and management at university want to run their own business after they graduate. 'This is a startling figure and appears to signal a move away from the trend of most youngsters wanting to work for big-name corporations,' says the chief executive of the association, Dr Jonathon Slack. 'Perhaps the influence of role models and the government's positive stance in support of entrepreneurship in Britain are having a positive effect on the way young people view the future,' he says. When asked which well-known business person they admired most, 45 per cent said Richard Branson, 25 per cent Bill Gates and 4 per cent Anita Roddick.

For the unemployed, there have been numerous measures, but perhaps the most radical in the United Kingdom was the Enterprise Allowance Scheme (EAS). Introduced in 1983, it provided approximately £40 per week for one year to those over the age of 18 with a valid business proposition who had been unemployed for at least 13 weeks (reduced to 8 weeks in April 1986) and had access to £1000 to invest in the business. This was intended to offset the loss of unemployment benefit experienced once the enterprise was established. Thus the whole objective of the scheme was to help unemployed people in receipt of benefit to start their own business and thereby create new businesses that otherwise would not have existed. As Gray and Stanworth (1986: 5) have observed, 'in essence the EAS represents an open invitation to Britain's unemployed to create their own jobs'. In 1991–92, the EAS was re-named the Business Start-up Scheme, and some of the restrictions were removed. For example, applicants no longer needed to have £1000 to invest in the business or to be in receipt of unemployment benefit, and the duration of the payment could be varied.

From its inception, the scheme proved to be popular, generally exceeding the rate of take-up the government had targeted. In 1987 and 1988, at its peak, over 100,000 people registered on it. However, questions have been raised about the quality, suitability and permanence of many of the businesses started, especially as the £40 per week 'subsidy' enabled the new firms to 'undercut' their competitors, frequently forcing them out of business. In particular, Storey (1994) has suggested that there were two main criticisms—that the failure rates of businesses started under the EAS were high (once the subsidy had been removed), suggesting an inefficient use of public funds, and that 60 per cent of the jobs in firms developed under the EAS were created by only 4 per cent of the firms that were originally started under the scheme. Even so, there is little doubt that the scheme did much to change workforce attitudes towards self-employment, which became, for many, a realistic alternative to unemployment.

Facilitating entry

Both 'hard' and 'soft' support have been made available to help 'entrepreneurs' create new ventures. Dealing with hard support first, this has ranged from finance to premises and space. Apart from the Enterprise Allowance Scheme referred to above, the UK government introduced, in 1981, the Loan Guarantee Scheme. This provided a government guarantee to banks (initially 70 per cent of the amount outstanding) on loans to potentially viable small firms that otherwise would not receive debt finance on commercial terms. The scheme required all applicants to prepare a business plan and pay an annual premium to the bank, which ranged, initially (1983), from 5 per cent to, subsequently (1986), 2.5 per cent of the amount covered by the guarantee. In 1993, the scheme was modified considerably. The premium was reduced to 1.5 per cent while the guarantee was increased to 85 per cent.

Take-up varied considerably, and Barrett et al. (1990) have suggested that this was largely in response to the changes in the scheme's terms and conditions. After the success of the initial pilot (when 80 per cent of the loan was guaranteed and the premium was at 3 per cent), take-up dropped dramatically. This probably reflected, at least in part, the high failure rates of the businesses on the scheme, but it was noticeable that following the changes to both the guarantee (70 per cent) and premium (5 per cent) in 1985, which made the scheme significantly less attractive, the take-up dropped to just 35 loans per month in the first part of 1986. However, the 1986 reduction in premium appeared to raise take-up by a factor of three or four and, by 1987, take-up rates had increased to almost 100 a month. Even so, Storey (1994) has concluded that the scheme's impact on the small business sector as a whole was minimal, since even at its peak in 1982/83, the scheme was relevant to no more than 0.6 per cent of the country's small firms. Despite this, there can be little doubt that in the early 1980s, the scheme did demonstrate to the clearing banks that there were opportunities for profitable lending to the small business sector. Having succeeded in its educational role, then clearly it should no longer be needed, as Barrett *et al.* (1990) have recognized.

Among the initiatives intended to provide space and accommodation for new small firms were the Enterprise Zones of the mid-1980s. As mentioned earlier in this chapter, these are essentially 'tax-free' havens where firms do not have to pay local authority rates and are exempt from certain regulatory restrictions, in particular planning constraints. Each zone, which was created for a period of 10 years, was intended to foster the growth of new businesses, but they were somewhat less than successful. Often there was a tendency for established businesses to 'decant' from other parts of the region in order to take advantage of the relaxed fiscal and other regulations and, as Amin and Tomaney (1991) demonstrated in the north-east of England, frequently the investment went into property development and the service sector rather than the intended manufacturing and new small firms. In particular, the zones were especially attractive to retailing. At the time, planning restrictions were being imposed on out-of-town shopping centre development. With the relaxation of land use planning controls in the Enterprise Zones, many became, in effect, out-of-town regional shopping centres or retail theme parks (Thomas and Bromley, 1987). Indeed, Europe's largest regional shopping centre, the Metro Centre at Gateshead in the north-east of England, was developed in the Dunston Enterprise Zone. Building work started in 1984 and the first phase of the centre started trading in April 1986.

Managed Workspace and business incubators are two other forms of support intended to facilitate the birth and development of new ventures. Pioneered by British Steel (Industry) Ltd, the Managed Workspace is a form of property development that provides both space and support for conventional new businesses. Normally rents are subsidized and the support available is in the form of secretarial and office services, security and business advice. There are no entry conditions and there is no graduation policy. As a consequence, the workspace is normally occupied by a wide range of businesses, attracted by the flexible rents and space, and tenants are encouraged to stay, more space being provided if needed. This contrasts with the incubator, which is defined as:

66 99 . . . a property with small units which provides an instructive and supportive environment to investors and entrepreneurs at start-up and during the early stages of businesses. Its aim is to maximize the formation and survival of businesses with the potential for growth.

(Enterprise Panel, 1996: 3)

The four key features of an incubator are that:

1. there is some form of selection or entry qualification to judge the viability of the business and its ability to grow
2. there is a close, hands-on relationship between the incubator director and his/her business clients
3. clients are encouraged to leave the incubator when they are sufficiently established
4. its performance is not judged by the number of client businesses but by the performance of its clients.

Details of the UK's incubator units are available at **www.ukbi.co.uk**. Suffice it to say here that the Enterprise Panel (1996) concluded from its investigation of British incubators that they do help start-up businesses with high growth potential to succeed and are an effective way of helping technology transfer, by developing innovation and local jobs. However, they also recognized that while there was considerable activity in the UK, incubator operators felt isolated and there needed to be more networking and greater access to best practice, new ideas, training, etc. Indeed this concept of isolation appears to be critical. According to Bennet and McCoshan (1993) when units are not integrated into the local innovation strategy or lack the support of the key local enterprise organizations, they become no more than Managed Workspaces, and integration is at the heart of the science park concept (**www.ukspa.org.uk**). This has been developed primarily, but not exclusively, to help academics become entrepreneurs through commercializing the results of their research. It is an attempt to recreate the sort of clusters of high-technology new firms that have emerged in Silicon Valley (California) and along Route 128 (Boston, Massachusetts). In Britain, most universities now have their own science park, though their success is variable, and Massey *et al*. (1992) have questioned the role they play in local economic development. Similarly, the work of Westhead and Storey (1994) suggests that there is little difference in the performance of firms on and off science parks, though they do conclude that science parks are important to the supply of high-technology firms as the founders of such firms require the highest possible academic qualifications. Probably the most successful initiative, known as the 'Cambridge Phenomenon', has been the cluster of high-technology small firms that has developed in association with Cambridge University (Segal Quince Wicksteed, 1990). The Cambridge Science Park has been in existence since the early 1980s and it is possible that, over time, other science parks will replicate its level of success. According to Westhead and Batstone (1999: 148), however, there are considerable differences in the way science parks are managed and in the role of the manager, and much closer attention needs to be paid to 'the mechanisms that engender trust, co-operation and community amongst tenant (and freehold) firms located on managed as well as non-managed science parks'.

Apart from hard support in the form of science parks and incubation units, soft support is available through a network of Business Innovation Centres. This is essentially a European Union concept, launched by the Directorate-General for Regional Policy in 1984. Each centre is designed to meet the unique needs of its region, though there is a standard mission, which is to support both the creation of innovative new enterprises and the modernization, innovation and diversification of existing enterprises. To achieve this, the centres offer a range of services intended to maximize the survival rate of innovative business ideas and act as an interface between the needs of entrepreneurs/SMEs and the specialist services available to them. Although each centre is unique, essential common services are believed by the Commission to be:

- the constant promotion of innovation and entrepreneurship
- the identification, evaluation and selection of innovative business projects
- support in the preparation of business plans, including issues relating to technical matters, finance, management, marketing, organization
- proactive post-start-up support
- support to existing firms for modernization, diversification and innovation
- support for business-to-business co-operation, locally, regionally, nationally or internationally
- guidance in the financing of innovative business projects
- support to regional firms wishing to internationalize
- provision of management training
- access to specialized advisory services
- accommodation of new business projects and provision of shared services.

Clearly the centres are not just intended to facilitate entry and are not confined to the UK, but they do provide a network of 'soft' support to new and existing enterprises that complements both the hard support and the existing soft support. Details of the network of Business Innovation Centres, of which there are 11 in the UK, are available at **www.ebn.be**.

As Storey (1994: 318) has recognized, 'for much of the 1980s the focus of small business policy was to encourage the start-up of new firms'. From 1977 onwards, therefore, numerous training initiatives were developed, largely by the then Department of Employment, that were intended to facilitate entry into business. However, the programme was somewhat piecemeal without any coherent framework, and was frequently based on individuals' perceptions rather than the objective analysis of needs (Kirby, 1991). By the mid-1980s the whole programme was under review and, by the late 1980s and early 1990s, the emphasis had shifted from business start-up to business growth.

Facilitating growth

This mainly takes the form, certainly in the UK, of making available the requisite funding and know-how to enable expansion to occur. Possibly the most significant fiscal measure taken to support the growth of small firms has been the Business Expansion Scheme. This was introduced in 1983 to provide tax relief to individuals investing in growth-oriented small and medium-sized enterprises. Tax relief was granted at the highest marginal rate, so providing an incentive to high income earners and making the real price of the equity sold significantly higher than it would have been without the benefit.

From the research evidence available (Mason and Harrison, 1991) it would seem that the scheme failed to achieve its objective of making available small amounts of equity capital. Indeed, the average investment under the scheme rose from £147,000 in 1983/84 to £245,000 in 1987/88. At the end of 1993, therefore, it was abolished. However, it did encourage financial institutions to take an interest in small firms and stimulate investment in them, as well as educating some small business owner-managers about the benefits of external equity. Even so, it came as something of a surprise when, in his Budget statement of 30 November 1993, the Chancellor of the Exchequer announced an almost identical scheme (the Enterprise Investment Scheme), giving tax relief on investments in shares of unquoted trading companies on sums of up to £100,000 per annum and allowing the investors to become paid directors. Interest in the scheme has not been great.

More targeted financial assistance has been given to facilitate innovation in small and medium-sized enterprises. The two most popular schemes have been SMART (the Small Firms Merit Award for Research and Technology) and SPUR (Support for Products Under Research). The SMART awards were introduced in 1986. They take the form of an annual competition open to firms with fewer than 50 employees. They are intended to stimulate highly innovative and marketable technology through, in Stage 1, a competitive award of 75 per cent of eligible project costs up to a maximum grant of £45,000 for a technical and commercial feasibility study into innovative technology. In Stage 2 the successful firms receive 30 per cent of the eligible project costs up to a maximum of €200,000 for the development up to pre-production prototype stage of a new product or process that involves significant technological advance. From 1997, Stage 2 has been absorbed into SPUR, which aids firms with fewer than 500 employees in developing new products and processes that involve a significant technological advancement.

'Know-how' schemes have involved both training and consultancy. Over the years in the UK a wide range of training programmes has been provided, intended to improve the managerial performance and growth prospects of small and medium-sized enterprises. These are summarized in Kirby (1991) and Matlay (2000). However, the government has attempted to standardize provision through the introduction of standard programmes, such as the Private Enterprise Programme and its successor the Business Growth Training programme, as well as through a programme of National Vocational Qualifications (NVQs). Business Growth Training was introduced in 1989 to overcome the scepticism of owner-managers as to the value of training (Kirby, 1990). Under Option 3 it provided smaller firms with up to half of the cost of engaging someone to train and develop their management staff, up to a maximum of £15,000. Though the take-up of training was increased, its effectiveness in terms of improving business performance has been difficult to ascertain and, from a survey of the literature, Storey and Westhead (1996) have concluded that there is little evidence of any link between formal training and improved business performance.

Apart from the quality of the research methodologies used (Patton *et al.*, 2000), one of the reasons for this could be the variability of the training provision and the inappropriateness of much of the training from a small business perspective. As Kirby (1990) and, more recently, Gibb (1997) have recognized, owner-managers have very specific preferences about what and how they wish to learn. These are very different from the traditional approaches to programme provision, and an unsuitable training experience is unlikely either to prove beneficial to the firm or to convince often sceptical owner-managers of the potential benefits of training. Hence the proposal that trainer training and trainer accreditation might be necessary (Kirby, 1990), and the emergence of the Institute of Business Advisers (**www.iba.org.uk**), 'the recognized professional body responsible for the accreditation of and continuing development of Business Advisers, Business Counsellors, Business Mentors, Trainers and support staff helping small firms world-wide'. Another possibility, however, which Storey and Westhead (1996) appear to have ignored, is that, without training, small firms could have grown smaller, not larger. Indeed they could have joined the ranks of those many firms that failed to survive, especially in a recession. As Stanworth *et al.* (1992: 5) observed in their study of a sample of firms attending business development training workshops, 'even under the difficult conditions prevailing, the overall failure rate amongst the sample was very low indeed (around 10 per cent over 3 years) and 2 out of every 5 firms actually held their workforce size during the period of the study or even expanded'.

Perhaps one of the most radical government initiatives to promote know-how in small and medium-sized enterprises was the Consultancy Initiative, the main component of the then government's Enterprise Initiative. Launched in 1988, the scheme provided financial assistance (a 50 per cent subsidy) to firms with fewer than 500 employees for the engagement of independent, private-sector consultants who would help enhance their capability in such areas as business planning, design, financial and information systems, manufacturing, marketing and quality. While the main objective of the exercise was to improve the survival chances and growth prospects of small and medium-sized enterprises, an important secondary objective was to encourage small firms to use the expertise of private-sector consultants. According to Bannock (1991: 26), the 'Consultancy Initiative (CI) scheme provided a concrete means for firms to address business development issues . . . and over one-third of companies would not otherwise have proceeded with the assisted project in the absence of CI support.' However, Storey (1994) has questioned the validity of this finding, suggesting that the method used by the researchers (Segal Quince Wicksteed, 1989; 1991a; 1991b) for determining the 'additionality' of the scheme was not robust. This involved asking the users of the Consultancy Initiative whether they would have proceeded if the consultancy had not been available. Given the factors involved, Storey argues, 'the measures of "additionality" estimated by Segal Quince Wicksteed . . . are open to question' (1994: 294). Whatever the validity of this criticism, it would seem that in less than two years (13 January 1988 to 1 December 1989) 28,000 small and medium-sized enterprises utilized the services of a private-sector consultant and most, according to the research, benefited accordingly. Given the reluctance of small firms to seek external support in general, and to use the services of consultants in particular, this in itself was an important outcome of the exercise. As Bennett and Robson (1999: 161) have observed, 'consultants are a key aspect of the advice sources available to SMEs, and their role has been stimulated by government initiatives (particularly the Enterprise Initiative)'.

Other measures intended to provide small firms with the know-how to grow have been targeted at opening up new markets, especially overseas. Numerous schemes have been introduced to help UK firms win overseas business, and details can be found at **www.dti.gov.uk/ots/publications**. As an example, there is a network of Export Development Counsellors that provides information and advice to help firms expand into overseas markets and that can assist potential exporters in paying for such services as translation, training or website development using match-funding up to £1000. Assistance with research prior to making the decision to export is available through the Export Marketing Research Scheme, which provides financial support for approved marketing research studies overseas. Additionally there are schemes to assist UK small and medium-sized enterprises in finding joint venture partners in Asia, Latin America, the Mediterranean countries and South Africa, as well as Russia and the transition economies of central and eastern Europe. On top of this, there is an annual Export Award for Smaller Businesses under which the winners receive £5000 and professional advice.

Private-sector support

Apart from trade associations and such cross-sector business organizations as the Confederation of British Industry (**www.cbi.org.uk**), the Federation of Small Businesses (**www.fsb.co.uk**), the Forum of Private Businesses (**www.fpb. co.uk**) and the Institute of Directors (**www.iod.co.uk**), the private sector includes a range of commercial organizations. Some of these have a direct interest in the small firm sector, others an indirect interest. They include financial service institutions, professional services, large organizations, and small firm networks and alliances. We will now look at each of these in turn.

Financial service institutions

The primary task of the banks and other financial institutions is to meet the funding needs of their clients by re-deploying the funds of their investors and savers. In a country like Britain, though, the traditional emphasis has been on directing such funds to the larger, safer, longer-established enterprises. This has long been recognized as a weakness of the British banking system and although they remain cautious, often demanding high levels of security, most of the major clearing banks have re-appraised their lending portfolios and developed a better understanding of the needs of small and medium-sized enterprises and of how to appraise small firm funding proposals. To achieve this, several of the banks have trained their staff in the principles of running a small business and have set up special small business units offering advice and guidance, in addition to money.

Additionally new lending schemes have had to be introduced. Apart from the Loan Guarantee Scheme referred to above, new institutions have emerged. In particular there has been a growth in venture capital companies (see **www. brainstorm.co.uk/BVCA**). These are specialist financial institutions set up to fund 'risky' investments in unlisted companies. On average the sums invested are between £1 million and £2 million and, according to Arnold (1998), most venture capital has been invested not in new venture creation or growing an existing business, but in management buyouts or management buyins. Given this propensity of the banks and the formal venture capital companies to invest in the larger initiatives, there has emerged, as in the USA, a growing informal venture capital sector. Commonly known as 'business angels', informal venture capitalists are individuals rather than institutions. Typically they invest sums of up to £10,000 and while they tend not to look for quick returns, they do appear to be somewhat selective in their choice of ventures, apparently rejecting over 90 per cent of the proposals put to them by TECs and Business Link. At the same time it would seem that 'too few firms that would benefit from raising venture capital seek this type of finance, and many of the businesses that do seek venture capital are not "investment ready"' (Mason and Harrison, 2000a: 26). Even so, it would seem that in the UK, as elsewhere, the informal venture capital market 'is of growing significance in the financing of the entrepreneurial start-up and growth business' (Mason and Harrison, 2000b: 234).

Professional services

Most countries have witnessed a spectacular growth in the provision of business services in recent years and the UK is no exception. As a consequence, there has been a very considerable increase in the availability of advice to small and medium-sized enterprises, especially in the private sector where 'the chief sources of advice in rank order are accountants, next either banks or solicitors, and then business associations, or consultants' (Bennett and Robson, 1999: 156). Though self-regulated, both the accounting and the legal professions have recognized that the needs of small and medium-sized enterprises are not confined solely to preparing annual accounts and assisting with contractual matters. Accordingly, they have extended the range of services they offer to small firms, though often there remains something of a misalignment between what they offer and what they are perceived to be capable of offering (Kirby and Travis, 1995; Kirby and King, 1997; Kirby et al., 1998). Even so, accountants and solicitors are perceived to provide 'a professional status, level of trust and quality control of advice that is not likely to be achievable in most other areas . . .' (Bennett and Robson, 1999: 160), making them one of the most important providers of expertise to the small firm sector. Interestingly, consultancy has been one of the fastest-growing sectors in recent years. As mentioned earlier (in Chapter 2), Keeble et al. (1991) have pointed to the growth of management and marketing consultants, while Jones-Evans and Kirby (1994) have drawn attention to the growth of technical consultants, both as a specialist form of entrepreneurship and as a source of advice and expertise. Under such circumstances, as Bennett and Robson (1999: 161) have recognized, 'consultants range over a wide variety of different intensities of relationships with their clients, from short-term and very specific advice to broader advice on management strategy, product development, marketing, technology, etc.'. Kirby and Jones-Evans (1997) show, moreover, that the consultant's objectives and approach can vary considerably. Hence it is not surprising that consultants traditionally have had a relatively low level of use by SMEs. In recent years, however, their use has increased (aided by the Consultancy Initiative) and new small, independent consultancies have emerged as a consequence of this newly recognized market opportunity.

Large organizations

Large organizations have assisted the promotion of enterprise and small business development in a number of ways, both directly and indirectly. First, they have often formed local partnerships between themselves and the small firms in their region. Often these have involved helping small-firm suppliers/contractors through the supply chain by creating strategic alliances or preferred supplier partnerships. Second, they have sponsored various initiatives intended to help promote the creation and development of small and medium-sized enterprises. In particular, they have played an important role in the establishment and management of Local Enterprise Agencies, as discussed below. More specifically, several have established schemes to set up new businesses. For example, both British Steel and British Coal established initiatives (British Steel plc and British Coal Enterprise Ltd) to assist people in creating new ventures in areas affected by job losses in their industries. The assistance took the form of loans, Managed Workspaces, training and advice, and although often criticized the schemes did appear to offer valued support. As Stanworth and Barker (1988) discovered in a survey of businesses receiving assistance from the British Steel programme, over 80 per cent could be deemed as growth businesses and as many as 43 per cent of the sample felt that the help they had received had speeded their development. A final way in which large firms have helped promote entrepreneurship in recent years is through the re-organization of their own operations. As a consequence of company downsizing/rightsizing, and concentrating on their core activities, they have often spun out new enterprises. At the same time, many have re-organized internally, creating a culture more conducive to enterprise, with the organization being made up of a number of semi-autonomous entrepreneurial units. Such developments have occurred in both the private and public sectors.

A CASE EXAMPLE

Reuters' Greenhouse Project: an example of large-firm support for new ventures

Orchestream is a London-based software business supported by alliances with other companies in its aim of placing centralized controls on quality of service over the Internet. It was founded by Charlie Muirhead, 24, who left university one year into his computer science course to set up the company. Founded in 1996, by January 2000 Orchestream had neither revenues nor profits as its products were out on test. However, in the four years since launch it had attracted approximately £22 million of investment from 45 investors, including Reuters' Greenhouse Project. Greenhouse was started in 1994 by John Taysom while living in Silicon Valley in the USA. He observed how the enterprise climate and tax infrastructure there stimulated growth. Accordingly, he set up Reuters' Greenhouse, which invests in about 20 growing businesses, as he believes 'corporate alliances are essential. Large companies benefit by spending less heavily on R&D; they stay nimble and get into new markets. Smaller firms get access to money, a brand name, a global presence. It's symbiotic.'

Small firm networks and alliances

It is not just links with large organizations that are important. As Birley (1985: 108) has recognized, the 'help and guidance received from both formal networks (banks, accountants, lawyers, SBA) and the informal networks (family, friends, business contacts) will influence the nature of the firm substantially'. However, it is not just the nature of the firm that is affected, and the findings of Larson (1991) have suggested that the entrepreneur's ability to identify, cultivate and manage a network partnership is an essential condition for survival and success. It is unclear, however, whether it is the formal or the informal networks that are the most critical. According to Johannisson (1998: 299), 'personal resource should be mobilized to enact new ventures that are alien to the market and generally struck by liabilities of newness'; while Huggins (2000) suggests that it is the formal groups that are the most potent success factors in networking, though they are probably best facilitated through an initially informal structure. This is a view reinforced by the work of Bryson *et al.* (1993: 268) who contend that 'the informal networks, including those embodied within formal relationships (for example, with clients or banks), identified by Birley appear to be the most important'. They suggest that these networks can be divided into three types—demand-related, supply-related and support—and conclude their examination of small information-intensive business services by suggesting that networking appears to have been an important element in the recent growth of such small firms.

A CASE EXAMPLE

First Tuesday

First Tuesday (**www.firsttuesday.com**) is the world's premier web networking organization. It runs monthly networking and special events in over 100 cities across five continents, providing online services that include:

- a daily e-mail newsletter on the Internet industry in Europe

- an e-mail newsletter on the Internet industry in Latin America

- an online discussion forum where entrepreneurs can ask questions of other First Tuesday members, and give advice

- an online marketplace for jobs or talent

- an online 'swapshop' for office space

- summaries of the speakers at recent events

- real-time newsfeeds on the Internet sector—e-commerce, wireless, etc.

The initiative, which was founded by entrepreneurs John Browning, Nick Denton, Adam Gold and Julie Meyer, started out as a gathering of 50 friends and contacts, a casual get-together for UK web entrepreneurs, venture capitalists and all those in between. It held its first event in a basement bar in Soho, London, in October 1998, and met regularly thereafter—on the first Tuesday of every month, hence its name. The first participants were invited to e-mail invitations to their friends and, by the autumn of 2000, it was represented in 85 cities in 42 countries. At its peak it had 25,000 members of which 10,000 were British and 8000 European. In July 2000, the founders sold it to Yazam, an Israeli-based Internet investor.

Other support: the not for profit sector

The expansion in the UK of the not for profit sector's support for small and medium-sized enterprises was possibly most marked in the 1980s. In part, this reflected a determination on the part of the British government to create the sort of environment that prevails in the United States, whereby the large corporations re-invest part of their profits in the local community and/or the community infra-structure. Partly, it reflected a recognition on the part of the large corporations that their own future depended, to a large extent, on the health of the small business sector, and its influence on the economy. Thus the growth of the not for profit sector might be seen to be the result of increased social awareness and enlightened self-interest on the part of major industrialists, prompted by government. The result was a whole range of initiatives, including programmes to assist different sectors of the population in establishing their own businesses and/or finding employment in small and medium-sized enterprises. For example:

- Instant Muscle provided younger manual workers with basic management skills
- Project Full Employ helped minority group members set up their own business or find employment
- Livewire (**www.shell-livewire.org**) and the Prince's Youth Business Trust (**www.wiredup.net**) provide finance for promising new businesses operated by young people
- STEP—the Shell Technology Enterprise Programme (**www.shell-step.org.uk**)—enables penultimate-year undergraduates to experience employment in a small enterprise.

Probably the single most important initiative was the creation of (Local) Enterprise Agencies or Trusts, bringing together private- and public-sector resources to support local enterprise/small business development. The agencies varied considerably in their origins, size, scope and activities but they were all embedded within their local communities. Typically they focused on business start-up, provided a signposting service, training, consultancy and advice on sources of finance, with the larger ones providing incubator facilities and/or Managed Workspace. In almost all cases the agencies were established with the support of the private sector, be it one firm or a consortium, and secondees from large firms were usually integral to the success of the venture. However, they were very much dependent on public funding and when this was withdrawn in 1989, the number of agencies declined from approximately 400 in 1991 to 160 in 1998. Those that have remained have diversified their activities away from start-up and frequently away from the local community, often selling their services overseas, particularly to support restructuring and enterprise development in the transition economies of central and eastern Europe.

However, not all of the not for profit associations have been newly created. Some, like trade associations and the Chambers of Commerce/Trade, are long established. Unlike their counterparts elsewhere, membership of the Chambers of Commerce is not compulsory in Britain and, with only 10 per cent of the business population being members (usually the larger firms), the Chambers have tended not to play a major part in the promotion of enterprise and small business development. However, as Bennett and McCoshan (1993) have noted, the role and influence of the Chambers varied greatly throughout the country and it was largely because of this that the government introduced the network of Training and Enterprise Councils (TECs). Largely since then, and undoubtedly in response to the competition from the TECs, the Chambers have begun to broaden the scope of their activities. They have become more proactive in the area of enterprise support, and frequently offer training courses, seminars, consultancy and counselling services to small and medium-sized enterprises. Some have merged with the TECs to form Chambers of Commerce, Training and Enterprise (CCTEs). This has often been a sound symbiotic relationship as some of the Chambers have had difficulty establishing themselves in the small business community, while some of the TECs have suffered from being perceived by the small firm sector as just another bureaucratic government agency. Even so, it would seem to remain the case that in the Chambers, as in the Trade Associations, 'SMEs are the sector that is probably suffering most adversely . . . because of their generally less satisfactory representation' (Bennett, 1998: 258).

Evaluation

Overall, the UK has developed an extremely comprehensive package of support for entrepreneurship since 1979, which involves a wide range of agencies and measures. The result is a comprehensive national system of support that has helped create a culture of enterprise. However, it has to be said that there is a 'general pattern of fragmentation and overlaps which is confusing, complex and offers no assurance that quality networks can be constructed' (Bennett and McCoshan, 1993: 78). At the same time, the take-up of public support has been low, leading Curran (2000: 45) to observe that 'Too few small businesses appear willing to accept the support and, among those that do, the evidence of any significant impact on the performance of the businesses helped appears scanty.' This leads him to suggest that as it is difficult to show any overall positive impact on UK economic performance, it is questionable whether there is any need for such support.

Support for such an argument is provided by research on small firms (Organisation for Economic Co-operation and Development, 1985; Storey and Johnson, 1987), which suggests that the contribution small firms make to economic recovery is not as great as had been anticipated. As few new firms either survive or grow, this has led researchers such as Storey et al. (1987: 325) to conclude that 'a policy towards small business has to recognise from the outset that it will only have a modest impact on employment in a country such as the UK over a period of one or two decades'. Accordingly, such findings throw up questions about how public policy might best assist small firm growth and development. In particular there has emerged a school of thought which suggests that providing general support for business start-up is counter-productive and public policy should focus on supporting growth firms (Storey, 1994) and those few individuals that 'have either the ability or the desire to be the engine of economic recovery' (Storey et al., 1987: 326).

Clearly such an argument has considerable appeal, and it is one that has been recognized elsewhere (Birch, 1979); however, its implementation would be surrounded by various problems. First, there is the question of whether it is possible to 'pick winners'. As Birch (1979: 22) has recognized, 'rifle shooting requires a kind of knowledge that we simply have not had' and it would seem from British research that 'contrary to expectation, it proves impossible to pinpoint any distinguishing feature of fast growth firms compared with no growth firms' (Hakim, 1989: 41). This suggests that a selective support policy simply is not feasible.

Second, there is the ethical problem of whether public resources should be directed at a small group to the exclusion of the majority, particularly those least in need. As Westhead (1988) has observed, there is a need to determine the purpose of public policy. Clearly, if the objective is 'social equity', government assistance should be targeted not at those new and small businesses most likely to survive and grow, but at those experiencing the greatest difficulties. The alternative to a targeted policy is a non-selective approach to business start-up, which is what appears to be the norm in most countries, though there is evidence that policies are targeted at particular sectors such as, for example, the new technology sectors.

Whatever the situation, there can be little doubt that there is more of an enterprise culture in Britain now than there was in the 1980s. More people are aware of the opportunities afforded by self-employment and appear more prepared to start up a new venture than previously. Thus, while there may be little evidence to prove the effectiveness of the individual measures, it would seem that, as is so often the case, the whole is greater than the sum of its constituent parts—that, in total, the different measures and agencies involved have contributed to the re-creation of a culture of enterprise within the country. Despite the various questionings of the appropriateness of such a strategy, the British government remains committed to the further development of an enterprise culture and, at the turn of the century, its aim was 'to create a broadly-based entrepreneurial culture in which more people of all ages and backgrounds start their own businesses' (Department of Trade and Industry, 1998: 14–15).

However, a true culture of enterprise is one in which individuals take ownership/responsibility for their own destinies and are able to harness the potential that is within them for the benefit of themselves, their families, their employers, their communities and their society. It is not simply about self-employment, new venture creation or small business growth and development. These are one set of manifestations of an enterprise culture. Equally, an enterprise culture is not simply about being business-like and introducing 'children and students to business experience and to the relevance of commercial skills, whatever career they pursue (Institute for Public Policy Research, 1998). Rather it is, as Gibb (2000: 16) has recognized, about understanding how:

> . . . entrepreneurship relates to ways in which people, in all kinds of organisations, behave in order to cope with and take advantage of uncertainty and complexity, and how in turn this becomes embodied in ways of doing things; ways of seeing things; ways of feeling things; ways of communicating things; and ways of learning things.

While Curran (2000) may be correct, therefore, to question the continued support of an enterprise policy in the UK intended solely to promote the creation and development of small businesses, there can be little doubt about the need for a policy that supports the promotion of enterprise in its broadest sense. As Leadbeater (1997) has observed, it seems inevitable that in the twenty-first century social entrepreneurs will be as important to the UK as business entrepreneurs were in the last two decades of the twentieth century. That is the entrepreneurial challenge now facing the country: to extend the concept of entrepreneurship out of business and into the social and community arena. Interestingly, this was recognized by the Prime Minister, Rt Hon Tony Blair, in his first policy speech, on 2 June 1997, when he made the point that the government would 'be backing thousands of "social entrepreneurs", those people who bring to social problems the same enterprise and imagination that business entrepreneurs bring to wealth creation'.

Exercise 4.1

Evaluate the attempts to promote an enterprise culture in Britain. What, in your view are its strengths and what do you think might have been done differently or better? Overall, do you think it has been successful? Justify your answer. How do you think it should develop in the future?

PAUSE FOR THOUGHT

Review the recommendations you made to your government in the 'Pragmatist' Learning Style Activity in Chapter 3. How do your recommendations compare with those provided in the UK? Do you have anything that is extra? Is there anything missing?

Chapter Review

➡ As large firms fail to sustain the rate of growth capable of providing the required levels of employment, many countries have begun to recognize the importance of entrepreneurship.

➡ Various measures have been taken to break the dependency culture and create an enterprise culture.

➡ Public support measures have included:

– raising awareness of entrepreneurship through the education system

– hard and soft measures to facilitate entry, including the provision of premises and finance

– measures—such as funding initiatives and know-how—to facilitate growth.

➡ Private support has involved:

– the banks

– the professional services sector

– large corporations.

➡ Other support has included the not for profit sector.

➡ There have been criticisms of the measures introduced in the UK and not all measures have been a success, but there is evidence to suggest that an enterprise culture is beginning to emerge in the UK.

Quick Revision

(Answers at the end of this section)

1. What might you expect to see if an enterprise culture is working?
   (a) more new ventures, small firms and self-employment than previously
   (b) more 'community' enterprise
   (c) more management buyouts
   (d) more small firms going bankrupt

2. Which country has not enacted legislation to promote and protect small firms?
   (a) United Kingdom
   (b) United States of America
   (c) Germany
   (d) Japan

3. 'Hard support' refers to the knowledge and guidance available to help the creation, survival and growth of new ventures. Is this:
   (a) true
   (b) false?

4. How have large organizations assisted the promotion of enterprise and small business development in the UK?
   (a) by sponsoring various enterprise initiatives
   (b) by creating unemployment
   (c) by developing partnerships with SMEs
   (d) by spinning out new enterprises

Answers to Quick Revision: 1–a, b and c; 2–a; 3–b; 4–a, c and d

Learning Style Activities

➡ **Activist:** Find out what is being done in the area where you live or work to promote new venture creation and small business development.

➡ **Reflector:** Relate the theory to the practice. How do the two relate to each other?

➡ **Theorist:** In the light of your experiences and your reflections on the theory and practice, how robust is the theory? Does it need to be changed to accommodate activities not accounted for?

➡ **Pragmatist:** On the basis of your understanding of the needs of new and growing small firms, what extra needs to be done in your area, if anything?

Reading

Amin, A. and J. Tomaney (1991) Creating an Enterprise Culture in the North East? The Impact of Urban and Regional Policies of the 1980s. *Regional Studies* **25** (5), 479–87.

Arnold, G. (1998) *Corporate Financial Management*. London: Pitman Publishing.

Bannock, G. (1991) Change and Continuity in Small Firm Policy since Bolton, in Stanworth, J. and C. Gray (eds) *Bolton 20 Years on: The Small Firm in the 1990s*. London: Paul Chapman Publishing Ltd.

Barrett, S., D. Colenutt, R. Foster, D. Glynn, S. Jaffer, I. Jones and D. Ridyard (1990) *An Evaluation of the Loan Guarantee Scheme: Research Paper No. 74*. London: Department of Employment.

Bennett, R.J. (1998) Business Associations and their Potential Contribution to the Competitiveness of SMEs. *Entrepreneurship and Regional Development* **10** (3), 243–58.

Bennett, R.J. and A. McCoshan (1993) *Enterprise and Human Resource Development: Local Capacity Building*. London: Paul Chapman Publishing Ltd.

Bennett, R.J. and P.J.A. Robson (1999) The Use of External Business Advice by SMEs in Britain. *Entrepreneurship and Regional Development* **11** (2), 155–80.

Birch, D. (1979) *The Job Generation Process*. Cambridge MA: MIT Program on Neighbourhood and Regional Change.

Birley, S. (1985) The Role of Networks in the Entrepreneurial Business Process. *Journal of Business Venturing* **1**, 107–17.

Bryson, J., P. Wood and D. Keeble (1993) Business Networks, Small Flexibility and Regional Development in UK Business Services. *Entrepreneurship and Regional Development* **5** (3), 265–78.

Cannon, T. (1991) *Enterprise: Creation, Development and Growth*. Oxford: Butterworth-Heinemann.

Crequer, N. (1988) Grants Turn Colleges into Enterprise Zones. *The Independent*. Autumn.

Curran, J. (2000) What is Small Business Policy in the UK for? Evaluating and Assessing Small Business Support Policies. *International Small Business Journal* **18** (3), 36–50, 71.

Curran, J. and R.A. Blackburn (1994) *Small Firms and Local Networks: The Death of the Local Economy*. London: Paul Chapman Publishing Ltd.

Department of Trade and Industry (1998) *Our Competitive Future: Building the Knowledge Driven Economy* (Cmnd 4176). London: HMSO.

Down, S. and M. Bresnen (1997) The Impact of Training and Enterprise Councils on the Provision of Small Business Support: Case Studies in London and the Midlands. *Local Economy* **11** (4), 317–32.

Enterprise Panel (1996) *Growing Success: Helping Companies to Generate Wealth and Create Jobs Through Business Incubation*. London: Midland Bank plc.

Gibb, A.A. (1997) Small Firms Training and Industrial Competitiveness: Building on the Small Firm as a Learning Organisation. *International Small Business Journal* **15** (3), 13–29.

Gibb, A.A. (2000) SME Policy, Academic Research and the Growth of Ignorance: Mythical Concepts, Myths, Assumptions, Rituals and Confusions. *International Small Business Journal* **18** (3), 13–35, 71.

Glancey, K.S. and R.W. McQuaid (2000) *Entrepreneurial Economics*. Basingstoke: Macmillan Press Ltd.

Gray, C. and J. Stanworth (1986) *Allowing for Enterprise: A Qualitative Assessment of the Enterprise Allowance Scheme*. London: Small Business Research Trust.

Gronmo, S., D.A. Kirby and K. Ekhaugen (1980) State Support to Small Stores: A Nordic Form of Consumer Policy. *Journal of Consumer Policy* **4** (3), 195–211.

Hague, D. and K. Oakley (2000) *Spin-offs and Start-ups in UK Universities*. London: Committee of Vice Chancellors and Principals.

Hakim, C. (1989) Identifying Fast Growth Small Firms. *Employment Gazette*, January, 29–41.

Hawkins, P. and J. Winter (1997) *Mastering Change: Learning the Lessons of the Enterprise in Higher Education Initiative*. Sheffield: Department for Education and Employment.

Huggins, R. (2000) The Success and Failure of Policy-implemented Inter-firm Network Initiatives: Motivations, Processes and Structure. *Entrepreneurship and Regional Development* **12**, 111–35.

Institute for Public Policy Research (1998) *The Entrepreneurial Society*. London: Institute for Policy Research.

Johannisson, B. (1998) Personal Networks in Emerging Knowledge-based Firms: Spatial and Functional Patterns. *Entrepreneurship and Regional Development* **10**, 297–312.

Johnson, S., L. Sear and A. Jenkins (2000) Small Business Policy, Support and Governance, in Carter, S. and D. Jones-Evans (eds) *Enterprise and Small Business: Principles, Practice and Policy.* London: Prentice Hall.

Jones-Evans, D. and D.A. Kirby (1994) Technical Entrepreneurs in the Service Sector: The Growth of Small Technical Consultancies in the UK, in F. Chittenden, M. Robertson and D. Watkins (eds) *Small Firms: Recession and Recovery.* London: Paul Chapman Publishing Ltd.

Keeble, D., J. Bryson and D. Wood (1991) Small Firms, Business Service Growth and Regional Development in the UK: Some Empirical Findings. *Regional Studies* **25**, 439–57.

Kirby, D.A. (1984) Government Policies Towards the Small Retail Business in Japan. *International Small Business Journal* **2** (3), 28–41.

Kirby, D.A. (1989) Enterprise in Higher Education in a Funded Institution. *Training and Development Bulletin* **36**, Cambridge: Careers Research Advisory Centre.

Kirby, D.A. (1990) Management Education and Small Business Development. *Journal of Small Business Management* **28** (4), 78–87.

Kirby, D.A. (1991) Management Training and Support, in Stanworth, J. and C. Gray (eds) *Bolton 20 Years On: The Small Firm in the 1990s.* London: Paul Chapman Publishing Ltd.

Kirby, D.A. (1992) Developing Graduate Entrepreneurs: The UK Graduate Enterprise Programme. *Entrepreneurship, Innovation and Change* **1** (2), 161–75.

Kirby, D.A. (1995) The Development of the Service Sector, in Evans, L., P. Johnson and B. Thomas (eds) *The Northern Region Economy: Progress and Prospects in the North of England.* Mansell.

Kirby, D.A. and D. Jones-Evans (1997) Small Technology-based Professional Consultancy Services in the UK—A Qualitative Study in the North-east of England. *Service Industries Journal* **17** (1), 155–72.

Kirby, D.A. and S.H. King. (1997) Accountants and Small Firm Development: Filling the Expectation Gap. *Service Industries Journal* **17** (2), 294–304.

Kirby, D.A. and D.C. Mullen (1989) Developing Enterprising Graduates. *Journal of European Industrial Training* **14** (2), 27–32.

Kirby, D.A. and D.C. Mullen (1991) Education for the Growth Company, in Gibb, A.A. and L. Davies (eds) *Recent Research in Entrepreneurship: The Third International EIASM Workshop.* Aldershot: Gower.

Kirby, D.A. and L. Travis (1995) Marketing and the Small Service Business: Solicitor's Practices in England, in Hill, G.E., D.F. Muzyka, G.S. Omura and G.A. Knight (eds) *Research at the Marketing/Entrepreneurship Interface.* Chicago: University of Illinois at Chicago.

Kirby, D.A., F. Greene and B. Najak (1998) *Accounting for Growth: The Ways Accountants Add Value to Small Businesses.* London: Institute of Chartered Accountants.

Larson, A. (1991) Network Dyads in Entrepreneurial Settings: A Study of the Governance of Exchange Relationships. *Administrative Science Quarterly* **37**, 76–104.

Leadbeater, C. (1997) *The Rise of the Social Entrepreneur.* London: Demos.

Mason, C.M. and R.T. Harrison (2000a) Influences on the Supply of Informal Venture Capital in the UK: An Exploratory Study of Investor Attitudes. *International Small Business Journal* **18** (4), 11–28.

Mason, C.M. and R.T. Harrison (2000b) Informal Venture Capital and the Financing of Emergent Growth Businesses, in Sexton, D.L. and H. Landstrom (eds) *The Blackwell Handbook of Entrepreneurship.* Oxford: Blackwell Publishers Ltd.

Mason, C.M. and R.T. Harrison (1991) The Small Firm Equity Gap since Bolton, in Stanworth, J. and C. Gray (eds) *Bolton 20 Years On: The Small Firm in the 1990s.* London: Paul Chapman Publishing Ltd.

Massey, D., P. Quintas and D. Wield (1992) *High Tech Fantasies: Science Parks in Society, Science and Space.* London: Routledge.

Matlay, H. (2000) Training and the Small Firm, in Carter, S. and D. Jones-Evans (eds) *Enterprise and Small Business: Principles, Practice and Policy.* Harlow: Prentice Hall.

Mugler, J. (2000) The Climate for Entrepreneurship in European Countries in Transition, in Sexton, D.L. and H. Landstrom (eds) *The Blackwell Handbook of Entrepreneurship.* Oxford: Blackwell Publishers Ltd.

Organisation for Economic Co-operation and Development (1985) Employment in Small and Large Firms: Where Have the Jobs Come From? *OECD Employment Review*, September, 64–82.

Patton, D., S. Marlow and P. Hannon (2000) The Relationship Between Training and Small Firm Performance: Research Frameworks and Lost Quests. *International Small Business Journal* **19** (1), 11–27.

Roche, B. (1997) *Enhanced Business Links: A Vision for the 21st Century*. London: Department of Trade and Industry.

Segal Quince Wicksteed (1985) *The Cambridge Phenomenon*. London: Segal Quince Wicksteed.

Segal Quince Wicksteed (1989) *Evaluation of the Consultancy Initiatives*. London: HMSO.

Segal Quince Wicksteed (1991a) *Evaluation of the Consultancy Initiatives—Second Stage*. London: HMSO.

Segal Quince Wicksteed (1991b) *Evaluation of the Consultancy Initiatives—Third Stage*. London: HMSO.

Stanworth, J. and G. Barker (1988) *BSC Industry Assistance in Steel Closure Areas*. London: Small Business Research Trust.

Stanworth, J., D. Purdy and D.A. Kirby (1992) *The Management of Success in 'Growth Corridor' Small Firms*. Milton Keynes: Small Business Research Trust.

Storey, D. (1994) Should We Abandon Support to Start-up Businesses?, in Chittendon, F. and M. Robertson (eds) *Small Firms: Recession and Recovery*. London: Paul Chapman Publishing Ltd.

Storey, D., K. Keasey, R. Watson and P. Wynarczyk (1987) *The Performance of Small Firms: Profits, Jobs and Failures*. London: Croom Helm.

Storey, D. and P. Westhead (1996) *Management Training and Small Firm Performance*. Coventry: Warwick Business School, Centre for Small and Medium Sized Enterprises, Working Paper 18.

Storey, D.J. and S. Johnson (1987) *Job Generation and Labour Market Change*. London: Macmillan.

Summon, P. (1998) Business Link Impact and Future Challenges. *Small Business and Enterprise Development* **5** (1), 49–59.

Thomas, C.J. and R.D.F. Bromley (1987) The Growth and Functioning of an Unplanned Retail Park: The Swansea Enterprise Zone. *Regional Studies* **21**, 287–300.

Westhead, P. (1988) *New Manufacturing Firms in the Economy of Wales*. Unpublished PhD thesis, University of Wales.

Westhead, P. (1997) *Students in Small Businesses: An Assessment of the 1994 STEP Student Placement Scheme*. Milton Keynes: Small Business Research Trust.

Westhead, P. and D.J. Storey (1994) *An Assessment of Firms Located on and off Science Parks in the UK*. London: HMSO.

Westhead, P. and S. Batstone (1999) Perceived Benefits of a Managed Science Park Location. *Entrepreneurship and Regional Development* **11** (2), 129–54.

Section **2**

Entrepreneurship and the Person

Chapter 5

The Nature, Characteristics and Behaviour of the Entrepreneur

Learning Outcomes

On completion of this chapter, the reader will:

● be familiar with the major theoretical approaches to the psychological study of entrepreneurial personality and behaviour

● have some initial insight into the strengths and weaknesses of the various approaches and the opportunities for further research

● be aware of the more recent cognitive approaches to the psychological study of entrepreneurial behaviour

● appreciate how entrepreneurship can be developed, from a psychological perspective, in both society and the individual

● have begun to appreciate his/her own entrepreneurial tendencies and how these might be developed further.

Introduction

As mentioned in Chapter 1, there is no single, uniform definition of entrepreneurship, and past attempts to identify and define the archetypal entrepreneur have not met with a great deal of success. Indeed, this led Kilby (1971) to suggest that the entrepreneur has much in common with the Heffalump in A.A. Milne's Winnie the Pooh stories, in that nobody has 'captured' him and those who have seen him disagree on his particulars. Despite years of further research, the situation appeared to be little better in 1986, when Brockhaus and Horwitz recognized that, 'the literature appears to support the argument that there is no generic definition of the entrepreneur'. More recently, Kuratko and Hodgetts (2001: 28) have suggested that, 'Although no single definition of "entrepreneur" exists and no one profile can represent today's entrepreneur, research is providing an increasingly sharper focus on the subject.'

Certainly the subject has evolved and it is generally recognized that the early attempts to classify entrepreneurial types and/or identify the archetypal entrepreneur were at best incomplete and fixed in both time and space. Being based very largely on western (usually American) research conducted mainly around the third quarter of the twentieth century, the findings had somewhat limited utility, but they very much influenced entrepreneurship thinking and clearly must be considered in any treatise on the subject. Accordingly, they constitute the focus of this chapter, which attempts to consider the attributes and ways of behaving that the reader will need to develop if he/she is to become more entrepreneurial.

The entrepreneurial personality

So, there is no uniform, standardized definition of 'the entrepreneur' and, in all probability, there is no one stereotypical model. However, it is frequently contended that entrepreneurs display certain similar characteristics and patterns of behaviour (traits). The problem is that there is no agreement over how many there are or what form they take. For example, Hornaday (1982) identifies more than 40 traits associated with entrepreneurs, Gibb (1990) identifies 12 and Timmons *et al.* (1985) 19. Some of them are similar or constant, but not all. The Timmons *et al.* attributes are:

- total commitment, determination and perseverance
- drive to achieve and grow
- orientation to goals and opportunities
- taking initiative and personal responsibility
- persistence in problem-solving
- veridical awareness and a sense of humour
- seeking and using feedback
- internal locus of control
- tolerance of ambiguity, stress and uncertainty
- calculated risk-taking and risk-sharing
- low need for status and power
- integrity and reliability
- decisiveness, urgency and patience
- dealing with failure
- team builder and hero maker
- high energy, health and emotional stability
- creativity and innovativeness
- high intelligence and conceptual ability
- vision and capacity to inspire.

According to Timmons *et al.*, these behaviours vary according to the situation in which the entrepreneur is found, and can be learned or acquired. Clearly this is important as it suggests that entrepreneurs can be developed. However, there are problems. Not only are the findings inconsistent but they are based very largely on American research and could be culturally biased (Kirby and Fan, 1995; Spence, 1985; Stimpson *et al.*, 1990). Also, it is not clear whether entrepreneurs *possess* these attributes or whether they *acquire* them as a result of being an entrepreneur. According to Chell (2000) whereas the traditional trait model suggested that P (trait) causes B (behaviour), the more recent social constructionist model suggests that B (behaviour) is construed and categorized before being ascribed to the person (P) as a behavioural descriptor or trait ascription. Finally, very few entrepreneurs possess all of the attributes or, if they do, they are combined in different ways. This has led Lessem (1986b) to suggest that there are various types of entrepreneur resulting from how the various personality traits combine. He identifies seven entrepreneurial types, as shown in Table 5.1.

Lessem's innovator type, Sir Terence Conran, started out making furniture, and diversified into home furnishings and household accessories through the development of a chain of retail outlets. According to Lessem he transformed a whole industry. Similarly, Mary Quant, his designer type, transformed women's fashion in the 1960s, sensing intuitively what people wanted and ensuring that the right products were developed at the right time. In contrast, Sir John Harvey Jones, the leader type, did not develop something. Rather, under his leadership and direction the image, profitability and productivity of Britain's largest chemicals com-

Table 5.1: Entrepreneurial types (after Lessem, 1986b)

Entrepreneurship type	Personality type	Attributes
Innovator (Sir Terence Conran)	Imagination	Originality, inspiration, love, transformation
New designer/enabler (Mary Quant)	Intuition	Evolution, development, symbiosis, connection
Leader (Sir John Harvey Jones)	Authority	Direction, responsibility, structure, control
New entrepreneur (Jack Dangoor)	Will	Achievement, opportunity, risk-taking, power
Animateur (Nelli Eichner)	Sociability	Informality, shared values, community, culture
Adventurer (Anita Roddick)	Energy	Movement, work, health, activity
Change agent (Steve Shirley)	Flexibility	Adaptability, curiosity, intelligence

pany, ICI, was improved. Likewise, Jack Dangoor, the new entrepreneur type, converted an existing product into a cheaper, higher-performing product. In the process, though, he created his own company, Advance Technology, by the age of 28. Meanwhile, Lessem's change agent type, Steve Shirley, created a new form of business organization, F International, in order to meet the career needs of women who had the responsibility for caring for their families, while his animateur type, Nelli Eichner, created a similar type of organization, Interlingua, which not only employed her family but developed into 'a family of nations'. Finally, his adventurer type is Anita Roddick, the founder of The Body Shop, who created a franchised chain of retail outlets selling products developed from natural ingredients from around the world. Apart from behaving in different ways and doing different things, each of these enterprising individuals has a very different and distinct personality. As Lessem points out, an entrepreneur is very much his or her own person.

Exercise 5.1

Complete Lessem's (1986a) Spectral Inventory, which is to be found in his book *Enterprise Development* (Aldershot: Gower). Which of his seven entrepreneurial types best represents you?

PAUSE FOR THOUGHT

Consider any entrepreneurs known to you. What attributes do they display? Do they display the same attributes or different ones? How do the attributes they display compare with those suggested by the literature?

The individual characteristics of entrepreneurs

The work of Lessem is important because it:

- reasserts that entrepreneurs can be found within large as well as small organizations
- denies the over-simplistic notion of the single entrepreneurial type
- focuses attention on the attributes of the entrepreneur.

Clearly he was not the first either to recognize that there are different entrepreneurial types or to focus on the psychological characteristics of entrepreneurs. For example, early research by Smith (1967) identified three types of entrepreneur—craftsmen, opportunists and inventors—the fundamental distinction being between the entrepreneur as 'opportunist' and the entrepreneur as 'craftsperson' or artisan. Whereas the archetypal craftsperson is a loner who values his/her independence, and whose social and commercial links are limited, the opportunist possesses considerable self-confidence, has an outgoing, cosmopolitan personality and is concerned more with the market than with production. In contrast Chell *et al.* (1991), drawing on an analogy from the biological classification system, have suggested that within the 'family' of business owners, it is possible to distinguish between the entrepreneurial intentions of those members of the family and to identify four different species: entrepreneurs, quasi-entrepreneurs, administrators and caretakers. The prototypical 'caretaker', they suggest, has little strategic focus and little or no desire to grow or change the business, whereas the business owned by the prototypical 'entrepreneur' is typified by growth and change. This distinction between those business owners who wish to grow their business (possess entrepreneurial intention) and those for whom self-employment is a way of life that enables them to fulfil their own personal goals (or non-entrepreneurial intentions) appears to have acquired quite widespread support. Indeed, it forms the basis for several of the various typologies that have been developed over the years.

From the literature, the main psychological characteristics of the entrepreneur would appear to be risk-taking ability, need for achievement ('nAch'), locus of control, desire for autonomy, deviancy, creativity and opportunism, and intuition. We will now look at each of these in turn.

Risk-taking ability

As noted in Chapter 1, classical economic theory suggests that entrepreneurs are risk-takers. By the very nature of their activities and roles in economy and society, it is clear that entrepreneurs cannot be averse to risk. Indeed, the research of Koh (1996) suggests that people who are entrepreneurially inclined have higher risk scores than those who are not. This appears to contradict the earlier findings of Brockhaus (1980) whose work indicates that there are no significant differences in their risk-taking ability between entrepreneurs, managers or the general population, while Miner (1997) argues that a key entrepreneurial task is that of avoiding risk. Thus, there is no apparent consensus with respect to risk-taking, though the prevailing belief appears to be that entrepreneurs are more predisposed to taking calculated risks than are other sectors of society (Caird, 1991; Cromie and O'Donoghue, 1992), and that they are more able to cope with the consequent ambiguity and uncertainty than are non-entrepreneurs (Koh, 1996). Interestingly the work of Busenitz (1999) indicates that entrepreneurs are more confident than managers in large organizations and as a consequence tend to distort their perceptions of risk. This introduces a further concept, that of self-confidence, which Koh (1996) believes to be a prerequisite for successful entrepreneurship, and which Ho and Koh (1992) regard as being linked to both a tolerance for ambiguity and creativity.

Need for achievement (nAch)

First propounded by McClelland in 1961, this suggests that entrepreneurs have a high need for achievement and that achievers will choose situations that are characterized by:

- individual responsibility
- moderate (not high) risk-taking
- knowledge of results of decisions
- novel instrumental activity
- anticipation of future possibilities.

It is the prospect of achievement (not money) that motivates them. Money is only important as a measure of success.

Empirical research support for McClelland's theory of nAch (1961) has been somewhat conflicting. While the work of Cromie and Johns (1983), Cromie *et al.* (1992) and Koh (1996) has suggested that entrepreneurs have consistently higher nAch scores than some population groups, they appear not to have significantly higher scores than others (such as managers and university professors). Thus it is generally held that 'although people with a strong need to achieve might well act entrepreneurially, there are problems with elevating nAch to a central position in explaining entrepreneurial motivation' (Cromie, 2000: 17).

However, within this statement there is a probable clue to reasons for the different findings. People can act entrepreneurially in all walks of life, as Van Gelderen (2000) has demonstrated. It does not mean that because they are not classified as 'entrepreneurs' (however defined), people do not behave entrepreneurially. Conversely, people who start a business, need not necessarily be entrepreneurs (Hull *et al.*, 1980). It is the nature of the activity, rather than its title, that needs to be measured. Entrepreneurship is a way of thinking and behaving, and entrepreneurial behaviour is not confined solely to the act of starting and running a small enterprise, as has been shown.

Locus of control

This is based on the work of Rotter (1966). Essentially a person who believes in internal control believes that the achievement of a goal is dependent on his/her own behaviour or individual characteristics. A person who believes it is the result of luck or other people's actions believes in external control. Entrepreneurs are believed to possess a high internal locus of control. However, the results of empirical research into this are inconclusive. Some (Cromie, 1987; Cromie and Johns, 1983) have found significantly higher 'internal' scores compared to experienced managers, while others (Brockhaus and Nord, 1979; Cromie *et al.*, 1992) have found no differences between the scores of these two groups. Additionally, it has been suggested, as Cromie (2000) has recognized, that high achievers will also exhibit these behaviours, and there is conflicting evidence (Chen *et al.*, 1998; Hull *et al.*, 1980) about whether locus of control or need for achievement is the more fundamental entrepreneurial attribute.

Desire for autonomy

Entrepreneurs want to be in control—hence they have been found to have a higher need for autonomy and a greater fear of external control than many other occupational groups (Caird, 1991; Cromie and O'Donoghue, 1992). They value individualism and freedom more than do either the general public or managers, and they have a dislike of rules, procedures and social norms. As a consequence they have difficulty functioning in constraining environments that stifle creativity, and can experience difficulty relating to others. As Cromie (2000) observes, some are even regarded as deviants (see below).

This desire to manage or take ownership of one's own life is a central feature of entrepreneurship, but given the findings with respect to locus of control it is difficult to explain.

Deviancy

This is based on the work of Kets de Vries (1977), who argues that entrepreneurial behaviour is the result of negative characteristics and drives, and its financial benefits and drives do not always lead to personal satisfaction and happiness. According to him, an entrepreneur is 'an anxious individual, a non-conformist poorly organised and not a stranger to self-destructive behaviour' (1977: 41). Such behaviour, he asserts, is the result of a very disturbed childhood where the father is often absent. As a consequence the entrepreneur becomes a person:

- with low self-esteem
- who lacks the ability to reflect critically
- who dreams of being in total control, and independent of everything and everyone.

This would thus explain why entrepreneurs become engaged in risky activities and choose to create their own organizations. However, research suggests that entrepreneurs are no more troubled than anyone else, and that they come from families that are stable financially and emotionally.

Creativity and opportunism

Much of the entrepreneurial literature suggests that entrepreneurs are more creative than others (Timmons, 1989; Whiting, 1988). Certainly entrepreneurs tend to think in non-conventional ways, to challenge existing assumptions, and to be flexible and adaptable in their problem-solving. All of these are integral to creativity and the creative process (Kirton, 1976; Solomon and Winslow, 1988), though some would argue that entrepreneurs are not so much creative as opportunistic. Rather than creating the new idea, they see opportunities and make them happen. Indeed some authors (Holt, 1983; Rogers, 1983) have distinguished between inventing something new (creativity) and adopting or using it (innovation). For Drucker (1985), innovation is the core of entrepreneurship, and more attention will be paid to this and its relationship with creativity in Chapter 6. For the present, suffice it to say that there is a difference of opinion over whether creativity and innovativeness are personality traits or processes. While Drucker suggests that innovation is a systematic process, Koh (1996) takes the alternative view, and others (Caird, 1991; Cromie and O'Donoghue, 1992; Cromie et al., 1992) have found that owner-managers are more creative than undergraduates or managers, and that innovation is an important aspect of entrepreneurial self-efficacy (Chen et al., 1998). Whatever, research by Utsch and Rauch (2000) suggests that there is a powerful link between innovativeness and venture performance, and that innovativeness is linked to achievement orientation. Whereas people with a low achievement orientation avoid innovation, give up quickly, demonstrate little effort and lack self-confidence, entrepreneurs with high achievement orientation exert considerable effort and persist in the face of problems and barriers. Hence they conclude that, 'an entrepreneur need not be high in achievement orientation to be successful, but it is helpful to be innovative. Especially in fast-growing areas or in high technology areas . . . a high achievement orientation is important' (2000: 59).

Intuition

It has been contested (Carland, 1982) that entrepreneurs are intuitive rather than rational thinkers. Instead of adopting a structured, analytical approach to problem-solving, which requires attention to detail, adherence to rules and systematic investigation, it is believed that they prefer a more intuitive approach that requires more holism and synthesis, lateral rather than sequential reasoning and random methods of exploration. However, others contest that although intuition is important, it is more important for certain situations than for others and for certain types of entrepreneur. For example, it is frequently contended that intuition is important in the invention phase of the entrepreneurial process, although Miner (1997) suggests that of the four types of entrepreneur he identifies, intuition is an important characteristic of just one: the 'expert idea generators'. In an interesting piece of research based on the 437 founders of high growth companies listed in the role model publication *Local Heroes* (Scottish Enterprise, 1997) referred to in Chapter 3, Allinson *et al.* (2000) compare the 156 responses to a questionnaire survey with an earlier survey (using the same questionnaire) of 546 managers from various organizations. The results reveal that entrepreneurs in high growth firms are more intuitive than members of the general population of managers, and middle and junior managers in particular, but are no different in their cognitive style from senior managers and executives.

While recognizing that this is a pilot investigation based on a convenience sample, the authors conclude that the findings 'provide empirical support for the widely held view that successful entrepreneurs adopt an intuitive approach to information processing' (2000: 41). At the same time they challenge the view that entrepreneurs process information differently from all categories of salaried managers, which is consistent with the view that entrepreneurial behaviour is not confined to the self-employed. More attention will be paid to intuition and entrepreneurial activity in Chapter 6 in the consideration of creativity and innovation.

PAUSE FOR THOUGHT

Consider the various psychological models referred to above and attempt to relate them to entrepreneurs known to you. How well do they fit? Are there other possible explanations for their behaviour?

Measuring the entrepreneurial personality

As mentioned in Chapter 2, most new ventures fail and many do not grow. Accordingly, there has been considerable interest in the concept of 'picking winners' (Chapter 4)—those businesses that are likely to succeed and grow. Not unnaturally, given the importance of the person in business success, much atten-

A CASE EXAMPLE

Charlie Muirhead: a successful entrepreneur

As noted in Chapter 4, Charlie Muirhead, 24, is founder and president of Orchestream, one of Britain's biggest commercial hopes of the e-era. Established in 1996 above a garage in the Old Brompton Road in London, the company's vision is 'to become the leading software company in Internet Protocol network management'. Within four years of its foundation, the company employed over 80 staff out of offices in London and New York, and counted among its customers operators of public telecom and cable networks (e.g. NTT Europe), service providers such as Inter Digital Networks and other major businesses, such as Toys 'R' Us.

Like Bill Gates, Charlie 'dropped out' of university at the end of his first year when, according to him, he realized that computers were just machines and he understood enough about how a microprocessor worked to ensure he was not afraid of them. At school, he was always fanatical about things, whether it was skateboarding, Dungeons and Dragons, BMX bikes or playing the electric guitar. He was not always good at them by any means. For example, he was terrible at skateboarding and playing the guitar. So, instead, he built a skateboard ramp for his friends to use, and set up the amplifiers and recording equipment for the school band. It was Charlie, also, who petitioned his headmaster for two years for £5000 to buy a sound system so that the school could hold its own rock concerts.

On leaving school, he spent a gap year not backpacking around the world with his peers, but working at Hilton Sound (a London business that leased audio equipment to pop groups) and re-sitting his Maths A-level to give him the entrance grade he needed for university. When he started at university he began to think about how it might be possible to improve the speed of the Internet in order to improve audio quality. While studying, he also worked part-time at Prime Time Video, Petplan Insurance and as a freelance Internet consultant, for £15 per hour. At the same time, he was 'playing' with his idea for a premium Internet.

On leaving university in 1995, Muirhead's ambition was to emulate Netscape which, that year, was floated on Nasdaq for US$2.9 billion. He thinks big! 'Whereas Netscape is a software company that lets you look for information,' he says, 'it doesn't solve the performance issues of the Internet. We saw ourselves as an equally powerful technology.' This is part of the reason for the firm's success: Muirhead's ambition and drive. Another factor is his undoubted ability to network and make contacts. However, possibly most important of all is his self-awareness and judgement. Recognizing that the business had grown faster than he was able to manage it, he bought in experienced business names—Alan Bates the former chief executive of Bell Cable Media as chairman and Ashley Ward, the former head of Anite Networks, as chief executive. This not only brought in experience but, as Muirhead recognizes, 'an obsession with customers to a company that didn't have a sales director'. At the same time, it enabled him to concentrate on what he is good at: product development, partnerships and acquisitions. 'I don't want to drive the ship,' he says, 'I'm much more the entrepreneur—it's about ideas, having the technical understanding, knowing how to raise funds and how to present concepts . . . '.

tion has been focused on the measurement of the entrepreneurial personality in an attempt to identify those persons most likely to succeed. Over the years, therefore, numerous measures have been developed, the most common of which are those based on responses to a series of statements about the attribute being measured. In particular, various measures have been developed to test for nAch (Lynn, 1969; Smith, 1973; Steers and Braunstein, 1976; Tziner and Elizur, 1985). While most of the instruments ask respondents questions about general tasks and conceive of nAch as a unitary concept, the Steers and Braunstein test focuses on work-related activities, while Tziner and Elizur conceive of nAch as having six separate components. Similarly, the original instrument developed by Rotter (1966) to test for locus of control was unidimensional, but Levenson (1973) developed a multi-dimensional scale to assess control over events by self, powerful others and chance, while the measure developed by Paulhus (1983) was intended to examine control over others in groups and over social and political events, but not entrepreneurial activity.

Some of these instruments are simple to complete, some are complex, and their reliability and validity is questionable. However, according to Cromie (2000), one of the most useful, comprehensive, accessible and easy to administer and score is the General Enterprising Tendency (GET) test, developed by staff at Durham University Business School. This is a 54-item questionnaire designed to assess five dimensions of personality: Need for Achievement (12 items); Autonomy (6 items); Drive and Determination (12 items); Risk Taking (12 items); and Creativity (6 items). Each item is a statement and participants are required either to agree or disagree with it. Each dimension receives a score of 0–12 (0–6 for the Autonomy dimension) with a composite score for the test of 0–54. The complete test takes about 10 minutes to complete and although Cromie believes it requires further work to verify its psychometric properties, it would appear to have 'criterion and convergent validity and good internal consistency', though one exception 'is the lack of correlation between locus of control and creativity' (2000: 22).

Most recently, Stormer *et al.* (1999) have applied the GET test to 128 owners of new (75) and successful (53) small businesses. Their results indicate that although the total GET test 'had reliabilities that were acceptable for research purposes . . . it . . . was poor at predicting small business success' (1999: 51) while the subscales were not at all predictive. This leads them to suggest that either the scale needs refining in order to improve its psychometric properties and to produce a better way of identifying those individuals who will be successful, or attention needs to be focused less on personality-based factors and more on task-based factors such as previous work experience, the thoroughness of the market research, the clarity of the business plan, the amount of working capital and so on.

Exercise 5.2

Complete the questionnaire to be found in Appendix 5.1 at the end of this chapter, which can also be accessed electronically at **www.flametree.co.uk/work/start-your-business/intro/courage**.

Cognitive models of entrepreneurial behaviour

In recent years the traits approach to entrepreneurship has received considerable criticism. This has taken various forms, as outlined below.

- There is no agreement on how to measure entrepreneurial traits or on which instruments to use.
- The lack of a standardized definition of the entrepreneur and entrepreneurship,

and the use of a variety of definitions, make it difficult to compare the findings from the various studies, even when the same instruments have been used.

- Given that there are different types of entrepreneur, different instruments are needed to measure each type.
- Even if there were a perfectly validated and measured entrepreneurial personality profile, there are a number of intervening variables that affect the propensity to behave entrepreneurially. As Cromie (2000: 25) has recognized, 'Personal attributes are important but not all pervading determinants of behaviour.'

Given the limitations of the simple trait theories approach, entrepreneurship research has turned to more cognitive theories. These are better able to explain the complexity inherent in entrepreneurial behaviour. They assume that individuals do not possess a perfect knowledge of the world and that they have to select and interpret information. Since they are different and have different experiences, they view the world differently. An opportunity for one person is a problem for another.

With the use of cognitive theory there is a shift away from the personality of the entrepreneur to studying the situations that lead to entrepreneurial behaviour. In psychological terms, behaviour patterns are the result of two processes. The first operates through the selection of environments, the second through the production of environments with individual characteristics acting as precursor traits that help determine how experiences are weighted and how the individual reacts to those experiences. Thus it is believed that individuals will only activate their entrepreneurial potential if they have:

- a specific ability—a sensitivity
- environmental possibilities
- social support.

All three prerequisites must be fulfilled if entrepreneurship is to take place. Hence the measures to promote and support entrepreneurship outlined in Chapter 4.

Essentially, there are two groups of cognitive models, namely attitude models and achievement models, as well as intrinsic motivation. We will now look at each of these in turn.

Attitude models

These are concerned with how an individual's attitude towards entrepreneurship shapes his/her behaviour. Within the field of entrepreneurship, two attitude concepts have received most widespread attention:

- why individuals become self-employed or start a business
- why some individuals want to grow a business (though most do not).

The model most used to explain these is Ajzen's (1991) theory of planned behaviour. This proposes that behaviour is determined by the individual's intention to act, which, in turn, is influenced by attitudes (social norms). According to the theory, a person will start or grow a business if he/she has:

- enough information to form an opinion

- an opinion favourable to the behaviour of starting a business
- the intention to start a business
- sufficient support/encouragement.

However, attitudes and social norms are not sufficient. There is a third factor: the perceived degree of difficulty involved in performing the behaviour. The theory proposes that a person's intention to perform the behaviour will increase with perceived behavioural control.

When tested empirically, it would appear that:

- attitudes are unable to predict whether a person will start or grow a business
- social norms have even less predictive power
- perceived behavioural control is the strongest predictor—people will try to start a business if they believe they have the ability and knowledge to do it.

Clearly such findings suggest that entrepreneurs are not necessarily born, and that they can be made. This is important for both educators and policy-makers, as well as for society in general. More attention will be paid to this in Chapter 6.

Achievement models

These are concerned with motivation and why individuals behave as they do, risking failure. Two models—perceived self-efficacy and intrinsic motivation—are believed to be of particular significance.

Perceived self-efficacy refers to 'the strength of an individual's belief that he or she is capable of successfully performing the roles and tasks of an entrepreneur' (Chen *et al.*, 1998: 301). It is related to the concept of perceived behavioural control and has its roots in the concept of locus of control discussed earlier. However, Chen *et al.* argue that it is more appropriate than either locus of control or nAch in identifying entrepreneurs. Essentially it proposes that people with a high level of self-efficacy (self-belief) approach difficult tasks as challenging goals and maintain strong commitment to them. They:

- are persistent even when faced with failure
- are objective and analytical
- attribute failure to insufficient effort and poor knowledge.

People with low self-efficacy:

- shy away from difficult tasks, perceiving them as personal threats
- have low aspiration levels and personal goals
- are not analytical
- give up easily
- attribute failure to external obstacles and personal deficiencies.

A person's level of self-efficacy is often affected by his/her previous experiences— success breeds success, and vice versa.

Entrepreneurship research indicates that perceived self-efficacy affects the strategies and performances of businesses and that entrepreneurs found to possess high levels of self-efficacy achieve a higher performance for their firms than those low in perceived self-efficacy.

Intrinsic motivation

This is often connected with interest and enjoyment. It is an action engaged in for its own sake. It contrasts with extrinsic motivation, which involves external influences. Generally, people who are intrinsically motivated outperform those who focus on behaviours for their extrinsic benefits. Hence, it is believed that entrepreneurs are intrinsically motivated—that they are successful because they enjoy what they do—the challenge of creating something new or of growing a business. They do what they do because they want to, not because they are forced to or because of the opportunity to become wealthy.

This shift in emphasis from personal traits to understanding what triggers the entrepreneurial process in people has important implications for the economy and society. It suggests that if entrepreneurship is to be encouraged, it is necessary for:

- society to have favourable attitudes towards such an objective
- individuals to believe they have the ability to do it
- people to believe it is intrinsically rewarding.

Even then, people with the propensity to act entrepreneurially may not do so. Indeed, Krueger and Brazeal (1994) have suggested that in many cases the latent capacity for entrepreneurship is not activated until there is a precipitating event, such as unemployment. Clearly this is a further reason why it is dangerous to believe, as discussed in Chapter 3, that those who are precipitated into entrepreneurship by redundancy (forced entrepreneurship) are any less successful than those who are not.

PAUSE FOR THOUGHT

Are all the entrepreneurs known to you successful people? Have they always been successful? How do they handle failure? How should we treat 'failure'? Do they appear to be enjoying themselves? What do you think motivates them?

A CASE EXAMPLE

Sir Richard Branson: a Virgin entrepreneur?

With a knighthood (for 'services to entrepreneurship'), an entry in the *Guinness Book of Records* (as the first man to cross the Atlantic in a hot air balloon) and a reported personal wealth of £2.4 billion (from his 150 business ventures), Richard Branson is perceived as a typical entrepreneur. Certainly he demonstrates many of the personality characteristics and patterns of behaviour traditionally associated with the 'entrepreneur' and propounded in the various theories of entrepreneurship.

Born in 1950, he had a somewhat unusual but privileged upbringing. For example, determined to develop her son's self-reliance, his mother, Eve, is reputed to have pushed her four-year-old son from the car one day and told him to find his own way home. Some distance from home, he got himself completely lost and had to knock on the door of a complete stranger to ask the way. Again, while other parents banned their children from climbing the tree on the village green where Branson was brought up, his mother made him climb right to the top. Such experiences developed his self-confidence and self-belief so, although he suffered from dyslexia and did not excel at Stowe, the top public school he attended, he grew up confident in his own ability. As Bower (2001: 13–14) has recognized, Branson's mother's exhortations 'created an obedient son convinced he could do no wrong and that self-doubt was a sin', while according to her, 'bringing him up was like riding a thorough-bred horse. He needed guiding but you were afraid to pull the reins too hard in case you stamped out the adventure and wildness.' As a result, he emerged as a doer rather than an observer, excited by intellectual stimulation and someone who has a healthy disdain for authority and is impervious to criticism.

Although he is reputed to have been frustrated by the rigidity of the formal education system and did not excel at school, he developed an interest in journalism and the possibility of publishing a magazine for sixth-formers. The concept was quite simple. It would be focused on students and would carry features written by well-known personalities, including rock stars, movie stars, intellectuals and leading politicians. It would sell advertising to major corporations. So, he began writing to celebrities requesting interviews. Somewhat surprisingly, he received replies, many of them positive. At the age of 16, therefore, with six O-levels, he persuaded his barrister father to let him leave school to start a publishing business, with his schoolfriend Jonny Gems. On the eve of Branson's departure from Stowe, his headteacher is reputed to have predicted that Richard would either become a millionaire or go to prison.

With a rumoured £4 donation from Richard's mother to help cover postage and telephone expenses, the business (Connaught Publications) was launched from his office on the top floor of a house his parents had leased in the Bayswater area of London. Branson persuaded a respected magazine designer to work for no fee and his friends to work for the magazine for £12 per week. At the same time, he negotiated a printing contract for 50,000 copies. The first edition of Student was published in January 1968, carrying a picture of a student drawn by Peter Blake, the cover designer for The Beatles' Sgt Pepper album. 'While others only talked about

the idea, Branson's energetic self-confidence could make Student a reality' (Bower, 2001: 14).

However, the venture was not a success. Like so many start-up businesses it had cashflow problems. So, in April 1970, together with two colleagues, John Varnon and Tony Mellor, Branson established his second business—Virgin Records—selling records by mail order. Since the British government had abolished Retail Price Maintenance on records, it was possible to sell them at discount prices, undercutting the main retail outlets. An advertisement in what was to be the last edition of Student produced an encouraging trickle of orders with payment in advance of delivery. Subsequent full-page advertisements in Melody Maker turned the trickle into a flood and Branson again exercised his persuasive skills to convince first the staff of Student to work for the spinout discount record company, and then the owner of a shoe store to let them use the upper floor of the outlet, free of charge. The venture was highly successful. Shortly after it was started, with orders flooding in from overseas, Branson drove a van to Dover intending to export a consignment of records to the continent. This was a particularly lucrative initiative as records sold overseas did not attract the 33 per cent purchase tax levied on goods sold within the UK. On arrival at Dover, he obtained a PT999 form, confirming that the records had left the country and boarded the ferry. Because of a strike in France, however, the sailing was cancelled and he returned to London with his records officially cleared of purchase tax. He was not slow to realize that he could sell them, via his mail order company, to British customers and save the tax.

Having discovered how easy it was, it is claimed that he set out deliberately and systematically to defraud Customs & Excise. The extent of the fraud is not clear, but Bower (2001) suggests that the van was driven regularly to Dover, and reports that not only were records supposedly exported in batches of at least 10,000 to every country in western Europe and to the United States, but that, on two occasions, Branson supposedly exported 30,000 records in a Land Rover! Once the official stamp had been secured on the tax exemption form, the van then returned to London. On occasions, Bower claims, Branson did not even bother to send a van to the port. To save money, he is said to have bought a cheap 'awayday ticket', caught a train to Dover, presented a certificate for 10,000 records and gone home.

When Branson was eventually caught, he spent a night in jail. Initially he claimed he was innocent; then, apparently with the support of his parents, but particularly his mother, he persuaded the authorities to settle out of court. The scale of the crime is reputed to have been in the order of £40,000 in unpaid taxes (the equivalent of £370,000 at 2000 prices) and Branson appears to have agreed to pay this, plus a fine of £20,000 (£185,000). Following negotiations, it would appear that Customs & Excise agreed to him paying £15,000 up front and the rest over a 15-month period.

Branson has never denied the fraud, but his explanations of it have varied. In 1986, he apparently told the *Sun* newspaper that he escaped imprisonment 'by convincing the court that he didn't know it was illegal'. However, in his own 1998 autobiography, he claims that he did it deliberately to cover debts amounting to £35,000. According to Bower (2001: 11) 'all those variations were a smokescreen. He had simply played the game and, unforgivably, he had lost.' Branson himself is reputed to have proclaimed 'I have always thought rules were there to be broken.'

From these humble and somewhat dubious beginnings, the current Virgin group of companies has evolved (see Chapter 9). In the process, numerous businesses were created, several of which failed. Branson recognizes that he 'is good at spotting opportunities in the market and filling them'. Often, when such opportunities arise 'we don't even do the figures in advance. We just feel there's room in the market or a need for something and we'll get it going' (quoted in Bower, 2001: 33). However, behind this apparently relaxed attitude, and a reputation for partying and fun, is a true determination to succeed.

Case example exercise

Review the two case examples in this chapter, of Charlie Muirhead and Richard Branson. Identify the attributes or traits they demonstrate and evaluate the validity of the various trait theories. Determine the value of the cognitive models in these specific contexts. How do the two theoretical approaches (the trait approach and the cognitive models approach) help advance our understanding of these two very different entrepreneurs?

PAUSE FOR THOUGHT

Review Chapter 4 in the light of the lessons learned from Chapter 5. Is there anything further you could do if you were required to promote entrepreneurship in your society/economy?

Exercise 5.3

How do you rate against the attributes and behaviours purportedly possessed by the entrepreneur? Which attributes do you believe you possess and which do you feel you will need to acquire?

Appendix 5.2, which you will find at the end of this chapter, contains a self-administered questionnaire. It originates from the research of Morris (1975) who has argued that managers need to be more resourceful. According to him, resourceful or enterprising managers are people who:

● can cope decisively with new situations
● use whatever information is obtainable to develop broad, but practical, plans with room for contingencies
● work with, and through, other people

- plan for themselves rather than fit into other people's plans
- take ownership of their own development.

Usually, they are characterized by the following characteristics or attributes:

- flexible intelligence
- technical ability
- emotional resilience
- drive for continued effectiveness
- effective judgement in situations of uncertainty
- commitment to fundamental values.

Whether you are working for someone else or intending to set up and run your own business, you will need to possess these attributes. So complete the exercise in Appendix 5.2 to see how you measure up against the criteria and how you will need to develop.

Chapter Review

➡ Successful entrepreneurs are believed to possess a special set of personal abilities and characteristics (traits).

➡ There is no agreement over these and in all probability they combine in different ways to produce not one archetypal entrepreneur but several.

➡ The psychological literature suggests that the main characteristics of an entrepreneur are his/her:

   – risk-taking ability

   – need for achievement (nAch)

   – internal locus of control

   – desire for autonomy

   – deviancy.

➡ More recently, cognitive theory has shifted the emphasis from studying the personality of the entrepreneur to studying the situations that lead to entrepreneurial behaviour.

➡ Essentially there are two types of cognitive model:

   – attitude models—concerned with how an individual's attitude shapes his/her behaviour

   – achievement models—concerned with why individuals behave as they do.

➡ Cognitive research suggests that if entrepreneurship is to be encouraged, it is necessary for:

   – society to have favourable attitudes towards such an objective

   – individuals to believe they have the ability to do it

   – people to believe it is intrinsically rewarding.

➡ Such findings have important implications for the development of entrepreneurship in both society and the individual.

Quick Revision

(Answers at the end of this section)

1. What is the significance of the attributes identified by Timmons *et al.* (1985)?

   (a) they are more comprehensive than those identified by other researchers

   (b) they can be learned or acquired

   (c) they are all possessed by the entrepreneur

2. According to McClelland (1961), what motivates the entrepreneur?

   (a) money

   (b) success

   (c) achievement

   (d) desire for autonomy

3. Cognitive theory better enables us to explain the complexity inherent within entrepreneurial behaviour by focusing on the personality of the entrepreneur? Is this:

   (a) true

   (b) false?

4. Entrepreneurs are successful because they enjoy what they do. What term describes this phenomenon?

   (a) self-efficacy

   (b) intrinsic motivation

Answers to Quick Revision: 1–b; 2–c; 3–a; 4–b

Learning Style Activities

➡ **Activist:** Re-read the Richard Branson case example and list all of the personality and behavioural characteristics he displays.

➡ **Reflector:** Relate these characteristics to the various theories of entrepreneurial behaviour.

➡ **Theorist:** Consider the extent to which the existing psychological theories explain Branson's personality and behaviour.

➡ **Pragmatist:** On the basis of your deliberations, what do you believe can or should be done to help people become more entrepreneurial?

Reading

Ajzen, I. (1991) The Theory of Planned Behaviour. *Organisational Behavior and Human Decision Processes* **50**, 179–211.

Allinson, C.W., E. Chell and J. Hayes (2000) Intuition and Entrepreneurial Behaviour. *European Journal of Work and Organisational Psychology* **9** (1), 31–43.

Bower, T. (2001) *Branson*. London: Fourth Estate.

Brockhaus, R.H. (1980) Risk Taking Propensity of Entrepreneurs. *Academy of Management Journal* **23**, 509–20.

Brockhaus, R.H. and P.S. Horwitz (1986) The Psychology of the Entrepreneur, in Sexton, D.L. and R.W. Smilor (eds) *The Art and Science of Entrepreneurship*. Cambridge: Ballinger Publishing Company.

Brockhaus, R.H. and W.R. Nord (1979) An Exploration of Factors Affecting the Entrepreneurial Decision: Personal Characteristics Versus Environmental Conditions. *Proceedings of the Academy of Management* **10**, 509–20.

Busenitz, L.W. (1999) Entrepreneurial Risk and Strategic Decision Making: It's a Matter of Perspective. *Journal of Applied Behavioural Science* **35** (3), 325–40.

Caird, S. (1991) The Enterprising Tendency of Occupational Groups. *International Small Business Journal* **9** (4), 75–81.

Carland, J.W. (1982) *Entrepreneurship in a Small Business Setting: An Exploratory Study*. Unpublished doctoral dissertation. Athens GA: University of Georgia.

Chell, E. (2000) Toward Researching the Opportunistic Entrepreneur: A Social Constructionist Approach and Research Agenda. *European Journal of Work and Organisational Psychology* **9** (1), 63–80.

Chell, E., J.M. Haworth and S.A. Brealey (1991) *The Entrepreneurial Personality: Concepts, Cases and Strategies*. London: Routledge.

Chen, P.C., P.G. Greene and A. Crick (1998) Does Entrepreneurial Self Efficacy Distinguish Entrepreneurs from Managers? *Journal of Business Venturing* **13**, 295–316.

Cromie, S. (2000) Assessing Entrepreneurial Implications: Some Approaches and Empirical Evidence. *European Journal of Work and Organisational Psychology* **9** (1), 7–30.

Cromie, S. and S. Johns (1983) Irish Entrepreneurs: Some Personal Characteristics. *Journal of Organisational Behaviour* **4**, 317–24.

Cromie, S. and J. O'Donoghue (1992) Assessing Entrepreneurial Inclinations. *International Small Business Journal* **10** (2), 66–73.

Cromie, S., I. Callaghan and M. Jansen (1992) The Entrepreneurial Tendencies of Managers: A Research Note. *British Journal of Management* **3**, 1–5.

Delmar, F. (2000) The Psychology of the Entrepreneur, in Carter, S and D. Jones-Evans (eds) *Enterprise and Small Business: Principles, Practice and Policy*. Harlow: Prentice Hall.

Drucker, P. (1985) *Innovation and Entrepreneurship*. London: Heinemann.

Gibb, A.A. (1990) Entrepreneurship and Intrapreneurship—Exploring the Differences, in Donckels, R. and A. Miettinen (eds) *New Findings and Perspectives in Entrepreneurship*. Aldershot: Gower.

Guirdham. M. and K. Tyler (1992) *Enterprise Skills for Students*. Oxford: Butterworth-Heinemann.

Ho, T.S. and Koh, H.C. (1992) Differences in Psychological Characteristics Between Entrepreneurially Inclined Accounting Graduates in Singapore. *Entrepreneurship, Innovation and Change* **1**, 243–54.

Holt, K. (1983) *Product Innovation Management*. London: Butterworth.

Hornaday, R. (1982) Research About Living Entrepreneurs, in Kent, C.A., D.L. Sexton and K.L. Vesper (eds) *Encyclopedia of Entrepreneurship*. Englewood-Cliffs NJ: Prentice Hall.

Hull, D.L., J.J. Bosley and G.G. Udell (1980) Renewing the Hunt for the Heffalump: Identifying Potential Entrepreneurs by Personality Characteristics. *Journal of Small Business* **18**, 11–18.

Kets de Vries, M.F.R. (1997) The Entrepreneurial Personality: A Person at the Crossroads. *Journal of Management Studies*, February, 34–57.

Kilby, P. (1971) Hunting the Heffalump, in Kilby, P. (ed.) *Entrepreneurship and Economic Development*. New York: Free Press.

Kirby, D.A. and Y. Fan (1995) Chinese Cultural Values and Entrepreneurship: A Preliminary Consideration. *Journal of Enterprising Culture* **3** (3), 245–60.

Kirton, M. (1976) Adaptors and Innovators: A Description and Measure. *Journal of Applied Psychology* **61**, 622–9.

Koh, H.C. (1996) Testing Hypotheses of Entrepreneurial Characteristics. *Journal of Managerial Psychology* **11**, 12–25.

Krueger, N.F. and Brazeal, D.V. (1994) Entrepreneurial Potential and Potential Entrepreneurs. *Entrepreneurship Theory and Practice* **18**, 91–104.

Kuratko, D.F. and R.M. Hodgetts (2001) *Entrepreneurship: A Contemporary Approach*. Orlando FL: Harcourt Inc.

Lessem, R. (1986a) *Enterprise Development*. Aldershot: Gower.

Lessem, R. (1986b) *Intrapreneurship: How to be a Successful Individual in a Successful Business*. Aldershot: Wildwood House.

Levenson, H. (1973) Multidimensional Locus of Control in Psychiatric Patients. *Journal of Consulting and Clinical Psychology* **41**, 397–404.

Lynn, R. (1969) An Achievement Motivation Questionnaire. *British Journal of Psychology* **60**, 529–34.

McClelland, D.C. (1961) *The Achieving Society*. Princeton NJ: Van Nostrand.

Miner, J.B. (1997) *A Psychological Typology of Successful Entrepreneurs*. London: Quorum Books.

Morris, J. (1975) Developing Resourceful Managers, in Taylor, B. and G.L. Lippit (eds) *Management Development and Training Handbook*. London: McGraw-Hill Book Company Ltd.

Olsen, P.D. (1995) Entrepreneurship: Process and Abilities. *Entrepreneurship Theory and Practice* **10** (1), 25–32.

Paulhus, D. (1983) Sphere-specific Measures of Perceived Control. *Journal of Personality and Social Psychology* **44**, 1253–65.

Rogers, E.M. (1983) *Diffusions of Innovations*. New York: Free Press.

Rotter, J.B. (1966) Generalised Expectancies for Internal Versus External Control of Reinforcement. *Psychological Monographs* **80** (whole No. 609).

Scottish Enterprise (1997) *Local Heroes*. Edinburgh: Insider Group.

Smith, J.M. (1973) A Quick Measure of Achievement Motivation. *British Journal of Social and Clinical Psychology* **12**, 18–27.

Smith, N.R. (1967) *The Entrepreneur and his Firm: The Relationship Between Type of Man and Type of Company*. East Lansing MI: Michigan State University.

Solomon, G.T. and E. Winslow (1988) Towards a Descriptive Profile of the Entrepreneur. *Journal of Creative Behaviour* **22**, 162–71.

Spence, J.T. (1985) Achievement American Style—The Rewards and Costs of Individualism. *American Psychologist* **40** (12), 1285–95.

Steers, R.M. and D.N. Braunstein (1976) A Behaviourally Based Measure of Manifest Needs in Work Settings. *Journal of Vocational Behaviour* **9**, 151–66.

Stimpson, D.V., P.B. Robinson, S. Waranusuntikule and R. Zheng (1990) Attitudinal Characteristics of Entrepreneurs and Non-entrepreneurs in the United States, Korea, Thailand and the People's Republic of China. *Entrepreneurship and Regional Development* **2**, 49–55.

Stormer, R., T. Kline and S. Goldenberg (1999) Measuring Entrepreneurship with the General Enterprising Tendency (GET) Test: Criterion-related Validity and Reliability. *Human Systems Management* **18** (1), 47–54.

Timmons, J.A. (1989) *The Entrepreneurial Mind*. Andover MA: Brick House Publishing.

Timmons, J.A., L.E. Smollen, A.L.M. Dingee (1985) *New Venture Creation*. Homewood IL: Irwin.

Tziner, A. and D. Elizur (1985) The Achievement Motive Construct. *Journal of Organizational Behaviour* **6**, 209–27.

Utsch, A. and A. Rauch (2000) Innovativeness and Initiative as Mediators Between Achievement Orientation and Venture Performance. *European Journal of Work and Organisational Psychology* **9** (1), 45–62.

Van Gelderen, M. (2000) Enterprising Behaviour of Ordinary People. *European Journal of Work and Organisational Psychology* **9** (1), 81–8.

Whiting, B.G. (1988) Creativity and Entrepreneurship: How do they Relate? *Journal of Creative Behavior* **22**, 178–83.

Entrepreneurial tendency test

Ring round your answer (Yes, Maybe or No) to each of the following questions, then check your score on the next page.

I am persistent	Yes	Maybe	No
When I'm interested in a project, I need less sleep	Yes	Maybe	No
When there's something I want, I keep my goal clearly in mind	Yes	Maybe	No
I examine mistakes and I learn from them	Yes	Maybe	No
I keep New Year's resolutions	Yes	Maybe	No
I have a strong personal need to succeed	Yes	Maybe	No
I have new and different ideas	Yes	Maybe	No
I am adaptable	Yes	Maybe	No
I am curious	Yes	Maybe	No
I am intuitive	Yes	Maybe	No
If something can't be done, I find a way	Yes	Maybe	No
I see problems as challenges	Yes	Maybe	No
I take chances	Yes	Maybe	No
I'll gamble on a good idea, even if it isn't a sure thing	Yes	Maybe	No
To learn something new, I explore unfamiliar subjects	Yes	Maybe	No
I can recover from emotional setbacks	Yes	Maybe	No
I feel sure of myself	Yes	Maybe	No
I'm a positive person	Yes	Maybe	No
I experiment with new ways to do things	Yes	Maybe	No
I'm willing to undergo sacrifices to gain possible long-term rewards	Yes	Maybe	No
I usually do things my own way	Yes	Maybe	No
I tend to rebel against authority	Yes	Maybe	No
I often enjoy being alone	Yes	Maybe	No
I like to be in control	Yes	Maybe	No
I have a reputation for being stubborn	Yes	Maybe	No

Once you have answered all the questions, give yourself 3 points for every 'Yes' answer, 2 for every 'Maybe' and 1 for every 'No'. Add up your score.

60–75 points

You possess the attributes of the entrepreneur. You can start your business plan immediately.

48–59 points

You have potential but need to develop yourself. You may want either to improve your skills in your weaker areas or hire someone with these skills.

37–47 points

You may not want to start a business alone. Look for a business partner who can complement you in the areas where you are weak.

37 points and under

The entrepreneurial life may not be for you. You will probably be happier and more successful working for an established company. If you still hanker after doing your own thing, remember there are organizations that reward those employees who take an entrepreneurial approach in a corporate context.

Targets for self-development

The form on the following pages is designed to help you set targets for your own self-development. It should stimulate your thinking about your personal skills, qualities and attributes as a manager. Read through the list of points and consider the attributes of the entrepreneur and the entrepreneurial manager. Are there any important points that have not been listed under the various headings? If you believe this to be the case, include your own points on the blank lines provided. Then, decide whether, in your view, you:

- are sufficiently developed in this area
- require further development.

Look again at the form, consider each response and place a tick in the relevant column for each: either 'Sufficiently developed' or 'Further development required'.

Having done this, pick out six areas where you believe you are sufficiently developed, and provide demonstrable evidence of your capability in these areas. Then go on to identify six areas where you require further development. These are your main targets for self-development, which should appear in your 'Learning Contract'.

Once you have done this, evaluate the exercise. For example, how valuable was this self-assessment instrument? Could it be improved? If so, how? Has the exercise made you more self-aware as a manager? If so, how or, if not, why not? Do you believe it has enabled you to develop as a manager? Has it enabled you to perform your duties better as a manager? If so, how? What has the exercise taught you about entrepreneurship and your own entrepreneurial development?

The end product will be a personal development file or learning skills portfolio that provides evidence of the skills you possess and those you need to develop. It should include a 'Learning Contract' (which shows your learning objectives, how and when you will meet them and how you will know you have achieved them) as well as the evaluation.

	Sufficiently developed	Further development required
FLEXIBLE INTELLIGENCE		
Assessing changing situations	_____	_____
Sifting and evaluating new information	_____	_____
Putting theory into practice	_____	_____
Thinking on more than one level	_____	_____
Thinking on my feet	_____	_____
Finding new solutions	_____	_____
Evaluating my ideas critically	_____	_____
_____	_____	_____
_____	_____	_____
TECHNICAL ABILITIES		
Identifying gaps in my abilities	_____	_____
Finding the best way to gain expertise	_____	_____
Interested in detail	_____	_____
Putting effort into gaining know-how	_____	_____
Using initiative to build personal skills	_____	_____
Understanding how a business runs	_____	_____
_____	_____	_____
_____	_____	_____
SOCIAL ABILITIES		
Being aware of the effect of my actions on others	_____	_____
Sensing how others feel	_____	_____
Controlling my emotions	_____	_____
Communicating effectively	_____	_____
Listening	_____	_____
Standing up for myself	_____	_____
Trying out new ways of dealing with people	_____	_____
_____	_____	_____
_____	_____	_____
EMOTIONAL RESILIENCE		
Understanding my own feelings	_____	_____
Hiding my emotions	_____	_____
Being over-sensitive with others	_____	_____
Bouncing back when disappointed	_____	_____
Dealing well with anger and hostility	_____	_____
Being objective	_____	_____
Being honest	_____	_____
_____	_____	_____
_____	_____	_____

DRIVE FOR EFFECTIVENESS
Knowing where I'm going
Committed to achieving my targets
Having the courage to overcome difficulties
Using my initiative
Keeping my long-term targets in mind
Waiting for opportunities
Working to achieve results

_____

_____

EFFECTIVE JUDGEMENT
Weighing the key considerations
Being sure of the facts
Consulting others
Making decisions quickly
Trusting my own judgement
Making up my mind firmly
Following through

_____

_____

GENERAL
Pursuing important goals
Acting with integrity
Being loyal to others
Believing in my own ideas
Being at one with myself

_____

_____

Chapter **6**

Entrepreneurship, Creativity and Innovation

Learning Outcomes

On completion of this chapter, the reader will:

- be able to differentiate between the twin concepts of creativity and innovation, and appreciate their significance for the development of entrepreneurship
- understand the barriers to innovation within organizations and the measures that, according to theory, need to be taken to increase the innovative capacity of the enterprise
- appreciate the barriers to creativity in people and how the creative mind can be developed
- understand how organizations can foster a creative culture and develop creativity in their staff
- recognize their own creative strengths and limitations.

Introduction

Various authors (Peters, 1987; Drucker, 1989; Handy, 1990) have talked about the need for and importance of change and, in an age demanding innovation, organizations that cannot innovate and change will experience problems. Indeed, Cortese (2001: 49) reports that, 'The incredible period of experimentation and creativity of the past five years has changed the business environment irrevocably. . . . Upstarts such as Amazon.com Inc., no matter how financially challenged, have raised consumer expectations for customer service.' However, many people and organizations find innovation unsettling and it 'may seem like a flimsy life-line for companies tossed about by forces of creative destruction' (2001: 50). In an era of very rapid change, though, innovation has become essential or, as Paul Saffo, director of the California-based Institute for the Future, has stated, 'Innovation has moved from a good idea to an imperative.' To survive, organizations will need to embrace change and adopt a more proactive approach to innovation—and this is the domain of the entrepreneur.

According to Drucker (1985: 17), 'Innovation is the specific tool of entrepreneurs, the means by which they exploit change as an opportunity for a different business or a different service.' Thus it is hardly surprising that entrepreneurs and entrepreneurship have become the focus of so much attention. From a reading of Chapter 1 it is apparent that, for economists such as Schumpeter, innovation and entrepreneurship are inter-linked. Entrepreneurship sets the innovation process in motion, the reward being profit. However, the concept is much more involved than this might imply and Drucker actually goes on to say that entrepreneurs need 'to know and to apply the principles of successful innovation', implying that perhaps these are not something possessed naturally by the entrepreneur.

Numerous difficulties surround the concept, as the term innovation is not easy to define. For some it equates with high technology. For others it is the process of change. Here it is used to mean the application of creativity to solve problems and to exploit opportunities. It can relate to the end products (the goods or services created) or the process by which the products are created. This conforms with Schmookler's (1996) definition:

> . . . when an enterprise produces a good or service or uses a method or input that is new to it, it makes a technical change. The first enterprise to make a given technical change is an innovator. Its action is innovation.

However, it is more than simply invention as this quotation might imply. It is, rather, the ability to apply creative solutions to problems to enhance or to enrich people's lives, by improving the efficiency or effectiveness of a system (Whiting, 1988). Thus it is linked closely with creativity and it might be possible to think of creativity as the ability *think* new things while innovation is the ability to *do* new things.

As Kirton (1976) has shown, creativity is not always about having original ideas. Sometimes it involves generating something from nothing. More frequently it results from elaborating on the present, from putting old things together in new ways, or from taking something away to create something simpler or better. The systematic process of applying creativity and innovation in the marketplace results in entrepreneurship. It involves applying focused strategies to new ideas to create a product or service that satisfies customers' needs or solves their problems. Entrepreneurs are those who marry their creative ideas with purposeful action. Thus successful entrepreneurship is a constant process that relies on creativity, innovation and application in the marketplace.

Barriers to innovation

Following the work of Galbraith (1967), it is generally held that entrepreneurs are at a disadvantage, when compared with large firms, in the innovation process. Galbraith argued that the costs of invention could only be undertaken with the

A CASE EXAMPLE

Iglu.com: a better way of doing things

To fulfil her passion for skiing, Emmanuelle Drouet used to work for the French government inspecting chalets in the French Alps. Though the pay was not good and prospects were limited, she had a comfortable life, and was able to go skiing at the weekends. She was married to Herve, a management consultant, who was studying for an MBA in London.

While carrying out her duties as a chalet inspector, an idea began to dawn on her. If customers could 'experience' the holiday on their computers, they would be more likely to book. So, she embarked on developing a website where customers could tour virtual chalets, ski down virtual runs and book a holiday in over 300 resorts, at any time of the day or night. In October 1998, she and her business partner, former City analyst Richard Downs, launched Iglu.com at the *Daily Mail* ski show in London. With a business plan in place it had taken just three months to raise the £3 million venture capital required, funding coming from the London Business School, David Potter of Psion and Chris Ingham of CIA Media.

Initially the business earned no money and life was extremely stressful. Fortunately, Drouet's husband was able to support her though, as she recognizes, they 'had a very low level of life. We ate a lot of pasta.' Since then, things have improved somewhat. They have been able to raise first-round financing from US venture capitalist Geocapital, which has enabled them to hire a professional management team, upgrade the website, and expand into France and Germany. Subsequently Iglu has grown through aggressive marketing, and partnerships with portals and ISPs such as Yahoo!, World Online, Lycos, France Telecom, etc., so that by March 2000, the business was employing 40 staff and was acclaimed as Europe's leading e-commerce website for skiing and snowboard travel and accommodation.

Inevitably, Drouet herself still works extremely hard. Despite selling skiing holidays, she now finds little time to indulge in her passion and her planned summer break ended up with her working in London and Herve going on his own to Greece. Ideas have to be worked at. Iglu.com has brought a new concept to the booking of winter holidays and has proved that its multilingual website and pan-European operation can add value in the industry and extract substantial commission revenue in the process. It intends to build on its premier position in the market by expanding into the Asian and North American markets, as well as by launching a summer business version.

Case example exercise

Review the case of Iglu.com in the context of the previous discussion. What does it teach us about creativity and innovation, and their role in entrepreneurship?

resources at the disposal of the large firm. In addition, economies of scale were believed to exist in research and development (R&D), which meant that large firms could develop new products more cheaply than small firms.

Despite these supposed advantages, there is long-standing evidence (Rothwell, 1983; 1984; 1989; Dunphy and Herbig, 1997) that small and new enterprises are more efficient in the technological and innovatory process than are large firms. More recent research by Barrett and Storey (2000) in the UK suggests that the most highly innovative medium-sized enterprises:

- are characterized by committed, involved leaders with vision and enthusiasm
- are future oriented
- exploit opportunities for inward investment and information gathering
- demonstrate 'active strategic commitment to research and technological change' (Motwani *et al.*, 1999)

- creatively configure their customer relationships in order to secure long-term knowledge and financial resources
- see innovation as part of their long-term organizational evolution
- give priority to human resource development.

Additionally, small and medium-sized enterprises are believed to possess such unique advantages as a lack of bureaucracy, rapid decision-making and short decision chains, risk-taking, motivated and committed management, motivated labour, rapid and effective communications, flexibility and adaptability, and closeness to market (Vossen, 1998). Thus Davis (1991: 145) is able to write:

> Small and medium-sized companies tend to be more innovative than entrenched large ones. They are more flexible, more willing to try new ideas and approaches. New product development is a crucial factor in determining their financial success, and they have the attacker's advantage. Management–employee relationships are better because people feel more closely involved, have a greater sense of achievement and spend less time on corporate in-fighting. Communication resembles consultation rather than command. The leaders of such companies usually have considerable entrepreneurial flair. Bright, creative people tend to perform well in that kind of environment.

Clearly, this is a somewhat sweeping generalization and, apart from the evidence on the lack of innovation in the great majority of small and medium-sized enterprises (see Chapter 2), it is apparent that both entrepreneurs and small firms do experience difficulties when attempting to innovate. Indeed, Freel (2000) has suggested that they can be broken down into four sets—finance, management and marketing, skilled labour, and information—though he concurs with Oakey (1997: 20–1) that 'all . . . concerns are directly or indirectly influenced by shortages of capital'. The reasons for this are numerous:

- banks are not prepared to lend seed capital
- banks face increased problems in risk assessment owing to the increased uncertainty with respect to new technology or high technology
- entrepreneurs may not be able to protect their investments through patents
- banks do not place any value on R&D in the balance sheet, regarding it as an intangible asset.

Thus to promote innovation, especially in new and small firms, increasing attention is being paid to it as part of regional policy. According to Landabaso (1997: 22):

> One practical way to approach this problem may be to encourage regions to develop regional innovation strategies. These strategies should aim at promoting public/private and inter-firm co-operation and creating the institutional conditions . . . for a more efficient use of scarce public and private sector resources for the promotion of innovation . . .

Often, however, strategies to promote innovation have been piecemeal and confined, for example, to new methods of funding or the development of environments that are intended to be conducive to innovation. Examples of the former include the State Investment Bank (KfW) in Germany, or the SMART awards in the

UK (see Chapter 4), while examples of the special supportive environments that have been created are science parks and incubators. Although 'incubator centres vary with respect to sponsorship type, funding source, services provided, facilities, tenant composition and management schemes' (Gatewood *et al.*, 1989: 359), essentially an incubator is a dedicated building intended to nurture emerging small firms. It is based on the principle of sharing resources and know-how, including:

- typing, copying, computer, telephone and occupancy space at reduced rates
- building maintenance, conference/meeting rooms, reception facilities, furnishings, etc.
- networking.

As a resource provider intended to facilitate innovation, the incubator:

- offers specific input to support the growing firm that is resource-constrained—help with cashflow/property costs, suitable prestige premises and advice
- brokers partnerships and alliances that are essential to firms by encouraging inter-tenant contact, acting as a gateway to other services.

The evidence on the success of such initiatives is not conclusive (Smith, 1991). In many cases, incubators appear to be little more than Managed Workspaces, contributing little to the innovation process. Where they are successful, however, is when either:

- they have strong linkages with academic institutions, symbiotically existing off academic spinouts and resources (MacPherson, 1998), or
- they specialize in particular sectors, creating effective innovative elements of pre-existing industrial clusters.

Creating a corporate capacity for innovation

While it might be possible to stimulate innovation through enhancing the external support structure, essentially the key is to encourage firms to develop their internal corporate capacity for innovation. According to Peters (1987), this is encouraged by four key strategies and four principal management tactics, as described below.

Key strategies

1. Use multi-function teams for all development activities. Draw members from design/engineering, marketing, manufacturing/operations, finance, purchasing and sales. From the outset, use full-time people to staff such teams and avoid the trap of 'shared resources'. As far as possible, involve outsiders—suppliers, distributors and customers—in product development from an early date.

2. Encourage pilots. Replace written proposals with pilots and prototypes, and find trial sites and field champions for new programmes/projects/products as far from headquarters as possible. Piloting needs to become a way of life.

3. **Practise 'creative swiping'.** Learn to copy from the best, with unique adaptation/enhancement as far as possible. Use market intelligence on competitors and non-competitors both at home and overseas. Fight the 'Not Invented Here' syndrome and become a determined copycat.

4. **Make word-of-mouth marketing systematic.** Purchasers buy new products based principally upon the perceptions of respected peers who have already purchased or tried them. Getting people to talk about the product can be systematically organized in exactly the same way as an advertising campaign can be planned and orchestrated. As the number of competitors and their product offerings increase and the product life cycle decreases, such programmes are increasingly important.

Principal management tactics

1. **Support committed champions.** As any innovation project has a low chance of success, it is important to cherish those with a passionate enough attachment to a new idea to push for it, even though most projects will fail and most of the champions will appear unreasonable and are likely to cause disruption. Champions must be drawn from all parts of the organization. Everybody must believe they can become a champion. The manager's task is to become an 'executive champion'—someone who nurtures, protects and facilitates as many energetic champions as can be induced to come forward.

2. **Model innovation (practise purposeful impatience).** Managers must demand innovation and personally symbolize innovativeness in their daily lives, being seen to be associated with, and supportive of, the innovators. When would-be champions see that managers support constant innovation, they will be encouraged, even if the process is somewhat disruptive. It is important that innovators are recognized at all levels and in all functions of the organization, and that their efforts and achievements are celebrated. Those in the support functions, who help the innovators, should also get credit.

3. **Support fast failures.** In order to reduce the innovation cycle time it is necessary to make more mistakes, faster. In innovative organizations, failure must not be something that is punished. Failed efforts that were well thought out, executed speedily, quickly adjusted and thoroughly learned from should be rewarded, as should constructive defiance of bureaucratic rules and regulations. Entrepreneurial managers should remove any obstacles that cause delay and cannot be cleared by the champions themselves.

4. **Measure innovation.** Since what gets measured gets done, it is necessary to set quantifiable innovation targets.

It is through these and other measures that innovation is promoted in organizations and people. Innovation needs to become a way of life for everyone in the organization. Change and innovation need to be welcomed, not resisted, and everyone should be continuously seeking out new ideas or new and improved ways of doing things. This is what the Japanese call 'Kaizen', the never-ending quest for perfection. To achieve this sort of organizational culture, however, people must have a sense of belonging or ownership and be able to identify their own personal success with the success of the company. Kanter (1983) has termed this 'cultures of pride and climates of success'. As she recognizes, 'pride-in-company, coupled with knowing that innovation is mainstream rather than countercultural, provides an incentive for initiative' (1983: 149). If this can be achieved and the employees at the bottom of the organization are given 'the same chance to contribute to innovation . . . that they get at the middle and top' (1983: 181), it is inevitable that the corporate capacity for innovation and change will be increased.

PAUSE FOR THOUGHT

Think of an organization with which you are familiar. Would you describe it as innovative? How would it measure up against such criteria?

A CASE EXAMPLE

Against the odds: Dame Stephanie Shirley, Xansa plc

Stephanie Shirley regards herself as different from most other people. First, though naturalized and extremely chauvinistic, she is not 'true blue' British. She was a refugee who came to Britain from Germany when she was five years old in 1939. Second, she is a campaigner. Even as an 18 year old, her passions were different from those of her peers. She was an extremist who championed the case for homosexual law reform, who campaigned for birth control and who lobbied for reform of the law on suicide. Indeed, she claims that in founding what is now Xansa her objective was to prove a point—to liberate women from the constraints of motherhood.

Though regarded as a risk-taker, her first job was with the Post Office Research Station, which she saw as a secure job offering her the opportunity to further her education. While working there she acquired a BSc in Maths and a husband, Derek. On marrying in 1959, she resigned and took up an appointment as a software engineer with Computer Developments Ltd, partly because she wanted to work with computers and partly because she believed a husband and wife need to work separately. At the age of 29, although she enjoyed her work and was good at it, she left. She wanted to start a family but actually reached her decision when, in response to a suggestion she made, was told 'that has nothing to do with you, you're technical'.

She went freelance, but for three months had no work. Then she got a break. A former colleague introduced her to a management consultancy that asked her to design management controls for data processing. By the time she had finished the contract she was about to give birth to her son and for three months after his birth she lost interest in work. In 1964 she incorporated Freelance Programmers and, as business was building up, she developed a panel of homeworkers, wherever possible utilizing the services of people like herself who were unable to work in a conventional environment. By the mid-1960s there was a panel of 60 and she had introduced a profit-sharing scheme. However, the business struggled until the mid-1970s and she even had to take out a second mortgage on her home in order to ensure it survived. In 1971/72, in the depths of the economic recession and after a manager had left with a substantial part of the business, it made an operating loss of £4000. She was determined, though, that it should not fail, not least because it would discredit this new way of organizing work. By 1972/73, it was back in profit, but with a reduced turnover. It was at this point that the decision to go international was made and F International was created as the parent company. The first subsidiary was opened in Denmark followed by The Netherlands and the USA, though by the 1980s some 90 per cent of its c. £6 million turnover still came from the UK. By 2002, when revenue was in excess of £0.5 billion, this had dropped to a healthier 80 per cent.

When 'Steve' Shirley (early on she had changed her name to the more 'acceptable' masculine form) retired and left the board in 1993 to become life president, the Group (which had been renamed in 1988 and rebranded again in 2001) was run by her chosen successor, Hilary Cropper, as a highly successful and profitable operation. Starting in 1981, some 24 per cent of the shares were put in trust for the staff, at no cost to them, and in 1991 they were all given the opportunity to buy shares. In 1996 Xansa floated on the London Stock Exchange, entering the FTSE 250 on 24 March 1997. As Lessem (1986: 9) recognizes, she had:

> . . . created a business out of a social cause. She had freed women, including herself, from having to choose between home and career, by providing them with the opportunity to do both. Through F International, she has established the kind of flexible structures and systems that enable 800 women, as systems analysts and computer programmers, to work in amenable locations on chosen projects.

Since then, Dame Stephanie has continued to innovate and in 'retirement' this serial entrepreneur has achieved a number of firsts. These have included the first disability conference on the web (1999) and sponsorship of the inter-disciplinary Oxford Internet Institute (2001), dedicated to the study of the effects of the Internet on society.

Case example exercise

Consider the odds that were against Dame Stephanie. How did she overcome them? Do you think they restricted or stimulated her creativity? What can you learn about entrepreneurship and creativity from this case example?

Creativity: a necessity for survival

In this fiercely competitive, fast-paced, global economy, creativity and innovation are important both for survival and for building competitive advantage. Although not every creative business opportunity that entrepreneurs take will be successful, many who are willing to go beyond conventional wisdom will be rewarded for their efforts. Successful entrepreneurs are those that are constantly finding creative solutions to problems. Merely generating one successful creative solution is not sufficient to keep an entrepreneurial venture successful in the long term. Success—even survival—requires entrepreneurs to tap their creativity (and that of their employees) constantly.

For many years, conventional wisdom held that a person was either creative (imaginative, free-spirited, entrepreneurial) or not (logical, narrow-minded, rigid). More recent research suggests that this is not the case and that almost anyone can *learn* to be creative. The problem is that most people have never been taught —or expected—to be creative. Most people never tap into their innate creativity.

Exercise 6.1

Test your creativity by completing the questionnaire in Randsepp (1981) or Whetton and Cameron (1984). (You will find full details of these texts in the Reading section towards the end of this chapter.)

Barriers to creativity

There are numerous potential barriers to creativity. Perhaps the most potent are the ones people place upon themselves. These include:

- searching for the one right answer
- focusing on being logical
- blindly following 'the rules'
- constantly being practical
- viewing play as frivolous
- becoming over-specialized
- avoiding ambiguity
- fearing you will look foolish
- fearing mistakes and failure
- believing that you are not creative.

All are patterns of behaviour that are conditioned by society and/or the education system. They can be removed through training.

The last one—believing that you are not creative—is particularly interesting. From a neuro-psychological perspective (Sperry, 1968; Ornstein, 1977), it would appear that the brain is divided into two hemispheres, as described below.

- The left side handles language, logic and symbols. It processes information in a step-by-step fashion. Left-brain thinking is narrowly focused and systematic, proceeding in a highly logical fashion from one point to the next.
- The right side takes care of the body's emotional, intuitive and spatial functions. It processes information intuitively, relying heavily on images. Right-brain thinking is lateral, unconventional, unsystematic and unstructured. It is this right-brain lateral thinking that is at the heart of the creative process.

According to Lewis (1987: 38–9):

. . . while the left brain requires hard facts before reaching a conclusion, the right is happier dealing with uncertainties and elusive knowledge. It favours open-ended questions, problems for which there are many answers rather than a single, correct solution. . . . The left specializes in precise descriptions and exact explanations; the right enjoys analogies, similes and metaphors. The left demands structure and certainty; the right thrives on spontaneity and ambiguity.

Thus, those who have learned to develop their right-brain thinking skills tend to:

- ask if there is a better way of doing things
- challenge custom, routine and tradition
- be reflective—often deep in thought
- play mental games, trying to see an issue from a different perspective
- realize that there may be more than one 'right' answer
- see mistakes and failures as pitstops on the route to success

- relate seemingly unrelated ideas to a problem to generate a solution
- see an issue from a broader perspective, but have the ability to focus on an area in need of change.

Although the two halves normally complement each other, on occasion they compete, or one half may choose not to participate. Importantly, also, most formal education systems since the time of the ancient Greeks have tended to develop in their students left-brain capabilities. As Lewis (1987: 41) has recognized:

66 99 In class, students are expected to acquire knowledge one step at a time, adding methodically to their storehouse of facts until they have sufficient to pass an examination. This demands left-brain skills. The problems students are given to solve more often demand an analytical than an intuitive approach. This, too . . . is a task for the left hemisphere. Written work, by which ability is chiefly evaluated, must be organized, well argued and logically structured . . . all left-brain skills. The students considered most intelligent and successful are those who strive after academic goals, can control their emotions in class, follow instructions, do not ask awkward questions, are punctual and hand in class assignments on time. Goal-setting, emotional restraint, time-keeping and matching your behaviour to other people's expectations are all left-brain skills. Children are meant to learn by listening, keeping notes and reading books. All these, too, of course, are tasks in which the left hemisphere specializes.

This may well explain why so many successful entrepreneurs appear not to have succeeded in the formal education system and why Gibb (1996) has argued that if the education system is to develop entrepreneurs, or more enterprising individuals, there needs to be a shift in focus (see Table 6.1).

Similarly, it explains the call by Chia (1996: 426) for university business schools to adopt 'a deliberate educational strategy which privileges the "weakening" of thought processes so as to encourage and stimulate the entrepreneurial imagination'. It could well explain, also, why so many entrepreneurs—such as Sir Richard Branson (see Chapter 5) and Ingvar Kamprad (see Chapter 11)—are dyslexic. As the language functions of the brain are on the left-hand side, it could be that those individuals, like entrepreneurs, in which the right brain tends to be more dominant are more prone to dyslexia. However, according to a report in the *Economist* (24 February 2001: 129), it would appear that dyslexia can result from 'defects in the language centres' of the brain and that when dyslexics were enrolled on an intensive training programme designed to improve their reading,

Table 6.1: Conventional and enterprising teaching approaches

Conventional approach	Enterprising approach
Major focus on content	Major focus on process delivery
Led and dominated by teacher	Ownership of learning by participants
Expert hands down knowledge	Teacher as fellow learner/facilitator
Emphasis on 'know-what'	Emphasis on 'know-how' and 'know-who'
Participants passively receiving knowledge	Participants generating knowledge
Sessions heavily programmed	Sessions flexible and responsive to needs
Learning objectives imposed	Learning objectives negotiated
Mistakes looked down upon	Mistakes to be learned from
Emphasis on theory	Emphasis on practice
Subject/functional focus	Problem/multi-disciplinary focus

Source: Gibb (1996: 315)

enhanced brain activity was identified 'in areas on the right-hand side exactly corresponding to the language centres in the opposite hemisphere'. The reading programme had somehow 'recruited' suitable batches of nerve cells in a place not normally associated with language-processing'. Interestingly, a 1999 Channel 4 television programme on dyslexia (**http://channel4.com/nextstep/dyslexia**) told the story of a 37-year-old small business owner, Oliver. It went as follows:

I run my own business making medical models mainly for the fields of orthopaedics and cardiology. It's a business I've built up over the last five years, starting in a garden shed and working up and up with new innovations. It's just grown and grown.

When I was seven I was at a rather posh prep school where it became increasingly obvious that I didn't fit in. I couldn't really read, and they used to send me out of Latin lessons to set the tables for lunch. Unfortunately I couldn't even do that. I set everything the wrong way round.

My mother eventually realized that something was wrong and I was sent off for all sorts of tests. I think I can remember them using the word 'dyslexia' but that didn't mean much. I was eventually sent to the local primary school and the family paid for a tutor at home. I don't think anyone suggested any help at school. I got by with the other boys because I was good at football.

At secondary school I didn't want to stand out from everyone else so the tutoring stopped and, of course, everything just got worse. I hated school and left at 16 with one O-level in geography. My poor parents simply didn't know what to do with me.

In the end I went off to France for a year to work as an assistant shepherd, though it was more sheepdog than shepherd really. But it changed my life. I'd found something I could do. I got very fit. There was a gorgeous French girl. I suddenly found some self-esteem.

I've worked ever since, first for a small firm, which grew very big and eventually bored me. And then in my own business.

Clearly much more research is needed to determine whether there is a link between entrepreneurial ability and dyslexia, but it would seem that there certainly appears to be a link with right-brain dominance and the process of learning. Clearly, despite various initiatives (see Chapter 4), changing the process of learning will take time and, inevitably, will be resisted. Thus, if creativity is to be developed without a change in the learning paradigm, it is important to recognize that the individual can learn both to develop his/her creativity and to control which side of the brain is dominant in a given situation. Indeed, it is possible to 'turn down' the left hemisphere and 'turn up' the right, thereby tapping the pool of creativity that lies hidden within the right side of the brain. It is this ability to shift from one brain hemisphere to the other that unleashes both the creative capacity of entrepreneurs and their ability to think strategically. Thus it would appear that successful entrepreneurs are those able to co-ordinate the complementary functions of each hemisphere of the brain, thereby using their brain's full creative powers.

Exercise 6.2

Complete the exercise in Appendix 6.1, which you will find at the end of this chapter, to test your left-brain/right-brain functioning. It can also be found at

 www.angelfire.com/wi/2brains.

There are numerous similar tests. You might like to try those at **www.web-us.com/ brain/LRBrain.html** or **http://utenti.tripo.it/learning_paths/Questionnaire/ Lrquest.htm**, for example.

In all cases, note how they are interpreted.

A CASE EXAMPLE

The Academy of Contemporary Music

The Academy of Contemporary Music (**www. acm.ac.uk**) is Europe's leading school for rock and pop musicians. It opened in Guildford, Surrey, in 1995 with 100 students studying guitar, bass and drums. By 2002, it had a turnover in excess of £2.5 million, generated by 450 further education students and 75 degree-level students, as well as 350 students studying part-time in the evenings and at weekends. Its objective is to present education and the process of learning in an exciting and stimulating way, giving students, many previously disillusioned by established education, the opportunity to re-engage and to realize their full potential. Interestingly, approximately 15 per cent of the Academy's intake require educational support with dyslexia and dyspraxia. Often, although intelligent, their students have disengaged from their earlier studies and are looking for a programme that will develop them as artists and give them maximum vocational opportunity.

The Academy is the brainchild of its co-founders Peter Anderton (chairman) and managing director 33-year-old Phil Brookes. Phil left school at 16 with five O-level qualifications and Grade 8 passes in Classical Guitar and Music Theory. In 1993, at the age of 24 and with the support of a £1500 grant and a £1500 loan from the Princes Youth Business Trust (see Chapter 4), he set up The Guitar Studio in the garage of his mother's home in Woking. Here he taught both electrical and classical guitar, and soon became recognized as one of Surrey's leading guitar tutors. By the end of 1993, the studio was teaching 30 students a week and had 60 clients on its books. Additionally, the business was offering course design consultancy services to local FE colleges and, in 1994, Phil approached a local retailer (Andertons Music Company, Guildford) with a view to negotiating a discount plan for his students. It was at this time that he met his business partner,

Peter Anderton. Peter was looking to develop into the area of music education and, in particular, to work in schools. After initial discussions, they decided that a centre dedicated to the development of young musicians would be both educationally beneficial and commercially expedient.

From the outset, the vision for the Academy was to establish a vocational training centre committed to linking education with the popular music industry which, at this point, saw music education as irrelevant. 'We knew from the beginning,' says Phil, 'that many of the traditional methods for the delivery of education would not be appropriate to this particular vision, and indicative of this philosophy is the fact that we set out to recruit working professionals with high-profile careers as the faculty.' Additionally, especially in its early years, the Academy worked closely with leaders in the music industry such as Fender, Marshall, Roland and Yamaha, and developed a reputation among the top recording labels, management companies and production houses as a source of new musical talent. Over the years its educational philosophy has evolved. Rather than just linking music education to industry, the Academy now sees itself as an active training centre, developing the complete product for placement into industry. The mastering studio of Jiant (one of the UK's leading production teams) is established within the Academy and this had led to the students being given the opportunity to collaborate on numerous professional projects.

Further opportunities for such experience will be provided in the next phase of the Academy's development, which is intended to be a centre housing established production, management, TV, publishing and recording companies, as well as the Academy's new music technology training studios.

As some 30 per cent of the Academy's students progress to a professional career in the music industry, often in a self-employed capacity, the Academy is now exploring the opportunities for entrepreneurial training, recognizing that the creativity and right-brain thinking skills of many of its students could enable them to become gifted entrepreneurs if pointed in the right direction. However, the Academy's mission is much broader than that. As Phil recognizes, 'The Academy aims to widen participation in structured learning by harnessing the interest of the student and building on his/her creative ability through the medium of music education.' Interestingly, some 35 per cent of the Academy's students progress into higher education on completion of their initial studies.

Case example exercise

Look at the Academy's website and see for yourself what it is doing. Having reviewed both the website and the case example, consider the implications of the Academy's approach to learning for the development of entrepreneurs. Design an entrepreneurship course that would develop the right-brain abilities of those studying on it, as well as the left brain, and would be intended to result in the creation of more entrepreneurially inclined, creative participants.

The creative process

As mentioned above, Kirton (1976) has suggested that innovation takes two forms: the highly creative solution, whereby someone comes up with a completely new idea; and the adapted solution, whereby someone modifies an existing solution. These two processes, he suggests, involve different approaches to problem-solving, as Table 6.2 reveals.

Clearly, from what has been said already, it is apparent that the adaptor is much more left-brain oriented than is the innovator. However, creativity can be increased by engaging the left brain and adopting a systematic approach: the creativity process. This involves seven separate steps, as described below.

1. Preparation. Getting the mind ready for creative thinking. This involves some form of training, which provides the foundation for creativity and innovation. It might include:

   - realizing that education is a never-ending process and that every situation is an opportunity to learn
   - reading on a variety of subjects/topics
   - creating a file of interesting articles
   - taking time to discuss ideas with others, including those who know little about the subject
   - attending professional/trade association meetings, both to brainstorm with others having a similar interest and to learn how others have solved a particular problem
   - investing time in studying other countries and cultures to identify global opportunities
   - developing the ability to listen to and learn from others.

2. Investigation. Studying the problem and understanding its components.

3. Transformation. Identifying the similarities and differences in the information

Table 6.2: Two approaches to creative problem-solving

Adaptor	Innovator
Employs a disciplined, precise, methodological approach	Approaches tasks from unusual angles
Is concerned with solving, rather than finding, problems	Discovers problems and avenues of solutions
Attempts to refine current practices	Questions basic assumptions related to current practices
Tends to be means-oriented	Has little regard for means; is more interested in ends
Is capable of extended detailed work	Has little tolerance for routine work
Is sensitive to group cohesion and co-operation	Has little or no need for consensus; is often insensitive to others

Source: Kirton (1976)

collected. This involves convergent and divergent thinking. Convergent thinking is the ability to see similarities and connections. Divergent thinking is the ability to see the differences. The ability to transform information can be increased by:

- trying to see 'the big picture' rather than getting bogged down in the detail
- re-ordering the components of a situation to identify new patterns
- considering several approaches to a problem or opportunity simultaneously
- resisting the temptation to make snap decisions; the first approach may not be the best one.

4. Incubation. The subconscious needs time to reflect on the information collected. Incubation can be enhanced by:

- doing something totally unrelated to the problem/opportunity under investigation
- taking time to daydream (i.e. freeing the mind from restrictive paradigms and self-imposed restrictions)
- playing and relaxing
- thinking about the issue before going to sleep so that the subconscious can work on it during sleep
- working on the problem or opportunity in a different environment.

5. Illumination. Occurs, usually spontaneously, at some time during the incubation stage, when all the previous stages come together to create a 'breakthrough'.

6. Verification. May include experiments, simulations, test marketing, establishing small-scale pilot programmes, building prototypes, etc. Intended to verify that the new idea will work, is practical to implement and really is a better solution to a particular problem or opportunity.

7. Implementation. Transforming the idea into reality. This is what distinguishes the entrepreneur from the inventor.

Enhancing personal creativity

Every individual is creative to some degree, though clearly some are more creative than others. Though Chell (2001: 227) suggests that 'creative performance increases with intelligence up to an IQ level of 120', the creativity an individual displays would seem to have little to do with intelligence, and appears to depend on the extent to which the right brain is developed or engaged. Since the brain is a computer, it can be programmed and it is possible to develop the right-brain functions. There are a number of exercises for doing this, but before examining these it is necessary to appreciate the distinction between the terms 'critical' and 'creative' thinking.

Critical, or vertical, thinking is a function of the left brain—it is objective, analytical and logical, and results in one or, at most, only a few answers. In contrast, creative thinking is lateral, imaginative and emotional, resulting, through association, in more than one solution (de Bono, 1970). The two ways of thinking, as summarized in Fig. 6.1, are clearly complementary, though western society has traditionally emphasized critical thinking. In recent years, however, much more attention has been paid to the development of creative thinking and, in particular, to the linked concept of emotional intelligence. There is considerable confusion over this latter term but Caruso (2001: 40) defines it as 'the ability to identify emotions accurately, to access emotions to facilitate thinking, to understand emotional causes and transitions, and to integrate emotions into decisions'. However, not only is there confusion over the term, there is considerable debate over its existence. To some it cannot exist as it is a contradiction in terms since intelligence involves rational thinking and rational thinking is devoid of emotion. For others it simply does not exist because:

> . . . some of the most creative people—and perhaps the most powerful—seem to lack a high degree of emotional intelligence. They tend to be single-minded and not too bothered about their effect on others. Such people may not enjoy great interpersonal relationships, but they do enjoy success.
>
> *(Woodruffe, 2001: 29)*

Possibly these two quotations illustrate the misconceptions of the term and the failure to appreciate that creativity includes both critical and creative thinking.

Whatever, to develop entrepreneurial capability, both critical and creative thinking are needed and, as with critical thinking, people can be *trained* to think creatively. Indeed, there are many techniques for encouraging people to think laterally and to look at things in new ways but perhaps the most important is to maintain at all times an open and enquiring mind. This should be the role of education but all too frequently, however, it is not. As Lewis (1987: 240) has recognized:

> Under the domination of the present paradigm, schools teach *what* and *how* rather than *why*. Content is all-important, and the key to success lies in the acquisition of 'knowledge' and its accurate representation to teachers and examiners. Facts are true, truth is sacred and information lasts a lifetime.

Sadly this situation pertains not just in schools but at most levels of education. While it cannot be permitted to continue, particularly in an era of very rapid

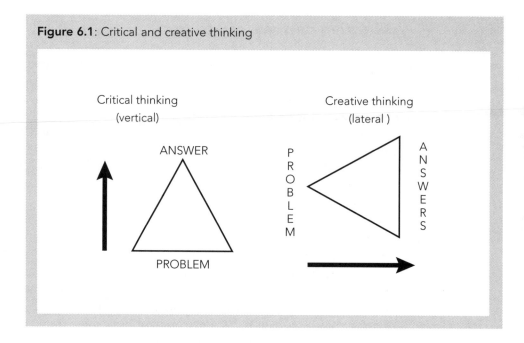

Figure 6.1: Critical and creative thinking

change where the life of the existing body of understanding will become increasingly shorter, it is likely to remain for some time, possibly fuelled by the trend towards online learning. Thus, until it changes, most people, even the most highly educated, will continue to accept the things they read and hear, without questioning or challenging them. However, nothing should go unchallenged and the words of Rudyard Kipling (in 'The Elephant's Child') need to be not just remembered, but also employed:

66 99

> I keep six honest serving-men,
> (They taught me all I know);
> Their names are What and Why and When
> And How and Where and Who.

Apart from reading and listening, it is important, also, to observe—to look for and to see opportunities. The Bible, once again, provides an insight into what is required here. In the Gospel according to St Matthew (7: 7–8) Christ advises us to:

66 99

> Ask and it will be given you;
> Seek, and you will find;
> Knock, and it will be opened up to you.
> For everyone who asks receives,
> And he who seeks finds.

It is an important part of creativity, therefore, not just to be open to new ideas but to seek them actively and, in order to get new ideas and become more creative, it is important to:

- read widely
- join and attend professional groups and associations
- travel widely
- talk to anyone and everyone

- scan newspapers, magazines and journals
- develop a 'reference' library/file
- record useful information and ideas in a notebook
- spend time following natural curiosities.

Interestingly, sleep occurs when the left side of the brain gets tired or bored. This means that, during sleep, the right brain is still active and this is why many people have their 'best ideas' when they are asleep. This being the case, it often helps to keep a notebook by the side of the bed so that ideas generated during sleep can be jotted down on wakening. It is reputed that Sir Paul McCartney (see Chapter 2) heard the tune for his chart-topping hit 'Yesterday' while coming out of sleep, and Albert Einstein (a dyslexic) identified the Theory of Relativity in the same way.

There are other, more formal and structured ways of developing creativity. These include brainstorming, forced associations, role play, multiple uses, and metaphors and analogies. We will now look at each of these in turn.

Brainstorming

This is one of the most commonly used methods of developing creativity and new ideas. It is a group activity that works on the principle of association and the avoidance of judgement. The intention is to create a situation where people feel free to express ideas, uninhibited by self-consciousness or 'what others will think' of them or their ideas. This means it is necessary to start from the premise that all ideas are valid and nobody voices criticism of them no matter how 'silly' or ridiculous they may appear. That is why you are 'brainstorming'—because sensible ideas have failed to resolve the problem or it is believed they can be improved—and, in any case, one person's 'silly' idea may trigger a new idea in someone else. Once this has been agreed, it is possible to start. Essentially, group members are required to shout out ideas and a scribe writes them down so that they can be read easily. They should not be judged or read back, and participants should not worry if the same idea is expressed more than once, the ideas should just be written down as they are expressed.

Normally the exercise commences by starting with a 'silly problem'. This is to get group members into the spirit of the exercise. Usually this takes no more than a few minutes before embarking on the real exercise. On occasions, though, individuals may wish to brainstorm in private before embarking on the exercise proper. Here the members of the group write down their initial thoughts and ideas before sharing them 'spontaneously' with the group. If this approach is adopted, it may be interesting to compare the number of ideas generated by the individual members (duplicates excluded) with those generated by the group. Whatever, brainstorming should continue until no new ideas are forthcoming, though it might be useful to set targets: a certain number of ideas in a given time period, say.

This is the creative or lateral thinking stage of the exercise. The next stage is the critical or vertical thinking stage. This is often referred to as the 'nominal group technique'. It involves the group, or a subgroup, taking away the ideas and selecting the most promising ones. This can be done in a number of ways, but usually this convergent stage of the exercise involves discussion and systematic voting to choose the best or most appropriate ideas.

You can find out more about brainstorming from either **www. brainstorming.co.uk** or **www.jpb.com/creative/brainstorming.html**.

Forced associations

There are various ways in which this might be done, but one of the most common, especially for those wishing to go into business, is to list all the areas in which a person has a particular interest against all of his/her particular skills or competences. By combining these, it might be possible to generate a new business proposition. For example, an interest in music, combined with an ability in computing led Charlie Muirhead to set up Orchestream (see Chapter 5). Such associations may be made within one person or between several, as was seen with Iglu.com earlier in this chapter. Equally, they can be made between products. Thus combination of the wheel with the internal combustion engine produced the motor car, for example. They can similarly be made between products and regions, and Ansoff's (1957) 'product/market expansion grid' (see Fig. 6.2) can be used to structure the associations, for example.

The grid is a four-way matrix of new and current products and markets. What everybody is looking for is the new product in the new market. That is rare, but it is possible to establish a successful business from bringing a new product to a current market or a current product to a new market. Indeed, it is possible to bring a current product to a current market, provided it is better or cheaper than the previous product and that of the competition, and Johnson and Jones (1957) have expanded the matrix into nine cells by adding modified products and modified markets. Thus the matrix can help people identify ideas and opportunities through forcing associations between products and markets. It should be recognized that all creative ideas do not have to be entirely new. Part of the skill of the entrepreneur is, in fact, to see opportunities and it is said of Sir Richard Branson (see Chapter 5), for example, that he is not the most creative of people—what he is good at, though, is seeing opportunities.

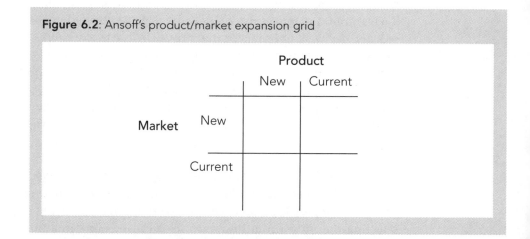

Figure 6.2: Ansoff's product/market expansion grid

Role play

This approach can take the following form. Either individually or in groups nominate a 'superhero' and then try to 'get inside' the person and determine how he/she might approach a problem. For example, identify a 'problem' and consider how Richard Branson might go about resolving it.

Multiple uses

A creative person tends to view things and people in terms of how they can satisfy their needs. To be more creative, therefore, it is important to look at things and people in non-conventional ways and to think of how they can complement you in your attempts to satisfy your own needs. Either privately or in a group (brainstorming) think of all the things you might do with a paper clip, for example. To assist you, look at **http:///members.ozemail.com.au/~caveman/ creative/Workout/newuses.htm**.

Metaphors and analogies

The use of metaphor—talking of something as if it is the thing it resembles—in the development of creativity depends upon there being some degree of difference between the objects or processes being compared. As Morgan (1991: 87) observes, 'it requires of its user a somewhat one-sided abstraction in which certain features are emphasised and others suppressed in a selective comparison'. Thus the effective use of metaphor is a creative expression that depends on constructive falsification to liberate the imagination. It is at its most effective when:

- the differences between the two phenomena are perceived to be significant but not total, and
- describing something that is less familiar with something that is more.

It is at its weakest when the subjects are perceived to be completely unalike and the imagery is nonsensical or only weak. Indeed, its unconscious use can cause problems as the assumptions upon which it is based are likely to be unclear. However, as Cameron (1999: 304) has recognized, 'conscious use of a range of metaphors can work in a similar way to forced associations. The potential is richer, as the metaphor will often carry a wider range of implications.'

Traditionally, understanding of the way organizations work, for example, has been aided by viewing them as either machines or organisms. However, viewing organizations on the basis of new or different metaphors makes it possible to interpret them in new or different ways. Thus, Morgan (1991) observes that the organization can be, and has been, viewed as a cybernetic system, loosely coupled system, ecological system, theatre, culture, political system, language game, text, psychic prison, instrument of domination, schismatic system, catastrophe, etc., and concludes that by so doing it has been 'possible to add rich and creative dimensions to organisation theory' (1991: 91). However, the use of metaphor is not confined solely to developing an understanding of the way organizations behave. It can be used to enhance understanding of any situation, and is an important aid to creativity and creative problem-solving.

Not surprisingly, given its importance to contemporary society, numerous agencies have been established, particularly in the private sector, to assist both individuals and organizations in developing their creative capability. One of the more interesting is Odyssey of the Mind (**www.odysseyofthemind.com**). This is an international organization based in the USA but with membership from 22 countries. It focuses specifically on challenging young people to develop divergent independent thinking skills, while working within the co-operative spirit of a team. Through its programmes, participants discover how to think divergently,

A CASE EXAMPLE

Dan Bricklin

Dan Bricklin, the 'father of the electronic spreadsheet', creator of VisiCalc, and founder and chief technology officer of Trellix Corporation in Concord, Massachusetts, provides an interesting example of someone who actively looks for new ideas. Born into a family business, Bricklin Press, in Philadelphia, he believes the entrepreneurial instinct was in his genes as growing up in a family business gave him respect for the paradox of running your own business, with the result that he never expected to work for a large corporation. Instead he 'was always looking for opportunities to turn some nifty idea into a business' (Bricklin, 2001), and though he knew that not all of his ideas would work, the risk did not stop him wanting to try as he knew that some would.

Interestingly, he proposes that much of his early entrepreneurial training came from the religious instruction he received during his school days. Apart from engendering a belief that God made the world incomplete so that we become partners in completing the act of creation, he suggests that Judaism taught him how to analyse complex problems and the importance of viewing a problem from different angles, sorting through the possibilities, testing different models and learning from them in the process. Also, he believes his early religious training helped him become comfortable with performing under pressure and speaking in public as he was frequently called upon to lead services.

As he suggests, he learned at an early age that he could make mistakes and would not be ripped to shreds. With this background when, at Harvard Business School, he became 'more than a little frustrated by having to manually calculate and re-calculate every single change on a spreadsheet' as he

worked through a case, he started designing a computer program to resolve the problem. It was this problem, and from this initial idea, that the 'first killer application of the PC industry' was developed. Clearly the idea had to be worked at and on. Bricklin collaborated with a partner, Bob Frankston, whom he had met as a fellow undergraduate at MIT, and it was not until 'after toiling for several months in the attic of Bob's home', that they developed the VisiCalc prototype. To do so, however, they had to make sacrifices. Neither drew a salary for about a year and they lived like students, borrowing US$25,000 from family members as a down-payment for the computer they needed to write the program and an advance on royalties (from a software publisher) to pay other expenses. Some 20 years later, after four start-ups, a lawsuit, lay-offs, two acquisitions and a failed start-up, Bricklin still enjoys creating tools that solve people's everyday problems and suggests that 'life as an entrepreneur, professional tinkerer, and technology and business commentator' has brought him many joys.

Case example exercise

Reflect on the case of Dan Bricklin and revisit Chapter 3. Do you believe that Bricklin's creativity and propensity for entrepreneurship are the product of 'nature or nurture'? Was he born naturally creative, has he acquired these attributes as a result of the influences to which he has been exposed or is it a combination of both? When you have evaluated the arguments for and against the nature versus nurture debate, consider the implications of the outcomes of your deliberations for the development of more creative and entrepreneurially disposed individuals.

identify challenges, evaluate ideas and think creatively to provide solutions to problems. In the process, they develop self-confidence, as well as an ability to work in teams and take calculated risks. Each year it holds a competition that culminates in a 'world final', usually held at a university campus in the USA.

Enhancing organizational creativity

Creativity does not just happen—it has to be encouraged. Entrepreneurs need to create organizational environments in which their own creativity can flourish as can that of their employees. As with innovation, this can be done in the following ways.

- Expecting creativity. Permit employees to be creative, to challenge existing ways of doing things and to come up with new ideas.
- Expecting and tolerating failure. Creativity involves taking chances. Managers must remove the fear of failure as not all creative ideas will succeed. The surest way of stifling creativity is to punish people who try something new and fail. People who never fail are usually not being creative.
- Encouraging curiosity. Asking 'what if' questions and taking a 'maybe we could . . .' attitude.
- Viewing problems as challenges. Every problem offers an opportunity.
- Providing creativity training.
- Providing support—giving employees the resources they need to be creative, including time. Allowing employees time to 'daydream' and 'play' is an important part of the creativity process.
- Rewarding creativity—with money, praise, recognition and celebration.
- Modelling creativity—setting an example by taking chances and challenging the status quo.

Importantly, it is necessary to create a convivial, collegial environment where people are happy to work, and where fun and humour are encouraged. Apart from the fact that the 'Thank God It's Friday' syndrome is a sad indictment on modern society and management, an organization that lacks humour and the opportunity to 'play' is not conducive to creativity. All too frequently, the emphasis on left-brain thinking has resulted in organizations in which:

- fantasy and reflection are perceived as a waste of time, a sign of laziness or 'shirking', or even eccentricity
- 'play' and humour are discouraged because problem-solving is perceived as a serious business
- emotion and feeling are seen as signs of weakness and a threat to objectivity
- intuition and insight are regarded as illogical and impractical.

If organizational and personal creativity is to be facilitated, this has to change. As the section on developing personal creativity demonstrated, for creativity to flourish, people need to feel secure, to be unafraid of 'looking silly' or 'failing', to be relaxed and to be able to experiment or play mental games with ideas. This does not mean to say that organizations must abandon, completely, the discipline that comes from left-brain thinking. As has been shown, creativity comes from a combination of the two forms of thinking and from the creative tension between them.

An organization in which 'play and fantasy' reign supreme may be an extremely exciting place in which to work but, as Cameron (1999: 307) has suggested, 'the results of such "unanchored" creativity may be disappointing or non-existent'. Creativity needs to be nested in a wider, more rational, structured context. This is probably what Kuratko and Hodgetts (2001: 122) mean when they claim that 'for creativity to occur, chaos is necessary but a structured and focused chaos'. This lack of structure could well explain why entrepreneurs are often such exciting, but frustrating, people to work for and with, and why so few university graduates, in particular, seek employment in small and medium-sized enterprises, though they often find them challenging and stimulating places in which to work.

PAUSE FOR THOUGHT

Consider an organization known to you. Would you regard it as creative? If it is, what factors contribute to that creativity? If it is not, what needs to be done?

Chapter Review

→ Innovation is the application of creativity to solving problems and exploiting opportunities. It relates both to the end product and the process by which products are created.

→ There are numerous barriers to innovation. These include:

- the cost of R&D

- the inadequacy of funding

- the inability to protect inventions through patents

- corporate culture.

→ Various measures have been taken to stimulate innovation. These include:

- new methods of funding

- the provision of science parks and incubator units.

→ Measures to increase the corporate capacity for innovation include:

- the use of multi-functional teams

- encouraging pilots

- creative swiping

- word-of-mouth marketing

- supporting product champions

- modelling innovation

- supporting fast failures

- measuring innovation.

→ Successful entrepreneurs find creative solutions to problems and tap the creativity of their employees.

➡ The are numerous barriers to creativity, but both personal and institutional creativity can be developed.

➡ The creative process involves:

  – preparation

  – investigation

  – transformation

  – incubation

  – illumination

  – verification

  – implementation.

➡ Creativity can be enhanced by:

  – expecting it

  – tolerating failure

  – encouraging curiosity

  – viewing problems as challenges

  – providing creativity training

  – providing support

  – modelling creativity

  – rewarding creativity.

➡ Creativity training requires developing the right-brain lateral thinking skills. This can be done by:

  – brainstorming

  – forced associations

  – identifying multiple uses

  – using metaphors and similes.

Quick Revision

(Answers at the end of this section)

1. Who said 'innovation is the specific tool of entrepreneurs'?

   (a) Schumpeter

   (b) Drucker

   (c) Schmookler

2. Incubators are intended simply to provide innovative small firms with cheap accommodation. Is this:

   (a) true

   (b) false?

3. How should 'failure' be treated in an innovative firm. Should it be:

   (a) punished as a waste of time and resources

(b) ignored

(c) rewarded and learned from?

4. The right side of the brain is at the heart of the creative process. Is this:

(a) true

(b) false?

5. Which of the steps in the creative process distinguishes the entrepreneur from the inventor?

6. Why is it important to allow employees to 'daydream' and 'play'?

(a) it relaxes them and minimizes stress

(b) it creates a more pleasurable atmosphere

(c) it stimulates creativity, new ideas and innovation

(d) it encourages bonding and team building

(e) it increases productivity

Answers to Quick Revision: 1–b; 2–b; 3–c; 4–a; 5–implementation; 6–c

Learning Style Activities

➡ **Activist:** Study the two pictures below: Picture A and Picture B. Picture A depicts two faces. Can you see them both? If so, what are they of? If not both, which one can you see? Picture B is a photograph of melting snow taken in China in the late 1930s. The pattern it portrays can be interpreted as a face. Can you see it? What 'face' does it portray?

Picture A   Picture B

➡ **Reflector:** Reflect on this exercise. What is its significance for entrepreneurship, innovation and creativity? What is the symbolic message of each picture?

➡ **Theorist:** What aspects of the theories of entrepreneurship and creativity apply to this exercise? Deal with each of the pictures separately.

➡ **Pragmatist:** How will the lessons you have learned from this exercise affect your future attitude and behaviour?

Reading

Ansoff, I. (1957) Strategies for Diversification. *Harvard Business Review*. September/October, 113–24.

Barrett, E. and J. Storey (2000) Managers' Accounts of Innovation Processes in Small and Medium-sized Enterprises. *Journal of Small Business and Enterprise Development* **7** (4), 315–24.

Bricklin, D. (2001) Natural-Born Entrepreneur. *Harvard Business Review*, September, 53–8.

Cameron, S. (1999) *The Business Student's Handbook: Developing Transferable Skills*. London: Pitman Publishing.

Caruso, D. (2001) Emotionally Challenged. *People Management* **7** (8), 40–1.

Chell, E. (2001) *Entrepreneurship: Globalization, Innovation and Development*. London: Thomson Learning.

Chia, R. (1996) Teaching Paradigm Shifting in Management Education: University Business Schools and the Entrepreneurial Imagination. *Journal of Management Studies* **33** (4), 409–28.

Cortese, A. (2001) Masters of Innovation. *Business Week*, 9 April, 48–51.

Davis, W. (1991) The Innovators, in Henry, J. and D. Walker (eds) *Managing Innovation*. London: Sage Publications.

de Bono, E. (1970) *Lateral Thinking: Creativity Step-by-Step*. New York: Harper and Row.

Drucker, P.F. (1985) *Innovation and Entrepreneurship*. Oxford: Butterworth-Heinemann.

Drucker, P.F. (1989) *The New Realities*. London: Heinemann.

Dunphy, S.M. and P.R. Herbig (1997) Seven Steps to Innovation. *Entrepreneurship, Innovation and Change* **6** (2), 109–26.

Economist (2001) Science and Technology: Reading Minds. *Economist*, 24 February, 129–30.

Freel, M.S. (2000) Barriers to Product Innovation in Small Manufacturing Firms. *International Small Business Journal* **18** (2), 60–80.

Galbraith, J.K. (1967) *The New Industrial State*. London: Hamilton.

Gatewood, E.J., L. Ogden, J.M. Humphreys and F. Hoy (1989) The Evolution of Business Incubation Centres: A Delphi Forecast. *Entrepreneurship and Regional Development* **1** (4), 357–70.

Gibb, A.A. (1996) Entrepreneurship and Small Business Management: Can We Afford to Neglect Them in the Twenty-first Century Business School? *British Journal of Management* **7** (4), 309–21.

Handy, C. (1990) *The Age of Unreason*. London: Random Century.

Johnson, S.C. and C. Jones (1957) How to Organize for New Products. *Harvard Business Review*, May/June, 49–62.

Kanter, R.M. (1983) *The Change Masters: Corporate Entrepreneurs at Work*. London: Unwin Hyman Ltd.

Kirton, M. (1976) Adaptors and Innovators: A Description and Measure. *Journal of Applied Psychology*, October, 622–9.

Kuratko, D.F. and R.M. Hodgetts (2001) *Entrepreneurship: A Contemporary Approach*. Orlando FL: Harcourt College Publishers.

Landabaso, M. (1997) The Promotion of Innovation in Regional Policy: Proposals for a Regional Innovation Strategy. *Entrepreneurship and Regional Development* **9** (1), 1–24.

Lessem, R. (1986) *Enterprise Development*. Aldershot: Gower.

Lewis, D. (1987) *Mind Skills: Giving Your Child a Brighter Future*. London: Souvenir Press.

MacPherson, A.D. (1998) Academic–Industry Linkages and Small Firm Innovation: Evidence from the Scientific Instruments Sector. *Entrepreneurship and Regional Development* **10** (4), 261–76.

Morgan, G. (1991) Paradigms, Metaphors and Puzzle Solving in Organisation Theory, in Henry, J. (ed.) *Creative Management*. London: Sage.

Motwani, J., T. Dandridge, J. Jiang and K. Soderquist (1999) Managing Innovation in French Small and Medium Enterprises. *Journal of Small Business Management* **37** (2), 106–14.

Oakey, R. (1997) *A Review of Policy and Practice Relating to High-technology Small Firms in the United Kingdom*, WP 359. Manchester: Manchester Business School.

Ornstein, R. (1977) *The Psychology of Consciousness*. New York: Harcourt Brace.

Peters, T. (1987) *Thriving on Chaos: Handbook for a Management Revolution*. London: Macmillan.

Randsepp, E. (1981) *How Creative are You?* New York: G. Putnam's Sons.

Rothwell, R. (1983) Innovation and Firm Size: A Case for Dynamic Complementarity; or is Small Really Beautiful? *Journal of General Management* **8** (3), 5–25.

Rothwell, R. (1984) The Role of Small Firms in the Emergence of New Technologies. *Omega* **12** (1), 19–29.

Rothwell, R. (1989) Small Firms, Innovation and Industrial Change. *Small Business Economics* **1** (1), 51–64.

Schmookler, J. (1996) *Invention and Economic Growth*. Massachusetts: Harvard University Press.

Smith, H.L. (1991) The Role of Incubators in Local Industrial Development: The Cryogenics Industry in Oxfordshire. *Entrepreneurship and Regional Development* **3** (2), 175–94.

Sperry, R.W. (1968) Hemisphere Deconnection and Unity in Conscious Awareness. *American Psychologist* **23**, 723–33.

Vossen, R.W. (1998) Relative Strengths and Weaknesses of Small Firms in Innovation. *International Small Business Journal* **16** (3), 88–94.

Whetton, D.A. and K.S. Cameron (1984) *Developing Management Skills*. Scott, Foresman and Company.

Whiting, B.G. (1988) Creativity and Entrepreneurship: How Do They Relate? *Journal of Creative Behaviour* **22** (3), 178–83.

Woodruffe, C. (2001) Promotional Intelligence. *People Management* **7** (1), 26–9.

Test for left-brain/right-brain dominance

Take a sheet of lined paper. Now read through the list below and, every time you read a description or characteristic that applies to you, write down its number on the page. There is no certain number of characteristics you must choose. After you have done this, use the key (which you will find at the end of this appendix) and write, next to every number on your paper, whether it was an L or an R. Count up the number of Ls and Rs. Whichever number is higher represents your left- or right-brain dominance. If the numbers are close, that means you use both sides of your brain equally.

1. I always wear a watch
2. I keep a diary
3. I believe there is a right and wrong way to do everything
4. I hate following directions
5. The expression 'Life is just a bowl of cherries' makes no sense to me
6. I find that sticking to a schedule is boring
7. I'd rather draw someone a map than tell them how to get somewhere
8. If I lost something, I'd try to remember where I saw it last
9. If I don't know which way to turn, I let my emotions guide me
10. I'm pretty good at maths
11. If I had to assemble something, I'd read the instructions first
12. I'm always late getting places
13. Some people think I'm psychic
14. Setting goals for myself helps keep me from slacking off
15. When somebody asks me a question, I turn my head to the left
16. If I have a tough decision to make, I write down the pros and the cons
17. I'd make a good detective
18. I am musically inclined
19. If I have a problem, I try to work it out by relating it to one I've had in the past

20. When I talk, I gesture a lot
21. If someone asks me a question, I turn my head to the right
22. I believe there are two sides to every story
23. I can tell if someone is guilty just by looking at them
24. I keep a 'to do' list
25. I feel comfortable expressing myself with words
26. Before I take a stand on an issue, I get all the facts
27. I've considered becoming a poet, a politician, an architect or a dancer
28. I lose track of time easily
29. If I forgot someone's name, I'd go through the alphabet until I remembered it
30. I like to draw
31. When I'm confused, I usually go with my gut instinct
32. I have considered becoming a lawyer, journalist or doctor

Key

1–L; 2–L; 3–L; 4–R; 5–L; 6–R; 7–R; 8–L; 9–R; 10–L; 11–L; 12–R; 13–R; 14–L;15–R; 16–L; 17–L; 18–R; 19–R; 20–R; 21–L; 22–R; 23–R; 24–L; 25–L; 26–L; 27–R; 28–R; 29– L; 30–R; 31–R; 32–L

Chapter 7

Entrepreneurship, Motivation and Leadership

Learning Outcomes

On completion of this chapter, the reader will:

- understand that as well as being a creative individual, the entrepreneur is someone who gets things done
- appreciate that he/she achieves this by being highly motivated and by motivating others
- know how to be self-motivated and capable of motivating others
- recognize the difference between transactional and transformational leaders
- be aware of how transformational leaders can be developed
- recognize the role of the entrepreneur as leader and how he/she achieves his/her objectives
- have begun to recognize his/her own leadership style.

Introduction

As has been discovered already (in Chapters 1 and 5) the entrepreneur is not just a creative or innovative individual but someone who can make things happen. It has been mentioned previously that the term is derived from the French verb *entreprendre*. The *Harraps Shorter French and English Dictionary* gives the English definition of *entreprendre* as 'to undertake; to take (something) in hand'. According to *The Pocket Oxford Dictionary*, the word 'undertake' is defined as follows: 'Bind oneself to perform, make oneself responsible for, enter upon (work &c); bind oneself to do; guarantee that . . . '. The meaning is clear. The entrepreneur is a doer. As mentioned earlier, Timmons (1989: 1) has suggested that:

" "   ... entrepreneurship is the ability to create and build something from practically nothing. It is initiating, doing, achieving and building an expertise or organization, rather than just watching, analysing or describing one. It is the knack for sensing opportunity where others see chaos, contradiction and confusion ...

Thus entrepreneurship is not just about being creative or innovative but about having the ability both to envision opportunities and to make them happen. The entrepreneur may work for and by himself or herself, harnessing the resources to enable his/her vision to be fulfilled, but increasingly he/she works as part of an entrepreneurial team, either as an owner-manager of a new venture or as part of a larger organization. Whatever, apart from being creative and innovative, the entrepreneur needs to be motivated and capable of motivating others. Hence this chapter looks at these issues and how they can be developed.

A good starting point for this, perhaps, is the work of Quinn (1988) who, in his book *Beyond Rational Management*, introduces the concept of the 'competing values framework'. He suggests that management can best be understood by considering two axes. The vertical axis ranges from flexibility at the top to control at the bottom, while the horizontal axis ranges from an internal organization focus on the left to an external organization focus on the right. This produces four quadrants which, working in a clockwise direction, he terms the Open Systems Model,

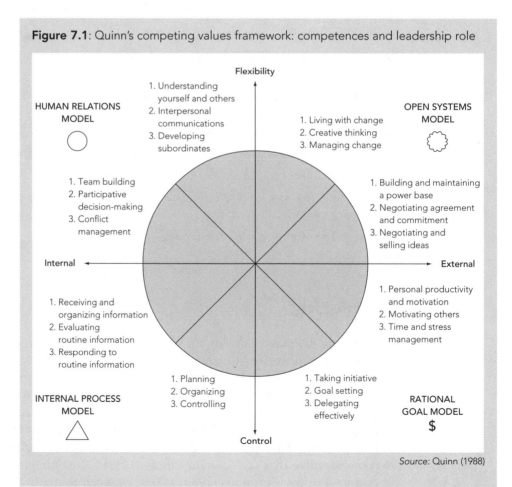

Figure 7.1: Quinn's competing values framework: competences and leadership role

Source: Quinn (1988)

the Rational Goal Model, the Internal Process Model and the Human Relations Model (see Fig. 7.1). Quinn suggests that the effective manager must be able to operate in all four segments. Undoubtedly this is true, equally, of the entrepreneur. However, probably the most important quality of the entrepreneur after his/her creativity, is the ability to get things done. Hence attention in this chapter is focused on Quinn's producer segment where the particular characteristics required are personal productivity and motivation, and the ability to motivate others. For Quinn *et al.* (1990: 16) producers are 'task oriented and work focused' with a 'high interest, motivation, energy and personal drive'. They 'accept responsibility, complete assignments, and maintain high personal productivity. This usually involves motivating members to increase production and to accomplish stated goals.' Clearly these are precisely the characteristics that the entrepreneur might be expected to possess, and attention is focused here on these two personal competences.

PAUSE FOR THOUGHT

Think of a time when you felt that you were performing extremely well. What factors brought about your high level of performance, do you believe?

Think about a time when you may have lost motivation. What caused you to stop trying?

Compare the two sets of factors. Are they similar or different?

Personal productivity and motivation

Theory: personal peak performance

Insight into how you can motivate yourself and achieve high levels of personal productivity can be obtained from the study of what is termed 'personal peak performance'. According to Garfield (1986) personal peak performance does not result from a specific personal talent or trait, nor from a particular set of behaviours; rather it appears to be the result of a combination of traits and attributes that include:

- a sense of personal mission (results orientation)
- the ability to work both independently (self-management) and as part of a team
- a capacity for self-correction and change management.

This concept is reinforced by the work of Adams (1984), who suggests that there are six conditions that stimulate personal peak performance. These are commitment, challenge, purpose, control, transcendence and balance. According to the research on personal peak performance, commitment is important because:

- it shields people from workload stress (Pines, 1980)
- high levels of performance require a significant involvement of time and emotion (Vaill, 1982)
- peak performers are known to care about the tasks they perform (Garfield, 1986).

It is this concept of 'commitment' that is behind the concepts of 'ownership' and 'empowerment'. It is argued that if individuals believe they 'own' an idea or are 'empowered' to make decisions, they are more likely to be committed.

However, commitment is not the only condition. Peak performers need, or desire, an appropriate challenge. They constantly search for new opportunities to 'stretch' themselves and set themselves targets or goals that are achievable but ambitious. They emphasize action—outcomes, results and solutions. Linked to this they have a sense of purpose and a clear vision, and they require both clear direction and the autonomy to pursue their vision without interference. They are in control. Linked to challenge and control, and associated with commitment, is a desire for continuous improvement or transcendence. This what the Japanese call Kaizen. Finally, according to Adams, there is balance. Peak performers are able to balance their private and their professional lives. All of these conditions have to be in place for personal peak performance to be sustained in the long term.

Practice: enhancing ability

Given that personal peak performance does not result from a personal talent or trait, it can be developed. As Virgil remarked over 2000 years ago (*The Aeneid*, Book 5, line 231), 'They can because they think they can.' We can do or achieve whatever we believe we can. Thus the starting point for enhancing our personal performance and motivating ourselves to achieve more and better is our imagination. As humans, our lives are not so much determined by our environment or by physical limitations but by our imagination. What we become and achieve is

Figure 7.2: Negative self-belief

Source: Roet (2001) *Positive Action for Health and Wellbeing*, Class Publishing

what we *imagine* ourselves becoming and achieving. Essentially our only limits are those we place upon ourselves. When we say we are not good at something and subsequently do badly at it we are living out a self-fulfilling prophecy (see Fig. 7.2).

Often it is more comfortable not to accept the challenge and the discomfort of failure, as Richard Bach (1972: 24) describes most vividly in *Jonathan Livingston Seagull*, his classic story of a seagull's attempt to perfect the art of flying. After several failed attempts, Jonathan decides to abandon his dream and immediately:

" "   He felt better for his decision to be just another one of the flock. There would be no ties now to the force that had driven him to learn, there would be no more challenge and no more failure. And it was pretty, just to stop thinking, and fly through the dark, towards the lights above the beach.

However, if you do decide not just to fly to eat, but to accept the challenge and strive to perfect the art of flying, like Jonathan, you will discover just how much more there is to life. As Jonathan discovered, 'we can lift ourselves out of ignorance, we can find ourselves as creatures of excellence and intelligence and skill. We can be free! We can learn to fly!' (1972: 27). To do so, however, we need to believe in ourselves, to believe we are good at something. If we do, our chances of success are improved dramatically.

According to Appell (1984), to increase our personal performance we need to engage our imagination by setting goals for ourselves. Most of us limit ourselves because we think too traditionally and fail to look beyond our present situation. Use your imagination. 'Dream' about what you would like to do in life. Brainstorm. Do not evaluate any idea at this stage. Simply write down any idea that comes to mind.

When you have completed your list of ideas, edit it. Put the things you want to do in preferential order. Modify or eliminate those that are clearly impossible, but make sure you do not get rid of any that are potentially achievable. Then set a series of long-term (i.e. longer than a year) goals that are achievable but stretching. Ensure these goals are clearly specified. Write them down in order of priority and, if necessary, set intermediate goals. Writing them down is important as not only does it force you to refine them but it helps implant them in your mind. Set targets for yourself, dates by when you expect to have achieved each goal. This will enable you to monitor your progress towards achieving your goals.

Once you have set your goals, you need to visualize them as already achieved. Clearly visualization does not relieve you of working to achieve your goals, but it will guide you towards achieving them. At all times visualization should be effortless. If you are to avoid burdening yourself with additional pressure and reinforcing a negative image, visualization must be natural and without effort. See yourself acting out the image according to your goal. Do not worry about achieving it. Worry is negative imagery and therefore destructive. To help your visualization work:

- be positive—you are concerned to achieve success rather than to avoid failure
- see your goals as being achieved—not something that will be achieved in the future

- see yourself in the visualization
- use the first person (I) rather than the third person
- feel good and be proud of your achievements.

Review your goals periodically and, as appropriate, revise them. You may decide that some goals are no longer relevant. That is not a problem. They are your goals and you can change them as you will. However, do replace them with others.

While goal setting is important and provides future direction, do not live in the future. Action must take place in the present. Even if you make mistakes it is important to take action. Mistakes are not a cause for concern. Use them to help you learn and then move on, focusing on your success.

Motivating others

In his book *Energising Your Enterprise*, Wickens (1999: 36) makes the point that:

" "

. . . manufacturers speak of the seven wastes—the wastes arising from overproduction, transportation, inappropriate processing, waiting, defects, unnecessary motions and unnecessary inventory. But there is an eighth waste, and it causes greater losses than the other seven put together. The waste of human potential arises when managers fail to realize they are not using people's abilities to the full, or worse, when they do realize but do nothing about it. In so many organizations, people switch off when they come to work or use their intelligence to thwart the system. Enabling 'people to perform to their full potential' is vital if we are truly to energise our enterprise.

The entrepreneur has this ability to energize an enterprise. He/she does it not just by motivating him/herself, but by motivating others. Indeed he/she gets them to perform not just to their full potential but, often, beyond it. To understand how he/she does this requires an understanding of motivation theory.

Motivation theory

There are numerous theories of motivation. They can be divided into content theories and process theories. Content theories include the work of Maslow (1943), Herzberg (1968), and McClelland and Burnham (1976), while process theories include the work of Skinner (1971) and Vroom (1964). While the former set of theories deals with the wants or needs that motivate individuals, the latter deals with the actions people take to satisfy their needs.

According to Maslow (1943) motivation comes from the desire of individuals to satisfy their needs (see Fig. 7.3). These he classifies into a hierarchy starting with the basic physiological needs to satisfy hunger and thirst. Once these needs have been met, they no longer operate as primary motivators and people concentrate on other needs. Moving up the hierarchy, these are, first, safety needs (including shelter and clothing as well as protection from all that is potentially dangerous or uncomfortable), followed by love needs (wanting to belong) and then the need for esteem followed finally by the need for personal growth or development, what Maslow terms self-actualizing. However, though Maslow asserts that an individual's lower level needs have to be satisfied before higher-

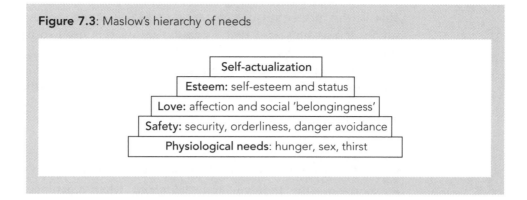

Figure 7.3: Maslow's hierarchy of needs

Self-actualization

Esteem: self-esteem and status

Love: affection and social 'belongingness'

Safety: security, orderliness, danger avoidance

Physiological needs: hunger, sex, thirst

level needs will be desired, an individual does not necessarily follow the sequence precisely. It is important, therefore, to recognize the precise needs that an individual has and what is actually motivating him/her.

Basing his observations on an analysis of 1685 employees, Herzberg (1968) proposed that it is possible to identify 'hygiene factors' (such as company policy, work conditions, salary, interpersonal relationships, status and security), which tend to work as dissatisfiers and motivators (achievement, recognition, the work itself, responsibility, advancement and growth) that encourage individuals to work harder. If this two-factor model is accepted, then it has a number of important implications as it suggests that:

- no matter how good the hygiene factors, people will not work effectively if the motivators are not in place
- so long as the motivators are in place, people will put up with deficiencies in the hygiene factors
- an increase in salary is unlikely to encourage people to work harder for a sustained period, even though most would claim that money is a motivator.

Mention has already been made of McClelland's (1961) work on the entrepreneur's need for achievement (nAch)—the need to overcome challenges. In his work with Burnham (McClelland and Burnham, 1976) he suggests that motivation results not just from the need for achievement, but from the need for affiliation and power. Affiliation motivation is the need to relate to other people, while power motivation is the need to have influence, over others and situations. Whereas achievers prefer to work with those who are competent, for affiliators interpersonal relationships are more important and they prefer working with those they can get on with. However, the research suggests that the strongest motivator of all is the need for power, and the desire to influence and lead others.

According to the process theories of motivation, behaviour that delivers desired outcomes is reinforced or encouraged, whereas behaviour that does not is discouraged. Such thinking, known as operant conditioning, is based on Freud's pain–pleasure principle. This states that individuals avoid those acts that give pain but repeat those that give pleasure. According to Skinner (1971), therefore, to motivate its workforce an enterprise needs to determine what it wants to happen and then set up a system of rewards and punishment to bring it about.

That is why in the previous chapter on the development of creativity and innovation, it was suggested that successful innovators need to be recognized, celebrated and rewarded.

Clearly operant conditioning is based on the premise that individuals choose the course of action that they expect will yield them the rewards they desire. This is expectancy theory. Vroom (1964) uses it in his work on motivation. He suggests that motivation can be broken down into the following parts:

- outcomes—what might be achieved
- valence—the individual's desire for a particular outcome
- expectancy—the individual's belief about what outcomes are likely to be achieved given the time and effort invested
- instrumentality—the perceived effectiveness of a course of action with respect to achieving a particular outcome.

He argues that a person's motivation can actually be measured by multiplying values for expectancy and valence (i.e. motivation = valence × expectancy).

Motivating in practice

It is possible to utilize the various theories of motivation to help you motivate others. If you are going to do this effectively you will need to do the following things.

- **Understand the needs and wants of individuals.** While you may not be able to meet them exactly, you may be able to adjust your approach to motivation to at least recognize them.
- **Set goals that are realistic and achievable but that stretch people.** Involve people in setting goals and targets for themselves and give them more responsibility/autonomy in planning work and innovating new processes.
- **Provide support.** Give people the opportunity to achieve their targets and goals in their own way, but never let them feel unsupported or isolated. Ensure the support is appropriate to the nature of the task and the person undertaking it.
- **Monitor outcomes.** Make it clear that individuals or groups are clearly accountable for achieving their targets and goals, and provide them with the control information that will enable them to evaluate their own performance.
- **Reward performance.** Money is an important prime motivator as it satisfies so many needs, including esteem, but it is not the only reward that people want or need. Rewards can take many forms but they must be appropriate (in nature and magnitude) and equitable. Importantly they must not be devalued by being given too frequently or inappropriately.
- **Ensure that the reward system is transparent.** Make it clear that performance will be rewarded, and ensure that the relationship between effort and reward is clearly defined—especially in financial reward systems or where promotion is involved. Make sure that people know what will happen if they do not perform effectively. This is not intended to be threatening or bullying but to ensure transparency. If people feel they have not been rewarded when they should

have been (because the criteria either have not been defined or communicated) they are likely to become demotivated. Similarly they will feel demotivated if they feel they have been sanctioned wrongly.

- **Adopt a positive approach to sanctioning.** When people under-perform, try to find out what is causing them to do so and, as appropriate, provide them with the requisite support to help them improve.

Once again, it is possible to discover from *Jonathan Livingston Seagull* what is needed. Having himself perfected the art of flying, Jonathan teaches the outcast gulls to do the same. On pages 79 and 82 of the book, Bach (1972) describes how:

> Every hour Jonathan was there at the side of each of his students, demonstrating, suggesting, pressuring, guiding. He flew with them through night and cloud and storm. . . . When the flying was done, the students relaxed on the sand, and in time they listened more closely to Jonathan. He had some crazy ideas that they couldn't understand, but then he had some good ones that they could.

If you are to motivate others, this is your role. You must be alongside your staff, through the good times and the bad, advising, demonstrating, encouraging, enthusing, inspiring and congratulating.

Leadership

Leadership theories

According to Whetten *et al.* (2000: 290), 'poor motivation is a lack of skilled leadership not a lack of desire within people'. This is an interesting assertion and it introduces McGregor's (1960) theories of motivation in the workplace. According to McGregor there are two extreme views about people's attitudes towards work. The first (Theory X) holds that people have an inherent dislike of work and do not want either to work hard or assume responsibility. Under such circumstances they have to be coerced, controlled, directed and punished in order to get them to perform well. The alternative (Theory Y) contests that people want to do a good job and assume more responsibility. If this is the case, the leader's role is that of enabling his/her workforce to achieve its potential by channelling the motivation to succeed.

All too frequently Theory X has tended to prevail. Emphasis is placed upon performance at the expense of how the employees feel. The leader gives the orders and the employees are required to implement them, irrespective of whether they agree with them, let alone understand them. As a consequence, 'many of us tend still to believe that "a leader" implies one person dominating another or a group of people' (Adair 1986: 116). This is not the case and while such a strategy can be extremely effective in the short term, it is not sustainable long term. Employees quickly begin to feel exploited, resulting in high levels of staff absenteeism, increased staff turnover, and even sabotage and aggression. The art of the entrepreneurial leader is to hold employees accountable for results while, at the same time, maintaining morale and employee satisfaction. Indeed, according to Wickens (1999: 52) leadership 'is about getting people to do what you want them to do because they want to do it for you', and for themselves.

There are various theories of leadership. They may be grouped into four broad categories: theories of leadership traits; theories of leadership style; situational theories; and integrative theories. We will now look at each of these in turn.

Theories of leadership traits

This is one of the earliest approaches to the study of leadership. It assumes that leaders have certain personal characteristics such as sociability, persistence, initiative, know-how, self-confidence, perception/insight, co-operativeness, popularity, adaptability, good communication skills, etc. While it has been recognized that such traits are important, over the years it has also become recognized that 'a person does not become a leader by virtue of the possession of some combination of traits, but by patterns of personal characteristics, activities and goals of the followers . . . ' (Stogdill, 1948: 64). Leadership is actually invested in a person by his/her followers based, as Wickens (1999) suggests, on their respect for his/her ability, their trust in him/her, their sharing of his/her goals and whether or not they are inspired by him/her.

Theories of leadership style

This is one of the most widely researched aspects of leadership. Generally attention has focused on the emphasis that the leader places on the task and the people undertaking it. Essentially there is thought to be a continuum with concern for production at one end and concern for people at the other. Using this concept, Tannenbaum and Schmidt (1973) have suggested that leaders can be classified as:

- autocratic—the leader dictates what he/she wants
- persuasive—the leader sells his/her ideas
- consultative/participative—the leader discusses with the team members before reaching his/her decision
- democratic—the leader involves the team members in both the discussion and the decision.

How the leader manages determines the kind of organizational climate that is created. However, it is generally accepted that the most effective leaders are open, candid and employee-centred, although the style of leadership depends on a range of situational factors.

Situational theories

These relate to the group environment, its physical setting, the size of the group, its technical abilities, the authority given to the leader by his/her superiors, etc. Perhaps the greatest attention has been focused on the role of communication in the group. The person at the centre of the communication system is often seen as the leader since group members come to him/her for information.

Integrative theories

These are the most comprehensive and realistic, but least precise or conclusive. They embrace a wide variety of variables and from them it is possible to ascertain that the successful leader is aware of the great many forces affecting his/her effectiveness and is able to determine the most important forces operating at any particular time. Possibly two of the most significant contributions to this field are Fiedler's (1967) contingency theory, and the work of Tannenbaum and Schmidt (1973), which identifies the factors or forces a leader needs to consider when deciding how to lead. The former suggests that the leader's performance can be improved by changing either his/her personality and motivation pattern or the favourableness of his/her situation. In contrast, the latter suggests that the way a leader should lead is decided by the forces invested in him/her (personal value system, confidence in his/her subordinates, own leadership inclinations, own feelings of security), his/her subordinates (their need for independence, their willingness to assume responsibility, their tolerance of ambiguity, their interest, their understanding of the group's goals and objectives, their knowledge and experience, their expectations with respect to the decision-making process) and the situation (the type of organization, the effectiveness of the group, the problem and the urgency).

Exercise 7.1

Complete the leadership style questionnaire in Appendix 7.1 (which you will find at the end of this chapter). It can also be accessed at **www.nwlink.com/~donclark/ leader/survstyl.html**.

PAUSE FOR THOUGHT

Think of someone you know whom you regard as a leader. What is it about them that makes you believe them to be a leader?

Leadership in practice

As mentioned earlier, the leader gets a task completed by developing good relationships with his/her colleagues and harnessing their combined resources. According to Appell (1984: 173), it is the leader's task to:

> . . . arouse and unite followers towards a common goal. A true leader fulfills this function by being aware of changing group needs, by arousing these needs so that they become transformed into demands . . . and by organizing the group so that these demands can be met through group action.

He/she 'arouses and unites' his/her colleagues by:

- listening to them and gaining their respect and trust
- being friendly and approachable but remaining sufficiently distant to exert authority
- treating them as equals without losing the capacity to exert authority
- paying attention to their individual as well as their collective needs
- involving them in agreeing objectives, reviewing results, solving problems, etc.
- representing their interests.

Their resources are harnessed by ensuring that they:

- fully understand their goals and objectives and, as far as possible, are involved in determining them
- know how they are going to achieve these objectives, and are party to deciding and agreeing the course of action to be taken
- are empowered to make decisions
- know and agree the control to be exercised over them
- are aware of the rewards and penalties of not achieving their objectives
- trust and respect the leader's judgement.

A CASE EXAMPLE

Nelson Mandela

Nelson Mandela, the first post-apartheid black president of the Republic of South Africa, was born on 18 July 1918 in the black homeland of the Transkei. The son of a farmer, he was brought up by the acting Regent of the Thembu people on the death of his father, and educated at the Missionary College of Fort Hare, where he became involved in student protests against the white colonial rule of the institution. On leaving the Missionary College, he 'fled' to Johannesburg (to avoid an arranged marriage) and joined a law firm as an apprentice. Here he witnessed the inhumanities of the apartheid system, which made him determined to 'change the world'. In a country where the political and military power, education and most of the wealth was controlled by the white minority population, he had little hope of success. However, he joined the Youth League of the African National Congress (ANC) and became involved in programmes of passive resistance against the laws that forced blacks to carry passes.

In 1956, in exasperation, the government charged 156 of its opponents, Mandela included, with treason. The resultant trial, which lasted for five years, acquitted all of the accused. By then, however, there had been the massacre of the peaceful black demonstrators at Sharpeville in March 1960, and the government banned the ANC and most of the other liberation movements. Mandela went 'underground' for a year and travelled abroad, enlisting support for the ANC. On his return, he was arrested and sentenced to five years' imprisonment on Robben Island. Shortly after, all of the leaders of the ANC were arrested, and Mandela was tried with them for advocating sabotage. At his trial he made the following statement:

> During my lifetime I have dedicated myself to the struggle of the African people. I have fought against white domination, and I have fought against black domination. I have cherished the ideal of a democratic and free society in which all persons live together in harmony and with equal opportunities. It is an ideal which I hope to live for and to achieve. But, if needs be, it is an ideal for which I am prepared to die.

Although it had been expected that, if convicted, he would face the death sentence, he was returned to Robben Island prison, where he remained until 1990. However, despite the harshness of the regime he had acquired and maintained a new dignity and status. His unswerving acceptance of his moral responsibility gained him the respect and trust of his peers, and conferred a moral dignity on his leadership.

After more than 20 years in prison, and careful preparation and planning, he opened up negotiations with the State President's Office, not just for his own release but for the abolition of apartheid. On 2 February 1990, the then President, F.W. de Klerk, lifted the ban on the ANC and announced that Mandela and his colleagues would be released. By 1994, despite many setbacks and various mistakes, he had been elected South Africa's first post-apartheid black president. He had not only won the support of the black people of South Africa, but that of the white population, who were likely to 'lose out' as a result of the changes. According to Professor Andre Brink of the University of Cape Town, this was achieved as a result of 'the patience, the wisdom, the visionary quality Mandela brought to the struggle, and above all the moral integrity with which he set about to unify a divided people'.

Although he received the Nobel Prize for Peace in 1993 (along with F.W. de Klerk) and has been feted throughout the world, he is not deluded by the adulation showered upon him. In his view, 'I was not a messiah, but an ordinary man who had become a leader because of extraordinary circumstances.'

Case example exercise

What made Nelson Mandela such an exceptional leader? Was it circumstance or situation as he implies? Was it his personality or was it the way he treated people? Evaluate the various leadership theories and consider which are most applicable in the case of Mandela.

Review Chapter 1. Would you regard Mandela as an entrepreneur? Compare him with Margaret Thatcher. What are the similarities and differences? Would you regard Margaret Thatcher as a leader? Justify your answer.

Leadership development

As with entrepreneurship itself, there is considerable debate over whether leaders are born or made. While it is generally accepted that the natural, truly inspirational leaders are probably born, there is a growing acceptance that leadership capability, as in other areas, can be developed and/or enhanced. Indeed, Handy (1997) has suggested that leaders are *grown*, not made.

Clearly, leaders need followers and in any organization aspiring 'leaders' can secure the hearts and minds of their employees quite easily using a series of recognized 'currencies'. These include buying support with:

- economic currencies—rewarding loyal colleagues fiscally, with promotion and/or with perks
- political currencies—rewarding loyal colleagues through protection or patronage
- psychological currencies—using anger and threats to create a climate of fear that encourages loyalty
- empowerment currencies—rewarding desired behaviour with increased authority and power.

Such 'transactional' leaders exist within most organizations and while they continue to have a role to play in many successful organizations, their long-term effectiveness is somewhat limited and their days are probably numbered. Their strength lies not in their true leadership abilities but in the power transferred to them, often by their positions in the organization. These are not powerful people in their own right but people who have either acquired power through, usually, the control of budgets and/or the misuse of their positional power. They have 'led' through fear and patronage rather than through trust and respect. Often they have not been agents for change in organizations but enforcers of the status quo, seeing their subordinates not as an aid to achieving their goals but as a threat.

However, not only are the needs of organizations changing but the contemporary workforce is very different. In an era of very rapid change, increasingly, organizations are needing leaders with vision, who can empower their colleagues and release the creativity within them to move an organization forward. Also, the workforce is becoming more sophisticated. Employees are becoming more independent, they are more knowledgeable and they are far more mobile than previously. Hence, they have to be managed very differently than in the past and under such circumstances it is the transformational, rather than the transactional, leader that is required and needs to be developed. Whereas the transactional leader is process- or means-oriented and uses transactions to maintain performance and, often, the status quo, the transformational leader is innovative, enthusiastic and concerned to empower others in order to create and achieve his/her vision. Transformational leaders provide a new sense of direction. They are the change agents—the true entrepreneurs. As McKenna (2000: 383) recognizes:

> This type of leadership needs to be fostered at all levels in the organisation when the organisation faces . . . a turbulent environment where products have a short shelf life; greater international competition and deregulation of markets; technology becoming obsolete before it is fully depreciated; and demographic changes are anticipated.

This is precisely the environment that most organizations find themselves in at the beginning of the millennium and it is for this reason that leadership training has emerged as a major growth industry, being provided by universities, private-sector consulting organizations and specialist training centres. Numerous bodies have emerged to help create the leaders of the future. Perhaps the one most worthy of note here is the United Nations Institute for Leadership Development based at York University in Canada (**www.ildglobal.org**). Founded in 1999, its mandate is to help define, shape and influence the critical issues concerning young professionals and young entrepreneurs (aged between 21 and 30) around the world. Using a variety of methods, it aims to develop positive attitudes, ethical understanding and a sense of responsibility in its participants, who come from diverse backgrounds, so that they become better decision- and policy-makers, and socially responsible agents for change. Perhaps a more modest, but none the less valuable initiative, is the UK's Common Purpose programme (**www.commonpurpose.org.uk**) founded in 1988 by a mother of five young children, Julia Middleton.

Essentially there are three forms of leadership development, as outlined below.

1. Formal training: most formal training is conducted by training professionals, is time-fixed (e.g. a short course) and is away from the place of work. It includes such techniques as behaviour role modelling, case discussion, games and simulations, which may be conducted in or out of doors. In recent years outdoor challenge programmes have become increasingly popular, but it is unclear how effective they are in improving leadership effectiveness.

2. Developmental activities: these are usually embedded within job assignments and the emphasis is on learning from experience. They can take many forms and include coaching, mentoring and multi-rater feedback, as well as special assignments and job rotation programmes that provide new challenges and the opportunity to develop the requisite skills. Although the research on developmental activities is inconclusive, 'the importance of learning from experience on the job is now widely acknowledged, and researchers have begun to map the

relationships between specific experiences and specific leadership competences' (Yukl, 2002: 397).

3. **Self-help activities:** as this heading suggests, these are carried out by the individual on his/her own. The activities range from reading books, viewing videos
   and listening to audio tapes, to using interactive computer programs. In some
   instances they are intended to be a substitute for formal training, while in others they are used either to supplement it or to facilitate learning from experience. Very little is known, unfortunately, about the effectiveness of such activities and there is scope for research into the extent to which such self-help
   activities can help individuals develop their leadership capability.

Interestingly, research conducted in the UK for the Council for Excellence in
Management and Leadership (Perren and Grant, 2001), reported a wide variety of
ways in which entrepreneurs acquired their leadership and management skills,
covering all three of the above methods. Most prominent, however, were informal methods, which ranged from observation to informal mentoring by business
colleagues or a former lecturer. Examples were given of how more formal management courses had helped, though such courses were not portrayed as a substitute for the informal mechanisms. Again, when asked how the support for management and leadership could be improved, the respondents very much emphasized the need for informal fora, where experiences could be shared, and for mentoring and business coaching. On the basis of this evidence, the report concludes
that while there has been an increase in the provision of formal support, there is
little demand for such schemes from entrepreneurs, at least in the UK. It recom-
mends, therefore, that leadership development activities should be an integral
part of the entrepreneurial life and need 'to tap seamlessly into the activities that
they [the entrepreneurs] would be undertaking as a normal part of running their
business' (2001: 16).

   Although understanding is still very much in its infancy, contemporary thinking, therefore, is that leaders are best developed in their own work situations,
where they can learn by doing. However, it is also recognized that if the leaders
of the future are to learn from experience, they need skilled coaching and counselling as well as accurate feedback. Also, they need to be given the opportunity
to widen their experience through broad job assignments, job rotation and lateral career moves, and to be put in positions where they have to move out of their
comfort zones and take risks. This suggests the following two conclusions.

   First, perhaps the most appropriate form of leadership development is a formal
programme of action learning (Revans, 1982). Essentially, action learning requires
the learner to consider problems for which there are no obvious solutions but
which can be resolved using prior experience. For Revans, action learning is a
process that requires the learner to appreciate that the existing body of knowledge
does not provide a solution to the problem under review and it is necessary, therefore, to rely on experience to provide questioning insights. Normally action learning programmes combine formal management training with learning from experience, the participants meeting periodically with a skilled facilitator to consider,
and learn from, their experiences. Much emphasis is placed on developing cognitive and interpersonal skills rather than technical knowledge, although the value
of action learning to the development of leadership skills is likely to be dependent

Table 7.1: Creating a climate for continuous learning

Job assignments that allow people to pursue their interests and learn new skills
Work schedules that allow sufficient free time to experiment with new methods
Financial support for continuing education
Specialist speakers and skill workshops
Sabbatical programmes
Career and self-awareness counselling
Voluntary skill assessment and feedback programmes
Pay increases linked to skill development
Awards for innovation and improvements
Symbols and slogans that embody values such as experimentation, flexibility, adaptation,
   self-development, continuous learning and innovation

Source: Yukl (2002)

on the project on which the learner is working. Unless the project involves considerable challenge, it is unlikely to provide much opportunity to develop the skills of leadership.

Second, the extent to which leadership competences are developed depends upon the conditions that prevail within the organization. Leadership development needs, first of all, to be consistent with the strategic aims of the organization and any developmental activity needs to be facilitated, supported and reinforced through a coherent and strong learning culture that emphasizes the importance of continuous learning and development. According to Yukl (2002) numerous things can be done to create such an environment (see Table 7.1).

The entrepreneurial leader

There are numerous definitions of what makes an entrepreneurial leader and, with reference to the work of Hitt *et al.* (1999), Kuratko and Hodgetts (2001: 516) have suggested that, 'entrepreneurial leadership can be defined as the ability to anticipate, envision, maintain flexibility, think strategically and work with others to initiate changes that will create a viable future for the organisation'. While there is much in such a definition that is good, it lacks something of the emotional nature of leadership. As Tichy and Cohen (1998: 21) have recognized, 'leadership is more about thinking, judging, acting and motivating than about strategies, methodologies and tools'.

Good entrepreneurial leaders care about their organizations and their people. They do not impose their solutions on their teams, or exclude or suppress potential. Rather they encourage their staff to be creative and to find their own solutions to problems. In some ways, the modern entrepreneurial leader is like the leader of a jazz band. He/she decides on the music to be played, gathers around him/her the musicians to play it and then allows them to improvise and use their creativity to interact with each other to create the required sounds. In the process, they have much fun and it is the role of the band's leader to bring out the best in the group.

As in the world of jazz, the authority of entrepreneurial leaders comes from their expertise and values rather that from their position, and they lead by example, empowering their teams and nurturing leaders at all levels. By so doing, they ensure that the organization is successful even when they are not around. They do this by the following means.

- Having a vision: entrepreneurial leaders constantly challenge the status quo to see whether they are doing the right things or if what they are doing can be done better or cheaper. They do not just identify the problem, they determine the solution and ensure the required actions get it implemented. Thus they see both the problem and the solution.

- Setting the tone and determining the values of the organization: they are careful to ensure that everything they do reflects the values they espouse and they encourage their people to examine their own values.

- Developing others: they have ideas that they can express and teach others about, coupled with well-developed coaching and teaching skills, as well as a willingness to admit to, and learn from, their mistakes.

- Exhibiting and creating positive energy: they work hard, with a determination that shows they care about the goal the organization is attempting to achieve. While they never tire, they never use their energy to intimidate. Rather their enthusiasm enthuses others and encourages people to join them. To energize others, leaders:

  - create a sense of urgency—the problem is not going to go away unless something is done

  - identify a mission worth achieving—the future looks better than the present

  - set goals that stretch people's abilities—but are achievable

  - develop a spirit of teamwork—risks are shared

  - engender a realistic expectation that the team can succeed—they build confidence.

- Facing up to reality and making tough decisions, often with imperfect information: frequently such decisions are not popular in the short term but the good entrepreneurial leader does not let the difficulty of the decision deter him/her from doing that which will improve the organization, even though it may be frightening or painful.

Thus, they may be regarded as 'patient leaders, capable of instilling tangible visions and managing for the long haul. The entrepreneur is at once a learner and a teacher, a doer and a visionary' (Timmons 1999: 221). However if there is no immediate problem, entrepreneurial leaders will often 'stir things up' by breaking down established bureaucratic procedures or setting new, stretching, targets and goals.

According to McGrath and MacMillan (2000), the entrepreneurial leader will know he/she has succeeded when everyone in the organization:

- takes it for granted that business success is about a continual search for new opportunities and a continual letting go of less productive activities

- feels that he or she has not only the right but the obligation to seek out new opportunities and make them happen

- comes to work excited and is proud to be associated with it

and when the value created within the organization translates into stakeholder wealth. They suggest that, to facilitate this, the entrepreneur needs to set the work climate, orchestrate the process of seeking and realizing opportunities, and become actively involved in identifying and developing new ventures. Setting the climate involves creating a pervasive sense of urgency to be working on the next new initiative. To achieve this, the entrepreneur has to model the sort of behaviour he/she requires 'consistently, predictably and relentlessly', and to dedicate a disproportionate share of his/her time, attention and discretionary resources to creating new business propositions. Orchestration involves defining the entrepreneurial directions that can be taken, minimizing investment and launch costs until the returns have been fully demonstrated, and implanting a discovery-driven philosophy into the organization by which it is not a crime to fail, only to fail expensively and without learning. Getting involved in identifying and developing new ventures requires that the entrepreneur is not just involved in identifying entrepreneurial insights and converting them into business propositions, but that he/she:

- builds resolve (i.e. gets people to commit to the launching of a new initiative)
- practises leadership by setting realistic but challenging targets, absorbing uncertainty, defining what must and cannot be accepted, clearing away any obstacles that may arise and by underwriting the proposition
- keeps a finger on the pulse to monitor progress
- constantly checks for market acceptance
- secures deals with key stakeholders
- pushes the team to
  - initiate revenue flows ahead of cost flows
  - be realistic in identifying skill deficiencies
- orchestrates market entry
- keeps the focus on learning
- makes sure the team continues to monitor critical sensitivities.

Clearly not all initiatives will succeed and the entrepreneurial leader's role is as critical in failure as it is to success. According to McGrath and MacMillan (2000), the leadership role in the case of failure is, first, to conduct constructive postmortems to distinguish projects that have failed through bad luck from those that have failed because of bad decision-making. Second, the entrepreneurial leader needs to recoup all the benefits from the failed initiative, in particular emphasizing to the team that it was the venture that failed, not them. Finally, he/she may have to shut down a project if the team is entrapped in a 'welter of optimism' that prevents it from seeing that it is doomed.

While the role of the entrepreneurial leader is clearly not easy, it is never too early or too late either to develop the skills or to help develop them in others. Entrepreneurial leaders do not have all the answers and they are not dictators. Rather, being a successful entrepreneurial leader is about:

- developing your own power by making the people around you more powerful
- being truthful and sincere, thereby building trust and respect
- providing direction, not the precise route
- recognizing that your colleagues may have some of the best ideas, especially if they are doing the job every day

- supporting your staff when they 'fail' and celebrating their achievements when they succeed
- learning from failure
- facilitating change but protecting fundamental values
- brokering people and harnessing the ideas that come from unlikely encounters
- building relationships
- exposing your colleagues to reality, but protecting them from danger
- leading by example
- creating more leaders.

If you can achieve this, you will be well on the way to becoming a successful entrepreneurial leader.

Chapter Review

➡ As well as being creative and innovative, entrepreneurs are highly motivated and able to motivate others.

➡ They have imagination and set challenging targets for themselves and others, which they review periodically.

➡ To motivate others they:
  – understand their needs and wants
  – set stretching goals that are realistic and achievable
  – provide support
  – monitor outcomes
  – openly reward performance
  – adopt a positive approach to sanctioning.

➡ They are transformational rather than transactional leaders, whose leadership capabilities can be developed through:
  – formal training
  – self-help activities
  – on-the-job development/action learning.

➡ The entrepreneur creates a successful organization by:
  – having a vision
  – determining the values of the organization
  – leading by example
  – exhibiting and creating positive energy
  – empowering his/her staff
  – creating leaders at all levels in the organization
  – facing up to reality and making tough decisions.

Quick Revision

(Answers at the end of this section)

1. What, apart from being creative and innovative, does the entrepreneur need to have?
   (a) money
   (b) motivation
   (c) the ability to motivate others
   (d) a degree

2. Personal peak performance results from a specific personal talent or trait. Is this:
   (a) true
   (b) false?

3. If you are going to motivate others, which of the following do you not need to do (i.e. which is the odd one out)?
   (a) understand the individual's needs and wants
   (b) set the individual stretching goals that are realistic and achievable
   (c) provide the individual with support
   (d) monitor the individual's achievements
   (e) reward the individual's performance
   (f) punish those individuals that under-achieve

4. Democratic leaders involve their team members in discussion before they reach their decision. Is this:
   (a) true
   (b) false?

5. Which of the following is most similar to the entrepreneurial leader?
   (a) the conductor of the orchestra who co-ordinates the activities of its members and ensures they play in harmony
   (b) the jazz band leader who allows the members of the group to improvise and use their creativity

Answers to Quick Revision: 1–b and c; 2–b; 3–f; 4–b; 5–b

 **Learning Style Activities**

➡ **Activist:** Identify a problem that needs to be resolved and gather around you a team of people to help you resolve it. It may be a work-related problem, a course-related problem or something unrelated to either.
➡ **Reflector:** Identify the skills you used both to establish and motivate the team.
➡ **Theorist:** How did theory help you? Did your experience corroborate or refute the theory? Do you need to modify or extend the theory on the basis of your experience?
➡ **Pragmatist:** What would you do differently next time?

Reading

Adair, J. (1986) *Effective Team Building.* Aldershot: Gower.

Adams, J.D. (1984) Achieving and Maintaining Personal Peak Performance, in Adams, J.D. (ed.) *Transforming Work.* Alexandria VA: Miles River Press.

Appell, A.L. (1984) *A Practical Approach to Human Behaviour in Business.* Columbus Ohio: Charles E. Merrill Publishing Co.

Bach, R. (1972) *Jonathan Livingston Seagull: A Story.* London: Pan Books.

Belbin, M. (1981) *Management Teams: Why They Succeed or Fail.* Oxford: Butterworth-Heinemann.

Fiedler, F.E. (1967) *A Theory of Leadership Effectiveness.* New York: McGraw-Hill.

Garfield, C.S. (1986) *Peak Performers.* New York: Avon Books.

Handy, C. (1997) New Language of Organising. *Executive Excellence,* May, 13–14.

Herzberg, F. (1968) How Do You Motivate Employees? *Harvard Business Review,* January/February.

Hitt, M.A., R.D. Ireland and R.E. Hoskisson (1999) *Strategic Management: Competitiveness and Globalisation.* Cincinnati OH: Southwestern Publishing.

Kurakto, D.F. and R.M. Hodgetts (2001) *Entrepreneurship: A Contemporary Approach.* Orlando FL: Harcourt College Publishers.

McClelland, D.C. (1961) *The Achieving Society.* Princeton NJ: Van Nostrand.

McClelland, D.C. and D.H. Burnham (1976) Power is the Great Motivator. *Harvard Business Review,* March/April, 100–10.

McGrath, R.G and I. MacMillan (2000) *The Entrepreneurial Mindset: Strategies for Continuously Creating Opportunity in an Age of Uncertainty.* Boston MA: Harvard Business School Press.

McGregor, R. (1960) *The Human Side of Enterprise.* New York: McGraw-Hill.

McKenna, E. (2000) *Business Psychology and Organisational Behaviour: A Student's Handbook.* Hove, East Sussex: Psychology Press.

Maslow, A.H. (1943) A Theory of Human Motivation. *Psychological Review* **50**, 370–96.

Perren, L. and P. Grant (2001) *Management and Leadership in UK SMEs: Witness Testimonies from the World of Entrepreneurs and SME Managers.* London: Council for Excellence in Leadership and Management.

Pines, M. (1980) Psychological Hardiness: The Role of Challenge and Health. *Psychology Today,* December, 34–44.

Quinn, R.E. (1988) *Beyond Rational Management.* San Francisco: Josey-Bass, Inc.

Quinn, R.E., S.R. Faerman, M.P. Thompson and M.R. McGrath (1990) *Becoming a Master Manager: A Competency Framework.* New York: John Wiley.

Revans, R.W. (1982) *The Origin and Growth of Action Learning.* Hunt: Chatwell-Bratt.

Roet, B. (2001) *Positive Action for Health and Wellbeing: The Practical Guide to Taking Control of Your Life and Health.* London: Class Publishing.

Skinner, B.F. (1971) *Beyond Freedom and Dignity.* New York: Alfred A. Knopf.

Stogdill, R.M. (1948) Personal Factors Associated with Leadership: A Survey of the Literature. *Journal of Psychology* **25**, 35–71.

Tannenbaum, R. and W.H. Schmidt (1973) How to Choose a Leadership Pattern. *Harvard Business Review,* May/June, 162–80.

Thomas, I. (1992) *The Power of the Pride.* Benmore RSA: Ian Thomas.

Tichy, N.M. and E. Cohen (1998) *The Leadership Engine: How Winning Companies Build Leaders at Every Level.* Dallas TX: Pritchett & Associates, Inc.

Timmons, J.A. (1989) *The Entrepreneurial Mind.* Andover MA: Brick House Publishing.

Timmons, J.A. (1999) *New Venture Creation: Entrepreneurship for the 21st Century.* Boston MA: Irwin McGraw-Hill.

Vaill, P.B. (1982) The Purposing of High Performing Systems. *Organisational Dynamics* **11** (2), 23–39.

Vroom, V.A. (1964) *Work and Motivation.* New York: John Wiley and Sons.

Whetten, D., K. Cameron and M. Woods (2000) *Developing Management Skills for Europe.* Harlow, Essex: Pearson Education Ltd.

Wickens, P. (1999) *Energise Your Enterprise.* Hampshire, Basingstoke: Macmillan.

Yukl, G. (2002) *Leadership in Organizations.* Upper Saddle River NJ: Prentice Hall.

Leadership style questionnaire

This questionnaire contains statements about leadership style beliefs. Under each statement, circle the number (1–5) that represents how strongly you feel about the statement, using the following scoring system.

1 Almost never true

2 Seldom true

3 Occasionally true

4 Frequently true

5 Almost always true

Be honest about your choices as there are no 'right' or 'wrong' answers—it is only for your own self-assessment.

1. I always retain the final decision-making authority within my department or team.

   1   2   3   4   5

2. I always try to include one or more employees in determining what to do and how to do it. However, I maintain the final decision-making authority.

   1   2   3   4   5

3. I and my employees always vote whenever a major decision has to be made.

   1   2   3   4   5

4. I do not consider suggestions made by my employees as I do not have the time for them.

   1   2   3   4   5

5. I ask for employee ideas and input on upcoming plans and projects.

  1   2   3   4   5

6. For a major decision to pass in my department, it must have the approval of each individual or the majority.

  1   2   3   4   5

7. I tell my employees what has to be done and how to do it.

  1   2   3   4   5

8. When things go wrong and I need to create a strategy to keep a project or process running on schedule, I call a meeting to get my employees' advice.

  1   2   3   4   5

9. To get information out, I send it by e-mail, memos, or voicemail; very rarely is a meeting called. My employees are then expected to act upon the information.

  1   2   3   4   5

10. When someone makes a mistake, I tell them not to ever do that again, and make a note of it.

  1   2   3   4   5

11. I want to create an environment where the employees take ownership of the project. I allow them to participate in the decision-making process.

  1   2   3   4   5

12. I allow my employees to determine what needs to be done and how to do it.

  1   2   3   4   5

13. New hirees are not allowed to make any decisions unless approved by me first.

  1   2   3   4   5

14. I ask employees for their vision of where they see their jobs going and then use their vision where appropriate.

  1   2   3   4   5

15. My workers know more about their jobs than me, so I allow them to carry out the decisions to do their job.

  1   2   3   4   5

16. When something goes wrong, I tell my employees that a procedure is not working correctly and I establish a new one.

1   2   3   4   5

17. I allow my employees to set priorities with my guidance.

1   2   3   4   5

18. I delegate tasks in order to implement a new procedure or process.

1   2   3   4   5

19. I monitor my employees closely to ensure they are performing correctly.

1   2   3   4   5

20. When there are differences in role expectations, I work with them to resolve the differences.

1   2   3   4   5

21. Each individual is responsible for defining their job.

1   2   3   4   5

22. I like the power that my leadership position holds over subordinates.

1   2   3   4   5

23. I like to use my leadership power to help subordinates grow.

1   2   3   4   5

24. I like to share my leadership power with my subordinates.

1   2   3   4   5

25. Employees must be directed or threatened with punishment in order to get them to achieve organizational objectives.

1   2   3   4   5

26. Employees will exercise self-direction if they are committed to the objectives.

1   2   3   4   5

27. Employees have the right to determine their own organizational objectives.

1   2   3   4   5

28. Employees seek mainly security.

1   2   3   4   5

29. Employees know how to use creativity and ingenuity to solve organizational problems.

    1   2   3   4   5

30. My employees can lead themselves just as well as I can.

    1   2   3   4   5

Now, using the grid below, write down your score for each item on the questionnaire. For example, if you scored item 1 with a 3 (Occasionally true) then enter a 3 next to item 1 below. When you have entered all the scores for each question, total each of the three columns.

Item	Score	Item	Score	Item	Score
1		2		3	
4		5		6	
7		8		9	
10		11		12	
13		14		15	
16		17		18	
19		20		21	
22		23		24	
25		26		27	
28		29		30	
Total:		Total:		Total:	
	Authoritarian style		Delegative style		Participative style
	(autocratic)		(democratic)		(free rein)

This questionnaire aims to help you assess what leadership style you normally operate from. The lowest score possible for a stage is 10 (Almost never) while the highest score possible for a stage is 50 (Almost always).

The highest of the three scores indicates what style of leadership you normally use. If your highest score is 40 or more, it is a strong indicator of your normal style.

The lowest of the three scores is an indicator of the style you least use. If your lowest score is 20 or under, it is a strong indicator that you normally do not operate out of this mode.

If two of the scores are almost the same, you might be going through a transition phase, either personally or at work, except:

- if you score high in both the participative and the delegative columns, then you are probably a delegative leader
- if there is only a small difference between the three scores, then this indicates

that you have no clear perception of the mode you operate from, or you are a new leader and are trying to 'feel for' the correct style for you.

Normally, some of the best leaders operate out of the participative mode and use the other two modes as needed. The exception would be a leader who has a new crew or temporary workforce. That leader would probably be operating out of the authoritarian mode. On the other side, a leader who has a crew of professionals or a crew that knows more than she or he does, would probably operate out of the delegative mode.

Leaders who want their employees to grow, use a participative style of leadership. As they 'grow' into their jobs, they are gradually given more authority over their jobs (delegative).

Chapter **8**

Entrepreneurship, Team Building and Conflict Resolution

Learning Outcomes

On completion of this chapter, the reader will:

- appreciate the importance of building teams and team working to successful entrepreneurial management
- understand how teams are developed and the different roles people perform in teams
- recognize how teams are managed and the importance of self-management
- be aware of the way in which conflict can be managed in order to benefit the organization
- have begun to appreciate his/her own, preferred team working role(s) and conflict management style.

Introduction

Traditionally it has been held that the entrepreneur is not a good manager and that a manager is not an entrepreneur. Indeed, Galbraith (1971) has suggested that the great entrepreneur can be compared in life to the male *apis mellifera* (honey bee). He accomplishes the act of conception, at the expense of his own extinction. As will be shown in Chapter 11, this is, indeed, often the case, but increasingly there is evidence to suggest that successful entrepreneurial ventures are headed by entrepreneurs who are also effective managers. Unlike the traditional manager, though, who focuses largely on administrative efficiency, it would seem that the effective entrepreneurial manager needs to possess skills in building an entrepreneurial culture.

Entrepreneurial influencing skills

As has been shown already, the effective entrepreneurial manager needs to be able to:

- recognize and cope with innovation
- take risks
- respond quickly
- cope with 'failure' (absorb setbacks)
- find chaos and uncertainty challenging and stimulating.

Additionally, he/she must be able to:

- build motivated and committed teams
- use consensus to manage conflict.

To do this, entrepreneurs need good interpersonal/team working skills that involve the ability to:

- create a climate and spirit conducive to high performance, including rewarding work well done and encouraging creativity, innovation, initiative and calculated risk-taking
- understand the relationships present among tasks, and between the leader and followers
- lead in those situations where it is appropriate, including a willingness to manage actively, to supervise and to control the actions of others.

These interpersonal skills are normally termed 'entrepreneurial influencing skills' since they have to do with the way entrepreneurial managers exert influence over others. They include: leadership/vision/influence; helping, coaching and resolving conflict; and teamwork and people management. We will now look at each of these in turn.

Leadership/vision/influence

Entrepreneurial managers are skilful at:

- clarifying confusion, ambiguity and uncertainty
- gaining agreement.

They do this, as was seen in Chapter 7, in a way that builds motivation and commitment, not just to parochial interests but to cross-departmental and corporate goals. In the process they demonstrate a willingness to relinquish their personal priorities and power in the interest of an overall goal. They also possess an ability to ensure that the appropriate people are included in setting cross-functional or cross-departmental goals, and in decision-making. For some more traditional managers, used to dealing with subordinates, collaborating with peers and superiors might be an uncomfortable, disturbing or confusing experience. When things do not go smoothly, the most effective entrepreneurial managers work them through to agreement.

Helping, coaching and resolving conflict

The most effective entrepreneurial managers are creative and skilful in handling conflicts, generating consensus decisions and sharing their power and information. They:

- are able to get people to open up and share their views
- get problems aired and identified
- acknowledge, without being defensive, the views of others
- are aware that high-quality decisions require information flowing in all directions
- are comfortable with knowledge, competence, logic and evidence prevailing over official status or formal rank
- are able to get potential adversaries to be creative and to collaborate by reconciling viewpoints
- are constantly blending views, often risking their own vulnerability in the process by giving up their own power and resources.

In the short term, the benefits of such an approach are often difficult to identify, and it appears a painful way to manage. Longer term, however, the gains from the motivation, commitment and teamwork can be considerable, especially when grounded in consensus.

Teamwork and people management

Entrepreneurial managers build confidence by encouraging creativity, innovation and calculated risk-taking, rather than by criticizing and punishing. They encourage independent thinking by expecting and encouraging others to find and correct their own errors and to solve their own problems. This does not mean they are abandoning their colleagues to their own devices. Rather, they are perceived by their peers and other managers as:

- accessible and willing to help when needed
- facilitators, providing the resources that enable others to do their jobs more effectively
- champions who defend their peers and subordinates, even when they know they cannot always win
- hero-makers, ensuring that others receive the credit for their efforts, rather than accepting it themselves.

Through such actions, they have the capacity to generate trust. They reinforce this by being:

- straightforward—doing what they say they are going to do
- open and spontaneous
- honest and direct
- creative problem-solvers
- people developers.

Having looked at motivation and leadership in Chapter 7, attention in this chapter is focused on the entrepreneurial management competences of:

- building teams and team working
- managing conflict, resolving differences and developing consensus.

As seen in Fig. 7.1, this is Quinn's human relations model (the 'competing values framework'), particularly the role of his facilitator, who, he suggests, 'is expected to foster collective effort, build cohesion and teamwork and manage interpersonal conflict' (Quinn *et al.*, 1990: 17).

PAUSE FOR THOUGHT

Think of any team of which you have been a member. How did it function? Was it successful? Why did it succeed or fail? If it succeeded, was it successful from the outset?

Entrepreneurial team working

Traditionally the entrepreneur has been thought of as an individual who works alone to achieve his/her objectives, managing in a somewhat autocratic manner. Increasingly it is being realized that this is not the case, that the successful entrepreneur is not an autocratic leader but someone who can work with and through others to achieve his/her objectives. He/she is a team worker. According to Belbin (1981), effective team working requires that the team members fulfil various roles. These, he suggests, are as follows.

- **Chairperson:** the team's co-ordinator. He/she works primarily through others. The chair is mature, confident and trusting, with good interpersonal skills. He/she has a calming influence on the team, is able to clarify the team's goals and promotes decision-making. He/she can appear to be manipulative, however, and is not always the leader. Sets objectives and priorities for the team and co-ordinates effort. Is disciplined and dominant but not domineering. Easy communicator who can provide effective summaries when needed, and the casting vote.
- **Plant:** the ideas person, the team's chief source of new ideas. Such people are creative, imaginative and frequently unorthodox. Sometimes their ideas may seem impractical and they may seem distant and uncommunicative. They are usually dominant, introverted and creative, normally with a high intelligence quotient (IQ). Can be prickly and not good at accepting criticism. May withdraw if their ideas are not accepted and may need to be coaxed.
- **Shaper:** the person who stimulates the others to action. He/she is normally the self-elected task leader. Shapers are normally extrovert, dynamic, outgoing and argumentative with lots of nervous energy. They are outgoing and emotional, impulsive and impatient, and intolerant of 'woolliness'. They constantly seek ways around problems, they thrive under pressure and get things done. However, they are often bullies who are not liked.
- **Monitor-evaluator:** the person who assesses ideas. He/she explores all the options and is capable of thoroughly analysing large amounts of data. His/her judgements are good and rarely do they make the wrong decisions. Usually

monitor-evaluators are introverted, serious, strategic and discerning, often lacking drive. They are unlikely to inspire their colleagues and can have a negative effect on group morale. However, they are the most likely member of the team to stop it committing itself to a misguided project.

- **Resource investigator:** the team's 'fixer'. He/she has a wealth of contacts and is always busy, often exploring new opportunities or/and 'picking other people's brains'. They are usually positive, enthusiastic, extrovert and amiable, but can be undisciplined and can lose interest quickly. Hence they need pressure to keep to task.

- **Team worker:** holds the team together. This is the team's counsellor, the person who reconciles differences. They promote harmony especially at times of crisis. Usually they are mild-mannered and sensitive, which makes them aware of problems and difficulties within the team. They are good communicators who are popular and unassertive. They do not like confrontation and tend to counter-balance the frictions created by the shaper and the plant. While they are perceptive, they can, however, be indecisive.

- **Company worker:** the implementer—turns ideas into manageable tasks. Practical, gets on with the job and organizes his/her work logically and orderly. They are disciplined, reliable, loyal and conservative, but can be inflexible and slow to change. Recognized by their colleagues as being sincere and trustworthy.

- **Completer-finisher:** makes sure things get done. They have an eye for detail and a concern for deadlines and timetables. Hence they pick up on omissions and errors and have relentless 'follow-through'. Sometimes they simply cannot let up and often have difficulty delegating. They worry about what might go wrong and are always prepared to take personal responsibility. While not being assertive, they maintain a sense of urgency and are intolerant of the more casual members of the team. Can lose sight of the overall objectives of the team.

- **Specialist:** the team's technical expert. They are usually single-minded self-starters. While they are dedicated (to their specialism and the team), they are narrowly focused and tend not to make a broad contribution.

Clearly, for tasks to be progressed, all of these roles are needed. Hence the successful entrepreneur, whilst frequently possessing many of the qualities him/herself, frequently joins in partnership with others to ensure that the idea/concept is brought to fruition.

A classic example of this is the Consett-based Derwent Valley Foods, which was founded in 1982 by two friends. One was a former marketing director of Tudor Crisps, while the other had worked in international advertising. Together they decided on manufacturing and distributing corn-based snacks from around the world, which they sold under the brand name of Phileas Fogg, after the Jules Verne character in *Around the World in Eighty Days*. Shortly after founding the business they were joined by two other experienced managers with backgrounds in the food industry, and together they secured the requisite financial backing and distribution agreements for them to go into production. The workforce, the vast majority of whom had previously been unemployed, were keen for them to succeed and with their innovative new products they quickly gave them a 33 per cent share. In 1993 the business was bought by United Biscuits for £24 million. The initial founder has been described as 'disorganized but determined, erratic and single-minded . . . able to organize and inspire a team' (shaper, team worker). He has described himself as an ideas generator who can get people to be creative and, while being disorganized, is not a bad delegator (plant, chairperson). His founding partner was 'a questioner and deep thinker' (monitor-evaluator). The other two members of the team were 'a pusher who gets things done' (completer-finisher, shaper) and a 'creative overcomer' (company worker).

However, according to Wickens (1999: 125), real team working has little to do with structures and roles. Rather it is about working together to achieve shared goals. As he points out, this 'does not mean seeking the lowest common denominator solution on which everyone can agree', nor does it mean that everyone's pet solution is incorporated into the final outcome. Rather, it means challenging each others' ideas and finding the best solutions. Hence effective teams are not comfortable places. Some members will be disappointed when their ideas are not accepted but if they are committed members of the team they will recognize the better idea and will work equally vigorously to make it a success. He quotes from Thomas's (1992) study of lions, which concludes:

The pride has evolved as a potent example of teamwork for maximum effect. Their combined co-operative effort working towards a common objective leads to a winning team situation where both the pride and the individual thrive. The lesson from lions to business is—teams are successful because:

- Each individual member is powerful
- The total focus is on clear-cut goals
- Team members are alert to communication
- Incentives motivate and reward success
- Spirit consists of trust, confidence, respect and pride
- The structure is flat
- Strict selection ensures there are no passengers
- Training is intense
- Image enhances function
- Synergy—the pride is more powerful than the strength of its individuals.

The unremitting application of these ten power points puts the pride in a win-win situation: the pride and its members thrive.

Wickens (1999: 127) then goes on, himself, to add a further nine points based on his observations of a mother cheetah and her son hunting impala in Zimbabwe. He suggests that real team working requires:

- tremendous energy combined with patience
- clear leadership
- intense relationships
- total trust
- intuitive understanding between members
- rules of behaviour that are understood by the members

- learning from failure
- goals that are time-bounded
- keeping on going until the goals are achieved.

Exercise 8.1

Identify your preferred team working role(s) by completing Belbin's 'Self-Perception Inventory' either in his book (1981; full details may be found in the Reading section towards the end of this chapter) or online at **http://team-belbin.com**.

A CASE EXAMPLE

Nelli Eichner: Interlingua

Nelli Eichner is the founder of Interlingua, the international technical translation service. She was born in what is now the Czech Republic, where her interest in languages was developed listening to the stories of the Russian and Italian prisoners of war. At the age of four she then translated them for her younger sister. In Vienna, where she went to School, she learned German, French and English, and on leaving school she worked in Rome and Paris.

When World War II broke out in 1939, she came to England acting as a translator for the Czech Army. Following her marriage to Fred, a chemist, she embarked on raising a family. As money was tight, she used her linguistic capability to supplement their income, including translating a book her husband was writing. When the second of their children, Mike, fell ill with polio, the Eichners moved from their home in north London to a dilapidated house in rural Sussex. Fred continued as a consultant chemist but all of their money and spare time was spent renovating their home. They also raised and sold poultry and goats in order to help supplement their income. However, the translation side of their activities was increasing and they engaged a small network of local university-trained women to assist. They ensured that every translation was checked before being sent out.

As the business grew, their children became involved. They collected and delivered jobs, folded leaflets, answered the telephone, etc. When they won a contract with the British government to translate all the specifications for the Concorde aeroplane project into French, they decided to create Interlingua as a registered partnership. Shortly after, they scraped together £50 as a down-payment for a fax machine. The children all learned how to use it and they began to offer instant translations by Telex. Satisfied clients began to tell others, who tried out the new service. The newspapers heard about it and enquiries came pouring in. Within months Interlingua was an international company with some of the world's largest companies as its clients. It translated books, film scripts, communications between heads of state and even the Bible, using a network of translators.

When commissioned to translate into Eskimo, Interlingua had to purchase a special printer as no English printer could print the work. This enabled it, with suitably recruited staff, to print in any language. When the then Shah of Persia (now Iran) commissioned the company to translate the orders and menus for a function involving royalty, several thousand heads of state and international celebrities, it set up a dedicated Persian department, complete with in-house translators, typists, printing units, etc. The Eichner's eldest daughter, Jona, took responsibility for this, while one of their sons-in-law took responsibility for the establishment of a Russian section.

Then came the Japanese. As Japan became a force in international business, Nelli and her husband left the children to run their business and went to Tokyo to recruit a translator who not only helped them build a successful Japanese department but married the company's Italian translator. After Japan, they added an Arabic department, run by Jona, and a Chinese department. Eventually, with computers helping to make translation faster and better, Nelli and Fred were able to hand the business over to their children—their son Mike taking over as managing director. They had created a multi-national company based on the concept of 'one family, one group of people who pulled together for the common good'.

Case example exercise

Interlingua is a classic example of a successful family business. Using the analogy of a family, do as Thomas and Wickens have done and develop a set of characteristics of a successful team. Compare them with those derived by Thomas and Wickens from the study of lions and cheetahs.

What common characteristics did you identify? What differences were there? How might your analysis help us better understand (a) the success of family firms such as Interlingua and (b) team performance?

Team building

Effective teams tend not to occur naturally, they have to be worked at, and team building is the process of enhancing the effectiveness of teams. According to Tuckman (1965), groups pass through the following stages in the process of becoming an effective team.

1. **Forming:** at this stage the members focus on the way the group will behave in order to enable it to meet its objectives with the resources available. They look to their leader or a powerful figure for guidance.

2. **Storming:** the group begins to fragment. Often at this stage there are interpersonal difficulties, differences of opinion over what the job entails and/or resistance to the control exercised by the group leader. Members stress their own needs and concerns, and resist the influence of the group.

3. **Norming:** group cohension develops. The group members exchange views and feelings freely, and there is an emphasis on harmony and mutual support. There is a conscious effort to avoid conflict situations, and new roles and ways of working emerge.

4. **Performing:** the group has developed a way of working, and solutions to problems are emerging. Interpersonal problems have been resolved and the group's energy is channelled into the task.

5. **Adjourning:** the group is wound down.

Clearly, it can take a long time for this process to work through, and for teams to mature into efficient and effective units. Hence, the entrepreneur needs to be patient and to manage the process. At Stage 1, he/she needs to resolve the group's insecurities by assuming authority, and providing leadership and direction, concentrating on the task, its purpose and its content. At Stage 2, however, he/she needs to move away from this directive approach and to concentrate more on developing the team, making it clear why members have been included, their strengths and the roles they are to play in the team. However, teams often tend to remain at Stage 2, usually because:

- the members are allowed or, indeed, encouraged to compete with each other
- there is a mismatch between the roles the members are being required to play and their preferred styles of working
- the principles behind the task are not accepted by the members
- members do not accept the team values

- the decision-making style remains authoritarian
- the task is not clear.

In all probability, the entrepreneur may have to recognize that some individuals are not suited to the team and may need to be replaced if the team is to move to Stage 3. By this stage the role of the entrepreneur should be more that of trainer, coach or counsellor. The group will have begun to gel and the entrepreneur's role is to consult with the team to ensure that the requisite support is available to ensure that it functions effectively, thereby enabling it to progress to the mature stage. This may not occur, however, if:

- the group is allowed to modify the task
- the team's processes are not monitored
- the team members get along too well (there is no shaper or plant)
- consensus has become the way decisions are reached
- team membership is static.

Assuming that it does reach the mature stage, the entrepreneur's job is to continue to support the team, ensuring that the external culture of the organization recognizes its importance and is supportive of it. Provided that this is in place, and the team's task and membership have evolved together, there is no reason why the team cannot survive indefinitely. There are circumstances, however, when this is not the case and the team is dismembered. Under such circumstances, the role of the entrepreneur is to recognize the importance of the 'grieving process' and support the individual team members through it.

Not all team-building exercises are successful by any means, and Hackman (1994) identifies five common mistakes in building effective teams. These are:

1. treating the unit as a team but still dealing with the members on an individual basis
2. failing to strike the right balance between authority and democracy
3. leaving organizational structures unchanged and failing to create an enabling structure
4. leaving the teams unsupported
5. assuming that individuals are eager to work in teams and have the experience and skills to do so.

If teams are to be effective, these issues need to be addressed, and he suggests that the entrepreneur needs to:

- think clearly and spell out the tasks to be performed, the composition of the team and the appropriate group norms
- specify the ends but not the means to the ends
- issue clear instructions and directions
- recognize the importance of intrinsic motivation (see Chapter 5)
- create a supportive organizational context
- provide training and expert coaching, not least in the development of team-working skills.

This cannot be over-emphasized. It is not a case of leaving teams to get on with their task. They need to be supported, encouraged and monitored so that remedial action can be taken if they begin to falter. While Tuckman's model suggests an onward progression in the evolution of teams, it is possible for them to regress to an earlier stage. Hence, it is the role of the entrepreneurial manager to monitor their performance, ensuring that regression does not occur and that the team continues to function effectively, meeting its objectives and goals. As mentioned already (Chapter 7), it is also the role of the entrepreneur to coach his/her team and, in this context, Orth *et al.* (1987) have suggested that the entrepreneurial manager interested in the effectiveness of his/her team needs to:

- be continuously on the lookout for means to exploit the capabilities of team members with a view to improving their performance
- create a supportive climate in order to encourage the improvement of performance by offering advice and guidance, removing obstacles to improved performance and by helping identify the causes of any under-achievement
- encourage members to change their behaviour in order to continually improve
- model the qualities he/she would like the team members to embrace (e.g. enthusiasm, commitment, openness, sensitivity, efficiency, etc.) and demonstrate them.

Clearly this requires a close and effective working relationship between the entrepreneur and his/her team not, as is frequently assumed, a 'hands-off', distant and detached relationship. However, the entrepreneur must avoid the temptation to do the work of the team or to meddle in its affairs, telling the members how they should conduct their business. Most importantly he/she should avoid 'reverse delegation' (i.e. re-asserting control over a task that has previously been delegated). When support is required, it should be given, but ownership of the solution should remain with the team. It is a fine balance, requiring considerable skill.

Building and empowering the entrepreneurial team

As was shown in Chapter 2, many new small ventures either fail or do not grow. Though the reasons for this remain unclear, Timmons (1999: 278) has suggested that, 'The capacity of the lead entrepreneur to craft a vision, and then to lead, inspire, persuade and cajole key people to sign up for and deliver the dream makes an enormous difference between success and failure . . . '. This is most certainly the case and it is the role of the lead entrepreneur to bring this about. According to Peters (1987), to do this, the entrepreneur needs to:

- involve all personnel at all levels in all functions
- ensure there are no limits on their ability to contribute
- engage staff who are
  - committed
  - properly selected
  - well trained

– appropriately supported

– organized into self-managed teams.

This latter point is important. Not only has the concept of self-management gathered strength in recent years (Orsburn *et al.*, 1990) but it is seen as an important means of empowerment. Essentially self-managed teams (sometimes termed semi-autonomous work groups) take responsibility for their own activities. According to Gordon (1992), these include setting work schedules, dealing with external customers, setting performance targets, training, purchasing equipment or services, dealing with suppliers, preparing budgets, and hiring and firing team members. While any type of team can be 'self-managed' in this way, the research of Cohen and Bailey (1997) suggests that self-management is most appropriate for teams that perform the same type of operational task repeatedly, have a relatively stable membership over time and are composed of members with similar functional backgrounds. Essentially, these are what are known as functional teams. As the name implies they are made up of members with the same or a similar function within a business. Characteristically, this is the way work is organized in large firms. Increasingly, however, such organizations are tending to develop what are known as cross-functional teams. These are composed of representatives of each of the functional sub-units of a business and may even include members from outside the business, such as customers, suppliers, partners, etc.

The whole purpose of such teams is to improve the co-ordination of activities among the firm's specialist sub-units, but also to increase the firm's capacity for creativity, by bringing together people from different backgrounds with different perspectives and viewpoints to consider solutions to a particular problem or problems. Often such teams are temporary in the large organization, but in the small firm they are, inevitably, permanent. While they have numerous advantages, as indicated, they are not easy to lead or manage. While functional diversity increases creativity, it can also create tensions within the firm. Not only does each function have its own language and way of thinking, but team members often have different objectives, time horizons and priorities. Under such circumstances, decision-making can be difficult and time-consuming, especially if the loyalty of the members is to their functional unit rather than to the team. Not surprisingly in such circumstances, Barry (1991) has discovered that most successful cross-functional teams tend to be 'managed' by a designated leader who helps the team:

- envision its shared objective
- decide how it is going to attain it
- maintain its internal cohesion
- ensure its activities are compatible with the needs of the stakeholders outside of the team.

Often, however, the difficulties and obstacles facing cross-functional teams are so great that the official leader may be unable to carry out all of the relevant leadership roles, and other team members may be required to share them. Also, no matter how effective the team may be, its successful functioning requires that the entrepreneur provide a clear mission, necessary resources and political support (Cohen and Bailey, 1997).

However, whether uni- or cross-functional, teams that are self-managed are believed to possess a number of advantages over those managed by a team leader that is imposed on them and/or is part of the senior management. Among these are greater commitment, improved quality, improved efficiency, greater job satisfaction, greater flexibility, and lower labour turnover and absenteeism. Additionally, fewer managers are required, thereby reducing costs. In reality, there is little reliable empirical evidence either to refute or support the theoretical advantages of self-management. Much of the research is based on weak research methods and/or anecdotal reports, and the results of the little reliable research that has been conducted are inconsistent and do not substantiate the major performance improvements that have been claimed. What is known is that self-managed teams are difficult to implement, and require competent leadership and support if they are to stand any chance of success. Invariably this takes the form of leadership internal and external to the team. Typically the internal team leader is responsible for co-ordinating the activities of the team. Sometimes he/she is appointed by the organization. More often the internal leader is elected from amongst the team members and it is here that a difficulty can arise. In a dysfunctional team, the elected leader may not be the person who is going to lead the group forward but the person who is going to cause the least disruption. Whatever, whether the internal leader is appointed or selected, the whole concept of self-management means that the leader does not simply replace the former team manager. Rather, the responsibilities are shared by the members of the team and the team takes collective responsibility for its actions. Members have to understand and accept this role.

Often it is believed that self-managed teams have no need for an external leader or, if there is a need, it is only present when the team is forming. Once the team has been established, the requisite leadership functions will be carried out by the team members, making an external leader redundant. However, the external leader is vitally important to the success of most self-managed teams. Typically the external leader serves as a coach, facilitator and consultant to the team. At the outset, he/she will play an important role in helping the team members learn the requisite skills to plan and organize the work and acquire the very necessary interpersonal skills to function effectively as team members. During this period, an important function of the external leader is to develop the self-confidence of the team members. Once the group is established, the role of the external leader may change but throughout he/she is responsible for:

- setting the direction for the team by communicating objectives and priorities, and articulating a vision of what might be achieved
- communicating clear expectations about the new responsibility of team members for regulating their own behaviour
- championing the group and helping it obtain the necessary resources and political support to enable it to function effectively.

Certainly there is no way that the external leader can, or should, abrogate his/her responsibility to the team. This is a very essential and ongoing role if the team is not to feel abandoned and lost. However, as with the internal leader, the external leader must not take on the role of the former first-line manager, whose role

Table 8.1: First-line managers versus team leaders

Old responsibilities	New responsibilities
10 people reporting to him/her	50+ direct reports
Work scheduler	Coach, sounding board
	Leader/co-ordinator
	Skill developer/enhancer
Rule enforcer	Facilitator
Lots of planning	Lots of wandering
Focused up and down the structure	Focused across the structure
Transmitting management needs down	Selling team needs/ideas up
Providing new ideas for staff	Helping colleagues develop ideas

should disappear if the team is functioning effectively. Indeed, the role of the external manager *vis-à-vis* the first-line manager can be summarized as in Table 8.1.

The research on self-managed teams (Cohen and Bailey, 1997; Kirkman and Rosen, 1999) suggests that their potential advantages are more likely to be realized when certain conditions are fulfilled. These include the following.

- **The objectives must be clearly defined.** The team needs to know what is required of it, otherwise it will set its own objectives, which could be at variance with those of the organization.

- **The task must be complex and meaningful.** The task must be challenging, requiring a range of skills and knowledge to ensure its completion.

- **The team should be small and stable.** There is no optimum team size, although it is generally accepted that teams of between 8 and 15 people are best, as below or above these figures they lose their internal dynamic. Ideally membership should be stable and the members should be located in the same place as both stability and proximity aid team identification and cohesion.

- **The team should have authority and discretion**—the authority to carry out the task and the discretion to decide how it is going to organize itself in order to do it. There should be no external interference or 'meddling'.

- **Access to information.** The success of the team will depend, at least in part, on the information it has at its disposal. It may need access to sensitive or confidential information if it is to do its job properly.

- **Appropriate recognition and rewards.** The team should be rewarded for its contribution, with the members determining how the rewards should be distributed.

- **Strong support by senior management.** This may include the delegation of authority, the allocation of resources, the creation of a compatible organizational culture, etc., as well as political support.

- **Adequate interpersonal skills.** Members must be effective team workers. They should be able to listen, to communicate effectively and to resolve conflicts, as well as being able to use group decision-making techniques and influencing skills.

When you have been a member of a team, whether at work or outside, have you always agreed with your fellow team members about what should be done? If not, what did you do about it and how did you resolve any disagreements?

Managing conflict

According to Timmons (1999: 222), entrepreneurs are:

66 99   . . . adept at conflict resolution. They know when to use logic and when to persuade, when to make a concession, and when to exact one. To run a successful venture, an entrepreneur learns to get along with different constituencies, often with conflicting aims. . . . Success comes when the entrepreneur is a mediator, a negotiator, rather than a dictator.

Clearly any organization that is made up of different people from different backgrounds with different views on how the business should be run is likely to encounter conflict, irrespective of whether it is a new small venture or a large established organization, When such people are brought together, deliberately, it is inevitable that differences of opinion will occur, and the entrepreneur has to be good at managing the conflict that can ensue. Traditionally conflict has been seen as a negative force within organizations and the perceived wisdom has been that, if present, it needs to be eliminated. However, there is a more recent view that conflict is inevitable, given the differences in personalities, needs, goals and values, and that rather than being eliminated, it needs to be managed for the benefit of the organization. As mentioned already, the conflicting views of individuals can be a source of new ideas and, if managed effectively, conflict can be a positive force, within the business, for innovation and change. Therefore, conflict needs to be managed in a way that increases the likelihood that positive outcomes will emerge. Entrepreneurs do this, as Timmons has recognized, but the skill can be acquired.

Regardless of the cause of the conflict, it is generally accepted that there is a set sequence of stages or events. Initially the conflict is latent. Neither party recognizes it but the circumstances have created the potential for individual or group conflict. Once the potential conflict situation has been perceived, the second stage has been reached. This is marked by one or more of the parties reacting emotionally to the situation, usually by being angry, hostile, frustrated, anxious or in pain. In the third stage, the conflict becomes overt. Individuals act either to escalate or resolve the conflict. Actions intended to escalate the conflict might include, for example, aggressive behaviour, purposefully frustrating the achievement of goals, attempting to get others to take sides, etc. In contrast, behaviour intended to resolve the conflict might include encouraging both parties to discuss their differences and identify a solution that would allow their needs and concerns to be heard and met. Clearly actions taken in this stage affect the outcomes of the fourth stage, which is the outcome or aftermath. These can be functional or dysfunctional. Functional outcomes include:

- a better understanding of the issues underlying the conflict
- improved quality of decisions

- increased attention to the use of creativity and innovation in solving and resolving future problems
- a positive approach to self-evaluation.

In contrast, dysfunctional outcomes include:

- continued anger and hostility
- reduced communication
- the destruction of team spirit
- the loss of morale
- mistrust
- further conflicts.

From the above it is clearly essential that conflict is managed effectively and to this end there are basically three strategies that can be adopted: non-confrontational strategies, control strategies and solution-oriented strategies.

- **Non-confrontational strategies:** these include both avoidance and accommodation. Avoidance means that conflict is recognized but neither party is prepared to confront the issues. This approach is often useful as a 'cooling off' strategy but long term it is unsatisfactory as the conflict is likely to simmer and, possibly, erupt at a later date. Also, avoidance often means failing to face up to what are frequently important organizational issues. In contrast, accommodation means that individuals abandon their own goals and work only to satisfy the other party's concerns. While preserving harmony in the short term, this is unlikely to be a long-term solution as individuals are rarely prepared to sacrifice their own personal needs and goals simply to maintain the relationship. Also, such accommodating approaches limit creativity, preventing the exploration of new ideas and solutions to the problem.

- **Control strategies:** these are essentially competing approaches, whereby the parties work only to achieve their own goals. Often these approaches result in dysfunctional outcomes as they result in a win-lose situation. However, they can be beneficial when quick, decisive action is needed or certain drastic actions must be taken for the benefit of the organization. Like accommodation, though, they generally limit creativity and the exploration of new ideas and solutions.

- **Solution-oriented strategies:** these embrace two approaches, namely compromise and collaboration. Compromise usually involves negotiation between the two parties with each giving up something in order to gain something else. The basic assumption of successful negotiation is that neither side will end up the loser, which is a major disadvantage of this approach as neither party ends up a winner either. Both tend to remember what they had to give up in order to gain what they wanted. In contrast, collaboration assumes that by addressing the problem creatively, a solution can be generated that will result in everyone being a winner. Clearly, if they can be achieved, such solutions can be extremely powerful, but they are time-consuming and they may not work.

While there are circumstances where the non-confrontational and control strategies might be appropriate, as discussed, it is generally accepted that a solution-oriented strategy leads to the best result, and that collaborative approaches are most frequently associated with positive outcomes. Clearly important by-products of the collaborative approach are the new ideas and creative solutions that can be generated in the process. However, negotiating such solutions requires skill and it is generally accepted that there is a set of procedures which, if followed, can aid the process. The first stage in the process is for both parties to recognize and acknowledge the conflict. They must be prepared to meet and talk about it, explaining their feelings, and they must be prepared to put aside any anger or hostility. Clearly this is not easy and the negotiator needs to consider beforehand how this situation will be handled. Throughout the process, however, it is the problem, not the person, that is being confronted.

When the meeting takes place, it should be non-threatening and, preferably, in a neutral environment. Feelings, as well as the source of the conflict, should be explored and the participants should express their views clearly and in a non-threatening manner. They should be prepared to listen and reflect on what they have heard. Once both parties have expressed their views on the conflict, they should agree a mutual definition of the conflict in terms of their needs. This is important as it must be clear that both parties share a common definition of the problem before moving on to the next stage, which is applying brainstorming techniques in order to identify solutions that will address the needs of both parties. When both parties have listed all of the possible solutions, they should identify their preferred solutions and say why these best meet their needs. The two parties should then see if any of the preferred solutions coincide and, if not, what compromises are needed to allow them to come to a solution that is mutually acceptable.

Once the solution has been identified, it is necessary to implement it. This requires an action or implementation plan that indicates what needs to be done, by whom and by when. At this stage, also, it is advisable to consider some sort of evaluation procedure that reviews the success of the solution and the learning that has occurred as a result of the exercise, focusing, in particular, on how the parties will avoid such situations arising in the future.

Exercise 8.2

To determine your conflict management style, complete the questionnaire you will find in Appendix 8.1 (at the end of this chapter). This can also be accessed at:

- www.careerbuilder.com/wl_ga_0012_conflictmanagement.html.
- Other similar tests can be found at www.queendom.com/tests/conflict.html or
- http://webhome.idirect.com/~kenhamilt/ipsyconstyle.html.

Try them out and see whether they give you the same results.

Chapter Review

➡ Entrepreneurial managers need to be able to:
- recognize and cope with innovation
- take risks
- respond quickly
- cope with 'failure'
- find chaos and uncertainty challenging
- build motivated and committed teams
- use consensus to manage conflict.

➡ They need to possess such influencing skills as:
- leadership and vision
- helping, coaching and resolving problems
- teamwork and people management.

➡ Effective teams are made up of 'individuals' (often from different backgrounds and with different experiences) performing different roles or functions. They are not developed immediately but go through a number of phases.

➡ The varied composition of teams almost inevitably results in conflict, especially in the early stages of team development.

➡ Conflict can be a positive source of creativity and new ideas, and the entrepreneurial manager needs to harness this for the benefit of the organization.

➡ To do this he/she should aim to adopt a solution-oriented strategy that reaches collaborative rather than compromise agreements.

Quick Revision

(Answers at the end of this section)

1. Within a team, the chairperson stimulates others to action. Is this:
   (a) true
   (b) false?

2. Which of the following is not one of the stages in team formation (i.e. which is the odd one out)?
   (a) forming
   (b) storming
   (c) norming
   (d) bonding
   (e) performing
   (f) adjourning

3. Self-management is probably most successful when teams are:

   (a) uni-functional

   (b) cross-functional?

4. Conflict can be good for an organization as it can stimulate creativity and new ideas. Is this:

   (a) true

   (b) false?

5. Collaboration is preferable to compromise as a means of conflict resolution as it results in 'win-win' situations. Is this:

   (a) true

   (b) false?

Answers to Quick Revision: 1–b; 2–d; 3–a; 4–a; 5–a

Learning Style Activities

➡ **Activist:** From your experience of the world of work, your family or any other situation relevant to you, identify a manager you know. How does he/she operate?

➡ **Reflector:** Reflect on the strengths and weaknesses of this person's managerial approach and relate it to the way entrepreneurs are expected to manage. How similar or different are they?

➡ **Theorist:** How do the theories of entrepreneurship help identify this person's managerial strengths or limitations?

➡ **Pragmatist:** How will your knowledge of this person affect you and the way you manage in the future?

Reading

Barry, D. (1991) Managing the Bossless Team: Lessons in Distributed Leadership. *Organisational Dynamics*, Summer, 31–47.

Belbin, M. (1981) Management Teams: Why they Succeed or Fail. Oxford: Butterworth-Heinemann.

Cohen, S.G. and D.E. Bailey (1997) What Makes Teams Work: Group Effectiveness Research from Shop Floor to Executive Suite. *Journal of Management* **23**, 239–90.

Galbraith, J.K. (1971) *The New Industrial State.* Boston: Houghton Mifflin.

Gordon, J. (1992) Work Teams. How Far Have They Come? *Training*, October, 59–65.

Hackman, J.R. (1994) Trip Wires in Designing and Leading Workgroups. *Occupational Psychologist* **23**, 3–8.

Kirkman, B.L. and B. Rosen (1999) Beyond Self-management: Antecedents and Consequences of Team Empowerment. *Academy of Management Journal* **42**, 58–74.

Orsburn, J.D., L. Moran, E. Musselwhite and J.H. Zenger (1990) *Self-directed Work Teams: The New American Challenge.* Homewood IL: Business One Irwin.

Orth, C.D., H.E. Wilkinson and R.C. Benfari (1987) The Manager's Role as Coach and Mentor. *Organisational Dynamics*, Spring, 67.

Peters, T (1987) *Thriving on Chaos: Handbook for a Management Revolution*. London: Macmillan.

Quinn, R.E., S.R. Faerman, M.P. Thompson and M.R. McGrath (1990) *Becoming a Master Manager: A Competency Framework*. New York: John Wiley & Sons.

Timmons, J.A. (1999) *New Venture Creation: Entrepreneurship for the 21st Century*. Boston MA: Irwin McGraw-Hill.

Tuckman, B.W. (1965) Development Sequence in Small Groups. *Psychological Bulletin* **63**, 384–99.

Wickens, P. (1999) *Energising our Enterprise*. Basingstoke: Macmillan.

What's your conflict management style?

By Kathy Simmons*

This simple test will help you handle confrontation like a pro.

Whenever people spend significant amounts of time together, conflict inevitably arises. The test of a true professional lies in the manner in which they handle such disputes in the workplace. An important first step is understanding your personal conflict management style. This quiz will help to determine yours.

1. When someone offends you, which of these best describes your typical reaction?

   (a) I ignore it
   (b) I try to understand why they are behaving badly
   (c) I try to reason with the person
   (d) I let them know how firmly I feel

2. Conflict is brewing between two of your co-workers. You would be most likely to:

   (a) avoid both of them until it is over
   (b) observe the situation carefully prior to acting
   (c) act as a mediator
   (d) let them know how disappointed you are.

3. Your boss makes an unreasonable work request on a Friday afternoon that will take you most of the weekend to complete. What would you do?

* *Kathy Simmons practises what she preaches as the assistant vice-president of Canada Life Assurance Company in Atlanta, where she is responsible for over 100 employees. She credits Art Sharp, her writing mentor, and Jim Freeman, her father, with providing the encouragement and inspiration needed to author many management and career articles.*

(a) Grin and bear it.

(b) Find out more about why it is necessary, then comply.

(c) Suggest alternatives to get the job done without working excessive hours.

(d) Laugh and let the boss know that you have a life outside of work.

4. If a client or a customer became angry and hostile, your reaction would be:

(a) remain quiet; after all, the customer is always right

(b) hear them out, trying to understand their perspective

(c) begin thinking about creative solutions to the problem

(d) ask them to calm down and then loudly explain your position.

5. You've just had a huge misunderstanding with a co-worker. How would you resolve it?

(a) leave it alone

(b) wait a few days before initiating contact; time will put things in perspective

(c) make an effort to talk through what happened

(d) try to get the person to understand your position

6. A co-worker is taking advantage of you. How do you react?

(a) I just accept it

(b) I try to figure out why he or she is acting this way

(c) I persuade them to change their ways

(d) I 'have it out' with them

7. A heated argument breaks out during one of your meetings. How would you handle it?

(a) adjourn the meeting and leave

(b) keep quiet and watch

(c) try to facilitate the discussion

(d) take sides with the person who agreed with me

8. My co-workers usually describe me as:

(a) quiet

(b) a good listener

(c) convincing

(d) bossy.

9. One of my greatest strengths is:

(a) the ability to stay out of trouble with people

(b) reading between the lines

(c) persuading others

(d) getting others to do what I want them to do.

10. When I have serious disagreements with someone, I often:

(a) remain quiet and hope it blows over soon

(b) listen and make sure I understand their point of view

(c) think of ways I can get the other side to understand my position

(d) continue talking until I am sure the other person understands.

Now add up all your (a), (b), (c) and (d) answers. Your conflict management style depends on which letter you choose most often. Read through the appropriate paragraph below.

(a) Avoidance
You avoid conflict at all costs and go to great extremes to keep the peace. You often resent others, but actually keep your feelings hidden and repressed. Good assertiveness skills training would help conquer your fear of conflict and turn you into an impact player at work.

(b) Analysing
You have the ability to remain calm in the face of conflict, and to understand or analyse other viewpoints. Listening is one of your strengths, but you do have a tendency to cave in to keep harmony. If you work on clearly communicating your emotions to others, then both parties can achieve a win-win solution.

(c) Assertive
You are persuasive and adept in matters of negotiation. You love to win people over to your side. Conflict does not scare you. You view it as a challenge and do not shy away from opportunities to manage it effectively. To improve your conflict management, try to focus on improving your listening skills.

(d) Aggressive
You like to have the upper hand. Conflict resolution is hampered by your need to control the situation. You tend to 'steamroll' over quieter individuals. To increase your successful conflict outcomes, work on softening your approach and listening to others. Remaining calm will actually give you more power.

   http://www.careerbuilder.com/wl_ga_0012_conflictmanagement.html

Section **3**

Entrepreneurship and the Organization

Chapter **9**

The Entrepreneurial New Venture

Learning Outcomes

On completion of this chapter, the reader will:

- appreciate the nature and character of the entrepreneurial new venture, and how it differs from more traditional enterprises
- understand that, strategically, it is managed differently from the large corporation and is more flexible
- recognize the organizational forms that are more suited to the creation of an entrepreneurial organization and culture
- appreciate the distinction between an entrepreneurial organizational culture and an administrative or bureaucratic culture
- recognize the importance of the reward system in shaping organizational culture, and the need for a reward system that reinforces the strategic orientation of the enterprise.

Introduction

Reference has already been made (in Chapters 2 and 3) to the fact that entrepreneurship is frequently equated with small businesses and new venture creation, and that new ventures are frequently seen as the manifestation of an enterprise culture. However, although the literature often fails to distinguish between the new venture and the entrepreneurial venture, it is generally accepted that there is a distinction between the two: not all small businesses can be regarded as being entrepreneurial and not all new ventures are the product of entrepreneurial activity. Indeed, Kao (1997: 237–8) has suggested that, '. . . even those who relate entrepreneurship with business undertakings have noted that only those who innovate and develop new combinations are entrepreneurs'. For him, therefore, innovation is the key and, as has been shown in previous chapters, creativity and innovation are certainly two of the distinguishing features of the entrepreneur. There are others, though, as has also been shown, and as the new, small business normally reflects the character and values of its founder, it might be expected that an entrepreneurial venture will portray the characteristics of the founding entrepreneur. Although there is no standard definition of the characteristics and attributes of the entrepreneur, as was shown in Chapter 5, it might be expected that the entrepreneurial venture, whether it is new or established, would portray many, if not all, of the 19 attributes identified by Timmons *et al.* (1985), for example. Thus, an entrepreneurial venture might display the following characteristics, among others:

- goal-oriented
- visionary
- motivated and committed to growth
- opportunistic
- proactive
- innovative
- flexible
- prepared to take risks and/or be able to cope with ambiguity and uncertainty
- tolerant of failure
- informal
- collegial
- an enjoyable (fun) place in which to work
- responsive to feedback.

Entrepreneurs do not necessarily possess all of the attributes identified by Timmons and his colleagues, however, and there is no agreement over whether these are, in fact the sole attributes. Hence, it is not quite as easy as it might seem to describe (or create) the entrepreneurial venture. Indeed, this might be why so many of the major entrepreneurship texts fail either to describe or distinguish between the entrepreneurial venture and the small business. If the two are not necessarily synonymous, as appears to be the case, clearly it is necessary to look into the nature and characteristics of the entrepreneurial venture in more detail and to decide, if at all possible, what it actually constitutes.

PAUSE FOR THOUGHT

Think of any new ventures with which you are familiar. Would you regard them all as entrepreneurial? If so, what distinguishes them from non-entrepreneurial, traditional ventures? If not, why are some different from others?

Entrepreneurial ventures

In Chapter 1, attention was paid to Schumpeter's (1934) theory that entrepreneurship is an economic process of creative destruction, in which wealth is created when entrepreneurs introduce new products or services that displace existing ones. Miller (1983) has taken this further and suggested that entrepreneurship is an organizational-level process and that businesses with an entrepreneurial orientation are innovative, proactive and prepared to take risks. He contends that the entrepreneurial orientation of a business is demonstrated by the extent to which it is inclined to continuously innovate in order to gain competitive advantage over its competitors, to proactively seize market opportunities and to take business-related risks.

It has long been known that innovation strategies are the surest way to gain a sustainable edge. So it might be expected that an entrepreneurial new venture is one that has an organizational culture that values innovation, is receptive to ideas and is willing to experiment in order to gain advantage over its competitors. In the process it will have to take risks and be prepared to tolerate failure as not all new ideas will succeed. Launching a new product (be it goods or services) is obviously a risky activity as it is difficult to predict with any certainty the reactions of either the customer or competitors. Hence, in order to minimize the risk, the enterprising venture needs to be close to the market, proactively seeking out new opportunities in response to customer feedback. This is consistent with the findings of von Hippel (1986), who reports that firms that are successful at innovation work closely with their customers. Indeed, it would suggest that entrepreneurial ventures are market oriented—they are responsive to market demand and in the process actively generate market intelligence (about customers, competitors, the market, etc.) and disseminate this information about the market throughout the organization (Kohli and Jaworski, 1990). Thus an entrepreneurial organization is one that is:

- innovative
- prepared to take risks
- proactive
- close to the market
- responsive to customer needs.

Gibb (1987) takes this a stage further by suggesting that central to the various essences of successful entrepreneurship in independent business is the concept of 'ownership'. By this he does not just mean ownership in the financial or legal sense, 'but the total self-identification with its success or failure' (1987: 24). At the heart of the concept of 'ownership' is, therefore, that of commitment—the motivation to see the project through to its (successful) conclusion. However, Gibb also identifies several other characteristics, or essences, of the successful entrepreneurial organization, as outlined below.

- Independence, flexibility and control—the freedom of the entrepreneur 'essentially to mix policy and practice, strategy and operational plan how he/she likes within the constraints of the market' (1987: 26).

- Holistic management. Often the resource constraints on the new venture mean that there is an absence of specialist functional managers. This not only gives the owner-manager an insight into the total operation of the business, but helps ensure that no one function dominates (see Chapter 12), and supports the 'necessary flexibility in the organisation' (1987: 26).

- Incrementality. This is the process of developing by taking small, rather than large, steps. It implies a process of continuous change in response to changing market needs and provides an opportunity for both 'learning from doing' and 'learning from failure'.

- Personal strategic and environmental awareness with rewards linked to the market. In the owner-managed entrepreneurial business, personal and business strategies are almost synonymous and 'the business strategy represents the personal commitment of the owner with close synonymity between family and business fortune' (1987: 27). Personal rewards are never seen as guaranteed but are linked to success in the marketplace.

Gibb's concept of 'successful entrepreneurship' has parallels with what Peters (1987) has called the 'winning look' of the successful firm. According to him, such firms will be:

- much faster at innovation
- more responsive
- oriented towards differentiation, producing high-value goods and services, creating niches
- quality-conscious
- service-conscious
- flatter (fewer layers of organizational structure)
- populated by more autonomous units
- users of highly trained, flexible people.

Attention has been paid, already, to the need for the entrepreneurial venture to be proactive and responsive to changes in the market. Clearly, all organizations, and especially new ventures, have limited resources. They are unable to take advantage of each and every opportunity that comes their way. As a consequence, if they are to succeed, they have to audit their own resources (i.e. identify their own strengths and weaknesses) and those of their competitors, and identify for themselves a niche in the marketplace, whereby they can differentiate themselves from the competition. In reality, most organizations adopt what might be termed a market sharing strategy—they try to identify established markets and determine how to gain a share of them (i.e. how they can take market share from the competition). If they cannot do this, either they do not enter the market or they withdraw. In contrast, the entrepreneurial organization is more likely, through innovation and creativity, to create new market opportunities, very largely through the application of technology, and a commitment to quality and service. Essentially, therefore, the more successful entrepreneurial organization differentiates itself from the competition by consistently identifying and creating new markets, rather than by finding ways of sharing the existing market. However, this does not mean that the only entrepreneurial firms are those that create new markets. Those that increase their share of the market by providing a product that is better or cheaper than that of the competition may also be regarded as entrepreneurial, and clearly innovations in technology, quality and service are all important here. Innovations that can improve the product and/or drive down the costs of its production are integral to this process, as are those that can increase customer satisfaction and delight.

To be fast at innovation, entrepreneurial organizations need an organizational structure that is different from the traditional vertical structures that typify many established organizations. With their sequential operations and co-ordination requirements, vertical structures frequently lengthen reaction times and hinder technological innovation. Equally, because they tend to follow traditional functional lines of responsibility, they tend to stultify the creativity that comes from cross-functional interaction and dialogue. As various authors have demonstrated (Hitt *et al.*, 1993; Woodman *et al.*, 1993), mixed-experience autonomous work teams are often more creative than single-function groups and develop new products faster. Thus an entrepreneurial organization needs to adopt a flatter, more horizontal organization, making it more time-efficient and productive (Hitt *et al.*, 1998b).

As Hitt and Reed (2000: 41) have recognized:

66 99 . . . firms that implement such structures, however, face the challenge of creating new mind-sets for workers familiar with the traditional vertical hierarchy. Independent frames of reference must be removed and replaced with a cross-functional, entrepreneurial view of the firm.

This is not easy, especially when it is appreciated that in the truly entrepreneurial venture, each of the employees is required to act as an entrepreneur. Not all employees have the ability to operate in this way, while some of those that have are simply more comfortable with the more traditional approaches to management:

66 99 They want to know what their job is, and they don't want a great deal of ambiguity in their daily work lives. They prefer to have an hourly rate, earn overtime, go home, and forget about the job. They like to have the ability to say no and to avoid responsibility.

(Miles et al., 2000: 111)

So, in Peters' terms, the successful entrepreneurial organization employs highly trained, flexible people who are capable of working in autonomous units. However, there is more to it than just identifying and employing them. Once they have been engaged, they need to be invested in. As Amit *et al.* (2000: 93) have recognized, 'organisations cannot expect their members to make informed decisions and be accountable for those decisions unless they have received an adequate level of training, education and autonomy'. This is important; successful entrepreneurial ventures do not just recruit highly trained, flexible staff in order to add value, they continue to train them. In this respect, therefore, the entrepreneurial venture is similar to Senge's (1990) learning organization in that 'characterised by adaptive structures, learning organisations meet the forces of change with multi-skilled incumbents who work relentlessly to improve their firm's strategic position' (Amit *et al.*, 2000: 93). However, while possessing such shared characteristics, an entrepreneurial organization is more than just a learning organization in that the intention is not to produce an organization that achieves competitive advantage through being smarter or more intelligent but through nurturing within it a culture of curiosity and innovation, in which individuals can act with autonomy. Thus an entrepreneurial organization is one that employs and empowers highly trained staff and continues to invest in them. In this respect the entrepreneurial venture is more like Handy's (1992) learning organization, which is characterized by four key factors: curiosity (to find the right answer), forgiveness (to encourage experimentation), trust (to avoid wasting time on checking things) and togetherness.

This concept of empowerment is equally difficult. According to Miles *et al.* (2000: 113) 'probably the most important notion in developing entrepreneurial competencies . . . is that workers at all levels of the organisation must have the opportunity and freedom to utilise them'. Many owner-managers are not ready to give up control of their businesses. Apart from losing control, however, many either do not trust their staff or believe they have the capability or role in the organization to 'think' and contribute to the development of the venture through idea generation. Their job is not to think but to carry out the management's decisions, for which incentives are required, primarily the stick but secondarily the carrot. Essentially, this is McGregor's (1960) Theory X. Not only does such a philosophy reveal a certain basic insecurity in the manager and his/her ability to lead, in reality it also demonstrates a lack of confidence in his/her ability to recruit quality staff. If the right staff have been recruited and trained appropriately, they will want to contribute to the success of the organization, and many will be capable of generating ideas that will help the organization. This is McGregor's Theory Y, which contends that employees want to work, enjoy their work, and have a sense of responsibility and commitment to their employer and to those they work with. Such people are motivated by recognition, praise and job challenge rather than monetary rewards.

All too frequently, though, this is not the case, even in ventures that purport to be entrepreneurial. As a consequence, by limiting the level at which entrepreneurial action takes place, invariably organizations are missing significant opportunities. Thus the truly entrepreneurial venture recognizes the entrepreneurial talent within its organization and creates a culture to harness it.

Entrepreneurial strategy: strategic management

Strategic management in the entrepreneurial venture is very different from that found in the more traditional types of organization. To understand it, and how it differs from the normative strategic management models, it is perhaps easiest to conceptualize the entrepreneurial venture in terms of Mintzberg's (1983) five-fold organizational typology. This identifies the following types of organization.

- The simple organization. This is characterized by informality, limited role definition and dependence on the founder (strategic head). In the absence of bureaucracy and 'red tape' it is responsive and innovative.

- The bureaucratic organization. This is characterized by a mechanistic approach to management, routinization and departmentalization. It is resistant to change and committed to meeting targets with respect to efficiency and effectiveness. Essentially it manifests itself in two forms—the machine bureaucracy and the professional bureaucracy. While the 'machine' bureaucracy (typified by the large manufacturing plant) is committed to standardization and mass production, the 'professional' bureaucracy (typified by public bodies) is about protecting professional standards and individual professional autonomy. In a machine bureaucracy, as the name implies, the management process is highly mechanistic with little opportunity for consultation and an emphasis on control. As Mintzberg (1983: 168) observes, 'the problem is not to develop an open atmosphere where people can talk things out, but to enforce a closed, tightly controlled one where work can get done despite them'. In contrast, in the professional bureaucracy—typified, perhaps, by the archetypal university—the professionals normally control their own work and although there is democracy, decisions are made by and through unwieldy and inflexible committees that reinforce the bureaucratic process, and protract decision-making and responsiveness.

- The **divisionalized organization** is typical of large corporations. Usually it comprises a head office, where the power lies, and one or more divisions, which have their own structures. As the divisional managers have little or no power and the autonomy of the divisions is limited, usually the divisions take the form of a machine bureaucracy, with the result that entrepreneurial and innovative behaviour is not encouraged and there tends to be a culture that resists growth and change.

- The **adhocracy** is a highly organic structure that pays little attention to the traditional principles of management and tends to be organized around a matrix structure (see below). It employs formally trained specialists and, in order to facilitate innovation and avoid bureaucracy, it pays little attention to traditional management principles and practices, adopting a facilitative approach that involves liaison, negotiation and co-ordination. The whole objective is to create novel solutions to problems, and accordingly managers, rather than supervising, tend to be part of the specialist teams that make up the organization. The environment tends to be somewhat unstructured and power is decentralized. As a consequence of the resultant role ambiguity, senior managers need to be capable of defusing conflicts. As might be anticipated, this is a difficult organizational form to sustain and the tendency is for it to develop into a bureaucracy, thereby destroying its innovative capability.

Thus, in Mintzberg's terms, entrepreneurial ventures are clearly characterized by simple structures and adhocracy. Indeed, it is possibly for this reason that they are frequently regarded as being somewhat chaotic. Typically, managers in such ventures 'find themselves going in many directions, trying to seize multiple opportunities, overcome staffing and financial problems, establish a presence in the marketplace, and keep afloat or manage greater-than-expected growth' (Eisenhardt *et al.*, 2000: 55). This leads Eisenhardt *et al.* (2000) to suggest that the strategic management of entrepreneurial organizations is essentially a balancing act on the edge of chaos. The alternative to the entrepreneurial venture is the bureaucracy, with its emphasis on structure, tight control, lack of flexibility and

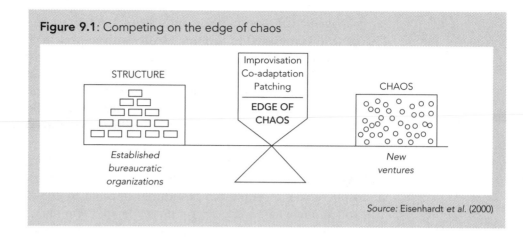

Figure 9.1: Competing on the edge of chaos

Source: Eisenhardt *et al.* (2000)

risk aversion. Such organizations do not easily adapt to change, while a 'chaotic' organization, with little or no structure, does not have the mechanisms in place to co-ordinate change. Thus neither is the optimum organizational form and, as a consequence, it is argued, the ideal position lies in between, at what Eisenhardt *et al.* call the 'edge of chaos' (see Fig. 9.1).

Additionally they suggest that a similar balance has to be struck with respect to time. Large, bureaucratic organizations have normally experienced past success and while this can assist the organization in terms of its progression along the learning curve, it can also block flexibility and the organization's responsiveness to changing conditions. In contrast, entrepreneurial ventures, and particularly new ones, tend to be focused on the future, with a lack of interest in the past and the lessons to be learned from it. Again, neither extreme is the optimum as an organization that focuses on the past has difficulty moving forward while one that focuses on the future tends to make mistakes that could have been avoided—history repeats itself. Thus the ideal position is in between, at the 'edge of time' (see Fig. 9.2), where managers can balance the past and the future, as well as the evolution between them.

Having identified the need to balance both chaos and time in managing the entrepreneurial venture, Eisenhardt *et al.* (2000: 56) go on to contest that in order to do this and make entrepreneurship a standard strategic practice, six processes need to be involved. These are as follows.

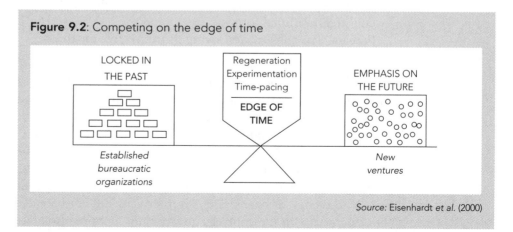

Figure 9.2: Competing on the edge of time

Source: Eisenhardt *et al.* (2000)

1. Improvisation—the ability for managers to operate flexibly within the constraints of minimum structures or rules. The analogy, here, is with the performing arts where the actors are 'fuelled' by the audience; and improvisation, when matched with the more traditional skills, results in innovation (Crossan *et al.*, 1996). In the business context, managers competing at the edge of chaos are fuelled by the dynamism of the market, but they can only adapt to it and innovate if they have strong, basic skills, operate with minimum structures and controls, and engage in real-time communication.

2. Co-adaptation or collaboration. Even though managers need to be autonomous, collaboration is important in order to extend the resources of the organization and capture the synergy that comes from effective networking, and the creation of strategic alliances and partnerships.

3. Patching. This is basically being aware of the 'holes' that appear in organizations as a result of market shifts, and being prepared to realign the business in order to match the market and 'patch' over the holes.

4. Regeneration. This recognizes that building on the past is critical for creating competitive advantage, but appreciates that it is necessary to abandon certain cash cows, while they are still profitable, in order to concentrate on new, often risky yet potentially higher-yielding opportunities. The goal is to provide a balance between old and new, and to create a stream of incremental, rather than revolutionary, changes. In the process, organizations are not only regenerated but can move into new competitive spaces.

5. Experimentation—trying things out (a) to see if they work and (b) to keep ahead of the competition and maintain first-mover advantage. Linked to this, clearly, is the ability to learn from failure.

6. Time-pacing. This implies that organizations change not as a result of some externally triggered event but proactively as a result of predetermined transition points. This 'helps managers avert the dangers of changing too frequently' (Brown and Eisenhardt, 1998: 67) yet, at the same time, introduces a minimum structure to ensure continuous innovation and allows for constant reassessment of an organization's actions.

Clearly such strategic management is very different from the traditional annual planning exercises and subsequent implementation activities requiring leadership, direction and control. Instead it is based on a set of temporal processes that encourages 'the rhythmic flow of change over time' (Eisenhardt *et al.*, 2000: 58) and eschews the temptation to build 'on the past along rigid lines of presumed strategic advantage' (2000: 58). Such an exercise is not easy, especially as finding the edge of chaos in new ventures usually requires putting discipline or structure into the organization, which can reduce its entrepreneurial capacity. However, this need not necessarily be the case, and the introduction of rules and appropriate enabling systems can actually permit greater creativity so that, when coupled with edge-of-time processes, the processes involved at the edge of chaos can create (according to Brown and Eisenhardt, 1998: 4) 'a "competing on the edge" strategy—an unpredictable, uncontrollable, and even inefficient strategy that nonetheless . . . works', facilitating reinvention, growth and market dominance.

Entrepreneurial strategy: strategic flexibility

The objective of strategic planning is to position the firm so that it has strategic advantage over its competitors. According to Porter (1980) competitive advantage is the competitive edge a firm has over its rivals based on its strengths or distinctive competences. Good strategy, therefore, produces sustainable competitive advantage and, according to Porter (1985), there are three generic strategies that can produce this effect. These are:

- 'low-cost leadership'—being cheaper than the competition
- 'differentiation'—being different from (usually better than) the competition, and
- 'focus or niche'—serving a segment of the market whose needs are not served well by the competition.

Clearly each strategy has a set of advantages and disadvantages, and the choice of strategy depends on the strengths of the organization relative to the competition (i.e. its distinctive competences). However, unless a new venture has invented a process for providing a product (be it goods or services) cheaper than the competition, thereby giving it a clear distinctive competence over its rivals, it is not usual for a new firm to enter the market via a low-cost strategy, as the costs of start-up require that prices are kept high. This suggests that most new ventures need to compete using either a differentiation or a focus strategy.

As discussed previously, one of the distinctive competences of the entrepreneurial venture is its innovativeness, and Sonfield and Lussier (1997) have suggested that a more helpful way of positioning the entrepreneurial venture, strategically, is in terms of innovation (its ability to create a unique and different product) and risk (the probability of major financial loss). As Fig. 9.3 reveals, by using this categorization ventures can be classified as being:

- high innovation–low risk (I-r)
- high innovation–high risk (I-R)
- low innovation–low risk (i-r)
- low innovation–high risk (i-R).

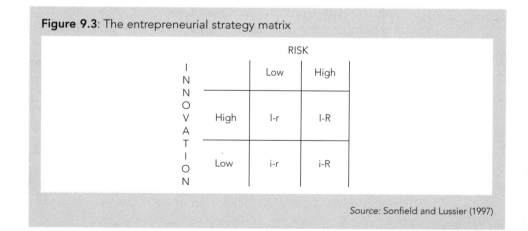

Figure 9.3: The entrepreneurial strategy matrix

Source: Sonfield and Lussier (1997)

Table 9.1: Appropriate entrepreneurial strategies

	RISK	
	Low	**High**
High	(I-r)	(I-R)
	Move quickly	Reduce risk by lowering investment and operating costs
	Protect innovation	Maintain innovation
	Lock in investment and operating costs via control systems, contracts and other measures	Outsource high-investment operations
		Joint venture options
INNOVATION	(i-r)	(i-R)
	Defend present position	Increase innovation; develop a competitive advantage
	Accept limited payback	Reduce risk
	Accept limited growth potential	Use business plan and object analysis
		Minimize investment
		Reduce financing costs
		Franchise option
		Abandon venture?
Low		

Source: Sonfield and Lussier (1997)

Clearly certain positions are more preferable (I-r) than others (i-R) and ventures require different strategies either to move from one position to another or to increase their propensity for innovation and reduce their exposure to risk. The appropriate strategies, according to Sonfield and Lussier (1997), are shown in Table 9.1.

Whichever strategy is adopted, however, to retain competitive advantage firms must be able to respond quickly to changing competitive conditions. To do this, they must be continuously rethinking their strategic actions and, importantly, developing their distinctive core competences—those resources that are non-imitable or for which there are no substitutes. Firms build competitive advantage by utilizing their distinctive core competences but those that 'do not invest in and update their core competences, in effect allowing them to become static, risk competences' becoming outdated, thus limiting their strategic options in the future' (Hitt and Reed, 2000, 36). Indeed, when a firm allows its core competences to become rigid, it not only restricts its strategic options but, quite frequently, has to develop an entirely new set in order to become competitive once more (Hitt *et al.*, 1998a). From the outset, therefore, the successful entrepreneurial new venture not only adopts an appropriate strategy, based on its core competences, to give it competitive advantage, but retains a considerable degree of strategic flexibility and continues to develop its core competences in order both to respond to changes in the environment and to keep ahead of the competition.

Organizational form

There is no one organizational form that typifies entrepreneurial ventures, other than, perhaps, the simple structure used by most small owner-managed firms, at least in the early stages of their development. Under such a structure all of the key decisions are made by the owner-manager and everything of significance affecting the business is referred to him/her. He/she provides the entrepreneurial dynamic for the organization and while it is natural for him/her to want to control the venture at the outset, it is unlikely that he/she will have expertise in all aspects of the business, which can be a limitation of this particular structure. Additionally, as the business grows, it is equally inevitable that the decision-making process will become too demanding and complex for one person, and the owner-manager usually has to relinquish some responsibilities. Normally these are the short-term decision-making processes, allowing him/her to concentrate on the more strategic aspects of developing the business. Whatever, a more formal structure begins to emerge, which can result in the organization losing its entrepreneurial dynamic (see Chapter 11).

Clearly, if this is to be avoided, the organizational form needs to give structure while, at the same time, providing the freedom to permit entrepreneurial action to take place anywhere in the organization. This means that some of the more traditional, mechanical forms of organizational structure are unlikely to be suitable as they are too rigid, routinized, hierarchical and formal to promote an entrepreneurial culture within the organization. Hence, it is the more flexible and fluid organic structures that are likely to foster the communication and innovation that is the prerequisite of the entrepreneurial venture (Burns and Stalker, 1961). However, there is no optimum structure for this purpose and it must be recognized that selection of the appropriate organizational structure is a strategic decision.

As entrepreneurial activity is typically a horizontal process that works best without management interference, it is important that the selected structure facilitates and supports lateral communication, co-ordinates entrepreneurial activity without senior management intervention, and encourages interaction between the organization and its environment. There are various organic structures that permit this, to a greater or lesser extent. These include the cellular structure, matrix structure, networked structure and the 'shamrock' structure. We will now look at each of these in turn.

The cellular structure

The concept of the cellular structure (or firms within firms) is borrowed from biological science (Miles et al., 1997) and, as such, carries with it two important notions:

- when cells combine, they create something (an organism) richer than the sum of the individual cells
- the idea of continuous evolution and growth.

As with living organisms, entrepreneurial ventures are made up of units (cells) that are self-governing, self-co-ordinating and self-initiating, enabling the organization (organism) to regenerate and expand its resources. Indeed, three characteristics that are integral to the success of the cellular organization are:

- acceptance of individual responsibility (taking ownership)
- commitment to self-organization and governance (permitting flexibility and strategic latitude)
- principles of individual and collective profitability (profit sharing).

While each cell (unit) has individual autonomy it must be working for the good of the organism (organization) as a whole. Equally, no cell is permitted to develop at the expense of another unless, as in the biological analogy, a cell is malfunctioning and needs treatment and/or removal. Such principles are apparent in the case example of the Burton Group under Sir Ralph Halpern (see Chapter 12), but it is in the knowledge industries where, according to Miles *et al.* (2000), the cellular form is emerging, since the generation and sharing of knowledge is particularly critical in this sector.

A CASE EXAMPLE

The Virgin empire

Although now a £3 billion operation with 200 companies employing 25,000 people, Sir Richard Branson's (see Chapter 5) Virgin group has no centralized Virgin headquarters, not even a corporate boardroom, as the company does not hold regular board meetings. Branson works as if he is running a start-up and communication is very informal as, according to him:

> One of the problems about formal meetings is that they lead to frustration. People who leave companies with formal structures don't leave because of salaries. If they come up with a good idea, they're told to wait until the next meeting. Then they're told they have to make another presentation to another group, then another. Then the board takes it on advisement. And he's gone off to another company. With Virgin, we make decisions on the phone. If you've got a good idea and I like it, you can get on with it.

For Branson, informality is crucial to the retention of an entrepreneurial, innovative culture, and a relatively informal system of communication is possible because the company is structured into 150 small companies. When any one of them itself grows large, it is split up. For example, Virgin Records, which became the largest recording label in the UK, was structured into 40 different companies before it was sold to Thorn EMI in 1992. However, according to Bower (2001) the real justification for such a cellular structure is the obfuscation of the company's finances.

> Under the guise of encouraging individual entrepreneurship, Virgin's different businesses had been spread in small offices around London, preventing his employees understanding his organization and blurring his juggling of money between companies.
>
> (Bower, 2001: 42)

According to Branson himself (in a 1997 interview with David Sheff of *Forbes* magazine), the company is structured this way in order to create a dynamic entrepreneurial culture within the organization.

> Each company has to stand on its own two feet, as if they are their own companies. Employees have a stake in their success. They feel—and are—crucial to their company because they are one in fifty or a hundred instead of tens of thousands. They indeed are all under the Virgin umbrella, but they are generally not subsidiaries. I'm over them to see if one company can't help another, but otherwise they are independent. Some people like the idea of growing fiefdoms—companies that brag about sales over $5 billion a year—but there is no logical reason to think there is anything good about huge companies. History, in fact, shows

the opposite. Those huge corporations with tentacles and divisions and departments become unwieldy, slow growing, stagnant. Some chairmen want them like that so that one division's loss can make up for another's profit, but we'd rather have a lot of exciting companies that are all making profits—as are all of ours.

It is neither informal communication nor organizational structure that, in Branson's view, is the most important element in the creation of a dynamic entrepreneurial venture. Clearly these are important, but for him the most important element is people—bringing in the best and keeping them motivated.

The girl who opened what will be the best bridal shop in Europe was flying on the airline as an air hostess. She came to me with an idea and I said, 'Go to it.' She did. Now it's Virgin Bride. By having the freedom to prove herself, she has excelled. Everyone you hire is important. You assume that every switchboard operator will excel and they will. Often people make mistakes, but you allow for that, too. Praise people—like

plants, they must be nurtured—and make it fun. Value them and give them the opportunity to contribute in ways that excite them. We're lucky because of the variety of places to go at Virgin. No one gets stagnant. When our people see an air hostess become managing director of her own business, there is motivation.

Interestingly, Branson has never read a business text nor taken a course in management. While recognizing that people can learn a lot from these, he regards himself as fortunate in that he has learned by experience—by trying and from making mistakes. As he says, 'I've learned every day by doing things different and new.'

Case example exercise

Review the Virgin case and the literature, and evaluate the benefits and limitations of cellular organizational structures. Do you believe that the Virgin group would have been as successful if it had adopted any other organizational form? Justify your answer.

The matrix structure

This enables greater co-ordination and co-operation across functions, and the formation of cross-functional teams as the organization is structured into a lattice composed of functions on the vertical axis and products or projects on the horizontal. When it works effectively, which requires expert management, such a structure:

- releases functional managers from routine tasks and enables them to focus on more strategic issues
- engages the staff as decisions are made at the level of the group, which become self-managed teams
- encourages flexibility, responsiveness and innovation.

The networked structure

This is either a collection of individuals or units from within an organization (intra-organizational networks) or collections of individual businesses (inter-organizational networks). Normally such networks are not flat but multi-levelled with clusters and different hierarchical structures. Although the individual members are independent, they recognize the benefits to be derived from collaboration and the links between them are strengthened through interaction. The intention is that by creating a system of loosely coupled units, the members can respond quickly to new opportunities in the marketplace. Thus the network members have common objectives and it is this unified purpose that holds them together. In reality, however, the network only responds as fast as the slowest member of the chain and it is found that the most suitable firms for membership of a network are those that 'make extensive use of teams and other lateral mechanisms both within the firm and between the firm and its partners, so that they are able to shift resources to meet the demands of the environment . . .' (Miles *et al.*, 2000: 105).

An emerging technological version of the network organization is the virtual corporation, which is a network of businesses, linked through information technology, that come together to share skills, costs and markets in order to exploit opportunities. The hub of the virtual corporation is the virtual web, which is an open-ended pool of partners who agree to form the members of the virtual corporation. While the corporation is the micro-level performing unit, the web is the macro-level organizational framework (Franke, 1999). Essentially the web has six attributes:

1. the partners have distinct resources and complementary core competences that facilitate the development of a world-class value chain

2. the ability to unite quickly to exploit a market opportunity

3. high levels of co-operation among the members, based on trust and complementarity

4. high levels of motivation among the members, based on the fear of letting down the other members of the web and not being invited to participate in future

5. joint planning, operation and control

6. few spatial constraints, resulting from the use of information technology and the Internet.

Crucial to the success of the virtual corporation is the net-broker, the facilitator of the organizational network. He/she acts as the catalyst and is responsible for identifying and creating business opportunities, as well as combining resources to form new ventures.

A CASE EXAMPLE

The Body Shop International plc

In 1976, The Body Shop was one small retail outlet in Brighton, England, selling 25 hand-mixed products. By 2000, it had evolved to a worldwide network of 1730 outlets employing in excess of 4000 people in 47 countries and with a turnover of £634.6 million and over 400 products. Of the total number of stores, 1300 are franchised operations and The Body Shop International owns the UK, US, French, German and Singaporean operations with the remaining 43 independently owned and operating through master franchises in each country. According to the company's homepage (**www.the-body-shop.com/uk**) 'franchising allowed for rapid

growth and international expansion as hundreds of entrepreneurs worldwide bought into the vision'.

The company was founded in March 1976 by Anita Roddick OBE, the current co-chair. Selling naturally based beauty products in low-cost refillable containers with no other packaging, the business captured the mood of the times and proved to be highly successful. However, without the resources to finance expansion, she decided to grow the business through what she now recognizes is franchising. As she has said (Lessem, 1986: 151) 'franchising is a fantastic motivator. In retailing the biggest problem is staff. Yet when people run their own business they discover untapped energies.'

Apart from growth through franchising, the company's success has been based in part on its commitment to corporate responsibility and its espousal of ethical values in business, and in part on ensuring that the members of its network have been properly trained, both in the products sold and in the way The Body Shop conducts its business. Herself a former teacher, Anita Roddick has a strong commitment to education and believes that 'you sell by having the knowledge'. However, The Body Shop staff, though knowledgeable, are not forceful and do not sell aggressively, only offering advice when it is requested. The company is very much a human enterprise and, as a consequence, has aroused commitment, enthusiasm and loyalty in those associated with it, as well as its customers.

Shortly after setting up the business Roddick said:

> Aside from developing new products, I've always enjoyed the momentum of the high street. There's a constant coming and going. You cannot stand still. The basic house in which you accommodate your product changes. The products don't. I love that change area. There's a buzz. I also love knowing that we have unique and individual strengths. . . . We'll always be adding new products.
>
> *(Lessem, 1988)*

Not surprisingly, The Body Shop has been, and remains, an extremely innovative organization. Not only did it pioneer natural products that had not been tested on animals, encouraging many of the leading retail companies (including Boots and the US Bath and Body Works chain) to copy it, but over the years it has drawn attention to important issues relating to the environment and human rights, as well as initiating new ventures. Among the latter have been the launch of *The Big Issue* newspaper in Australia, the UK and California, the establishment of the New Academy of Business (which offers an innovative management degree specializing in environmental, social and ethical issues) and the setting up of The Body Shop Foundation, a charity that funds human rights and environmental protection groups. Since 1998, Patrick Gourney, the former executive vice-president of Danone's North and South American Division, has been the company's CEO and, according to Roddick, the company has 'gone through a period of squashing one hell of a lot of entrepreneurial spirit' (**www.ltbn.com/tribroddick.html**). Even so, it has continued to grow and has remained innovative. It has sold its manufacturing business, re-organized its operating structure into four regional business units and entered into partnership with SOFTBANK Venture Capital which, for a 24 per cent share of the business, is investing US$15 million to develop the company's e-commerce activity. The Body Shop Digital, as it is known, is run as a separate operation by a management team with a proven Internet track record. It is led by Andy Slack who founded 'abuzz', an Internet-based expertise network that was sold in 1999 to The New York Times Digital. According to Gourney, 'the global strength of The Body Shop brand, together with the expertise, resources and networking opportunities provided by SOFTBANK will ensure a new, exciting and highly differentiated internet presence' (Chief Executive's Review, 2000: 10) that will extend The Body Shop brand into Internet sites and businesses that are complementary in theme and demographics.

Case example exercise

Review the discussion of franchising and other forms of networking in Chapter 3 and consider the benefits of such organizational forms for the growth of entrepreneurial ventures such as The Body Shop. Could The Body Shop have grown as swiftly and successfully if it had not adopted franchising?

From what you know of The Body Shop and franchising, do you believe that the present demise of The Body Shop is related to its organizational structure and the way it has grown? Justify your answer.

The 'shamrock' structure

First mooted by Handy (1993), the 'shamrock' organization (see Fig. 9.4) has three components:

1. the core personnel who maintain the strategy and core activities of the organization

Figure 9.4: The shamrock structure (after Handy, 1993)

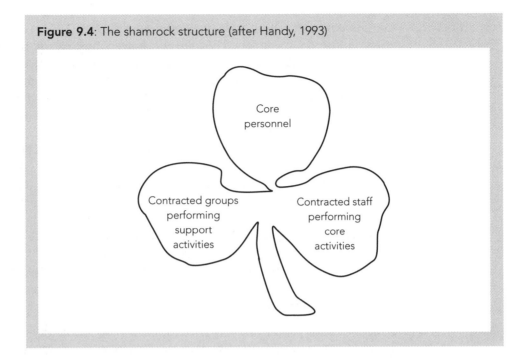

2. contracted or associate staff who perform the organization's core activities

3. outsourced bodies (contracted groups) that perform the 'support' activities.

While the core activities are outsourced to individuals (associates), not organizations, and the associates come together when necessary, increasingly such structures have the clear potential to be 'totally electronic, with no clear real-world, physical identity' (Barnatt, 1997: 37). They are favoured by entrepreneurs because of their relatively low operating costs, facilitating both market entry and start-up, their flexibility and ease of modification, and their growth potential. However, they are difficult to manage as it is not easy to sustain the relationship. Usually the agents on which the business relies for its core activities are 'free', often with portfolio careers and little loyalty to it. Additionally, innovation can be problematic as, unless specifically contracted to do so, the associates rarely engage in essential research and development, normally acting as outworkers commissioned to carry out very specific activities.

Entrepreneurial culture

Inevitably the culture of any venture is influenced, if not created, by the founder who imprints his/her values on to it. Hence if founded by a true entrepreneur, the culture of a new venture might be expected to be entrepreneurial. However, the culture of any organization is determined, also, by the organization's structure—by the way the founder delegates authority and divides up responsibilities. Hence the culture of the organization can be viewed as a result of its organizational form. As might be expected, therefore, from the discussion in the previous section, there are those cultures that encourage and reward innovation and initiative, and those that discourage it. These are what Kotter and Heskett (1992) term 'adaptive' and 'inert' cultures, respectively. They are epitomized most clearly by the Dell organization and IBM. At IBM, the culture of the firm not only led to the belief that mainframe computers would always be the dominant product design, but it encouraged conservatism, risk aversion and a reluctance to challenge the status quo. When the company did realize that this was not the case and that the future of the computer industry lay not in mainframes but in personal computers and interactive networking software, the company's hierarchical, centralized structure slowed the decision-making process and made it difficult to change. In contrast Michael Dell has always tried to keep the company as flat as possible and to create a customer-service culture. He has done this by decentralizing authority and decision-making, and by encouraging all employees to get as close to the customer as possible, to ensure both high-quality customer service and that the company is aware of, and responds to, changes in the market.

This leads to a consideration of the traits that characterize adaptive cultures; Peters and Waterman (1982) have suggested that there are essentially three sets of values, which ensure that the business:

- has a bias for action whereby the emphasis is on autonomy and initiative, and employees are encouraged to take risks; managers are not simply involved in strategic decision-making but in the day-to-day operation of the firm
- focuses on both what it does best and, importantly, on its customers as a means of improving its competitive position
- respects and motivates its employees to give of their best and gives them the latitude to make decisions and the support to enable them to succeed, yet at the same time is sufficiently centralized to ensure that the business pursues its strategic mission.

Table 9.2: Cultural attributes of entrepreneurial and administrative organizations (after Chell, 2000)

Entrepreneurial	Administrative
External focus	Internal focus
Task-oriented	Status-oriented
Risk-taking	Safety-conscious
Individuality	Conformity
Group rewards	Individual rewards
Collective decision-making	Individual decision-making
Decentralized decision-making	Centralized decision-making
'Adhocery'	Planning
Innovation	Stability
Competition	Co-operation
Simple organization	Complex organization
Informality	Formality
Commitment to the mission	Commitment to the organization
Knowledge valued	Procedures valued

Table 9.3: Organizational culture dimensions (after Hofstede *et al.*, 1990)

Entrepreneurial	**Administrative**
Results	Process
Job	Employee orientation
Parochial	Professional interest
Open	Closed system
Loose	Tight control
Pragmatic	Normative orientation

Though it is important, as the example of IBM demonstrates, that the enterprise does not become so focused (on either what it does best or its own customers) that it becomes blinkered and does not see the broad changes that are taking place in the market, these may be regarded as the main cultural values of the successful entrepreneurial venture. However, Chell (2000) lists 14 cultural attributes which, she suggests, differentiate the entrepreneurial organization from the non-entrepreneurial or administrative organization. These are shown in Table 9.2.

While some might argue with the precise content of the listing, it does provide a useful insight into what distinguishes an entrepreneurial organization from a non-entrepreneurial organization, in terms of culture. Also, as she observes, it is consistent with the six organizational cultural dimensions defined by Hofstede *et al.* (1990), as shown in Table 9.3.

Once again, while there might be some debate over the precise attributes (e.g. over whether an administrative organization is more employee-oriented than an entrepreneurial organization), there appears to be broad agreement between Hofstede's cultural dimensions and the cultural values of Peters and Waterman (1982) outlined above.

PAUSE FOR THOUGHT

Think about a time when you have been positively 'rewarded'. What did you learn as a result of the reward? How did the reward affect you, in particular the way you thought and behaved?

Entrepreneurial reward systems

As the attitude of the founder and the structure of the organization can affect the culture of the firm, so too can the reward system. Indeed, reward systems are used to control and shape the behaviour of employees in organizations, and to provide important signals as to how senior management expect them to behave. Thus, reward systems are an important aspect of an entrepreneurial culture though few observers comment on them, as is noticeable above. Some obververs have provided a framework for comparing the characteristics of entrepreneurial and administrative organizations based on five major factors—strategic orientation, commitment to seize opportunities, commitment of resources, control of resources and management structure. Interestingly, however, this only considers reward systems with respect to the administrative culture under the topic of management structure, though clearly it is something that affects both types of organization, and can be used to reinforce the strategic orientation of the firm and to encourage the commitment to seize opportunities, in particular.

Traditional reward systems have tended to be based on individual performance (measured by achievement of short-term goals) and responsibility or status in the organization (measured by the control of assets or resources). In organizations where such systems are in place, the reward tends to be promotion and increased responsibility, linked to higher pay. In the entrepreneurial organization, the tendency is to reward value creation and teams rather than individuals. Whereas in the traditional organization rewards are based on not making mistakes, in the entrepreneurial organization reward can be, and often is, is associated with risk-taking, even if the risk results in 'failure' rather than success. Additionally, in the entrepreneurial organization rewards are often not linked solely to money. As early as 1968, Hertzberg emphasized that people are often motivated not just by money and status, but by:

- the potential to contribute and achieve through the job
- recognition for effort and success
- promotion opportunities
- interesting work
- responsibility.

In addition to these, there are other influences, including the freedom to decide how to do things, the opportunity to work with certain types of people, especially if they are successful, the sense of achievement, the opportunity to learn and develop, etc. As a consequence, the entrepreneurial organization recognizes, as pointed out above, that employees at all levels are motivated not just by monetary rewards but by recognition, praise and job challenges. Indeed, Kanter (1983: 154) suggests that the reward system in entrepreneurial organizations, in which innovation flourishes:

" " . . . emphasises investment in people and projects rather than payment for past services—for example, moving people into jobs for which they must stretch or giving them resources to tackle projects they define. The other important conclusion about rewards is that they occur throughout the accomplishment process rather than at the end. In the initiation stage, the incentive is the very chance to 'do something' itself. Later, there are rewards for teamwork. And at completion . . . many of the most meaningful rewards are those which put people in a position to begin the accomplishment cycle again on a larger scale . . .

The entrepreneurial venture is very different, therefore, from what might be termed the traditional administrative organization. It is not just different in terms of some of the ways in which it conducts its business, but in almost every aspect, though, as might be expected, there is no clear and definitive statement of what constitutes an entrepreneurial venture. Possibly the closest definitive statement is Kanter's (1983) description of 'Chipco', her pseudonym for a record-breaking entrepreneurial computer manufacturing firm based in America. This is summarized in Table 9.4.

Table 9.4: General characteristics of 'Chipco' (after Kanter, 1983)

Structure:	matrix, decentralized
Information flow:	free
Communication emphasis:	horizontal
Culture:	clear, consistent, favours individual initiative
Emotional climate:	pride in company, team feeling
Attitude to change:	change 'normal', constant change in product generation; proliferating staff and units
Rewards:	abundant—include visibility, chance to do more challenging work in the future, get bigger budget for projects

Chapter Review

➡ Much of the literature on entrepreneurship fails to distinguish between the new venture and the entrepreneurial venture, though the two are not necessarily synonymous.

➡ While innovation is a key characteristic of entrepreneurial ventures, there are others, such as:

 – a preparedness to take risks

 – proactivity

 – closeness to the market

 – responsiveness to customer needs.

➡ Strategically entrepreneurial ventures are managed very differently from the more traditional types of organization, frequently being on the edge of chaos and time.

➡ Being more flexible than the traditional organization, entrepreneurial ventures adopt a range of more flexible structures, including:

 – the cellular structure

 – the matrix structure

 – the shamrock structure.

➡ The culture of the entrepreneurial organization is different from that of the traditional; and the reward system, which greatly influences the culture of the enterprise, is seen more as an investment in the future rather than as a payment for past performance.

Quick Revision

(Answers at the end of this section)

1. What, according to Kao (1997), is the key feature of an entrepreneurial venture?

 (a) its ability to innovate and develop new combinations

(b) its size

(c) its age

(d) its ownership

2. When Gibb (1987) refers to 'ownership', he is talking about it in the legal and financial sense. Is this:

(a) true

(b) false?

3. Which of his organizational forms does Mintzberg regard as being that of the entrepreneurial venture?

(a) the simple organization

(b) the bureaucratic organization

(c) the divisionalized organization

(d) the adhocracy

4. In an entrepreneurial organization it is important that the selected organizational structure supports communication that is:

(a) lateral

(b) vertical?

5. Which, according to Peters and Waterman (1982), are the values that are not characteristic of an adaptive culture?

(a) a bias for action

(b) a focus on core competences and customers

(c) a concern for corporate procedures

(d) staff respect

Answers to Quick Revision: 1–a; 2–b; 3–d; 4–a; 5–c

Learning Style Activities

➡ **Activist:** Identify a venture that you regard as entrepreneurial and find out as much about how it is organized and managed as you can. What makes it different from the traditional organization?

➡ **Reflector:** Consider the results of your investigations and try to produce a model of the entrepreneurial venture.

➡ **Theorist:** Compare your model with the accepted body of theory. Could it be extended, modified or improved?

➡ **Pragmatist:** You are going to set up a new venture. What are the implications of all this for you? If you want your venture to be entrepreneurial, what will you have to do?

Reading

Amit, R.H., K. Brigham and G.D. Markman (2000) Entrepreneurial Management as Strategy, in Meyer, G.D. and K.A. Heppard (eds) *Entrepreneurship as Strategy: Competing on the Entrepreneurial Edge*. Thousand Oaks CA: Sage Publications, Inc.

Barnatt, C. (1997) Virtual Organisation in the Small Business Centre: The Case of Cavendish Management Resources. *International Small Business Journal* **15** (4), 36–47.

Bower, T. (2001) *Branson*. London: Fourth Estate.

Brown, S.L. and K.M. Eisenhardt (1998) *Competing on the Edge: Strategy as Structured Chaos*. Boston MA: Harvard Business School Press.

Burns, T. and G.M. Stalker (1961) *The Management of Innovation*. London: Tavistock.

Chell, E. (2000) *Entrepreneurship: Globalisation, Innovation and Development*. London: Thomson Learning.

Crossan, M.M., R.E. White, H.W. Lane and L. Klus (1996) The Improvising Organisation: Where Planning Meets Opportunity. *Organisational Dynamics* **24** (4), 20–35.

Eisenhardt, K.M., S.L. Brown and H.M. Neck (2000) Competing on the Entrepreneurial Edge, in Meyer, G.D. and K.A. Heppard (eds) *Entrepreneurship as Strategy: Competing on the Entrepreneurial Edge*. Thousand Oaks CA: Sage Publications, Inc.

Franke, U.J. (1999) The Virtual Web as a New Entrepreneurial Approach to Network Organisations. *Entrepreneurship and Regional Development* **11** (3), 203–29.

Gibb, A.A. (1987) Enterprise Culture—its Meaning and Implications for Education and Training. *Journal of European Industrial Training* **11** (2), 2–38.

Handy, C. (1992) *Managing the Dream: The Learning Organisation*. London: Gemini Consulting.

Handy, C. (1993) *The Age of Unreason*. London: Hutchinson.

Hertzberg, F. (1968) One More Time How Do You Motivate Employees? *Harvard Business Review*, January/February, 53–62.

Hitt, M.A. and T.S. Reed (2000) Entrepreneurship in the New Competitive Landscape, in Meyer, G.D. and K.A. Heppard (eds) *Entrepreneurship as Strategy: Competing on the Entrepreneurial Edge*. Thousand Oaks CA: Sage Publications, Inc.

Hitt, M.A., R.E. Hoskisson and R.D. Nixon (1993) A Mid-range Theory of Interfunctional Integration, its Antecedents and Outcomes. *Journal of Engineering and Technology Management* **10**, 151–85.

Hitt, M.A., B.W. Keats and S.M. DeMarie (1998a) Navigating in the New Competitive Landscape: Building Strategic Flexibility and Competitive Advantage in the 21st Century. *Academy of Management Executive* **12** (4), 22–42.

Hitt, M.A., R.D. Nixon, R.E. Hoskisson and R. Kochhar (1998b) Corporate Entrepreneurship and Cross-Functional Fertilisation. Activation, Process and Disintegration of a New Product Design Team. *Entrepreneurship: Theory and Practice* **23** (3), 145–67.

Hofstede, G., B. Neuijen, D.D. Ohayv and G. Sanders (1990) Measuring Organisational Cultures: A Qualitative and Quantitative Study Across Twenty Cases. *Administrative Science Quarterly* **35**, 286–316.

Kanter, R. (1983) *The Change Masters: Corporate Entrepreneurs at Work*. London: Unwin Hyman Ltd.

Kao, R.W. (1997) *An Entrepreneurial Approach to Corporate Management*. London: Prentice Hall.

Kohli, A.K. and B.J. Jaworski (1990) Market Orientation: The Construct, Research Propositions and Managerial Implications. *Journal of Marketing* **54** (April), 1–18.

Kotter, J.P and J.L. Heskett (1992) *Corporate Culture and Performance*. New York: Free Press.

Lessem, R. (1986) *Enterprise Development*. Aldershot: Gower.

Lessem, R. (1988) *Intrapreneurship: How to be an Enterprising Individual in a Successful Business*. Aldershot: Wildwood House.

McGregor, D.M. (1960) *The Human Side of Enterprise*. New York: McGraw-Hill.

Miles, G., K.A. Heppard, R.E. Miles and C.C. Snow (2000) Entrepreneurial Strategies: The Critical Role of Top Management, in Meyer, G.D. and K.A. Heppard (eds) *Entrepreneurship as Strategy: Competing on the Entrepreneurial Edge*. Thousand Oaks CA: Sage Publications, Inc.

Miles, R.E., C. Snow, J. Mathews, G. Miles and H. Coleman Jr (1997) Organising in the Knowledge Age; Anticipating the Cellular Form. *Academy of Management Executive* **11** (40), 7–20.

Miller, D. (1983) The Correlates of Entrepreneurship in Three Types of Firms. *Management Science* **27** (July), 770–91.

Mintzberg, H. (1983) *Structure in Fives: Designing Effective Organisations*. Englewood-Cliffs NJ: Prentice Hall.

Peters, T. (1987) *Thriving on Chaos: Handbook for a Management Revolution*. London: Macmillan.

Peters, T.J. and R.H. Waterman (1982) *In Search of Excellence: Lessons from America's Best-Run Companies*. New York: Harper and Row.

Porter, M.E. (1980) *Competitive Strategy: Techniques for Analyzing Industries and Competitors*. New York: Free Press.

Porter, M.E. (1985) *Competitive Advantage: Creating and Sustaining Superior Performance*. New York: Free Press.

Schumpeter, J. (1934) *The Theory of Economic Development*. Cambridge MA: Harvard University Press.

Senge, P.M. (1990) *The Fifth Discipline*. New York: Doubleday.

Sonfield, M.C. and R.N. Lussier (1997) The Entrepreneurial Strategy Matrix: A Model for New and Ongoing Ventures. *Business Horizons*, May/June, 73–7.

Stevenson, H.H. and D.E. Gumpert (1985) The Heart of Entrepreneurship. *Harvard Business Review*, March, 85–94.

Timmons, J.A.E., L.E. Smollen and A.L.M. Dingee (1985) *New Venture Creation*. Homewood IL: Irwin.

Von Hippel, E. (1986) Lead Users: A Source of Novel Product Concepts. *Management Science* **32** (July), 791–805.

Woodman, R.W., J.E. Sawyer and R.W. Griffin (1993) Toward a Theory of Organisational Creativity. *Academy of Management Review* **18**, 293–321.

10

New Venture Planning and Creation

Learning Outcomes

On completion of this chapter, the reader will:

- understand the importance of the business plan and the roles it plays in new venture creation
- be able to produce a business plan for a new venture
- be in a position to decide on the feasibility, or otherwise, of a project and use the business plan to raise finance, if appropriate
- understand the different methods of financing a new venture and be able to identify possible sources
- negotiate funding for a commercially feasible new venture and launch the enterprise.

Introduction

As discussed in Chapter 2, many new ventures fail, especially within the first two years of start-up. The reasons for this are numerous but the ability of the entrepreneur to manage the venture is paramount. Many new ventures are created without the requisite planning and preparation, and without the owner-manager having established the feasibility of the venture or appreciated the difficulties involved in its operation. Frequently those who start new businesses possess the technical, but not the managerial, skills and understanding to make them work. They are convinced by their idea and believe that customers will want to buy their products, be they goods or services. Once the businesses are up and running their owner-managers have neither the knowledge nor the systems to control and manage them, with the result that the businesses go out of control and the owner-managers learn the hard way, by trial and error. Often, in an era of intense competition, errors can be fatal. Hence if new ventures are to succeed, it is important to establish their feasibility from the outset and to put in place the controls that will help navigate them to success. This is done through the business plan.

PAUSE FOR THOUGHT

Why is so much emphasis placed upon the business plan for new ventures?

The purpose of the business plan

As might be expected, 'perhaps the most important step in launching any new venture or expanding an existing one is the construction of a business plan' (Barrow *et al.*, 2001: 6). Given its importance, preparation of the business plan is something that cannot be taken too lightly and is not something that can be rushed. If it is, it is unlikely to be of any great use.

Essentially the purpose of the business plan is to help the business founder crystallize his/her ideas—to consider all aspects of the business and see how they fit together. In itself this is an invaluable exercise as, through it, it is possible to identify any mistakes that, if made in the marketplace, could prove fatal. However, once completed, the plan enables the founder to see where he/she is going and how to get there. So, although there is no standard format for a business plan, it should include:

- the short- and medium-term goals for the business
- a description of the products (be they goods or services)
- the market opportunities that have been identified
- the resources required to enable the goals for the business to be achieved.

Importantly, also, it should include details of the entrepreneur and any of his/her partners. The entrepreneur and any co-founders will be the main drivers of the business and not only is it important that they recognize their own strengths, but that they convince others that they have the experience and expertise to make the business a success. If they do not possess the requisite skills or expertise, they will need to make it clear how they are going to acquire them, which may be through training or recruitment.

There are other important functions of the business plan. They include establishing the feasibility of the new venture, determining the fiscal needs of the business, and raising finance. We will now look at each of these in turn.

Establishing the feasibility of the new venture

A business plan tests the viability of an idea and sets out what the business expects to achieve, together with the resources and actions required. Once developed, it acts as a map showing what is expected to be done and when. Thus not only does it check the commercial and technical viability of the idea, but it sets goals and objectives, and allows monitoring of actual progress. If the performance of the business varies from that identified in the plan, the reasons for this and the implications for the business need to be considered, and any remedial action taken.

Sadly this is one of the most neglected aspects of the business plan. Once produced the plan is often put away and never used again.

Determining the fiscal needs of the business

The plan should show:

- how much money is needed
- what it is needed for
- when, and for how long, it is required.

As discussed in Chapter 2, some of the main reasons why new and small businesses fail are under-capitalization and problems with cashflow. Many fail with full order books because they lack the resources to service them. A soundly prepared business plan can help avoid such difficulties.

Raising finance

This is a further, important function for the business plan—to persuade external financial institutions to fund the project. Often it is seen as the *only* reason for producing the business plan. It is not—as has been emphasized already—but potential financiers will want to see a plan for the proposed business. While the business plan is not necessarily a passport to finance, a good business plan should help raise the requisite funding, assuming the project is commercially viable. If nothing else, it should:

- enable the entrepreneur to demonstrate his/her understanding of the business and managerial capability
- give him/her an opportunity to present his/her ideas and self in a way that potential financiers will be able to understand.

So, what are financiers looking for in a business plan? According to Barrow *et al.* (2001), there are five main things.

1. **Evidence of market orientation and focus.** The plan must demonstrate that the needs of the potential customer have been recognized. Any plan that devotes more space to the product than it does to the market and marketing is unlikely to be well received.
2. **Evidence of customer acceptance.** It must provide a clear idea of how and to whom the product is to be sold, and that it is likely to sell in the numbers predicted.
3. **Proprietary position.** Potential financiers want to be assured that the competition has been limited, at least initially, by protecting the idea. Patents, copyright, trademark protection or licensing can help reduce the riskiness of the venture, at least from the financier's perspective.
4. **Return.** Financiers will want to see that the business is capable not only of servicing any loan but of providing a return on the investment. As will be shown,

there are two main investors—banks and venture capitalists. The two have very different requirements. Banks are probably less interested in rapid growth and the consequent capital gain than they are in a steady stream of earnings almost from the outset. In contrast, venture capitalists are looking for fast-growing companies in which they can take a substantial shareholding that they can eventually sell on in order to generate profit. Both will want to see how the performance of the business is to be monitored and controlled.

5. **Believable forecasts.** Clearly potential investors will want to see forecasts that will convince them that this is an attractive proposition, while the entrepreneur will want to convince them (and him/herself) of the attractiveness of the venture. Under such circumstances, there is a temptation to exaggerate forecasts. Potential investors deal with thousands of investment proposals each year and have a good idea of what is and is not achievable. If forecasts are beyond their expectations, they are likely to doubt them and the capability of the entrepreneur. So it is important to ensure that forecasts are realistic and can be supported with facts, whenever possible. If this is not possible:

- the assumptions should be stated upon which any forecasts are made
- a set of pessimistic, realistic and optimistic forecasts should be included.

If the forecasts are on the low side, the plan should be taken to a bank rather than to a venture capitalist. Often the banks see modest forecasts as a virtue, lending credibility to the proposition.

There is one further aspect of the business plan that potential financiers look at that Barrow *et al.* do not mention—that is the section that deals with the founder. Most potential financiers would prefer to see a bad idea with a good entrepreneur than a good idea with a bad entrepreneur. With a good entrepreneur, a bad idea has a chance of success, while a good idea can be ruined in the hands of a poor entrepreneur. So, it is important to convince them that the founder is a 'good entrepreneur'. Indeed, when assessing business propositions, one bank has an acronym—PARSER—that guides its evaluation of any proposition. The 'P' stands for 'Person' and indicates that this is what is looked at initially. Under this heading, it is looking at the founder's character (background, integrity, reliability), competence (training, qualifications, track record, experience) and capital (both financial and personal) resources. (For completeness, the other components of PARSER are the Amount of funding required, the method of Repayment, the Security and Expediency of the 'investment' and the level of Remuneration.)

Problems associated with the business plan

A business plan is an important document as it enhances understanding of the business and sets out a clear way forward to ensure continued commercial viability. There are problems with it, however.

- The quality of the analysis may be poor, or weaknesses may not be considered fully. Often, demand projections are over-estimated, for example, making the situation look more positive than it actually is.
- The plan may be used solely as a means to gain funding. Once this is achieved,

it is never referred to again. Conversely, it sometimes becomes a 'straitjacket', opportunities are missed and the business fails to change when changes occur in the environment.

Business plans, therefore, need to be well researched and prepared, used sensibly and seen as being flexible and capable of adapting to, and showing, changing circumstances.

The format of the business plan

While there is no single format, and a plan intended for raising finance may be somewhat different from a plan designed to establish the feasibility of a project, normally a business plan would contain the following sections:

- executive summary (this covers all the main points in the plan and is intended to convince the reader that the plan, itself, is worth reading)
- description of the business
- key personnel and their roles
- the market and the marketing plan
- operation and production plan
- human resources plan
- capital resources plan
- financial plan.

These may all affect the viability of the venture, as well as the amount of money required to fund it. It is appropriate, now, to look at each of these components of the business plan (with the exception of the executive summary).

7   Description of the business

Clearly in this section of the plan it is necessary to introduce the business idea and how it was arrived at. However, it is important, also, to consider:

- the mission and objectives of the business
- the name of the business
- the proposed legal status of the business.

The mission and objectives of the business

These must be realistic and achievable. They should fulfil the following criteria.

- Focused and capable of differentiating the business from its competitors. There must be something that makes people want to buy from it: a unique sales proposition (USP). Normally it is necessary to produce something cheaper or better than the competition, though it may be that the business is located more conveniently or customers prefer to deal with the proprietor as a person than with his/her competitors.

- Sufficiently broad to allow the business to grow and realize its potential. Clearly a new business has limited resources and many new businesses fail because they attempt to do too much and are unable to create a distinctive niche for themselves in the market. However, the objectives should not be so narrow as to restrict opportunities for development.

- Concise and capable of being memorized, not just by the entrepreneur but by the staff. Both parties need to know what the business is attempting to achieve so that both can be pulling in the right direction at all times. Many poor mission statements are so long and convoluted that nobody can remember them.

- Capable of explaining the business and its purpose. The strategic goals for the business—what it is intended that the business should achieve in the short term (one year) and in the medium term (two to five years). The ultimate size of the business is more a matter of judgement than forecast. Clearly it is not easy to forecast sales, especially before trading has started, but if a goal is not set for the business:

  – sales will be insufficient to cover fixed costs, which means the venture will probably fail, or

  – too much will be sold and the venture will start to over-trade, or

  – values and standards will be compromised.

Exercise 10.1

Barrow *et al.* (2001) give the following mission statement for a business called Blooming Marvellous.

> Arising out of our experiences, we intend to design, make and market a range of clothes for mothers-to-be that will make them feel they can still be fashionably dressed. We aim to serve a niche missed out by Mothercare, Marks & Spencer, etc., and so become a significant force in the mail order fashion for mothers-to-be market. We are aiming for a 5 per cent share of the market in the south east, and a 25 per cent return on assets employed within three years of starting up.

Consider the strengths and weaknesses of this statement and then write a mission statement for your business.

The name of the business

A business name is an identity. Ideally, it should indicate what the business does and how it does it. Essentially, a good name should summarize the marketing strategy and should help differentiate the business from the competition. It is not easy to find a good name and time should be devoted to doing this. It is helpful to work through the following stages.

- Pretend to be a potential customer. What is it about the business that will make the customer choose it? Whatever it is, the name should reflect it.

- Choose a word or words that is/are easy to say and that roll(s) off the tongue.

- Check potential names with relatives or friends. See which they prefer, which evoke the image being projected, and see whether they can come up with any others.

- Check the local telephone directory to ensure that nobody else has come up with the same or a similar name.

Finally, once a name has been decided upon, check with a trademark agent to see whether it can be protected. If a dot.com (Internet) business is being set up, a domain name will be needed. Hundreds of domain names are registered daily and clearly it will be necessary to have one that has not already been registered. There are several different registration options. It is possible to use:

- Nominet UK
- an Internet Service Provider (ISP), which will submit a domain name application on behalf of the business
- one of the hundreds of websites that now offer domain name registration online
- an Internet community—normally these offer web pages within their community space as well as a free domain name; usually such names have their own community name tagged on the end, making the business name rather long.

Exercise 10.2

Consider the name 'Blooming Marvellous'. Compare it with the mission statement for the business (as presented in Exercise 10.1). How appropriate do you feel it is for that particular business? Now design a name for your business.

The legal form of the business

There are four main forms that a business may take. One will need to be decided upon before trading starts and it will need to be indicated in the business plan.

Two of the forms (the sole trader and the partnership) are regarded as informal in that a business using either of these forms can be started without any formal procedure. The other two (the limited liability company and the co-operative) are both artificial creations. They can do anything that a person can do but have to be managed according to company law. Hence they are regarded as being formal arrangements. Generally it is better/easier to start informally and progress to a formal business set-up as the enterprise develops. However, it is also recommended that partnerships should be avoided as, in addition to the drawbacks associated with the sole trader option, the partnership has a number of its own. If a partnership is entered in to, it should be governed by a partnership agreement, drawn up by an experienced 'partnership lawyer'.

The informal route

Each of these forms has advantages and disadvantages. If the informal route is selected and the business is set up either as a sole trader or partnership, then the following factors apply.

- No advanced permission is required. Trading can start immediately, although a licence is required for certain types of business, such as a pet shop, public house/off-licence, retail pharmacy or dance hall, etc.

- No registration is required, although the business must be registered with the Inland Revenue.

- No publicity is required and it is possible not to disclose the profitability of the business. Clearly it will be necessary to publicize the business (if customers are to be attracted) and to disclose its profitability (if funding is to be secured).

- No accountant is required. Clearly it will be necessary to prepare accounts for the business, if only to meet the requirements of the Inland Revenue. However, the entrepreneur may prefer to produce these him/herself and, by so doing, will learn a lot about the business. It may be desirable, though, to seek the advice of an accountant and/or to have the accounts audited by him/her.

- There is no limit to the entrepreneur's personal liability or responsibility for the debts of the business. As a sole trader there is no distinction between the proprietor and the business. The business is seen as one of the proprietor's assets. If it fails, its creditors have a right not only to the assets of the business, but also to the proprietor's personal assets. However, provided that:

  – he/she was solvent when making the transfer, and

  – the business does not encounter difficulties within two years of the transfer being made

  it is possible to avoid the worst of these consequences by transferring all personal assets to the legal ownership of a spouse, against whom the creditors will have no claim.

The partnership

If it is decided to establish a partnership, it must be appreciated that although there may be more capital and skills available, the following factors apply.

- Each partner is jointly and severally liable for the other's activities and anyone entering into business with the partnership is entitled to assume that the partner he or she is dealing with has full authority. This means that if one of the partners were to incur a debt against the business, the other(s) would be liable for that debt. Similarly, if he/she became bankrupt, his/her creditors could seize an appropriate share of the partnership. One way around this is for the business to be registered as a limited partnership, whereby the risks are limited to the capital put into the business.

- Each partner is regarded as a sole trader for tax purposes.

- The Inland Revenue has a legal right to find out about the partners.

- The proprietor has an obligation to inform the Inland Revenue about the partners.

- If the partnership breaks up, for any reason, all business contacts need to be notified immediately and the proprietor needs to formally take 'public leave' of the arrangement. Otherwise he/she could remain liable for the partner's continued activities and end up being sued for his/her liabilities.

As mentioned already, it is important that if a partnership is decided upon there should be a partnership agreement. This should indicate the roles, responsibilities and liabilities of the partners and how the profits will be shared between them.

The formal route

It may be decided not to go down the informal route but to set up a legal business entity, either a limited liability company or a co-operative. Both have their advantages and disadvantages over the informal method.

The limited liability company

Provided that the business does not trade fraudulently, the main advantage here is that as the business has a legal identify of its own, separate from the proprietor's, the entrepreneur is not liable for the debts of the business beyond the paid-up value of the shares held in it. This means that in the event of failure, creditors' claims are restricted to the assets of the company. Additionally, it is possible to raise capital by selling shares. However there are disadvantages.

- Each company has to be registered and issued with a registration number. The cost of registration is about £500 and it takes between six and eight weeks to complete the registration. It is possible to reduce this by buying a company 'off the shelf' from a registration agent. This will cost approximately £250, but it will have to be adapted to suit the purposes of the business.
- There is no confidentiality. A chartered or certified accountant will have to be engaged and the company's accounts will have to be lodged at Companies House.
- There must be at least two shareholders and a board of directors, and a company secretary will have to be appointed.
- As a new business, with no track record, difficulties may be experienced in raising initial funds and finding suppliers and customers unless a personal guarantee is provided. In effect the business is then operating as a sole trader.

The co-operative

Like a limited liability company, a co-operative has limited liability for its members and must file annual accounts. Although it is not mandatory to register it with the Chief Registrar of Friendly Societies, the cost of which is £90, if this is not done the co-operative will be treated in law as a partnership with unlimited liability. While it has these benefits, this is not the legal form for anyone wanting to run their own business, take control of their own destiny or maximize their profits because:

- the principle of 'one member one vote' means that each member of the co-operative has equal control
- there must be at least seven members from the outset and membership must be open to anyone who satisfies the stipulated qualifications
- if profits are not retained in the business, they must be shared in proportion to the members' contribution and members should benefit, primarily, from their contribution to the business (e.g. the hours worked)

- even if the profits are high enough to permit a greater payment, interest on any loan or share capital has to be limited.

Exercise 10.3

Decide on the legal form of your business and give reasons for your choice.

Key personnel and their roles

From the perspective of a potential financier, the entrepreneur is critical to the success of the business. If the business is going to succeed, clearly it will be necessary for the entrepreneur (and his/her team) to possess the requisite technical and entrepreneurial skills. Potential financiers will have to be convinced that the entrepreneur (and any colleagues) possess these attributes, or can acquire them. This can be done through the business plan, which can also enable the entrepreneur to assess him/herself and the entrepreneurial team to determine their suitability for setting up and running a business.

So, assuming the entrepreneur possesses the technical qualifications, skill and experience to run the business, what are the entrepreneurial skills and attributes that will be required?

Exercise 10.4

Consider the attributes identified by Timmons and his colleagues (see Chapter 5). How do you rate against them? Which attributes do you believe you possess and which do you feel you will need to acquire?

Be honest with yourself. Apart from the fact that many people who set out to start their own business deceive themselves into believing they are the 'right sort of person', you will never develop your entrepreneurial capability unless you are aware of your limitations.

Once you have done this, complete Exercise 5.2 if you have not done so already. Repeat the whole exercise with any colleagues you may have.

Finally, having done this:

- determine which members of the entrepreneurial team will be responsible for which functions and explain why they are most suited to these positions
- identify any gaps that will need to be filled and explain how you intend to fill them—through recruitment, training or 'buying in' the expertise as and when it is needed
- consider how you and your colleagues will be reimbursed for your efforts, what it will cost and when.

The market and the marketing plan

Few topics are more important for the new small business than the marketing plan. Not only does it identify the customers for the business, but it formulates the marketing strategies that ensure the customers' needs are satisfied and the resources of the business are utilized most effectively. Essentially it is a systematic document that proceeds from a general assessment of the marketing environment through to a detailed summary of the marketing budget. Normally it comprises four stages:

1. review (where are we now?)

2. objectives (where do we want to get to?)

3. strategy (how are we going to get there?)

4. plan (how can we put strategy into action?).

The plan

A detailed marketing plan will need to be prepared for the business that covers all four stages, but only a summary need appear in the main body of the business plan. The full marketing plan usually appears as an appendix. Each stage of the marketing plan will now be dealt with in some detail.

Market review

This sets the scene. It provides a factual basis for determining the marketing objectives of the business and the marketing strategies to be followed. It is based on a detailed analysis of:

- the market—its size, trends, segments, the elasticity of demand (for the product), the likely impact of political, economic, social or technological changes, and so on.
- the competition (both direct and indirect), focusing on their strengths and weaknesses, and the opportunities and threats that they pose
- potential consumers, their number, frequency of purchase, purchasing habits, and so on.
- the business itself, its strengths and weaknesses.

Marketing objectives

The resultant analysis should make it possible to determine the target markets the business is best equipped to enter. These are the market objectives for the business. In addition, the proprietor's own personal objectives will need to be specified, as follows.

- How fast does he/she want the business to grow? Does he/she want short-term profits or long-term growth?
- What will be the sales objectives? What share of the market is being aimed for? Over what period?
- What money will be required to enable these objectives to be met?

This section of the plan should be brief and the objectives should be:

- realistic and achievable, given the resources and present marketing position
- specific—measurable
- actionable—activities that can be undertaken to achieve the objectives.

Marketing strategy

This section details how the various objectives are to be met. Each market segment is composed of consumers with different needs. A separate strategy should be developed for each segment in which it is intended that the business should trade.

In this section a summary statement is being made of how the resources of the business are going to be used to take advantage of the market opportunities and meet the marketing objectives. Therefore the strategy statement(s) should be broad and succinct, and should summarize the total offer being made to each segment. It should deal with the 'four Ps' of the marketing mix, ensuring that they are consistent and reinforce each other. This involves:

- specifying the characteristics of the Product and differentiating it from other competitor products
- determining the Price at which the product is to be sold
- identifying how the product is to be Promoted
- considering the Place from where the product is to be sold and/or how it is to be distributed.

The following is an example of a strategy statement.

" We intend to produce a premium product sold at 5 per cent above the price of the market leader. It will be backed by advertising that stresses the high product quality and first-class after-sales service. It will be sold direct through an existing network of agents who will provide a full delivery, installation and maintenance service.

Action plan

This is a summary of the actions needed to put the strategy into effect. Having decided on the product and the support to be provided, it is necessary to decide on the price to be charged. Which of the following will it be?

- Cost-based—that is, will a fixed margin be added to the cost of the product to cover overheads and profit requirements? If so, it is possible to calculate the price to be charged from the following equation.

$$\text{Sales price} = \frac{\text{fixed costs} + \text{profit objective}}{\text{breakeven profit point}} + \text{unit variable cost}$$

This will be discussed in more detail later in the chapter but say, for example:

– fixed costs = £10,000

– profit objective = £4000

– unit variable cost = £3.00

– breakeven profit point = 7000 units

The sale price would be £5.00. That is:

Sale price = $\dfrac{10,000 + 4000}{7000} + 3$

$= 2 + 3$

$= 5$

- Demand-based—that is, what the market will bear. How much will customers be prepared to pay for the product?
- A combination of both.

Whichever pricing strategy is adopted, it is important to consider how the proposed prices will compare with the competition and how they will enable the business to meet its marketing objectives. It is not advisable to charge a price that is attractive to customers and lower than that charged by the competition if it does not contribute to the profit objectives of the business. What credit facilities will be provided, if any, and will discounts be offered for bulk purchases or early payments, for example? If so, what will be the cost of these to the business?

The way the product(s) will be promoted

Under this heading it is necessary to consider how, when and where the product will be promoted. There are various methods of promotion, including public relations, advertising, trade shows/exhibitions, promotional literature and, of course, the Internet. Each has its own strengths and weaknesses. Generally, however, the weakest form of promotion is media advertising and the most effective is word-

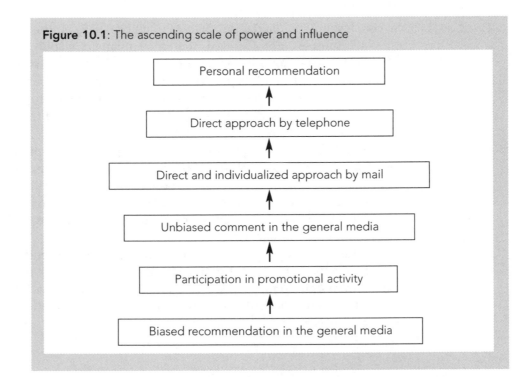

Figure 10.1: The ascending scale of power and influence

Personal recommendation

↑

Direct approach by telephone

↑

Direct and individualized approach by mail

↑

Unbiased comment in the general media

↑

Participation in promotional activity

↑

Biased recommendation in the general media

of-mouth. Indeed, there is what is known as an ascending scale of power and influence (see Fig. 10.1).

With each there are costs involved and it is necessary to decide not only on the promotional strategy, but on the resources to be devoted to promotion and how the benefits derived from the promotional activity are to be identified and monitored. All too frequently, new small firms do not do this and large amounts of money are wasted on ineffective promotion, yet promotion is essential to the new business. So it is important to get it right and to know that the money that is being spent is, indeed, benefiting the business.

The place where the product will be sold

Here it is necessary to consider where and how the products will be sold and distributed.

- Will the business have its own outlet? If so, where will it be located? Will it be owned or leased? How much will it cost?

- Will the products be delivered to the consumer or will the consumer be expected to collect them? Alternatively, will a third party be used, such as the mail service? How will the appropriate distribution channel be selected and how much will it cost?

- How will the product be sold in the first place? Will the business have its own sales force? If so, how big will it be? How will it be paid and how much will it cost?

Remember, the way the product is sold and distributed affects its image.

To sum up

In conclusion, the marketing plan is a crucial part of the business plan. If estimated sales are not achieved, the entire financial viability of the project is affected. Similarly, an over-optimistic sales forecast can make the plan appear financially viable when it is not. Therefore it should always be written down and used as a management tool to monitor progress. If it is used properly, it is possible to see as soon as the business goes off-course, if it does, and the necessary remedial action can be taken.

Undoubtedly backers will want to see that appropriate attention has been paid to the necessary market considerations. Clearly this is not an easy exercise and in a rapidly changing environment doubtless the plan will require frequent updating and revision. However, the time and cost involved in producing a robust and effective plan will be more than repaid by the benefits derived from increased efficiency and performance.

Towards the end of the plan all of the proposed expenditures should be brought together. This budget summary should cover no more than one page and should always group major related expenditures. It should be followed by a calendar of marketing activities, showing how the various activities fit together and when they occur.

Exercise 10.5

Produce a marketing plan for your business together with a summary. The summary will appear in the main body of the business plan, with the full marketing plan as an appendix.

Operation and production plan

This section of the plan describes how the goods or services will be manufactured or provided. Essentially it focuses on all of the activities required to implement the business strategy, although, as the previous section has shown, sales, distribution and promotional activity normally appear in the marketing plan.

All firms, whether they operate in manufacturing or the service sector, have to consider how they will operate as this is the basis for determining their resource needs. However, it is not untypical for the service-based company to think that it does not need to consider the production process, while the textbooks tend to focus on manufacturing production.

Irrespective of whether the intention is to open a manufacturing or a service business, the three key features of any successful business are that:

- work is completed on time and delivery dates are met
- quality standards are set and maintained
- resources (equipment, materials and employees) are used effectively and costs are kept within budget.

Thus an operational plan is an integral part of the business plan.

The plan

Although the operation of the business must be considered in the business plan, it need not show the complete detail as to how every operational activity will be implemented. The proprietor and his/her colleagues will need to know this, but it is sufficient to show, in the business plan, that account has been taken of the principal matters that concern the venture.

Clearly, the main production process will need to be described and it is necessary to consider how much of the process will be:

- produced in-house
- sourced externally.

However, it is necessary not only to describe the production process but to explain why it has been chosen. Often new firms can secure an advantage over their competitors by doing things differently from them, thereby reducing costs and/or improving the quality of the finished product. It is important to compare the operation with its main competitors or rivals, therefore. In particular, attention should be paid to:

- what work will need to be done

- when it is to be done
- where it is to be done
- how it is to be done
- by whom it is to be done.

Consideration will also have to be given to the development of systems which will ensure that:

- the customer's requirements are made clear
- the work is planned to ensure that
  - delivery schedules are met
  - employees and machines are being used effectively
  - the sequence of operations is such as to minimize travel distances.

Additionally, it will be necessary to explain what materials will be required and how they will be sourced. The choice of supplier(s) will have to be justified and details of the stock it is intended that the business will hold will have to be provided. As stock is a cost to the business it is important to keep stockholding to a minimum.

At the same time, it is important to demonstrate that through the ordering and supply systems, the business is never likely to be out of stock, certainly of the high-demand items. That is why the Japanese have introduced the 'just-in-time' (JIT) concept, and why many firms have begun to enter into strategic alliances with their suppliers and subcontractors. If it is intended that the business should enter into such a relationship or relationships, details should be indicated in the plan.

Last but not least, it is important to state how the quality of the production process is to be monitored and controlled. In a highly competitive market it is important that quality standards are not only maintained but improved. Failure to maintain quality can be costly. A high level of returned products means not only less money flowing through the business, but a large number of dissatisfied customers who may:

- transfer their custom to the competition
- damage the image and reputation of the business by telling others of their experiences.

It is necessary to show, therefore, how it is intended to ensure the quality of the product and to this end there are a number of quality standards that might be helpful. In particular, the BS/ISO 9000 series of standards can help ensure that the operating procedure delivers a standard of products (both goods and services) that is consistent and acceptable to the customers of the business. Indeed, some large organizations will not deal with organizations that do not meet one of these quality standards.

Prospective financiers will want to see that not only have such operational aspects of the business been considered, but that their cost implications have been considered too. Indeed, they will expect that a costing system has been developed that accurately predicts the costs of production at different capacity levels.

Exercise 10.6

Write an operations plan for your business. You will need to:

- describe and explain your proposed production process, including a comparison with that of your principal competitor(s); if your process is different from theirs, explain why this is the case

- show what resources you will require and the suppliers you will use, explaining your choice

- demonstrate that you are aware of the need to keep stockholding to a minimum and outline the measures you have taken to ensure this

- explain your procedures for monitoring and controlling quality, and costing production.

Human resources plan

People are the most important resource of any business. No matter how good the idea is or how well thought-through the business plan, it is people that are responsible for how well the business functions. If the business is to grow and develop, it will need staff other than the entrepreneurial (management) team. However, many businesses fail to grow and either employ nobody other than the owner-manager or engage only a small number of people, usually family members or friends. If it is intended that the business should grow, even by engaging family and friends, it is important that it is done professionally as even the best-planned businesses can fail because of the engagement of just one poor employee. It is the function of the human resources plan to determine the number and type of staff needed, when they will be recruited, how they will be managed and used, and the costs involved in their employment.

The plan

As indicated above, the human resources plan should identify the people required, other than the entrepreneurial team, to set up and develop the business. It should indicate:

- when they will be required
- the functions they will perform (job specification)
- duties/responsibilities
- level of authority
    - reporting to
    - responsible for
- hours of work
    - full-time
    - part-time

- the experience, qualifications and expertise they will possess (the person specification)
- age
- educational level
- previous experience
- special skills
- personality
- physical aspects
- location and travel
- how they will be remunerated and at what level
  - pay
  - salary/commission
  - hourly/weekly monthly
- overtime
  - rates
  - amount
- bonus/incentive schemes
- holiday entitlement
- sickness pay
- pension
- expenses/allowances
- lunches and breaks
- notice period
- career prospects
- staff development expectations
- working environment
- equipment (tools, machines, desk, telephone, computer, vehicle, etc.)
- welfare facilities (eating, washing, toilets, lockers, lighting, heating, rest rooms, etc.)
- health and safety (medical facilities, protective clothing, extractors, etc.).

Once all this has been determined, it will be necessary to consider the following factors.

How will people be recruited?
Will the post(s) be advertised or will prospective employees be 'headhunted'. If the former, where will the advertisements be placed? If the latter, will personal contacts be used or will a specialist agency be engaged?

How will people be administered/managed?
It will be necessary to develop:

- company rules
- disciplinary/grievance procedures
- contract(s) of employment
- systems to administer wages
- record systems
  - holiday
  - accident
  - personal.

The costs of employment

Employment costs are not just the cost of the wage or salary, but all of the costs involved in the employment of the staff. As an example, it is possible to take on an office junior at a salary of £6000 per annum. The true allocated cost of employing that person is probably nearer to £9320 per annum, as follows:

- salary £6000
- National Insurance £540
- office space £1000
- desk/chair £60
- word processor/stationery £200
- filing cabinets £50
- telephone £20
- lighting £100
- heating £200
- lunch/tea/coffee breaks £100
- temporary cover/holidays £500
- sickness £250
- office cleaning/decorating £50
- bonus payment £100
- recruitment costs £50
- toilet/washroom, etc. £100.

This is probably one of the main reasons why so few new businesses grow and take on staff—the costs are high, the procedures are complex and the process is somewhat less than efficient. While the overall objective is to match the person to the job requirements and ensure they fit with the style of business, all too frequently the recruitment process results in a mismatch, which can be difficult and expensive to rectify. In many cases, though, the reason for the poor recruitment is lack of appropriate preparation and planning. Over a five-year period, the cost to the business of an office junior, using the above example, would be an estimated £47,000. The average owner-manager would probably take weeks or even months to decide on a £47,000 piece of equipment that would be written off over a five-year period. For an office junior, however, he/she would probably devote no more than a few hours or a day at the most to recruiting him/her. Yet the wrong person could destroy the business. So, it is important either to give full consideration to the recruitment strategy or to adopt a no-growth strategy, which is what so many new ventures do.

Exercise 10.7

Develop a human resource plan for your business. What employees will you need, what will they do, how will you recruit them, how much will they cost you?

Capital resources plan

All businesses require capital resources. Even if there is no need for any significant investment in machinery and plant, inevitably there will be some equipment requirements. So, once it is known how the business is to operate, and the number of people required, it will be necessary to determine the capital resources needed to enable the business to achieve its objectives.

The plan

Premises
Probably the first thing to be considered is the premises from which the business will operate. As discussed earlier, the choice of premises is important as it impacts on the image of the business. To some businesses, such as shops, restaurants and hotels, it can be quite critical, as the location of the premises can mean success or failure. So, depending on the type of business to be started, it may be necessary to choose the location of the premises very carefully indeed.

Clearly the type of premises the business occupies can reflect the type of business that has been established. However, if the business is not particularly sensitive to either location or image, it is advisable to keep the occupancy costs as low as possible at start-up. Indeed, it is worth noting that this is exactly how Richard Branson started out (see Chapter 5)—from the basement of his parents' home in Bayswater. Assuming that there are no restrictions on its use, the home is a good place to start certain types of business but it is necessary to check with the local council to ensure that planning regulations are not being breached. Indeed one of the first things to do is check the planning regulations on any premises that might seem appropriate, to ensure they cover the proposed business operations. If they do not, it will be necessary to apply for 'change of use', which will take a month at the very least, assuming permission is granted.

Whatever premises are chosen, they must enable the business to operate according to the operational plan, so it is necessary to ensure they are the right size and are configured appropriately. If not, alterations may have to be made, which are likely not only to incur unwanted expenses, but also to require planning permission. To determine how much space will be needed, a scale drawing should be prepared that indicates the optimum layout for any equipment required, allowing adequate circulation space. By a process of trial and error it is normally possible to arrive at an appropriate layout.

Generally it is not advisable to use valuable cash on acquiring unnecessary accommodation, but equally, if the objective is to grow the business, it is not desirable to move too soon. This is both costly and disruptive. Normally, it is advisable to think small and secure premises that will satisfy the expected needs of the business for the first two or three years of operation. However, it might be possible to acquire larger premises and sublet the surplus accommodation on a short-term lease, so that there is space for subsequent expansion.

Having decided on the type, location and size of the premises, it is necessary to determine the cost and whether the premises will be bought or leased. Rarely does it make sense for a start-up business to buy a property from the outset, not least because the repayments on the borrowings will usually be more than the rental payments. However, there are problems with leasing. Potential financiers will want to see a lease that is sufficiently long to establish the business before it has to move on or renegotiate the terms. If a long lease is entered into, though, the lessee (the tenant) remains personally responsible for payments over the whole life of the lease. To overcome this problem, business incubators and science parks have been developed with the intention of providing specialist short-term accommodation for new and small businesses (see Chapter 4). Such opportunities, if appropriate, should be explored as, often, they provide additional services and equipment that can be paid for on a use-only basis. This can prove extremely valuable to start-up businesses with limited cash.

Exercise 10.8

Sketch the layout of the premises you require, showing the overall layout, the layout of equipment and the 'production path'. Identify any specialist features that you may require and consider the most suitable location for the premises, explaining your eventual choice. State whether the premises will be bought or leased, and indicate the cost.

Web development

For those intending to start an e-commerce business, premises are not so important. However, an effective web presence is required that will attract customers to it and encourage them to buy. Although it may not appear to be the case, location is just as important as it is with physical premises, as is the design of the site itself. Essentially in designing an effective website it is necessary to:

- minimize the number of clicks, especially in the ordering process
- ensure that the 'add to basket' button is in front of the consumer as quickly as possible
- allay the consumer's concerns in order to encourage purchasing
- apply to organizations such as Uktrust or Webtrader for quality assurance trademarks.

While there are advantages in building the site in-house on a dedicated server, this is an expensive solution. Alternatively it is possible to buy a packaged solution. A number of options are available on the Internet. These include such low-cost providers as IBM's HomePage Creator (**www.ibm.com/hpc/uk**) and BT Storefront (**www.btwebworld.co.uk**). Using these, you can create a site for your business in just a few hours. However, it is important to realize that valuable information on your customers and their requirements is being left on a third party's computer.

Equipment

Apart from premises, you will require plant and equipment. This can range from expensive scientific instruments or machinery to relatively cheap items of office equipment, such as chairs and filing cabinets. It may also include transportation, such as a van or car; but avoid the temptation of indulging yourself by buying too expensive a car at the outset.

If the amount of equipment and plant required is extensive, it is probably worth listing it in an appendix, indicating:

- the piece of equipment
- its function
- the number of items required
- whether it is possessed already or has to be purchased
- its cost
- how it will be acquired (purchased/leased, new/second-hand).

Having identified the capital resource needs—premises and equipment—it is necessary to cost them out and to determine when and how payments will be made. Prospective financiers will want to see these calculations in the business plan and to see that they are based on actual estimates. Hence they will want to see the cost of actual premises and 'quotations' from actual suppliers.

Exercise 10.9

Produce a fully costed capital plan for your business that includes both premises and equipment. Identify potential suppliers.

Financial plan

All of these aspects will have financial implications for the business, which will need to be considered in the business plan. While any forecasts may turn out to be wrong, it is important to demonstrate that the factors that will have an impact on performance have been thought through.

The starting point is a forecast of sales and the cost of sales. This is the trading account. It can be extended to identify the fixed cost (overheads) involved in running the business, which shows the profits or losses that the business is likely to make over a given period, usually a year. This is the profit and loss account.

In addition to the projected profit and loss account, the following paperwork will be needed.

- Cashflow statement (showing the estimated flow of money in to and out of the business). This is normally done on a monthly basis and is vitally important to demonstrate when the business is likely to run out of cash and require an overdraft facility. Businesses often go bankrupt with full order books, simply because they lack the cash to pay their creditors.
- Balance sheet (showing the assets of the business—where they come from and where they go to).
- Breakeven analysis. This shows the point at which the business will start to make a profit.
- Sensitivity analysis. This forecasts the likely impact of, for instance, lower sales turnover, higher material costs, the business opening later than forecast, etc.

These may all affect the viability of a venture, as well as the amount of money required to fund it. Hence each will now be discussed in a little more detail.

The projected profit and loss account

This records how well the business is doing in terms of sales, costs and profitability. Normally it is produced for an accounting period of a year but, often, it is produced on a monthly basis so that the performance of the business can be monitored and any corrective action necessary can be taken.

The starting point is the forecast of sales for the period. This is probably the most important forecast of the exercise as it will have an impact on the whole of the business. If it is wrong—and it is for most new businesses—it could affect not only the profitability of the business but whether it is possible to raise finance. So, the sales forecast needs to be as accurate as possible. To help make an accurate forecast it is necessary:

- to check the sales of competitors and other similar new ventures
- to use any industry norms or 'rules of thumb' that might apply to the business
- to consider any seasonal effects and the impact they may have on the new venture
- to relate the sales figures to the activity required to generate the sales (e.g. the number of calls needed to generate a sale)
- not to forecast over too long a period; most textbooks will advise that forecasts should be over a three- to five-year period—there are very good reasons for this
    - most new ventures fail in the early years and such medium-term planning should help overcome the problems that are likely to bring about the downfall of the business
    - potential investors are interested in how the business is likely to perform in the medium term.

However, it is very difficult to predict with any accuracy over such a period. If an adviser or a prospective investor requires that financial projections be made for three to five years then clearly they will have to be done, but:

- more accurate forecasts are likely to be made once the business has been operational for some time

- in an era of very rapid change, it is not possible to make accurate predictions over such a time-span.

Once the sales have been forecast, it is necessary to subtract from this figure the cost of the goods sold. This includes:

- the cost of the materials used, plus
- the cost of any labour used in manufacturing the product.

The amount remaining, once the cost of the goods sold has been subtracted from the forecasted sales, is the forecasted gross profit. This is the trading account.

By extending this and subtracting the fixed costs (overheads or expenses), it is possible to forecast the net profit or loss for the business over the period. Thus a detailed 'trading and profit and loss account' looks like that shown in Fig. 10.2.

Figure 10.2: Trading and profit and loss account

	£	£	%
Sales		24,500	100
Purchases	20,189		
+ opening stock	3,760		
	23,949		
– closing stock	4,000		
= Cost of sales		19,949	(81.4)
Gross profit		£4,551	(18.6)
Less fixed costs			
Wages and Social Security	1,415		
Rates	300		
Electricity and gas	170		
Insurance	45		
Repairs and maintenance	64		
Telephone	28		
Printing, postage and stationery	130		
Sundry expenses	27		
Motor expenses	220		
Bank charges and interest	248		
Hire purchase interest	210		
Accountancy and audit fees	78		
Legal charges	15		
Depreciation	547		
		£3,497	
Net profit		£1,054	(4.3)

The projected cashflow statement

Like the profit and loss account, the cashflow statement also records how well the business is doing, but on this occasion in terms of cash generation. It is similar to the profit and loss account, but reflects the effect of credit taken from the supplier and given to the customer. It is essential for short-term planning as it shows the cashflow surplus or deficit each month and the result on the cash balance or overdraft of the business, indicating the maximum overdraft facility required.

It is a relatively simple document to prepare. All that is needed is:

- a list of the income (sales, loans, etc.) that is expected
- a list of the expenditure that is expected
- an indication, for each month of the year, of
  - the income expected
  - the expected expenditure.

For each month the expenditure should be subtracted from the income to give any cash surplus or deficit (overdraft). Additionally, any existing overdraft should be subtracted from the cash surplus or added to the month's deficit and carried forward to the following month. So, a typical cashflow statement would look like that shown in Fig. 10.3.

From this example, it is clear that the overdraft requirement would be greatest in October when a sum of £60,750 would be required. This would enable negotiations to be opened up with the bank to arrange an overdraft facility for this amount. Thus, for the cashflow forecast to be meaningful, income and expenditure has always be recorded in the month it is expected.

Figure 10.3: Projected cashflow statement

RECEIPTS	January	February	March	April	May	June	July	August	September	October	November	December
Sales receipts	66,000	78,000	81,000	70,500	69,600	49,200	21,000	21,000	16,200	16,200	45,000	81,900
Related VAT	9,000	11,700	12,150	10,575	10,440	7,380	3,150	3,150	2,430	2,430	6,750	12,285
Sales of assets												
Loans received												
Total receipts (A)	75,900	89,700	93,150	81,075	80,040	56,580	24,150	24,150	18,630	18,630	51,750	94,185
PAYMENTS												
Purchases	26,312	26,312	20,309	26,312	33,856	33,856	33,856	33,856	33,856	18,078	33,856	33,856
Direct labour	10,290	10,290	14,319	14,319	14,319	14,319	14,319	14,319	14,319	14,319	14,319	14,319
Capital expenditure			12,000									
Related VAT			18,000									
VAT payments to C&E			4,668			432				420		28,416
Corporation tax										27,500		
Dividends												
Interest payments												
Loan payments												
Total payments (B)	36,602	36,602	177,296	40,631	48,175	48,607	48,175	48,175	76,095	32,397	48,175	76,591
Surplus (deficit) (A) – (B)	39,298	53,098	84,146	40,444	31,865	7,973	−24.025	−24.025	−57,465	−13,767	3,575	17,594
Cash (overdraft) b/f	−30,000	9,298	62,396	−21,750	18,694	50,559	58,532	34,507	10,482	−46,983	−60,750	−57,175
Cash (overdraft) c/f	9,298	62,396	−21,750	−18,694	50,559	58,532	34,507	10,482	−46,983	−60,750	−57,175	−39,581

For example, if an annual rates bill is expected in June, the full amount should be indicated in June, and not averaged over the 12-month period. However, if the plan was to pay it in 12 monthly instalments, then an equal amount would be indicated each month. Similarly, if £10,000 worth of goods were sold in March, but payment was not expected until June, the £10,000 would be entered in the column for June.

The projected balance sheet

This measures the growth of the business over a particular period, usually a year. It shows where the money came from (share capital, generated profit, loans, etc.) and on what it was spent (fixed assets, stocks, debtors, cash reserves, etc.) over a given period. Therefore, it should always be dated as it provides a picture of the business at that particular point in time. So, a balance sheet looks like that shown in Fig. 10.4.

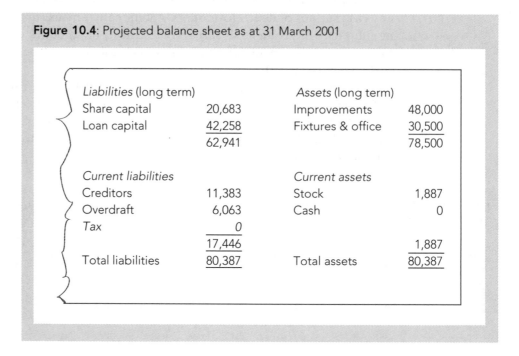

Figure 10.4: Projected balance sheet as at 31 March 2001

Liabilities (long term)		Assets (long term)	
Share capital	20,683	Improvements	48,000
Loan capital	42,258	Fixtures & office	30,500
	62,941		78,500
Current liabilities		Current assets	
Creditors	11,383	Stock	1,887
Overdraft	6,063	Cash	0
Tax	0		
	17,446		1,887
Total liabilities	80,387	Total assets	80,387

Breakeven analysis

This reveals the level of sales required to generate sufficient gross profit to cover the fixed costs or overheads of the business (i.e. to break even). Once this level of sales has been reached, further sales should result in profit. The breakeven point can be calculated from the following equation.

$$\text{Breakeven point} = \frac{\text{Fixed costs}}{\text{Selling price - unit variable cost}}$$

Assuming fixed costs of £10,000, unit costs of £3 per unit and a sales price of £5.00 per unit, the breakeven point is 5000 units—that is:

$$\text{Breakeven point} = \frac{10,000}{5 - 3} = 5000$$

This formula can be modified to identify the number of units that need to be sold to make any desired profit, as follows:

$$\text{Breakeven profit point} = \frac{\text{Fixed costs} + \text{profit objective}}{\text{Sales price} - \text{unit variable cost}}$$

So, if the same example is taken and a profit of £4000 is desired, it would be necessary to sell 7000 not 5000 units:

$$\text{Breakeven profit point} = \frac{10,000 + 4000}{5 - 3} = 7000$$

This is a very useful formula. As was shown in the marketing section of this chapter, if the fixed costs, unit costs and the desired level of profit are known, it is possible to calculate the price that needs to be charged, for example.

Sensitivity analysis

Clearly the estimates need to be as accurate and realistic as possible. However, before the business has started to trade it is difficult to predict accurately. Also, circumstances may change in ways that could not have been predicted, especially in an era of very rapid change. As a consequence, it could be that the forecasts—particularly, but not exclusively, the sales forecasts—are likely to be wrong. Under such circumstances, it is worth asking, 'what happens if . . . ?'. By asking this and calculating the effects (of a 20 per cent reduction in sales or a 10 per cent increase in costs, for example) it is often possible both to pre-empt any awkward questions from potential financiers and to plan for different contingencies. With modern technology and the use of spreadsheets, this is often a very simple, and not very time-consuming, exercise, but care should be taken to appreciate the full significance of the results.

These are the main financial forecasts that need to appear in the business plan. They are not easy to produce but they will be a lot easier if:

- each of the previous sections of the plan has been costed out, and
- the assumptions on which the estimates have been made are clear.

Not only will this help compile financial projections, it will help the reader see how they have been derived and, hopefully, convince him/her that they are accurate and reliable. Clearly, if this is not done, it is easy to forget how they were derived, which could be extremely embarrassing. If the assumptions are not clear and there is no indication of how the estimates have been derived, it is possible that a potential financier will work them out for him/herself (assuming he/she has the time/interest) and come to some very different results!

Exercise 10.10

Produce a set of financial forecasts for your business and then merge the results of Exercises 10.1 to 10.10 to produce a business plan for your new venture.

Alternatively, use the results of these exercises to help you complete one of the pro-forma (possibly electronic) business plans provided by banks. HSBC, for example, has one available on disk that can be obtained from any local branch.

Financing the new venture

Financing the venture can be one of the most challenging tasks facing the entrepreneur. As with Boo.com (see Chapter 2), new ventures are frequently under-capitalized and seldom is sufficient capital available to launch a venture optimally. Indeed most new ventures are continually limited by scarce resources.

Obtaining capital for the new venture is particularly difficult because it has no track record and, in addition, the entrepreneur may be somewhat inexperienced. Accordingly, most lenders take a somewhat conservative approach to new venture lending and it is perhaps appropriate that they should, as most new businesses fail. However, it is possible that if such businesses were properly funded from the outset, more would survive.

PAUSE FOR THOUGHT

If you were a potential investor in a new venture, what would you be looking for? How would you reach your decision on whether or not to invest? What criteria would you use?

As mentioned already, one of the most important things that potential investors are looking at in the proposition is the person. How convincing is the proposed founder as a potential entrepreneur? Assuming the applicant is convincing, the next thing the financiers will look at, probably, is the quality of the idea and the robustness of the business plan. How likely is it to be a viable proposition? Finally, though not necessarily of least importance, they will look at the proposition from their perspective. How is the proposal going to help them meet their objectives?

If money is going to be raised for the business, therefore, it will be necessary for the proposed founder to convince potential financiers that he/she has the requisite technical and business acumen, that the proposal is sound and that there is something in it for them. The business plan will help here, but it is important to explain:

- why the money is needed
- the type of funding required
- when the money will be needed
- the deal being offered
- the exit routes open to investors in the business.

Clearly, potential investors will be able to work all this out for themselves, especially with the help of a well-thought-out business plan, but why should they?

They are busy people and there are a lot of applicants competing for very limited funds. So, it is important to make it easy for them.

Why the money is needed

Essentially, new ventures require funding at the following stages.

- Before start-up. Here the requirement is normally for funding prototype development, research and development, market research, business plan preparation and, possibly, site acquisition.
- Start-up. The funding required at this stage is usually for inventory, plant and equipment, advertising, professional fees, and the opening. Such funds are required before, during and after launch.
- After start-up, and growth. Continued funding is needed for advertising, sales expenses, wages and salaries, rent, utilities, additional inventories, and seasonal/cyclical cashflow needs.

In all probability, the turnover of the business will not be sufficient, initially, to cover such costs. Over time, hopefully, it will build up to a level where such costs are covered. However, further funding will be required if the business is to grow.

The type of funding required

Under such circumstances, new ventures normally require two types of funding:

- short-term capital to launch the venture or to finance development costs before the venture is formally launched
- long-term capital to finance fixed equipment and facilities.

There are basically two types of financing available for such purposes:

- equity financing—capital provided in exchange for ownership
- debt financing—capital provided in exchange for interest payments.

Some suppliers of capital may prefer one type of financing over another, but often the type is determined through the negotiation process, particularly with the less formal funding sources. For any new venture the main sources of capital are as follows.

- Own capital. The money that the entrepreneur owns—savings, windfall, redundancy payments, etc. Investors like to see the entrepreneur putting some of his/her own capital into the business and normally the banks, for example, will be looking at a gearing of 1:1 for a new business with no previous track record— that is, £1 of their money for £1 of the founder's.
- Informal investors. These include family and friends. Normally the lending arrangements are informal or semi-formal, though this is not advisable and can lead to a variety of problems.
- Internal capital networks. These are normally community based and are found most commonly in developed economies in minority communities or sectors

of society that feel disadvantaged or discriminated against. In the emerging economies, they frequently provide important conduits for inward investment. Though informal in a legal sense, they have clear rules, which are often based on culture and tradition.

- Retained capital. Once a new venture is profitable, it can re-invest in itself. Usually, however, such profits are the property of the investors funding the venture and they may want to consider other investment opportunities before reaching their decision.

- Informal venture capital ('business angels'). These are individuals or small groups of individuals who offer their own capital to fund new ventures. They are termed informal only to distinguish them from the institutional forms of venture capital. Agreements are formalized and clear, though the investment structure and return expectations vary. Usually they are equity based and the investors like to be involved in the ventures. As a result, they tend to seek opportunities in ventures where their knowledge or business skills are applicable.

- Venture capital. Usually venture capital companies seek large (in excess of £0.5 million) investment opportunities characterized by the potential for a fast, high rate of return. Typically they seek annual returns in excess of 50 per cent, harvested over a five-year period. Usually the deals are equity based and complex but with a clear exit strategy enabling the investment to be liquidated quickly.

- Retail (high street) banking. Relatively small amounts are available from this source, normally in the form of loan capital with clear terms detailing the rates

---

A CASE EXAMPLE

Charlie's angels: a new form of informal venture capital

Not content with running his own leading-edge Internet software company, 24-year-old Charlie Muirhead has teamed up with other leading e-business names to start a technology investment fund that will invite up to 50 start-up companies a year to benefit from 'high-risk angel capital' worth between £62,500 and £312,000. The fund, known as igabriel, describes itself as an economic network of seasoned technology and Internet industry leaders, who want others to benefit from their experience and contacts as they push forward the spirit of entrepreneurship in the new economy.

The group provides early-stage companies with strategic advice, money and access to high-placed individuals as they seek to establish their ventures. By providing access to the right people at the right time, igabriel aims to guide entrepreneurs through the process of raising money, building strategic alliances, and marketing their products or services. In return igabriel expects a small stake in the company it helps jumpstart, thereby ensuring a continuous and unbiased working relationship with igabriel's membership community.

In addition to providing a relationship with key industry executives, igabriel also links start-ups with venture capital firms and incubators active in the Internet and new technologies.

According to Trinny Woodall, co-founder of Ready2shop.com (one of the clients of igabriel), 'Charlie's experience of setting up a business from scratch helped provide us with part of the funding we needed to get off the ground. He taught us what pitfalls to avoid and what goals were achievable.'

of return and the duration of the loan. As outlined above, the banks will normally require the entrepreneur to have invested in the venture and/or put up some form of collateral.

- Corporate banking. Offers larger amounts, usually of loan funding, though some equity opportunities do exist. Deals may be complex, offering, for example, conversions between the two types of funding. Returns may be over longer periods than those offered by the retail banking sector but normally the banks will expect to see commitment on the part of the entrepreneur and some form of asset security.

- Public flotation. Capital is raised by offering shares in the venture to a pool of private investors. These can be bought and sold in an open stock market. Apart from the established stock markets (London, New York and Tokyo, for example), there are:

  - the emerging markets that trade stock from companies in the emerging and transitional (former communist) economies

  - the special stock markets for smaller businesses; in Europe possibly the most important is the London-based Alternative Investments Market (AIM), which has 265 companies listed and a capitalization of c. US$10 billion; other important European small business markets are the Nouveau Marche in Paris, Easdaq in Brussels and the Neuer Markt in Frankfurt; in America, small and fast-growing business investment occurs through the Nasdaq market.

- Government. Most governments invest in business start-ups, though the nature of the support varies. In recent years there has been a tendency in some countries to invest in growth rather than new venture creation as observed already, and generally direct government investment appears to be in decline. However, there are often a number of quasi-government agencies (e.g. the former Training and Enterprise Councils (TECs) in the UK or the Small Business Administration in the USA), which direct grants towards the new venture. In addition, governments often assist new ventures and small firms through tax breaks. (The support provided by the UK government was examined in Chapter 4.)

- Commercial partnerships. Existing businesses are a potential source of investment, especially if the established business has a strategic interest in the success of the venture—for example, if it is a supplier of a particularly innovative product. There are a variety of ways in which such partnerships can be structured, ranging from take-over to various forms of strategic alliance.

When the money is needed

It is likely that not everything will be needed at once. Money will probably be needed for different things and for different stages in the life cycle of the business. So, potential investors will not expect to be asked for everything at once. Equally, however, they will not welcome being asked for more and more money. As with Boo.com (see Chapter 2) investors lose confidence when they are continuously asked for money, as it gives the impression that the entrepreneur does not know what he/she is doing.

It is necessary, therefore, to prepare a statement showing when the money will be needed. For example the cashflow forecast shown earlier (Fig. 10.3) revealed that that particular business would run out of cash in September and would require an overdraft facility for the rest of the year. In that particular instance, the proprietor would be advised to go to the bank well before September to negotiate the requisite overdraft, and to make it clear that the cashflow showed that the peak requirement would be in October, when c. £61,000 would be needed. After that, the requirement would tail off to about £40,000 in December.

The deal being offered

The funding of a new venture is essentially a buying and selling process. The proprietor is trying to sell the business as an investment opportunity, and the investor is looking to buy an opportunity that will provide a good return on his/her investment. According to Tyebjee and Bruno (1984), there are five key stages in the investment process.

1. **Deal origination.** The process by which the proprietor and the investor become aware of each other. Few investors actually search for new opportunities. Most wait for the entrepreneur or a third party to contact them. Business angels are often informed about investment opportunities through informal networks.

2. **Deal screening.** The potential investor evaluates the proposal to see whether it fits with his/her profile of activities. Normally the criteria for evaluation are:

   - the amount of investment being sought

   - the industry sector of the venture

   - the venture's stage of development.

   So, it is advisable to find out their criteria before making a proposal. This way it is possible not to waste time by applying to the wrong funding source, but also to strengthen the proposition by writing it so that it meets, directly, the evaluation criteria.

3. **Deal evaluation.** Assuming the proposal does fit, a more detailed evaluation now occurs. Here the objective is to compare the returns offered by the venture with the risks involved. Key issues are:

   - the potential for the venture in terms of the innovation it is offering

   - the conditions in the market it intends to develop

   - the competitive pressures it will face.

   If the potential appears good, then consideration will be paid to:

   - the ability of the entrepreneur and his/her team to manage the venture

   - any security being offered.

4. **Deal structuring.** These are the decisions that have to be made in relation to how the initial investment will be made and how the investor will ensure that he/she obtains the requisite returns on the investment. The critical issues here are:

   - how much funding is being sought

- the period of the proposed investment
- the return offered
- the time it will take for the return to materialize
- the form the return will take (e.g. cash or shares).

5. Post-investment activity. Investors, especially those with a significant interest in the venture, will usually retain a degree of involvement in it. Normally this takes two forms, as described below.

- Monitoring—the procedures that are put in place to enable the investor to evaluate the performance of the business and keep track of his/her investment. Legally this is done through the balance sheet and profit and loss account, but some investors may want to monitor more than just the financial performance of the business.

- Control mechanisms give the investor an active role in the venture and the power to influence decision-making. One common control mechanism is for the investor to be represented on the firm's management team, perhaps as a director.

The model is helpful since it should help focus on the sort of information any potential investor will need in order to make an effective investment decision. It can be seen to be operating in the actions of a group of business angels studied by Mason and Harrison (1996).

The exit routes open to investors

While the entrepreneur is probably seeing the business, certainly at this stage, as a long-term business opportunity, potential investors are unlikely to be seeing it this way. Hence they will want to identify a possible exit strategy prior to investing in the business. Thus it is worth recognizing this and suggesting the preferred strategy at this point in time. Generally there are three options: the business is sold when the time comes, the investor is bought out or the business is floated on the stock market or the AIM.

A CASE EXAMPLE

Lastminute.com: a successful new venture funding programme?

Lastminute.com was founded in 1998 by two young entrepreneurs, Martha Lane Fox and Brent Hoberman, in the sitting room of Hoberman's home and with money borrowed from Lane Fox's parents. Two years later, on 14 March 2000, it was floated on the London Stock Exchange and the Nasdaq National Market with a valuation of about £316 million.

Essentially Lastminute.com, the brainchild of management consultant Brent Hoberman, aims 'to provide solutions and inspirations to its customers at short notice'. It works on the principle that airlines, hotels, theatres, gift companies, etc. always have surplus capacity that is worthless if unused, but profitable if sold, even at short notice. Meanwhile busy, spontaneous consumers with limited time for comparison shopping are looking for a brand they can trust. The Internet can bring the two together. So, according to Lane Fox, the concept is to 'create a global e-commerce brand which is part of people's everyday lives'. However, when she first read Hoberman's proposal to sell excess inventory at short notice, she is reputed to have dismissed it as 'hopeless'. She was eventually won over, though, and with a 6000-line Excel spreadsheet they went about raising finance. Given Lane Fox's initial scepticism, it was not surprising that hard-nosed financiers were difficult to persuade and, as she admits, 'would I have believed me 12 months ago, 18 months ago? Probably not. I don't begrudge anyone who put the phone down on me because I might have done the same thing.'

Even so, the venture grew rapidly, moving out of Hoberman's sitting room and into the back of Lane Fox's mother's office in the Portobello Road area of London before moving into its present office accommodation behind Oxford Street in central London, where it employs some 200 telephone and computer operators. Immediately prior to its flotation, figures released by the company showed that for the last quarter of 1999, sales were £409,000, up from £119,000 in the third quarter. By 30 June 2000, the number of registered subscribers had risen to 2.1 million (from 189,000 the previous year) and the total transaction value for the three-month period was £9.6 million, representing a 34 per cent increase on the quarter ending 31 March 2000 (£7.2 million), an increase of over 17 times compared to the equivalent period for the previous year. Similarly the gross profit (£950,000) was up 34 per cent on that (£707,000) of the period ending 31 March 2000, and over 23 times that of the corresponding period in 1999. According to Hoberman, such results placed 'Lastminute.com ahead of plan on all key metrics—brand strength, product range and depth, subscriber base, customers, total transaction value and gross profit'.

Despite such growth and considerable over-subscription at the time of the flotation, the price of Lastminute.com shares dropped significantly after flotation, from an offer price of 380p in March 2000 to 154p in August of the same year. Commenting on the situation in March 2000, Hoberman made the point that 'the float achieved one of the prime aims of the company. It raised the capital [£113 million] to enable us to go forward'. While clearly being disappointed by the share price, he recognized that other stocks—notably Amazon and Freeserve—fell below their issue price and reputedly argues that he and Lane Fox 'should be running the business, not staring at stock price volatility'.

However, the problems for Lastminute.com have continued. In October 2000 it purchased Degriftour, a French online travel site for £51.5 million. This helped it increase its 'registered subscribers' to 2.9 million by the end of the year but in the last three months of the year its quarterly loss more than doubled to £15.4 million. Even so it ended the year with a cash surplus of £70.9 million and, with sales rising from £409,000 to £2.9 million, it believes this reserve will see it through to profitability, which is expected to be towards the end of 2002. In February 2001 it announced an alliance with the international travel agency Thomas Cook. Under this arrangement customers from the Lastminute.com website will be directed to Thomas Cook's site if they are looking to buy more than six weeks in advance of travel. In return, Thomas Cook will refer its customers to the Lastminute.com site for items such as theatre tickets and restaurant bookings.

Case example exercise

Review the Lastminute.com case example. From it you will see that Lastminute.com appeared to have difficulty raising finance, initially. Why do you think that was? Do you think that if it had had a proper business plan instead of a '6000-line Excel spreadsheet':

(a) it would have been any more successful and, if so, why

(b) the problems it subsequently encountered might have been anticipated and/or reduced

(c) it would have purchased Degriftour and entered into the alliance with Thomas Cook?

Evaluate how a business plan might have helped and hindered its development.

Exercise 10.11

Identify a number of potential funding sources for your proposed business. Find out more about them. On the basis of the research, select one that looks as if there is a good match between their portfolio and what you want to do. Then, draft a proposal to them for the funding you will require.

Launching the new venture

The business start-up or new venture creation process can be perceived as a number of discrete but overlapping stages. At each stage there are a number of factors that either facilitate or limit development. The stages are normally regarded as follows.

- **Idea formulation.** Each business start-up is a unique event. Often there is a considerable time-lag, however, between having the initial idea and the launch of the business. This is because it takes time to:
  - research, refine and formulate ideas
  - raise funding
  - find partners.

  There is no single source of ideas. Apart from activities to increase creativity and generate ideas (discussed in Chapter 6), it is possible to generate ideas from a number of sources, including:
  - being observant—looking for new opportunities or ways to do things better, listening to what people say, etc. (these may include customers, distributors and wholesalers, competitors)
  - franchise opportunities
  - patents
  - product licensing
  - corporations
  - research institutes
  - universities
  - trade shows
  - former employers
  - professional contacts
  - consulting
  - networking.

- **Opportunity recognition.** Converting an idea into a business opportunity is the critical element in the process of business creation. The economic environment has to be conducive, there must be an appropriate culture supportive of risk-taking and the nascent entrepreneur must have the confidence to ensure that the idea fulfils its potential. Role models (see Chapter 3) help in this process as they demonstrate what can be achieved and what efforts are needed to ensure success.

- Pre-start planning and preparation. This is vital to the success of the venture. Included here is:
  - research—both technical and market research
  - determining an appropriate entry strategy
  - raising sufficient finance
  - assembling the entrepreneurial team
  - identifying suppliers
  - establishing the feasibility of the project.
- Entry and launch. Clearly, the timing of entry is important, particularly if the product or process is new and requires patenting. While there are advantages for first movers, moving too early can result in insufficient customers/clients, and can alert competitors.
- Post-entry development. While few new businesses grow, for those that do this is a crucial stage for the inexperienced entrepreneur. Many see growth as a symbol of success and grow too rapidly (namely some of the recent dot.com collapses).

Strategies for entry and launch

Developing a strategy for the new or emerging venture is one of the most important tasks to be undertaken. All other activities are dependent on the selected strategy, and considerable time has to be devoted to developing the venture strategy and the functional strategies that support it.

Essentially the strategic planning process comprises four stages, as the business plan section of this chapter has shown. These are as follows.

- Premise stage:
  - determine the nature of the venture.
- Analysis stage:
  - analyse opportunities
  - analyse the venture's capabilities
  - identify distinctive competences.
- Strategy development stage:
  - develop the venture strategy
  - develop supporting strategies.
- Implementation stage:
  - assemble the necessary resources
  - establish controls
  - begin action.

New and emerging businesses essentially have three generic strategy types to select from, namely differentiation strategies, low-cost leadership and focus strategies. We will now look at each of these in turn.

Differentiation strategies

These create value for the customer beyond that available from competing products. They are useful since they permit a premium price to be charged for the product. The high profit margins either allow costing errors to be absorbed or permit re-investment in the business, either to refine the product or exploit it further.

Low-cost leadership

Normally this strategy would not be appropriate for the majority of new ventures as it requires high relative market share. However, if the new venture can reduce production costs (through introducing a cheaper, more efficient method of production, for example) or reduce overheads, then it is possible, but once embarked upon, it is necessary to continue to reduce the cost of the product if the venture is to retain its low-cost leadership position. This must not be at the expense of quality, though.

Focus strategies

These combine parts of both the differentiation and low-cost leadership strategies. Focus strategies are not market share-oriented. Rather, they are oriented towards serving a small target market in the best way possible. The right sort of customers will willingly pay a premium for the specialized attention they receive and the strategy is protectable because the business continues to provide the specialized attention.

Choosing the appropriate market entry strategy

The appropriate strategy for the business is determined through the formulation of the marketing plan. Once this has been done, it is necessary to decide upon an appropriate market entry strategy. According to Vesper (1990), there are 14 possible entry strategies or, in his terms, 'entry wedges'. These are as follows.

- **New product or service.** The development of a completely new product or service that has never been used before. Very rare.
- **Parallel competition.** More frequent. The entrepreneur begins a venture that is similar to one already in existence, although the product or service may be marginally different in some way.
- **Franchise.** A frequently used entry wedge, used by both the franchisor and the franchisee.
- **Geographical transfer.** Frequently a potential entrepreneur will spot a venture or an opportunity while travelling and will implement it on returning home.
- **Supply shortage.** This wedge opportunity occurs when demand exceeds supply. A vacuum is created and the entrepreneur moves quickly to fill it.
- **Tapping unused resources.** Here the entrepreneur controls a resource and starts a venture to supply that resource to a waiting market. The impetus behind the venture is the untapped resource, not the unmet demand.

- **Customer contract.** The entrepreneur enters into an agreement with a customer to supply the product before launching the venture. Hence he/she is assured of a significant customer.

- **Becoming an additional supplier.** Here the entrepreneur negotiates with the customer to become an additional supplier. Many firms are keen to have more than one supplier of a product in order to ensure an uninterrupted supply.

- **Joint ventures.** An existing company forms a new venture that is partly owned by the parent company and partly by the entrepreneur. The joint venture either makes products for the parent or produces products in which the parent has only a modest interest. Sometimes they are funded by the parent and operated by the entrepreneur.

- **Licensing.** An agreement is reached with an existing business whereby the new venture can produce the product using the name and trademark of the existing company.

- **Market relinquishment.** An existing, usually large, company may negotiate with some of its managers or other interested entrepreneurs to take over the product. Usually this happens when the market is too small to retain the interest of the original producer, or when labour problems make production of the product uneconomical. The new venture, being smaller, can make a profit by producing the product with a lower overhead or paying lower wages for non-union labour.

- **Sell-off of a division.** Rather than phase out a product, leaving a vacuum in the market, an existing firm may sell off a division, usually to its employees.

- **Favoured purchasing.** Government agencies often discriminate in favour of new and small ventures in order to help support the sector. This gives the new or small business an opportunity to enter the government contracting sector, which might have been difficult otherwise.

- **Rule changes.** Here the new venture takes advantage of a change in government regulations.

The first three of these are the main competitive entry wedges for new ventures, but selection depends on the nature of the business and the resources available

Exercise 10.12

Produce an action plan to enable you to enter the market. Your plan should identify:

- what will need to be done
- by whom it will be done
- any resources that might be needed
- the timing of the activities.

If you anticipate any difficulties you should state them and say how you intend they should be overcome.

Assuming your business proposition is commercially viable, and you have been able to assemble the requisite funding, you should now be in a position to launch your new enterprise. So *carpe diem*—seize the day!

Chapter Review

➡ The feasibility of the new venture is determined through the business plan. This provides:
- an executive summary
- a description of the business
- a marketing plan
- the methods of operation and/or production
- details of human resource requirements
- details of capital requirements
- financial forecasts.

➡ Once it has been determined that the project is commercially viable, it is necessary to raise funding. The business plan will be useful here.

➡ Essentially there are two forms of financing—equity financing and debt financing—and often there are many different sources that can be used. The type of funding and potential sources are usually determined by the funding amount, purpose and timing.

➡ Once funding has been negotiated it is possible to launch the business. There are a limited number of entry strategies but the process needs to be thoroughly planned and thought through.

Quick Revision

(Answers at the end of this section)

1. What is the purpose of the business plan?
   (a) to test the viability of an idea
   (b) to act as a 'route map' for the business
   (c) to raise funding for the business

2. Sensitivity analysis is an important part of business planning as it indicates when a new venture is likely to start making a profit. Is this:
   (a) true
   (b) false?

3. What is meant when it is said that 'the funding of a new venture is essentially a buying and selling process'? Does it mean that:
   (a) the entrepreneur is attempting to sell the new business to a prospective buyer
   (b) the entrepreneur is attempting to buy funding for his business, which the financiers are attempting to sell
   (c) the entrepreneur is attempting to sell an investment opportunity and the

investor is attempting to buy an opportunity that will provide a good return for his/her investment?

4. Which of the following is *not* one of the five key processes in the investment process according to Tyebjee and Bruno (1984)?

(a) deal origination

(b) deal screening

(c) deal evaluation

(d) deal structuring

(e) deal offering

(f) post-investment activity

Answers to Quick Revision: 1–a, b and c; 2–b; 3–c; 4–e

Learning Style Activities

Either

➡ **Activist:** Obtain and read a copy of a business plan. You will find a range of plans at www.Bplans.com/sp/index.cfm?a=bc.

➡ **Reflector:** Relate the plan to the above discussion on business plans. How well does the plan meet the various requirements?

➡ **Theorist:** What have you learned about the theory of business planning from your evaluation of the plan?

➡ **Pragmatist:** What have you learned that will help you produce a better business plan for your new venture?

Or

➡ **Activist:** Talk to people who have recently set up in business or who are about to launch a new enterprise. How did they raise or how are they raising the necessary finance? What problems or difficulties have they experienced?

➡ **Reflector:** Relate their experiences to what you have learned about funding a new venture. How do the two compare? Identify any similarities and differences between the two.

➡ **Theorist:** Consider the theory of new venture funding. Could it have helped the people you spoke to in any way? Do their experiences suggest that the theory ought to be modified?

➡ **Pragmatist:** If you were to set up a new venture, how would you go about raising finance given your knowledge of both the theory and the practice?

Reading

Barrow, C., P. Barrow and R. Brown (2001) *The Business Plan Workbook*. London: Kogan Page Ltd.

Clegg, G. and C. Barrow (1984) *How to Start and Run Your Own Business*. London: Macmillan.

Jones, G. (1988) *Starting Up*. London: Pitman Publishing.

McDonald, M.H. (1985) *Marketing Plans: How to Prepare Them. How to Use Them*. London: Heinemann.

Mason, C. and R. Harrison (1996) Why 'Business Angels' Say No: A Case Study of Opportunities Rejected by an Informal Investor Syndicate. *International Small Journal* **14** (2), 35–51.

Stapleton, J. (1984) *How to Prepare a Marketing Plan*. Aldershot: Gower.

Tyebjee T.T. and A.V. Bruno (1984) A Model of Venture Capital Investment Activity. *Management Science* **30** (9), 1051–66.

Vesper, K.H. (1990) *New Venture Strategies*. Englewood-Cliffs NJ: Prentice Hall.

West, A. (1988) *A Business Plan*. London: Pitman.

Chapter 11

Retaining Entrepreneurship as the Venture Grows

Learning Outcomes

On completion of this chapter, the reader will:

- appreciate the barriers to growth in small firms
- recognize the difficulties small firms are likely to face when they do grow
- be more aware of the changing management needs of small and medium-sized enterprises as they grow
- understand what needs to be done if the enterprise is to retain its entrepreneurial drive as it grows
- appreciate the difficulties of having to replace the founding entrepreneur, and how these can be overcome
- be aware of what needs to be done to create an entrepreneurial team that will grow the venture.

Introduction

A major problem facing all entrepreneurial new ventures is that when they grow, they tend to lose the entrepreneurial dynamic that is the hallmark of their success. In reality, however, few small businesses survive, let alone grow, and before examining the challenges of growth and how a growth business may retain its entrepreneurial dynamic, it is worth examining the barriers to growth in new and existing small firms.

There are numerous reasons why growth does not occur and there have been many studies of the barriers to growth in small firms. According to Barber *et al.* (1989), however, they can be grouped into three categories:

1. **management and motivation**—lack of management training, relatively low qualifications, reluctance to delegate, the need for new management skills as the organization grows, etc.

2. **resources**—access to finance, access to skilled labour and access to technology

3. **market opportunities and structure**—market growth rates, size and frequency of purchases, degree of segmentation, opportunities for collaboration or merger, etc.

However, a more recent study by the Institute of Chartered Accountants in England and Wales (1996) argues that there is a need to distinguish between firms on the basis of their size. The study revealed that for micro-businesses (with up to 10 employees) the main barrier to growth was funding, for small businesses (11–100 employees) it was compliance with UK regulations, and for medium-sized enterprises (101–500 employees) it was the impact of European legislation. However, the overall barrier to growth was funding. Although management was not the main barrier to growth for any of the size groupings, businesses of all sizes were found to experience a lack of management skills and the study argued for the provision of low-cost business management training for small and medium-sized enterprises in order to facilitate growth.

The importance of good management is probably identified most clearly in the Cranfield University study of growth in small and medium-sized enterprises (Barrow, 2000/2001). Based on a study of over 300 successful owner-managed firms over a 10-year period, the study suggests that the main barriers to growth are as follows.

- **The planning vacuum.** Both in Europe and across the UK, owner-managed firms with business plans perform better than those without. Both sales and profit growth for firms with business plans are likely to be higher than for others in their sector.

- **Muddled marketing.** A total of 88 per cent of the fastest growing and most profitable small and medium-sized enterprises achieved those results by selling more of their core products to broadly similar types of customer. Yet, less than half of the firms studied saw this as the way to future growth. Most saw entering new markets and launching new products as the way forward. The most successful growth businesses had a superior product or service, a superior reputation and a better understanding of customer needs. They achieved growth through focus and concentration rather than diffusion of effort.

- **Mis-managed change.** The research suggests that the main reason why most owner-managed firms fail to achieve their true potential is because they fail to recognize the different phases of growth through which firms pass, and to manage the transition. Each phase of growth calls for a different approach to managing the business but most founders tend to try to run their business in much the same way as it gets bigger as they did when it was small. As a consequence 'they end up with a small big company rather than the big small company that is required if successful growth is to be achieved' (2000/2001: 4).

- **Meddling and mis-spent time.** To grow a business successfully the day-to-day business operation has to be carried out effectively, business improvements have to be made and a business strategy has to be developed. In the most successful growth businesses, the owner-manager recruits a successful management team to run the business on a day-to-day basis and spends his/her time planning the future competitive strategy of the business and improving its performance. However, the research suggests that in most cases owner-managers spend only 10 per cent of their time on these tasks, preferring to focus on the day-to-day operation of the business, checking and overseeing the work they are paying others to do. The result of this 'meddling' is soaring overheads, unhappiness and a loss of motivation. For growth to be successful, the owner-manager needs to 'stop working and start thinking'.

- **The wrong objectives.** Most small and medium-sized firms have no clear objectives, 'muddling through' from year to year. Of those that do, many have the wrong objectives, commonly concentrating on sales or turnover growth, which usually brings more problems for the business including reduced profitability. The research suggests that less than a third of small and medium-sized enterprises across Europe set their objectives in terms of profits and margins, which is surprising as profit and profitability are the key measures of business success.

- **No financial strategy.** Few small and medium-sized enterprises have any strategy towards finance when attempting to grow the business. Most rely on the bank overdraft as the means of long-term finance and many either have no knowledge of alternative sources of funding or have the wrong impression of them. As a consequence, either they use the least appropriate sources of funding to finance growth or, as demonstrated in previous studies, find it difficult to raise the required funding. Often the situation is exacerbated by the lack of a business plan and/or an appropriate system of budgeting and control.

As can be seen, there are numerous factors that prevent new and small firms from growing and, as Chapter 4 demonstrated, various measures have been introduced in the UK, as elsewhere, to overcome such barriers, and to facilitate new and small firms' growth and development. However, there is one barrier that has not been considered, namely the motivation of the founder. Often the founder does not wish to grow the business and Birley (2000a) has suggested that there are, in fact, four types of owner-manager:

1. **the protectionist**–the owner-manager wants to maintain the business at its current size, thus protecting his/her investment

2. **the business-oriented**–the owner-manager wants to both grow and control the business in order to protect his/her income and investment

3. **the dynast**–the owner-manager wants to grow the business in order to protect the investment and pass it on to the next generation

4. **the family business**–the owner-manager wants to keep the business at its current size and pass it on to the next generation.

Thus not all businesses *want* to grow and it is wrong to assume that they should or must. However, some do and, of these, many fail. Therefore, it is important to look at the challenges that new and small firms face when attempting to grow and to consider, in particular, the way in which they can retain their entrepreneurial dynamic. In an era of very rapid and non-linear change, when flexibility, speed and focus are important to business success, it is important that growing businesses retain the entrepreneurial drive that so characterizes their initial success. Yet, frequently, growing businesses fail to do this.

Facing the strategic challenges of growth

When small firms do grow, they face various challenges. According to Greiner (1972), small growth firms pass through distinct periods of crisis as they shift from one phase of growth to another (see Fig. 11.1).

Greiner's growth model

Altogether he identifies five growth stages, which he describes as creativity, direction, delegation, co-ordination and collaboration. Each of these stages is followed by a period of crisis, as outlined below.

Crisis of leadership

When the firm moves from Stage 1 where growth comes through entrepreneurial creativity to Stage 2 where growth results from more strategic leadership, more sophisticated knowledge is required to operate larger production runs and manage an increasing workforce. Capital needs to be secured to underpin further growth, and financial controls are required. The firm has to hire additional executive resource, and to restructure to meet these challenges.

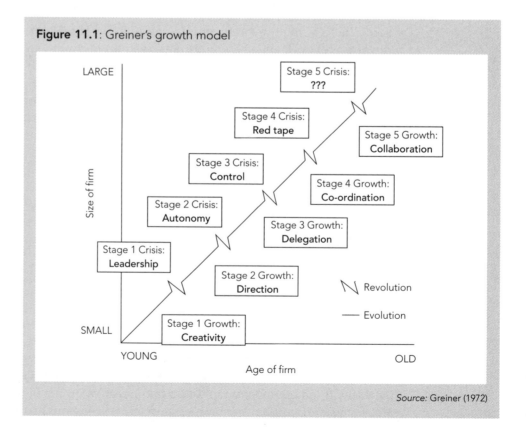

Figure 11.1: Greiner's growth model

Source: Greiner (1972)

Crisis of autonomy

The control mechanisms implemented to overcome the first crisis become less appropriate as the physical size of the firm increases. Line employees and line managers become frustrated with the bureaucracy attendant upon a centralized hierarchy. Line staff are more familiar with markets and machinery than executives, and become 'torn between following procedures and taking initiative' (1972: 42). It becomes necessary, therefore, for the firm to delegate to allow sufficient discretion in operating decision-making, and the passage from Stage 2 (direction) to Stage 3 (delegation) is marked by a crisis of autonomy.

Crisis of control

Top executives perceive a loss of control resulting from excessive discretion resting with lower and middle managers. There is little co-ordination across divisions, plants or functions. Top management needs to regain control through special co-ordination techniques, and Stage 4 (co-ordination) is entered.

Crisis of 'red tape'

By the time Stage 4 has been reached, the firm is likely to have lost much of its entrepreneurial drive. There are probably set procedures for doing things and the 'watchdog' approach adopted by senior management, together with the proliferation of systems and programmes, leads to a crisis of confidence and red tape. Line managers object to excessive direction, and senior managers view line managers as un-co-operative and disruptive. Both groups are unhappy with the cumbersome paper system that has evolved to meet the challenges of the previous period. The firm has become too large and complex to be managed through an extensive framework of formal procedures and controls. Movement to Stage 5 requires a shift to 'interpersonal collaboration'.

Crisis of ???

In the fifth stage, according to Greiner, the organization attempts to overcome the excessive bureaucracy of Stage 4 by getting people to work together through a sense of mission or purpose. However, the model suggests that, as in earlier phases, a new crisis emerges as the business evolves, though Greiner can find no 'consistent' empirical evidence that points to the nature of the crisis into which Stage 5 degenerates as it shifts into Stage 6. However, he hypothesizes that this crisis will revolve around the 'psychological saturation' of employees that will occur as a logical result of the information age. Consequently organizations will evolve with dual structures of 'habit' and 'reflection', allowing employees to move, periodically, between the two periods of rest—or some alternative format whereby 'spent' staff can refuel their energies. It could be, though, that this is the stage in which organizations revolt and begin to behave as they did when they were small, a topic that is considered in the next chapter.

Greiner's growth model in practice

As might be expected, each of the stages identified in Greiner's model requires a different management style. While Stage 1 requires an individualistic and entrepreneurial style, subsequent stages require a directive style, a delegative style, a watchdog style and, finally, a participative style. However, perhaps this is not the main point of Greiner's model. Rather it is the fact that new and small firms can quite quickly lose their entrepreneurial momentum as they grow. To prevent this happening, possibly the key is to evolve an organizational structure and style of management that prevents the business passing into Stage 4. Indeed, this is precisely what Richard Branson has done with his Virgin group, as was shown in Chapter 9. Not only did he develop it as a cellular structure of individual, autonomous new and small enterprises, but he actually breaks up the larger enterprises as they begin to lose their entrepreneurial dynamic. For example, when the growth of Virgin Records began to slow, Branson took the deputy managing director, the deputy sales director and the deputy marketing director and gave them responsibility for an entirely new company.

Since Greiner published his findings, other life cycle models have been produced (Churchill and Lewis, 1983; Scott and Bruce, 1987). All of them are similar but identify different stages, and all have been criticized for the following reasons:

- most firms experience little or no growth and are unlikely, therefore, to reach Stages 3, 4 or 5
- the models do not allow for backward movement or for the skipping of stages
- growth need not involve crises, and growth firms need not necessarily lurch from one crisis to the next.

While such criticisms are valid, possibly they miss the real point, that of focusing on the experiences that firms are likely to encounter when attempting to grow and develop. Possibly the models are too rigid and inflexible, but their value is that they do focus attention on the challenges facing small firms when they attempt to grow. Whether they face them sequentially, as the models suggest, is another matter. Equally whether all firms face the *same* crises is also to be contested. Whatever, whether they face all of them or just some, they are the sort of challenges that firms have to face when attempting to survive and grow. Thus the

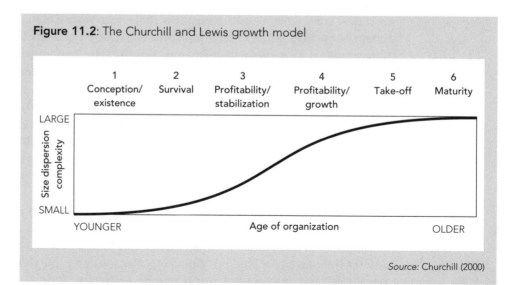

Figure 11.2: The Churchill and Lewis growth model

Source: Churchill (2000)

models are extremely valuable in addressing the issues facing growth businesses. Indeed, the Churchill and Lewis (1983) model is particularly helpful in that it focuses on the changing role of the entrepreneur and his/her requisite skill needs.

The Churchill and Lewis growth model

According to the Churchill and Lewis growth model (Fig. 11.2), there are six stages of development, as described below.

Stage 1: conception/existence

At this stage the business has not really come into existence. The owner *is* the business. He/she does everything. Systems and formal planning are minimal and the strategy is simply to survive. Many businesses actually fail at this stage and do not pass on to Stage 2.

Stage 2: survival

By Stage 2 the business has become a workable entity, though the major goal is still survival. The business retains a simple organizational structure and the owner remains synonymous with the business. However, it will probably have recruited a limited number of employees, including a sales manager or general foreman. Neither is able to make decisions, instead being required to carry out the orders of the owner-manager. Formal planning remains limited. Many businesses remain at the survival stage without passing on to Stage 3. Churchill and Lewis refer to these as 'hobby' businesses, though they might be equated with Birley's protectionist and family businesses. In many cases, however, the businesses do become profitable and move on to the next stage.

Stage 3: profitability and stabilization

By this stage the business has grown to a size where it requires functional managers to take over some of the responsibilities of the owner. At this stage, also, the business engages its first professional staff members, usually someone to control the office and a production scheduler. The owner, working through the management team, develops and monitors a strategy essentially intended to maintain the status quo. However, as the business matures, it and the owner move apart, so that the two are not synonymous with each other. In part this is because of the presence of the other managers.

Stage 4: profitability and growth

Many businesses stay for long periods in the stability stage before moving on to Stage 4, the time when the owner consolidates the business and marshals the resources for growth. At this stage the owner not only has to ensure that the business remains profitable but also to recruit a team of high-calibre managers capable of managing the business through the next stage of its development. Better systems are needed to facilitate further growth and the owner shares responsibility for the strategic development of the business with his/her senior managers.

Stage 5: take-off

This is a pivotal period in a firm's development. Often the founders are unsuccessful at managing the business through this stage, either because they try to grow the business too quickly or because they are unable to delegate effectively. If this is the case, and the founder recognizes his/her limitations early enough, the business may be sold. However, it is not uncommon at this stage for the firm's investors and/or creditors to have the founding entrepreneur replaced. If action is taken soon enough the business may be successful—if not, it may move back to Stage 4.

Stage 6: maturity

At this stage, the owner and the business are no longer remotely synonymous. The management is decentralized and the requisite systems are in place. The firm has the necessary resources in place for it to remain profitable and the main concern at this stage is for it to retain the advantages of small size, including flexibility of response and the entrepreneurial spirit. If it can do this, it will be a formidable force in the marketplace. If not, it is likely to ossify. Ossification is characterized, normally, by a lack of innovation and avoidance of risk.

Management needs in the Churchill and Lewis model

From this model, and Fig. 11.3, it is apparent that much of the success of the small firm is dependent on the skills of the owner-manager. In the early stages it is dependent on his/her ability to do the job (invent, produce, sell, manage, etc.). As the business grows, other people take over these responsibilities and the owner is required to spend less time doing and more time managing, which means he/she needs to delegate. However, many owners do find it difficult to let go, as the Cranfield research suggests, and this frequently explains why so few businesses are successful beyond the fourth stage

Figure 11.3: Management needs in the Churchill and Lewis model

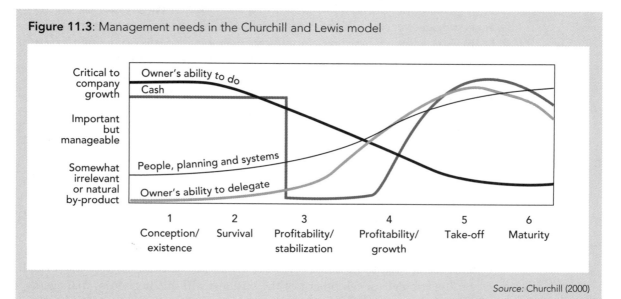

Source: Churchill (2000)

Clearly, the model can be criticized as pointed out above but it does focus attention on the challenges facing small businesses intent on growth. Importantly, also, it does introduce a number of important topics related to the growth of the small firm, namely how to maintain the entrepreneurial dynamic, how to replace the founder and how to create the entrepreneurial team. Each will be explored in more detail below, once you have considered the following 'Pause for Thought' section.

PAUSE FOR THOUGHT

Given your knowledge of growth firms, how representative are the models of the phases through which they pass and the problems they encounter?

A CASE EXAMPLE

Creative solution for Jensen Cars: the relaunch of a family business

At a time when the world car market is in a state of flux and the UK car industry is almost completely collapsed, the firm manufacturing one of the most famous marques of British motoring, the Jensen, is being relaunched. The first Jensen was manufactured in 1934 by West Bromwich entrepreneurs, Alan and Richard Jensen, who were essentially truck repairers. Since then, the business has had a somewhat chequered history. Until the mid-1960s, the car was extremely popular and the business attracted many high-profile customers, such as the film star Clark Gable. Though the business was successful it was becoming increasingly apparent that the *modus operandi* was somewhat dated and old-fashioned. In 1966, all that changed when the board appointed an Italian to design the firm's now famous Interceptor. This proved an unpopular move with the founders, 'Mr Alan' and 'Mr Richard' as they were known, and they resigned. Their departure did not prove to be too much of a problem, the Interceptor became the most successful Jensen of all time and in 1970 the company was bought by an American sports car salesman, Kjell Qvale. Jensens were heavy on fuel consumption and he was brilliant at selling them to US tycoons. However, with the energy crisis of the early 1970s and the consequent three-day working week, Jensen was losing £67,000 a day by August 1975. Thus, despite a full order book the firm was declared bankrupt in 1976, leaving 1500 people jobless. However, Jensen Parts and Service (JP&S) remained in existence, ensuring customers could still get spares. In 1981 it announced plans for the limited production of the Interceptor Mk IV. Production was costly and at more than £100,000 a car, it barely sold one a year. Eventually in 1992, the company, which was now owned by Stockport businessman Hugh Wainwright, was put into receivership once more. Potential purchasers came up against a major problem; while the business was for sale, the Jensen trademark was not. It was not until after Wainwright's death that the rights were acquired from his estate by Redditch firm Creative Design, in January 1998.

Formed in 1995, the Creative Group is a private automotive consultancy and tool-making company that has worked successfully on projects for major international customers including Chrysler, Nissan Western Star Trucks and Leyland Trucks. Within four years from start-up it had achieved annual sales of over £10 million and was employing over 100 staff. It has its own design studio and one of the largest privately owned tool rooms in the country. Its owners, Keith Rauer and Robin Bowyer, both have a lifetime's experience in the motor industry. Together, they have invested £2.9 million in Jensen motors for approximately 60 per cent of the equity, with management providing a further £500,000. The rest of the finance has come from about 20 private individuals and grants. The UK Department of Trade and Industry has contributed £400,000 through its regional development selective assistance programme, while Liverpool City Council has provided a grant of £250,000.

Rauer (who is managing director of the company) and Bowyer have been joined on the board by Graham Morris, as company chairman. Morris, the former chief executive of Rolls-Royce Motor Cars, claims they have relaunched the company because of 'inner belief, though not just the blind belief of car enthusiasts'. He claims the group has a sound business plan, which shows a cash breakeven at below 200 cars. Already, it has 100 orders for the car and plans to produce 600 a year, employing 60 people.

Case example exercise

Review the Jensen case and the theories relating to the life cycle of the firm. How do the theories help us understand the problems that firms such as Jensen experience during their life? Could they have helped predict some of the difficulties Jensen experienced and helped the founders and its subsequent owners overcome them? As a consultant to Jensen, what would you have advised the founders to do?

Once you have done this, read the Burton Group case example in Chapter 12 and repeat the exercise by considering Burton's development prior to Sir Ralph Halpern taking charge in 1981. What can you learn from the two cases?

Maintaining the entrepreneurial dynamic

In order to overcome such crises and to retain the entrepreneurial spirit as the firm grows and develops, the entrepreneur needs to ensure that all employees are aware of:

- customers' needs
- why they purchase
- the problems they face
- their specific needs and wants
- the importance of improvement.

According to Stevenson and Jarillo-Mossi (1986: 12) the very 'success of the entrepreneur and the methods by which that success is often achieved can lead to bureaucracy and stagnation' in the growing firm. They argue that not only do successful entrepreneurs often come, themselves, to a stage where they resist change and prefer the status quo, but their tendency to adopt an authoritarian style of management frequently results in the absence of any culture of change within the organization, employees feeling alienated from the change process and, often, resistant to it. Indeed, when the pressures for change come from lower down in the organization, they are often blocked by the entrepreneur, the result being frustration and/or the loss to the firm of a source of ideas and impetus for change.

In such situations, Stevenson and Jarillo-Mossi argue, entrepreneurship cannot be perpetuated by cloning the founder or by developing a mechanistic set of rules to ensure extensions of the brilliant thoughts of the leader. Rather, they suggest, it is necessary to create an 'adaptive organization'—an institution capable of facilitating the characteristics of the entrepreneur, namely to perceive and pursue opportunities, and to believe that success is possible.

To perceive opportunities, the business needs to be structured in such a way that:

- each function and each level in the organization knows what the market is demanding, and uses those market demands to structure its own set of goals and objectives

- individuals in the organization have a sense of ownership of the firm's broad objectives rather than the narrower objectives of their own functional specialism

- no individual function becomes dominant and it is recognized that success will be achieved only by balancing functional needs

- change becomes institutionalized and recognized as an organizational goal.

To pursue opportunities, the firm needs to:

- reward the pursuit of new ideas and encourage all its employees to try, especially as only a few will ever succeed

- recognize that the pursuit of new ideas needs patience, protection and faith, and create an environment where individuals are not afraid to innovate

- appreciate that, in an era of change and uncertainty, plans need to be flexible and organizations need to adapt speedily to changed circumstances.

However, as Vandermerwe (2000) has recognized, being entrepreneurial is more than just having new ideas and '. . . "seeing" things differently or seeing different things. It involves knowing how to articulate imaginative ideas into language and concepts that others can and want to understand and make actionable.' The key to success, as she recognizes, is customer focus. This is not just about orientating the business around the customer as in the traditional models of small firm marketing or reacting to expressed customer needs (Brown, 1985); rather, it is about being proactive and building deep and long-lasting relationships with customers in targeted markets in order to understand and anticipate their needs, and lock them on to the business. Often, especially but not exclusively in the high-tech industries, customers are not aware of what they want because they lack the detailed insights into the advances in technology. Thus, being customer-focused does not just mean responding to the expressed needs of customers, but anticipating their needs by having a close, intimate knowledge of them. By so doing customers become 'locked on' (rather than locked in) to a firm because it continuously gives them what they want. Thus customer focus is a way of thinking, an organizing logic, around which all decisions are made. It manifests itself in companies like Amazon.com and Virgin. The appeal of Amazon, for example, is not that it provides books cheaply but that it has taken the hassle out of book buying, thereby giving the customer more time. Similarly Virgin has minimized the hassle of getting to and from airports by offering limousine services to its first-class and business-class passengers, thereby locking them on to the airline. As Vandermerwe (2000: 269) suggests, being entrepreneurial is about:

66 99 . . . being precise, able, through the management of knowledge and use of new electronic technology, to know what customers want, and having the capability and flexibility to deliver that to them—instead of only what the company makes, has in stock, or is promoting at that moment in time.

Thus, to retain their entrepreneurial drive as they grow, firms need to remain focused on their customers, and capable of anticipating and responding to their needs.

Identify a growth firm and consider the problems it has experienced or is experiencing in attempting to maintain its entrepreneurial drive. What did it do or what should it have done to retain it?

A CASE EXAMPLE

Mary Quant OBE

Together with her husband, Alexander Plunket Green, Mary Quant (www.maryquant.co.uk), a shy, hesitant woman, revolutionized women's fashion in the 1960s and has continued to do so ever since. Born in London in 1934 to Welsh school teacher parents, she started her career ironing hat veils at a designer milliner's in London, after leaving school at the age of 16 and attending Goldsmith's College of Art. Shortly after her marriage to Alexander, whom she had met at art college, Mary opened a shop called Bazaar in the Chelsea area of London. It was the first boutique to be opened on the King's Road and was an instant success.

Mary's designs captured the mood of the times. In part, this was due to her intuition and flair but in part can be attributed to the way the business operated. She would buy her fabrics from Harrods (because she did not have to pay for them for a year), take them to the machinists to be made up to her designs, take the made-up clothes to the shop, sell them and start the cycle all over again. This kept her in close contact with her customers, as did the restaurant she and her husband opened beneath the shop, which became one of the most popular in London, frequented by film stars and the elite of London's trendy society. The Beatles bought clothes for their girlfriends from the store, and she made John Lennon's famous leather cap and the matching sheepskin coats that George Harrison and Pattie Boyd wore at their wedding.

Within seven years the business had expanded throughout Europe. Her designs began to penetrate the American market when, in 1962, she was signed up by the American retail giant JC Penney, and she designed the costumes for several popular films, including the Oscar-nominated Georgy Girl in 1966 and Audrey Hepburn's Two for the Road in 1967. 'The success just bowled us over,' she is reported to have said, 'we were terrified because the whole thing was going so fast.' Even so, in the second half of the 1960s she diversified into cosmetics. In the 1960s, she says, 'cosmetics were stuck on three shades of eye shadow. Brushes were a foot long and lipstick was pink, red and orange. I wanted a collection you could carry around in a small handbag.' So she created one.

Then, in the 1970s, she stopped manufacturing and diversified further into the design of household furnishings—bedding, duvets and wallpaper. The business continued to expand and, in 2000, was bought by a Japanese firm whose managing director reportedly declared she was 'not a good businesswoman'. Thereafter, the woman who had broken the stranglehold of Chanel, Dior and others on fashion, and caused the UK government to introduce new tax rules because of the millions it was losing in tax revenue from the revolution she had created, became a freelance design consultant to her former empire and a non-executive director for House of Fraser, working from her two homes—a mansion in Surrey and a country house in southwest France. According to Mary Riddell in a 2002 interview with Mary Quant, 'somewhere, far back down the years, time froze for Mary Quant. . . . At 67, she could pass for 50, maybe even less. The look is perfect, just as it always was.' Yet, in A.E. Hotchner's *Blown Away: The Rolling Stones and the Death of the Sixties*, Mary explains her success otherwise—by keeping abreast, if not ahead, of change: 'Good designers,' she says, 'know that to have any influence they must keep in step with public needs and that intangible "something in the air". They must catch the spirit of the day and interpret it in clothes before other designers . . .'.

Case example exercise.

Although she was supposed not to be a 'good businesswoman', Mary Quant created a successful business that is still successful more than 40 years after its foundation. Consider the factors that have contributed to its enduring success.

'Founder's disease'

As the earlier discussion has indicated, and the research of Buchelle (1967) and others has demonstrated, many entrepreneurs cannot, or will not, break old habits and learn new skills. As a consequence, the company goes out of control, profits turn to losses and what started as a successful business with a clear vision and full of promise becomes an enterprise that is confused, wandering and full of disappointment. This is the classic 'founder's disease'—founders are unable to adapt to the needs of the growing organization to the extent that if they continue to lead the business, performance tends to suffer. Under such circumstances many successful growth companies, according to Hambrick and Crozier (1985), bring in 'one or more senior level executives with big company experience' to supplement or replace the founding entrepreneur.

As firms grow, they become more complex and this complexity has to be managed. As complexity is increased, the founding entrepreneur normally experiences three areas of severe problems, namely the discovery that:

1. he/she cannot make all the decisions
2. science cannot clone the founder
3. the authority he/she has will never equal the degree of responsibility.

Under such circumstances, a new style of management is needed, often involving new information and control systems, and the introduction of a team-working approach to decision-making. All too frequently, it would seem, the founder is reluctant to lose control of the business, as Clifford and Cavanagh (1985) have observed, wanting: 'to do it all himself rather than manage others, so the growth potential of the business is strictly limited by his personal energy and capacity'.

However, research by Willard et al. (1991) on 126 manufacturing firms listed in the 100 fastest growing publicly held firms in the United States in the years 1985, 1986 and 1989 suggests that there is no statistically significant difference in performance between rapidly growing firms managed by founder chief executive officers (CEOs) and non-founder CEOs. While the research does not explain why this is the case or why some founder CEO firms perform well while others falter or fail, the authors do recognize that, increasingly, entrepreneurship is a team effort and the existence and composition of the entrepreneurial team is important. Indeed, this is a weakness of the literature on entrepreneurship. Most of the studies focus on entrepreneurs as individuals when, in reality, they are often part of a team.

This problem of succession is probably one of the greatest challenges facing the founding entrepreneur. Somewhat surprisingly, perhaps, it is most acute in the family firm. On the surface it might appear to be relatively easy—the entrepreneur simply chooses an heir who will inherit the business. Rarely is it so easy, however, and the change-over in the family business is often marked by:

- increased levels of inter-personal conflict, leading to a belittling of each others' goals
- attention to short-term profits rather than long-term goals
- ill-defined management procedures emphasizing the short term

- no defined process for integrating family members
- no career plans offering the younger generation some enticement
- failure to tap available financial resources from the external environment
- difficulty in valuing diverse contributions of family members to the firm, using conformity to avoid the strengths of diversity
- levelling off of growth and/or profits, probably an indicator of a lack of shared long-term goals.

In addition to all this, the founder frequently does not wish to relinquish his/her hold over the business and may view with hostility any attempts by the family to remove him or her. Conversely, the family may not want to confront the issue and so defer any action until it is unavoidable, by which time the business often has serious problems.

To avoid such problems, and to deal with the succession issue, it is variously held that planning should start well in advance (between 5 and 20 years) and that the entrepreneur should begin by considering the sort of successor that is required. The first point that needs to be considered is the type of successor needed—whether the business is looking for someone to provide the critical ideas for new product development and future initiatives (the entrepreneur) or someone interested in efficiency, internal control and effective use of resources (the manager). Often the founder is looking for a clone of him/herself, but it is important that the successor is appropriate for both the culture of the business being created and the stage of its development. However, it is important, also, that the founder and the successor are compatible. The heir must respect the founder's attachment to the venture and be sensitive to his/her feelings of ownership, while at the same time being able to initiate change. Conversely, the founder needs to be able to convert from being a leader to being a mentor or coach, from being a 'doer' to being an adviser.

Additionally, attention needs to be paid to the qualities and characteristics of the successor. Clearly these will depend on the particular circumstances that prevail but according to Chrisman et al. (1998) successors are most likely to possess at least some of the following attributes:

- a good knowledge of the business, or be in a good position from which to acquire one quickly
- fundamental honesty and capability
- good health, energy, alertness and perception
- enthusiasm about the enterprise
- a personality compatible with the business
- a high degree of perseverance
- stability and maturity
- a reasonable amount of aggressiveness
- thoroughness and a proper respect for detail
- an ability to solve problems
- resourcefulness

- an ability to plan and organize
- the talent to develop people
- the personality of both a starter and a finisher
- an appropriate agreement with the owner's philosophy about the business.

Clearly, the founder may be clear about who he/she wishes to succeed him/her but often this is not the case and it is generally accepted that the founder needs to design, and write down, a plan for succession very carefully. This should consider in some detail the duties and responsibilities of the successor, and the expertise and experience that he/she might possess, as well as any preferred abilities/attributes. In formulating the plan it is often helpful to bring into the discussions those people who are most likely to be affected by it. Not only does this introduce different perspectives and viewpoints, it can help to allay fears and create unity behind the successful candidate (Rue and Ibrahim, 1996).

On occasion the founder may not be the right person to decide on who should succeed him/her, especially if the business is not doing as well as perhaps it might. Alternatively, he/she might welcome help in selecting a successor. Under such circumstances it might be advisable, and desirable, to establish a board of advisers composed of people from outside the organization with no personal self-interest in the appointment. Whoever is appointed, it is normally advisable that a mentor is allocated and that if the successor is one of the founder's offspring, he/she has gained legitimacy through external employment and low-level entry, as the main issue is whether the successor can gain credibility with his/her colleagues.

Such issues are considered further in the research of Kirby and Lee (1996) on succession planning in family firms in the north-east of England. This concludes that, while firms do founder on the succession issue, many actually survive it 'without any formal mechanisms for choosing and training a successor and without the long-term strategic planning which is advocated by the theory' (1996: 80). They suggest that this happens because the entrepreneur acts intuitively and informally, and uses his/her networks and senses to identify a potential successor at an early stage. Subsequently, the candidate or candidates is/are groomed, through a combination of education and training, both in the company and outside. Hence, it is argued that, rather than attempting to impose a formal, bureaucratic system of succession planning on the firm that is alien to its entrepreneurial culture, it might be more appropriate to introduce a more general programme of human resource development, which identifies and grooms potential successors and more closely resembles the natural process of successor selection.

Even after such procedures have been followed there may be no clear successor. The founder may have no family members to pass the business on to or there may be no members of his family interested in taking it over. Under such circumstances he/she may decide to sell the business. Indeed, some founders may prefer to sell their business as a means of 'harvesting' their investment. Clearly, the final decision to sell will almost certainly, as Birley (2000b) recognizes, be related to the price the founder expects to receive from his/her equity, which may be above or below what the business is actually worth. This is determined by the size, profitability and track record of the business as well as the state of the market. However, it is generally held that the value of any business can be enhanced by adopting the tactics identified in Table 11.1.

Table 11.1: 10 tips for building the value of a business

1. Aim to increase the recurring profits of the business.
2. Focus on maintaining long-term sales growth.
3. Develop relationships with key customers to enhance the 'quality' of earnings.
4. Run the business with the same degree of governance and financial reporting as if it were a public company.
5. Adopt transparent and conservative accounting policies that are appropriate to the business sector.
6. Maintain flexibility by reconsidering major capital investment and through the ability to rent (rather than own) non-core assets.
7. Consider ways of compensating for the owner-manager's contribution to the success of the business if he/she will not be continuing to manage it. This may involve bringing in new management or transferring key business contacts to existing managers.
8. Make sure that any questions over the value of business assets, tax or other compliance issues are resolved in advance of the sale—if something is awry, the seller will lose credibility and this can decimate the business's value.
9. Identify and protect any intellectual property.
10. Get the timing right.

Source: Harrison (2000)

PAUSE FOR THOUGHT

Consider how any firm known to you has faced the problem of 'founder's disease' and how it coped with the issue of succession. What lessons can be learned from this experience?

A CASE EXAMPLE

The IKEA challenge: succession planning in a family firm

With 155 stores in 29 countries in North America, Asia, Australasia and the Middle East, as well as throughout Europe, furniture retailer IKEA is a truly global business. It has not always been like this, however. The original business, a mail-order company, was founded in Sweden in 1943 by 17-year-old dyslexic Ingvar Kamprad. Without a college education, but with considerable common sense, hard work and determination, Kamprad has turned the concept into a £5.7 billion empire employing approximately 50,000 people.

The first IKEA store opened in Sweden in 1958, followed in 1963 by a store in Norway and then, in 1969, by one in Denmark. In 1973, the first store outside of Scandinavia was opened, in Switzerland, and for the next two decades the company steadily expanded its operations to become the global

empire it is today. Essentially expansion took place through franchising, the owner and franchisor of the concept being IKEA Systems BV. However, the business remained very much a family affair.

At the age of 74, Kamprad has begun to think about retirement and who should inherit the family business. He has three sons: Peter, 36; Jonas, 33; and Matthias, 31. Peter works as the chief financial officer for IKEA's Belgian subsidiary; Jonas in the buying department of Habitat in Britain, which is part of the family empire; and Matthias outside of the family firm. Kamprad has worked with all three but does not believe that any of them is ready to take over. 'I admire my three sons,' he insists, 'They are very clever. But I don't think any of them is capable of running the company, at least not yet.' So, according to reports, he has decided to set them a test. Each of the three brothers is to be given, apparently, a part of the Habitat chain, which was bought in 1992 from the English entrepreneur, Sir Terence Conran and which owns 79 stores in Europe, employs 2500 staff and had a turnover in 1999 of £250 million. Whichever brother manages the business best will determine who takes over from the founding father. It could be years before the test is complete, especially as Kamprad senior has not spelt out publicly the business qualities he is looking for in his sons. Meanwhile, he remains in control. Hopefully both the family and the business will survive the succession exercise. 'At the moment, the three brothers seem very warm towards each other,' says Sir Terence Conran, founder of Habitat, 'it would be a shame if that changed.' If it is not to change, then the three brothers need to work together as a team.

According to Sir Terence, 'One might emerge as the leader but . . . they should each decide where their strengths lie and deploy them accordingly.'

Case example exercise

Imagine you are Ingvar Kamprad. You have been talking to Sir Terence Conran and you realize that this is not the way to find a successor for the company you have created. Not only might it break up the family you love, it could result in one of your sons taking over the firm who is not fully able to manage it and take it through to the next stage of its development, especially as he may not be able to rely on the support of his brothers. You have decided to scrap your original idea, but how are you going to find a successor? Consider the alternatives and justify your recruitment/selection strategy.

Creating the entrepreneurial team

From the models outlined above, it is clear that the quality of the entrepreneurial team is critical to the success of the growing business. Entrepreneurs will only succeed in growing their business if they create around them a quality management team with and through which they can function. Indeed, from the research of Muzyka *et al.* (2000), it is apparent that when looking to buy out (MBO) or buy into (MBI) a business, investors place considerable emphasis on the quality of the management team and its leadership. Indeed, as Table 11.2 shows, 6 out of the top 10 criteria are to do with the management team, and they conclude that 'management team factors reign supreme on the list of opportunity evaluation factors' (2000: 321). Having established the importance of the management team to potential investors in the business, the authors then go on to examine the char-

Table 11.2: Top 10 criteria for assessing opportunities for an MBO/MBI

1. Leadership capability of the management team
2. Track record of the management team
3. Sustained share-competitive position
4. Track record of team leader
5. Completeness and balance within management team
6. Complete business data
7. Leadership capability of team leader
8. Ease of cash out
9. Organizational/administrative capabilities of team
10. Expected rate of return

Source: Muzyka et al. (2000)

Table 11.3: Top 10 rankings of team criteria

1. Effectiveness of group decision-making
2. Ability of team to lead the organization
3. Previous profitable track record
4. Success in managing business-related conflicts
5. Trust within team
6. Commitment to group goals
7. Ability to manage interpersonal conflicts
8. Balance of team skills
9. Level of collective motivation
10. Team understanding of/commitment to investor's needs

Source: Muzyka et al. (2000)

acteristics looked for when such teams are being evaluated. The top 10 of these are ranked in Table 11.3, from which it can be seen that, from the perspective of a potential investor, the quality of the team is determined by its ability to identify what needs to be done and execute it successfully.

In many ways, these are the criteria for assessing the founding entrepreneur, also, the clarity of the vision and the ability to deliver. However, in creating the team, it is important that the entrepreneur does not simply appoint clones of him/herself. As in all team building (see Chapter 8 and Table 11.3) it is important that there is balance in the attributes that the members bring to the team. Also important, however, is the quality of the individuals recruited to the team. The entrepreneur needs to surround him/herself with people of the highest calibre with, as far as possible, a proven track record of achievement.

Often, however, it is difficult for small firms to attract quality staff, especially when they are new and there is uncertainty about their future. It is the role of the entrepreneur, however, to attract into the business the best people for the tasks in hand and it is not surprising to discover that in so doing:

- the entrepreneur often recruits the team, at least initially, through his/her personal contacts or family network
- there emerges over time an inner and outer team as the business grows and the new members are recruited, often based on their ability rather than their relationship to the founder.

Under such circumstances, one of the key challenges for the entrepreneur is to weld the two teams into one effective single unit, which clearly is not likely to be an easy task. Importantly, though, effective teams rarely just emerge—they have to be developed and often this takes time. As was shown in Chapter 8, it is generally accepted, following the work of Tuckman (1965), that there is a four-stage process in developing an effective team: forming, storming, norming and performing. Clearly the forming stage is important and the entrepreneur has to consider the composition of the team. In selecting team members he/she has to consider:

- their expertise—both their competence to do the job and their ability to plug skill gaps in the team
- their track record and experience—whether they have worked in a growth business previously
- whether they are likely to be credible with their fellow team members, employees and in the marketplace
- whether they are likely to fit into the culture of both the team and the organization
- their levels of motivation and reasons for wanting the job
- their contact networks.

Appointing the 'right' person for both the job and the team is not an easy task and despite the availability of a battery of pyschometric and other tests supposedly to aid the decision-making process, most entrepreneurs rely on instinct and intuition. Not surprisingly, mistakes are made, which in part explains the often impermanence of the entrepreneurial team.

Once formed, sufficient time needs to be set aside for building relationships if the team members are to work together effectively. As Cartwright and Cooper (2000) point out, there are numerous techniques that can be used to make teams perform more effectively. Most focus on developing team cohesiveness, but this should not be at the expense of creativity and constructive criticism. Hence the range of activities might include:

- setting time aside for building team relationships; this may include both social activities away from the workplace as well as the more traditional outdoor team-building exercises
- preventing the development of cliques and the development of set patterns of thinking by regularly changing the venue and seating arrangements at team meetings
- holding 'second chance' meetings before a final decision is reached to give the team an opportunity to reflect on the proposed solution
- ensuring that everyone is clear about what is to be done by recording the name of the person required to implement an agreed action in the minutes of team meetings
- requiring the person responsible for implementation to report back on their progress until the task is completed
- celebrating the successes of the team.

Often the entrepreneurial team will function, also, as the board of directors, possibly augmented by a small number of non-executive directors. On occasion, non-executives will be 'imposed' on the firm by investors and frequently are not welcomed by the management team, the belief being that they, the management team, will lose control of the business. However, given the responsibilities of the board, non-executives can be a valuable extra resource, bringing in additional experience, a different perspective and, often, a different set of contacts, which extends the firm's existing networks. Essentially the role of the board is to agree the strategy for the business and monitor its performance. Specifically it has responsibility for:

- planning the strategy
- approving the strategy in key areas
- changing the way the business operates or functions
- changing the organizational structure
- monitoring management performance
- determining remuneration levels
- providing appropriate accountability and approving the annual financial statements
- ensuring that the firm complies with all legal requirements
- managing succession
- all major decisions that affect the business and the way it operates.

Given the importance of these responsibilities to the firm, it is clear that an extended board of directors can be a major asset to the management team, complementing its expertise and experience. Indeed, as a study by the London-based accounting firm Kingston Smith (1994) has shown, those firms that take on a non-executive director are twice as likely to remain profitable during a recession as those that do not. Such is the importance of the board, and its executive and non-executive directors, to the success of the firm that the Institute of Management has published a guide to best practice (Allday, 1997). This includes a checklist of competences that the board should possess, grouped under the four main headings of strategy, culture, people and operations (see Table 11.4).

Table 11.4: Board-level competences

Strategy: guiding strategic direction	People: practising 'human' skills
Strategic thinking	Communicating
Systems thinking	Creating a personal impact
Awareness of external environment	Giving leadership
Entrepreneurial thinking	Promoting the development of others
Developing the vision	Networking
Initiating change	
Championing causes	
Culture: developing organization culture	**Operations: exercising executive control**
Customer focus	Governance
Quality focus	Decision-making
Teamwork focus	Contributing specialist knowledge
People resource focus	Managing performance
Organizational learning focus	Analysing situations
	Awareness of organizational structure

Source: Allday (1997)

A CASE EXAMPLE

Dixons

Dixons is arguably Europe's premier electrical retail operation. Worth something in the order of £5 billion it includes such famous high-street names as Currys, PC World and The Link. In addition, it has fledgling businesses in France and Spain, and in 2000 bought Elkjop, the leading Scandinavian electrical retail chain, and subsequently a stake in UniEuro, the second biggest electrical retailer in Italy.

The company was founded 55 years ago by Stanley Kalms who was knighted in 1996 for his services to the electrical retailing industry. Sir Stanley's father, a Jewish immigrant from Poland, owned a photographic studio in north London. When he left school in 1948 at the age of 16, Sir Stanley joined his father's business, Dixon's Studios, and it is from this single outlet that he built the Dixons empire. Shortly after joining the family firm he realized that he could earn more money from selling cameras than from taking photographs so he started to import and sell photographic equipment from the Far East. A growing interest in photography and innovative credit terms helped the firm expand and, by 1962, when the business was floated on the stock market, he had opened 16 outlets and profits were in the order of £160,000 per annum. However, much of the success of the business is down to Kalms' drive and aggression. Dixons has been his all-consuming passion built, as he recognizes, on rage and an incessant desire to win.

Under the aggressive Kalms, the business continued to grow very much as a result of his influence. As he acknowledges, for the first 20 years of his life he was an autocrat. However, as the business grew he recruited quality people around him and although he used to challenge them and 'wind them up' with his sarcasm, he did listen to them, otherwise they would, in his words, have 'toddled off'. From 1994, moreover, Dixons has been run by a chief executive, John Clare, based at the company's headquarters in Hemel Hempstead, with Sir Stanley acting as executive chairman 25 miles away in London. According to Clare, who joined the company in 1985 as marketing director after three years at Ladbrokes and twelve years at Mars, it is their contrasting styles, experiences and backgrounds that have helped make the relationship work well, together with the fact that they do not 'sit on top of each other'. Also, Clare suggests, Sir Stanley has recognized that the group is now so large that it requires a different set of skills from those he possesses. 'He is an absolutely superb retailer,' says Clare, 'but he doesn't show the same flair when it comes to IT system strategies and distribution logistic structures. There is a need for professional management, organization and disciplines that are not his strengths.' Possibly because of this, Kalms announced in April 2001 that he would retire in September 2002, shortly before his 70th birthday. As he said in an interview with Kate Rankin (*Daily Telegraph*, 12 January 2002: 30), 'I will never be made to admit that I haven't been running the business. I've been a seven days-a-week chairman, but the young turks are more and more in charge, and slowly the balance has moved towards John.'

Once Sir Stanley announced his intention to retire, the company engaged an international recruitment firm to search for a successor. In August 2001, it was announced that Sir John Collins, the chief executive of Vestey, was to take over as non-executive chairman. Collins, who joined Shell in 1964 and was chairman and chief executive of Shell UK from 1990–93, was the chairman of National Power who oversaw its break-up and was responsible for firing the company's chief executive after the group lost its way. Described by one of his former National Power colleagues as 'charming' and a 'strong leader', it would seem that, in Collins, Dixons has an appropriate successor to Sir Stanley. Certainly the City appears to believe so. On the announcement of Collins' appointment, Dixons' shares rose by 2p to 231p. If this is the case, Sir Stanley will have achieved what so few founders manage—an orderly succession. As he recognizes, it is not possible to buy perpetuity and everyone has to 'create space in due course. The secret is to create it when you're at your peak rather than when you're hanging on by your fingertips. There's nothing worse than leaders who are OTT and hang on too long.' Dixons has announced that Sir Stanley is to take up the presidency of the firm on his retirement.

Case example exercise

Review the Dixons and IKEA case examples. Evaluate the strategies of the two founders, Ingvar Kamprad and Sir Stanley Kalms, with respect to finding their successors. Consider the strengths and weaknesses of the two approaches, and determine the problems that the two businesses are likely to encounter when the two founders do finally 'retire'.

Which of the two firms do you believe is likely to be the more vulnerable and why?

If you were facing this situation, how would you go about finding a successor that would take your business on to the next, exciting stage of its development?

Chapter Review

➡ Few new ventures grow. The main barriers to growth are believed to be:
 – management and motivation
 – resources
 – market opportunities and structure.
➡ When businesses do grow, they tend to face various difficulties, such as:
 – crisis of leadership
 – crisis of autonomy
 – crisis of control
 – crisis of red tape
 – crisis of ???
➡ To overcome such crises it is necessary for the management of the firm to:
 – adapt so that the venture remains a customer-oriented, adaptive organization, capable of perceiving and pursuing opportunities
 – manage any succession problems that might arise
 – create an entrepreneurial team that will take the venture forward.

Quick Revision

(Answers at the end of this section)

1. Who suggested that the barriers to growth in small firms can be grouped into three categories (management and motivation, resources and market opportunities, and structure)?
   (a) Barber *et al.* (1989)
   (b) Barrow (2000/2001)

2. Which of these is *not* one of the stages in the Churchill and Lewis (1983) growth model (i.e. which is the odd one out)?
   (a) conception/existence
   (b) launch

(c) survival

(d) profitability and stabilization

(e) profitability and growth

(f) take-off

(g) maturity

3. To retain their entrepreneurial drive as they grow, firms need to remain focused on their customers, and capable of anticipating and responding to their needs? Is this:

(a) true

(b) false?

4. When should a firm begin to look for a successor to its founder?

(a) when the founder decides he or she wishes to retire

(b) 15–20 years in advance of the founder retiring

(c) only when it is absolutely necessary

5. When selecting members for the entrepreneurial team, the entrepreneur needs to consider their:

(i) expertise

(ii) track record

(iii) credibility

(iv) levels of motivation

(v) contact networks.

Is this:

(a) true

(b) false?

Answers to Quick Revision: 1–a; 2–b; 3–a; 4–b; 5–b (there is one criterion missing)

Learning Style Activities

➡ **Activist:** Draw up a list of questions you would like to ask a successful entrepreneur about the problems he/she encountered when growing his/her business. Identify an appropriate entrepreneur and interview him/her.

➡ **Reflector:** Consider the answers you receive. To what extent do they corroborate or refute the existing body of theory?

➡ **Theorist:** How relevant was or is the existing theory? Does it need to be modified or extended in any way? If so, how?

➡ **Pragmatist:** What have you learned from the exercise that would be of benefit to you if either (a) you wanted to grow your own business or (b) you were employed in a small or medium-sized enterprise that wished to grow but was afraid of losing its entrepreneurial dynamic?

Reading

Allday, D. (1997) *Check-a-Board: Helping Boards and Directors Become More Effective*. London: Institute of Management.

Barber, J., S. Metcalfe and M. Porteous (1989) *Barriers to Growth in Small Firms*. London: Routledge.

Barrow, C. (2000/2001) *Barriers to Growth*. Cranfield: School of Management, Cranfield University.

Birley, S. (2000a) To Grow or Not To Grow, in Birley, S. and D.F. Muzyka (eds) *Mastering Entrepreneurship: The Complete MBA Companion in Entrepreneurship*. London: Prentice Hall.

Birley, S. (2000b) Harvesting at the Right Price, in Birley, S. and D.F. Muzyka (eds) *Mastering Entrepreneurship: The Complete MBA Companion in Entrepreneurship*. London: Prentice Hall.

Brown, R. (1985) *Marketing for the Small Firm*. London: Holt, Rineheart and Winston.

Buchelle, R.B. (1967) *Business Policy in Growing Firms*. Chandler Publishing.

Cartwright, S. and G.L. Cooper (2000) Distilling a Strong Team Spirit, in Birley, S. and D.F. Muzyka (eds) *Mastering Entrepreneurship: The Complete MBA Companion in Entrepreneurship*. London: Prentice Hall.

Chrisman, J.J., J.H. Chua and P. Sharma (1998) Important Attributes of Successors in Family Business: An Exploratory Study. *Family Business Review*, March, 19–34.

Churchill, N. and V. Lewis (1983) The Five Stages of Small Business Growth. *Harvard Small Business Review* **61**, May/June, 30–50.

Churchill, N. (2000) The Six Key Phases of Company Growth, in Birley, S. and D.F. Muzyka (eds) *Mastering Entrepreneurship: The Complete MBA Companion in Entrepreneurship*. London: Prentice Hall.

Clifford, D.K. and R.E. Cavanagh (1985) *The Winning Performance*. Bantam Books.

Clifford, M., V. Nilakant and R.T. Hamilton (1991) Management Succession and the Stages of Small Business Development. *International Small Business Journal* **9** (4), 43–55.

Greiner, L. (1972) Evolution and Revolution as Organisations Grow. *Harvard Business Review* **50**, July/August, 37–46.

Hambrick, D.C. and L.M Crozier (1985) Stumblers and Stars in the Management of Rapid Growth. *Journal of Business Venturing* **1**, 31–45.

Harrison, C. (2000) Timing and Tenacity in a Business Sale, in Birley, S. and D.F. Muzyka (eds) *Mastering Entrepreneurship: The Complete MBA Companion in Entrepreneurship*. London: Prentice Hall.

Institute of Chartered Accountants in England and Wales (1996) *Barriers to Growth: A Report of the Enterprise Group of the Institute of Chartered Accountants in England and Wales*. London: Institute of Chartered Accountants in England and Wales.

Kingston Smith (1994) *How Companies Succeed in the Recession*. London: Kingston Smith.

Kirby, D.A. and T.J. Lee (1996) Succession Management in Family Firms in the North of England. *Family Business Review* **ix** (i), 75–85.

Muzyka, D., M. Hay and S. Birley (2000) A Management Team to Lure Investors, in Birley, S. and D.F. Muzyka (eds) *Mastering Entrepreneurship: The Complete MBA Companion in Entrepreneurship*. London: Prentice Hall.

Rue, L.W. and N.A. Ibrahim (1996) The Status of Planning in Smaller Family-owned Businesses. *Family Business Review*, Spring, 29–44.

Scott, M. and R. Bruce (1987) Five Stages of Growth in Small Business. *Long Range Planning* **20** (3), 45–52.

Stevenson H.H. and J.C. Jarillo-Mossi (1986) Preserving Entrepreneurship as Companies Grow. *Journal of Business Strategy*, 10–23.

Tuckman, B.W. (1965) Development Sequence in Small Groups. *Psychological Bulletin* **63**, 384–99.

Vandermerwe, S. (2000) The Customer-focussed Mission, in Birley, S. and D.F. Muzyka (eds) *Mastering Entrepreneurship: The Complete MBA Companion in Entrepreneurship*. London: Prentice Hall.

Willard, G.E., H.R. Freeser and D.A. Krueger (1991) In Order to Grow, Must the Founder Go? An Empirical Test of Conventional Wisdom, in Churchill, N.C. *et al.* (eds) *Frontiers of Entrepreneurship Research, 1990*. Boston MA: Babson College.

12

Intrapreneurship: Developing Entrepreneurship in Large Organizations

Learning Outcomes

On completion of this chapter, the reader will:

- appreciate the difference between entrepreneurship and intrapreneurship
- realize why intrapreneurship is important to contemporary society
- recognize the barriers to intrapreneurship within corporate culture
- understand the theory underpinning the development of intrapreneurship within large organizations, whether in the private or public sector
- know how to effect intrapreneurial change in organizations and how to institutionalize change within the established enterprise.

Introduction

Given the fast-changing nature of world markets, many large organizations are realizing that they need to be more innovative and flexible than perhaps they have been in the past. According to Hamel (2000a: 4–5):

> We now stand on the threshold of a new age—the age of revolution. In our minds, we know the new age has already arrived: in our bellies, we're not sure we like it. For we know it is going to be an age of upheaval, of tumult, of fortunes made and unmade at head-snapping speed. For change has changed. No longer is it additive. No longer does it move in a straight line. In the twenty-first century, change is discontinuous, abrupt, seditious.

As discussed earlier (in Chapter 2) such thinking is not new, but, under such circumstances, companies need to adopt a radical innovation agenda if they are to compete and survive. The fundamental challenge companies will face will be to re-invent themselves and their industries, not just in times of crisis but continuously. One way of doing this is to integrate the strengths of the entrepreneurial small firm (creativity, flexibility, innovativeness, closeness to market, etc.) with the market power and financial resources of the large organization. This has become known as 'intrapreneurship' and since the pioneering writing of Macrae (1976), there has been increasing interest in the concept, though some have questioned its relevance (Duncan, 1988). Whatever, a number of terms have been spawned to describe the concept in its various forms. The first, and most embracing, is organizational entrepreneurship. This refers to entrepreneurship in established organizations, irrespective of whether they are large corporations, government bodies, not for profit institutions or smaller businesses. Since most of the concern is with large corporations, the term corporate entrepreneurship has become popular, as has the term intrapreneurship. This is defined as the process in which innovative products or processes are developed by creating an entrepreneurial culture within an organization. It can take various forms and there are various ways in which it can operate.

The characteristics of entrepreneurial and intrapreneurial ventures

Many of the characteristics of intrapreneurship are similar to those of traditional entrepreneurship, namely both:

- focus on innovation (new products, processes or management methods)
- focus on the creation of value-added products
- require investment in 'risky' activities (activities for which the outcome is uncertain).

There are differences, however, namely:

- intrapreneurship is restorative, while entrepreneurship is developmental; restorative entrepreneurship is intended to counter stagnation within the organization (to restore the entrepreneurial culture); developmental entrepreneurship creates a process, product or even a venture where none existed before
- the enemy of the entrepreneur is the market, whereas the enemy of the intrapreneur is the corporate culture; while the entrepreneur is concerned to overcome obstacles in the market, the intrapreneur has to overcome corporate obstacles
- whereas funding is often a constraint on the entrepreneur, the funding available to the intrapreneur is usually very considerable.

PAUSE FOR THOUGHT

If it is so important for organizations to behave entrepreneurially, why do so many appear to have lost their entrepreneurial drive? What are the barriers to entrepreneurship within the corporate culture?

The barriers to intrapreneurship within the corporate culture

There are numerous reasons why large organizations have lost their entrepreneurial drive and have difficulty regaining it. These relate to the following factors.

The inherent nature of large organizations

Under this heading there are five factors that work against the development of an entrepreneurial culture, as outlined below.

1. **Impersonal relationship.** Once the entrepreneur loses contact with his/her employees, it is difficult to ensure that the appropriate level of entrepreneurship exists within the organization.

2. **Too many levels of approval.** Multiple levels of management tend to stultify innovation as each level has the potential to kill the project before it gets funded.

3. **Need for control.** In order to control the business, corporate management tends to establish fixed, quantifiable performance standards. Under such circumstances, there is a tendency for performance reports to take precedence over both planning and results, and for rules and standards to become more important than entrepreneurial behaviour.

4. **Corporate culture.** Corporate culture favours conservatism. According to Hisrich and Peters (1992: 534):

   > The guiding principles in a traditional corporate culture are: follow the instructions given; do not make any mistakes; do not fail; do not take initiative but wait for instructions; stay within your turf; and protect your backside. This restrictive environment is of course not conducive to creativity, flexibility, independence, and risk taking—the jargon of intrapreneurs.

5. **Specificity of the time dimension.** Budget cycles force managers to plan short-run cost reductions in order to stay within budget. Thus, even though an organization may have a 5–10-year planning horizon, its actual performance is measured over much shorter time periods. It is difficult to be creative under such circumstances.

The need for short-run profits

Short-run profits are an established organization's measure of success. They help keep stock prices up and attract investment. Thus senior managers are pressured into devising strategies for short-run performance rather than long-run investment. Entrepreneurial ventures tend to lose money initially and need to attract money in, without any guarantee of success.

Lack of entrepreneurial talent

Enterprising individuals are often not attracted to large organizations and tend not to be found in them. When they are, either they become worn down by bureaucracy or they leave. Often, large organizations see such people as loners rather than team players, or as eccentrics more interested in pet projects than corporate objectives. They are frequently viewed as cynics, rebels, free spirits, who are often late and responsible for sloppy work that does not conform to the standards set by the corporation. According to Duncan (1988):

> Creative people are, to be honest, a pain in the neck. They disrupt the established order by asking questions and experimenting with new ways of doing things when well-established procedures are available to provide direction. They come in late and leave early even if they do work three or four hours a night at home and most of the weekend.

Similarly, Sinetar (1985) suggests that entrepreneurs have difficulty working as team members because they tend to alienate others by their drive, focus on pet projects, their idiosyncrasies and even their thinking abilities. As a result they tend not to get promoted in large organizations, which contributes to their job dissatisfaction and departure.

Inappropriate compensation methods

Most large organizations have few ways to compensate creative employees. Neither monetary nor non-monetary methods of rewarding individuals recognize innovation. Even promotion seldom works for intrapreneurs as:

- talented individuals tend to be promoted into management, which takes them out of the arena in which they were innovative
- intrapreneurs typically do not have the temperament needed to be good corporate managers, and may cause problems that did not exist previously.

The theory of intrapreneurship development

Intrapreneurship theory suggests that if established organizations are to re-invent themselves, then a number of factors have to be in place. These include the following.

Committing the organization

Innovation is necessarily a bottom-up process. It can only work, however, when it is supported from the top. Top management commitment means that the CEO and his/her team are firm believers in the benefits of corporate entrepreneurship, making it possible, for example, to change the reward system, which will be necessary for the process to be successful.

Determining the corporate entrepreneurship model

Here there are five possibilities. The organization needs to decide which is the most appropriate. Briefly they are as follows.

1. Organic organization. The entire organization adopts intrapreneurship and an organic structure is developed, similar to the one developed by Richard Branson at Virgin (see Chapter 9). While a cellular structure inevitably results in a loss of the economies of scale, scale is not quite the advantage it used to be. In an era of rapid change, speed, flexibility and focus have become more important and a cellular structure permits this as each cell is seen as an autonomous entrepreneurial business unit that is close to its customers. Additionally, it is a structure that promotes flexibility and experimentation. Individual cells can grow or contract according to developments in the market, while risks can be taken without damaging the whole organization if they fail.

2. **New products group.** A multi-disciplinary 'new products division' is formally established at vice-presidential level to facilitate new product development and encourage others in the organization. The vice-president becomes the product champion.

3. **New products subsidiary.** This is established with a semi-autonomous structure. It accepts proposals from individuals, evaluates them and determines whether a project is worth funding.

4. **Corporate venture capital firm.** An autonomous company that underwrites and assists either internal or external proposals that meet formal venture capital criteria.

5. **A section within the HR function.** This trains managers in intrapreneurship or arranges for them to attend off-site seminars and conferences. However, it is likely to have only limited impact as a result of perceived limited commitment of senior management, and the lack of a structure and incentives.

Developing an intrapreneurial culture

If a corporation is to be truly intrapreneurial, the entire corporate culture must fit the intrapreneurial mode. This cannot normally be done immediately—it develops over time and, according to Pinchot (1985), involves 10 principles, as described below.

1. **Self-selection.** Intrapreneurs appoint themselves and pursue their own ideas. They are self-starters, not people who just carry out an assignment.

2. **No 'hand-offs'.** There is continuous involvement. The inventor or initiator is involved throughout the project's development. While other individuals may be brought in, the originator retains membership of the intrapreneurial team.

3. **The 'doer' decides.** The originator must be allowed to continue for as long as he/she believes the project to be viable.

4. **Corporate slack** refers to an excess of resources beyond those required for normal output. These are discretionary resources that can be channelled to an intrapreneur for a project that might not otherwise be funded.

5. **Ending the home run philosophy.** Realizing that not all projects will be a major success.

6. **Tolerance of risk, failure and mistakes.**

7. **'Patient money'**—the willingness to invest funds in intrapreneurial ventures without expecting an immediate return.

8. 'Freedom from turfiness'. The corporation is seen as a family of teams, all of whom work towards the same goals. Working together as a group is encouraged. Resources are shared, ideas are exchanged, moral support is provided and assistance is given without regard to ownership claims.

9. Cross-functional teams. For intrapreneurship to work at its best, individuals must be allowed to work in teams, irrespective of their specialities. Individuals with different specialities need to be encouraged to work together and to stay with the project throughout its development.

10. Multiple options. Often the requirements of a particular project are not known at the outset, which means that multiple options should be followed.

Identifying intrapreneurial talent

Once the intention to endorse corporate entrepreneurship has been made, some intrapreneurs will surface automatically. They may have projects they have been working on secretly or developing in their minds.

Others, who possess the ideas and managerial skills, will need to be identified. Not all aspiring intrapreneurs make good venture owners and not all creative individuals make good intrapreneurs, however. Good results can be achieved, though, by pairing a creative person with a good manager. The best intrapreneurs, as Ross and Unwalla (1986) have recognized, are results-oriented, ambitious, rational, competitive, questioning individuals who dislike bureaucracy and are challenged by innovation, but who understand the organization and believe in their colleagues, with the ability to resolve conflicts.

They need around them support staff with entrepreneurial tendencies who can work through the corporate system. These are people comfortable with the entrepreneurial culture, who can cope with uncertainty, long lead times, indefinite resources and new concepts or products.

Rewarding intrapreneurs

This is a complex issue. Unlike the entrepreneur, the intrapreneur is normally unwilling to give up a salaried position. At the same time, intrapreneurs believe that if they are to work on more risky projects, which have the potential to make large profits for the organization, they should benefit from that risk.

Designing an appropriate reward system requires that senior management understands the needs of both the intrapreneur and the more traditional employees. However, the reward system for intrapreneurs needs to be both:

- monetary—this may include bonuses, profit-sharing or intracapital (i.e. the freedom to use corporate resources to fund additional product development), and

- non-monetary—these might include formal recognition of performance (e.g. Halls of Fame), the provision of discretionary funds, the establishment of support groups or dual promotion systems that recognize performance in innovative project development.

An identifiable system for administering and evaluating projects

Importantly, the firm must establish some policy and report it to the staff. According to DeSarbo *et al.* (1987), there are eight variables that are important for managers when projects are evaluated. These are:

1. high corporate fit
2. low initial investment
3. experienced venture champion
4. experience with product
5. low competitive threat
6. proprietary technology
7. high gross margin
8. high rate of return.

Additionally there is the issue of corporate politics. Funding corporate entrepreneurship can never be as objective as funding decisions for new ventures because the firm can never divorce itself from the project. Political factors can therefore affect the acceptance process. Apart from proposals from individuals with a known, positive track record, proposals from known (visible) individuals are more likely to get funded. Similarly, in order not to discourage, an organization may decide not to invest in only the 'best' proposals, but to allocate acceptances to departments.

PAUSE FOR THOUGHT

Consider a large organization known to you. How entrepreneurial is it? What would you do to increase its entrepreneurial capacity?

A CASE EXAMPLE

Sir Ralph Halpern and the Burton Group plc

In 1990, the Burton Group plc consisted of 12 companies and 450 shops selling clothing for both sexes. It had not always been like this. In 1900 15-year-old Meshe David Osinsky fled to Britain from Russia. By 1904, he had opened his first store in Chesterfield offering cheap ready-made suits for men and boys under the Burton name. A second Burton shop was opened in 1908 and a third in 1909, and in 1910 Osinsky established the firm's headquarters at Elmwood Mills in Leeds. Between 1910 and 1919 the number of branches grew to 40, including eight shops in Northern Ireland, and the firm's operation included the production of clothing for both civilian needs and the armed forces. With the end of World War I, the firm had either to shelve half of its production capacity or expand its retail outlets. It chose the latter and by 1992, the number of shops had grown from 40 in 1919 to 140. By the mid-1920s the firm, which had become Montague Burton Ltd, made almost entirely wholesale bespoke male clothing, with the customer being measured in the branch shop, and the measurements being sent to the factory for manufacture into the appropriate garment.

Throughout the inter-war years, the firm expanded and by the outbreak of World War II the number of retail outlets had increased to 595. During World War II, progress as a manufacturer and retailer of men's bespoke clothing was restricted by the wartime shortages of materials, the disruption of the labour force in response to the demands of the armed forces and the rationing of clothes purchasing, which continued into the immediate post-war period. Also, the company threw itself, once more, into the war effort. Thus it was not until 1950 that the chairman was able to report to the shareholders that stocks had improved to pre-war standards. However, over £1 million was written off the value of the firm's stocks when prices fell and, in 1952, Sir Montague Burton, as he had become known, died. The following year, in an attempt to strengthen the management, the firm acquired Jackson the Tailor and the services of Sidney and Lionel Jacobsen, who had built a reputation for successful trading and who became directors. On their advice, the firm divested itself of its cloth-making activities. However, in an attempt to make itself more competitive, in 1958 it introduced credit and in 1963, having saturated the home market, it established itself in France, anticipating Britain's entry into the European Common Market. In 1964, after much detailed organization and planning, it launched Burton-by-Post, a mail-order venture that was never profitable and was sold in 1972.

With the exception of a small chain of women's shops (acquired in 1947) trading as Peter Robinson, the firm remained dependent on the sale of men's tailored clothing. However, in 1969, Greens Leisure Centre was acquired. This was a retail chain of 41 outlets specializing in photographic equipment. Rymans, a chain of office equipment shops, was also purchased but neither venture was successful—Greens was disposed of in 1976 and Rymans in 1981. Even so, the then chairman (Ladislas Rice) made it clear that the company:

> . . . is now on the way to becoming a group of specialist retail chains each with a clearly defined market and a distinctive face to the public. . . . We intend to maintain and develop our dominant position in the menswear market. However, we shall become less completely dependent on it as our newer retail activities grow.

In continued pursuit of this strategy, the company attempted to break into the children's market with the establishment of its Orange Hand shops. This initiative lasted for just four years.

Continued poor performance led to a policy of consolidation of existing units rather than continued broadening of the retail base and, in 1977, Rice resigned as chief executive following a boardroom struggle. The aim of his successor was to 'eliminate loss-making businesses' and modernize retail out-

lets. From 1977 to 1981, the company embarked on a programme of consolidation. In 1981 Ralph Halpern became chief executive and all that changed. Born in 1938, Halpern had joined the group in 1961 as one of three trainee managers at Peter Robinson. During the 1960s, he developed Top Shop, the first example of the market segmentation strategy for which the Burton Group became famous. In the 1970s he applied the strategy to the whole of the loss-making group, and in 1981 was appointed chairman and chief executive. The 1980s, the 'Halpern era', was a period of 'transformation and flux' (Jacobs, 1999: 47) for Burton. Halpern sought to refocus the business on fashion retailing. In his chairman's report of December 1981, he detailed the reasons why Burton had fallen behind British clothing retailers in general and then outlined his strategy for retrieving the situation. This included curtailing the company's manufacturing activity, applying the methods evolved at Top Shop to other company chains and shedding all of the loss-making activities.

Halpern operated by centralizing the major policy decisions in his senior management team. Implementation was then delegated to teams in each of the operational divisions. Change was always on the agenda and Halpern talked about 'institutionalizing change'. This required setting demanding targets and building the expectation for change into financial plans. It also required a positive attitude to risk-taking and a reward system that recognized the achievement of these objectives:

> We believe in high pay and incentives and we stress promotion from within for those who succeed. . . . For all our management and staff, substantial bonuses are linked to target plan. . . . A senior executive member of a divisional board can double his salary for outstanding performance.

Additionally he introduced a unique organizational structure that cut out divisional managing directors and had functional (shop operations, merchandising, concessions, finance, personnel and systems) executives reporting directly to functional managing directors in order to ensure that 'central management should keep in touch with every facet of the business. They can see what's happening down to the market place.'

As a consequence, by 1983 Burton showed sales of £300 million, pre-tax profits up to £39 million and a return on capital employment of 16 per cent, after a total of £29 million had been spent on new store openings and shop modernizations. Burton emerged as a group with different divisions specializing in different market segments. Two new chains of shops were added: Principles for Women in 1984 and Principles for Men in 1985. These specialized in high-quality clothing. Also in 1985, the group succeeded in a take-over bid for the Debenhams chain of 67 retail stores. Halpern promised, during the take-over battle, to sharpen up the Debenhams image. In his 1985 report to the group's employees, Halpern made the following point:

. . . think of Marks & Spencer. It stands for something. Burton stands for something. Or Next. Now think of Debenhams. If you've got a blank in your mind it's because the retailers have not successfully stamped a position and an image on the store.

By 1987 Halpern and his team were able to unveil their new concept in the main London store and Burton emerged as a group with different divisions specializing in different sectors of the market. In its corporate advertising in 1986, Burton described its various retail offerings using a mixture of demographic and psychographic labels (see Table 12.1).

The formula was highly successful and, by 1990, the group had a turnover just short of £2 billion and it is generally held that the strategies that Halpern introduced 'transformed Burton's retail presence and its performance' (Jacobs, 1999: 47). According to Halpern it all resulted from good management, which in his view is about: 'making complicated things simple. The first thing you have to decide is what business you are in. A high percentage of organizations are in decline because the original purpose is no longer relevant to the future.' However, the Halpern formula for the success of the Burton Group, as it became known in 1985, was

more than just this. He recognized the importance of change. 'Change,' he said, 'is always on the agenda. . . . Only the most visionary recognize the need to change a successful formula while it is still working.' According to him, we have to learn to welcome and manage change—to lose the fear and anxiety that has led to change being seen as a threat as opposed to an opportunity. Commenting on the group's performance he made the point that:

. . . people in my own group's business, like Dorothy Perkins and Evans, which were dying on their feet and more recently in Debenhams, which was seriously under-performing, suddenly started rushing about making profits. They're mostly the same people who were there before. So, what brought this about?

Nothing very mysterious. They acquired new skills and through encouragement, incentives and respect for their talent, we managed to realize a capacity for commitment and achievement that was always there but had simply been untapped.

(Halpern, 1987: 8)

Possibly the situation is somewhat more complicated than this might suggest. According to an article in The Sunday Times dated 18 November 1990, Halpern had created by 1988 the strongest and best retailing scheme in the whole industry. He had done it by being a megalomaniac and a listener, and by being able: 'to put together a strong team around him and right down through the organization. A lot of the credit for that can be given to the remuneration package and generous option scheme.'

Having revitalized the group and turned it into an enterprising organization, the man who 'transformed the firm of Burton almost beyond recognition' (Sigsworth, 1992: 22) resigned. Cracks were beginning to show and from 1992 the company re-entered a period of consolidation that included cost-cutting, downsizing (the loss of 2000 jobs) and

Table 12.1: The different Burton Group outlets

Dorothy Perkins	The Young Female Market
Principles	The Style Market
Top Shop/Top Man	The Teenage Market
Evans	The 'Larger' Market
Burton	The Men's Market
Harvey Nichols	The Knightsbridge Market
Debenhams	The Family Market

the demerger of Debenhams. It now trades under the name of Arcadia.

Case example exercise

Review the case study focusing, in particular, on the Burton Group during the post-1981 period when Sir Ralph Halpern was in charge. How far do the theories of intrapreneurship and the creation of an enterprise culture within large organizations explain what Halpern was able to achieve at Burtons in the period he was in charge? On the basis of this case, should the theories be modified in any way? How, having studied the theory, would you have turned Burtons into a more entrepreneurial organization? Would you have done anything differently and, if so, what and why?

If it is important for large organizations to possess an entrepreneurial culture if they wish to sustain their competitive advantage, why did 'cracks' begin to show in the early 1990s and the company begin to retrench? If Halpern had stayed on as chairman do you think things might have been different? In what way? Justify your answer.

Intrapreneurship in the public sector

As discussed in Chapter 1, Drucker (1985: 201) has observed that, 'public service institutions . . . need to be entrepreneurial and innovative fully as much as any business does'. Throughout the western world, and increasingly in the former eastern bloc countries (the transition economies), governments have begun to recognize the need for change in the provision of public services, whether at the local, regional or national levels. Invariably the process from a traditionally bureaucratic, supply-led culture to a more flexible, customer orientation is not easy for most public-sector organizations, particularly given the traditional philosophical beliefs that surround them, the absence of relevant management skills and the various misunderstandings about what, precisely, is involved. This latter point is manifest clearly in an early Australian deliberation on how to eliminate the barriers to making public enterprise enterprising. According to the then associate director of Rothschild Australia Ltd, Christopher Still, enterprising behaviour is about 'growth and efficiency' and not about 'showing courage and imaginativeness' as the *Oxford Dictionary* defines it (Still, 1989). Clearly while the ultimate objective of developing a more entrepreneurial or enterprising approach to public-sector management might be, as in the private sector, to obtain 'growth and efficiency', the priority is to develop an organization that has the 'courage and imaginativeness' to both cope with and initiate change in order to meet the needs of the consuming public, in 'an era of unprecedented uncertainty' (Peters, 1987: 7).

While the process of change in the public sector is often complex and there would appear to be no single standardized formula that can be followed to guarantee success, the results of an investigation into change in local government in the UK (Kirby et al., 1991) suggest that various conditions need to exist, or be created, if the process of change is to occur. Most are similar to those found in the private sector but how the conditions combine, and the extent to which they need to be present, appears to depend on local conditions and circumstances. However, from the research evidence it would seem that, irrespective of the status of the authority, its political control or the type of service provided, innovation was unlikely unless seven conditions were met, namely:

1. a culture for change

2. systems to enable change to take place

3. interaction with the environment

4. visionary leadership

5. empowered management

6. planning

7. resources.

Essentially what these results imply is that if the public sector is to adopt a more innovative, entrepreneurial approach to service delivery, then there needs to be consensus and commitment on the part of staff to the need for change. Largely this is achieved by creating an environment where staff feel valued and involved, and where they take 'ownership' of the innovation. Of major importance, also, to the achievement of this end is the setting of realistic objectives and the formulation of a vision for the organization that is communicated, understood and shared throughout it. Integral to the success of the project is the establishment of enabling systems, including sound channels of horizontal as well as vertical communication. To ensure that the appropriate systems and resources are in place to effect change requires planning. In turn, this requires a sound understanding of the external environment and the markets in which the organization operates, and of the way they are likely to change in the future. In particular, public-sector organizations need to possess a clear image of their 'customers' and of their changing needs and demands, not least with regard to the levels of service they require. At all levels, however, the key to successful innovation is people, and while the role of the 'leader' (usually the CEO) is important, it is his/her style of management and ability to motivate that is of significance, as is his/her ability to create a team with the requisite skills, attitudes and commitment to translate ideas into reality.

As in the private sector, leaders can occur at all levels in the public-sector organization. It is their responsibility, as intrapreneurs, to create the culture for change within their institutions—to dismantle 'dysfunctional old truths and to prepare people and organisations to deal with—to love, to develop affection for—change *per se*, as innovations are proposed, tested, rejected, modified and adopted' (Peters, 1987: 388). To achieve this, not only do such leaders need to have a vision, they need to ensure it is communicated and shared by the people for whom they are responsible (i.e. those they are expected to 'manage'). This requires that their staff are engaged and empowered to take initiatives on a day-to-day basis, aimed at improving and eventually transforming routine functions in order that service delivery best meets the needs of the consuming public. Thus it would seem that within the public sector, as within the large private-sector corporation, 'what it takes to get the innovating organisation up and running is essentially the same two things all vehicles need: a person in the driver's seat and a source of power' (Kanter, 1983: 209).

Effecting intrapreneurial change

The intrapreneur is both an entrepreneur and a good corporate manager. As has been recognized already, intrapreneurs are results-oriented, ambitious and competitive. They are motivated by problem-solving and rational decision-making as well as by change and innovation, believing that reward is in the work as much as in the pay. While they find bureaucratic systems frustrating and question the status quo, they understand the organization, can resolve conflicts, and have faith in their colleagues and staff. Thus they combine the qualities of the entrepreneur with those of the corporate manager. As such they effect change in the organizations in which they work, whether as CEO or employee. Indeed, the process of change in organizations is not always initiated from the top and, on occasion, senior management only become involved when the process is well under way. Whatever, the change process is a hazardous exercise, but especially for intrapreneurs lower down in the organizational structure. As Machiavelli (1999: 19) recognized almost 500 years ago:

> It should be borne in mind that there is nothing more difficult to handle, more doubtful of success, and more dangerous to carry through than initiating change in a state's constitution. The innovator makes enemies of all those who prospered under the old order, and only lukewarm support is forthcoming from those who would prosper under the new. Their support is lukewarm partly from fear of their adversaries, who have the existing laws on their side, and partly because men are generally incredulous, never really trusting new things unless they have tested them by experience. In consequence, whenever those who oppose the changes can do so, they attack vigorously, and the defence made by the others is only lukewarm. So both the innovator and his friends come to grief.

Under such circumstances, the intrapreneur needs the support of the most senior person(s) in the organization. Without it, the task becomes that much more difficult. It is not impossible but certainly much more hazardous, and from the work of Pinchot (1985), it is apparent that most intrapreneurs would do well to adopt the following ten commandments, in that they should:

1. come to work each day willing to be fired
2. circumvent any orders aimed at stopping them achieving their dream
3. do any job needed to make the project work, regardless of the job description
4. network with good people and enlist their support
5. build a spirited team of the best people
6. work underground for as long as possible as publicity triggers the corporate immune mechanism
7. be loyal and faithful to their sponsors
8. ask for forgiveness rather than permission
9. be true to their goals and realistic about how to achieve them
10. keep the vision strong.

Certainly there is much truth in such guiding principles and, by adhering to them, it is often surprising what aspiring intrapreneurs can achieve, especially when changing an organization from the bottom up. However, as the abundance of literature on change management demonstrates, there is a recognizable change process which, if followed, can increase the likelihood of success still further.

Efforts to implement change in an organization are more likely to be successful if the intrapreneur, whatever his/her position is in the organization, understands the barriers to change. According to Connor (1995), people resist change for the reasons described below.

Lack of trust

People distrust the person or persons who propose the change. Even if there is no obvious threat, people often imagine there are hidden implications that will only become obvious later in the change process. Mutual mistrust may encourage the intrapreneur to be secretive about the change, thereby stimulating further mistrust and resistance.

Belief that change is unnecessary

Change is frequently resisted if the current way of doing things is successful and there is no clear evidence of serious problems. This resistance may be further intensified if senior management has exaggerated how well the organization has been doing in order to maintain company morale and shareholder confidence. Even when a problem is finally recognized, it is unusual for large-scale change to be made, both the management and the employees preferring to make incremental adjustments. Rarely do organizations embrace change, as the Burton Group did under Halpern, and change a successful formula while it is still working.

Belief that change is not feasible

Even when problems are acknowledged, people often resist change because they believe that the proposed solution is unlikely to succeed, especially when the proposed change is radically different from that which has gone before. The failure of earlier change programmes creates cynicism and scepticism, making people doubt that the next change will prove to be any better.

Economic threats

People are likely to resist change if it is perceived to result in a loss of personal income or job security, even if it is likely to benefit the organization. This is especially true when people are being replaced with technology, or the change process is likely to result in productivity or efficiency gains. Earlier downsizing experiences increase the resistance to new proposals irrespective of the actual threat.

Relative high cost

Inevitably, change is costly and it is not always easy to identify the costs involved. Often, established routines are disrupted, extra resources are needed and existing resources are frequently lost. Thus, even though the benefits may be clear, resistance is often encountered because it is not possible to estimate, accurately, the true costs of the change process.

Fear of personal failure

People who lack self-confidence will oppose change as, inevitably, not only does it make some expertise redundant but they will be concerned whether they have the ability to cope with the new ways of working the change will bring about.

Loss of status and power

Change not only threatens those lower down the organizational hierarchy, it can also threaten those who have achieved high-ranking status, especially those responsible for activities that are likely to be cut back or eliminated. Such people are likely to oppose change and their concerns need to be recognized, not least because they are very real—major change usually does result in some shift in relative power and status for both sub-units and individuals.

Threats to values and ideals

Any threat to a person's values and ideals usually arouses strong emotions that can fuel resistance to change. If such values are embedded in a strong organizational culture, as is often the case in the public services sector for example, such resistance will be widespread rather than isolated and confined to a limited number of individuals.

Resentment of interference

Some people resist change because they do not want to be controlled by others. Usually most people resist change unless they acknowledge the need and perceive they have a choice in determining how to change. Attempts to force them or manipulate them tend to result in greater hostility, resentment and resistance.

Such concerns are only natural and need not only to be acknowledged and recognized but used to aid the change process. Whereas apathy with regard to change can suggest lack of interest, active resistance suggests commitment and concern, and it is the role of the intrapreneur to harness this for the benefit of the organization (Maurer, 1996). Apart from using his/her leadership skills and/or powers of persuasion, the successful intrapreneur can utilize proven change process theories and practices. One of the earliest, developed by Lewin (1951), is the 'force-field'. According to this theory, the change process can be seen to follow three phases: 'unfreezing', 'changing' and 'refreezing'. Unfreezing is about getting people to realize that the old ways of doing things are no longer appropriate. This may occur as a result of a crisis or simply by encouraging them to identify the threats and opportunities for themselves. Once this has occurred, the changing phase involves people identifying new ways of doing things and selecting the most promising. In the refreezing phase, the new approach(es) is/are implemented. Clearly all three phases are important to the successful implementation of change in the organization and must be progressed in sequence. Any attempt to move to the change phase without first unfreezing attitudes will inevitably lead to resistance, while any changes resulting from a weak diagnosis or insufficient attention to consensus building are likely to be temporary and reversed soon after implementation. According to the Lewin model, change may be achieved by:

- increasing the driving forces for change
- reducing the restraining forces that create resistance to change.

If there is little resistance to change then it is usually possible simply to increase the driving forces, but in those cases where there is strong opposition to change, a dual approach is normally necessary, as unless the restraining forces are overcome, any increase in the driving forces will only create further resistance and, possibly, conflict. Clearly, the key to the change process proposed by Lewin is an accurate listing of the driving and constraining factors.

A second approach is based on the reactions of people to changes imposed on them. According to Jick (1993) and others, people react to enforced change in the same way they might react to traumatic events. The initial reaction is to deny that change is necessary (denial). This is followed by resistance to the change, during which time there is anger and hostility with people looking for someone to blame. This second (anger) stage is followed by a third stage in which people acknowledge the inevitable and mourn the loss of what has been lost before moving on to the final stage (adaptation), whereby they accept the need to change and proceed to implement the required changes. Understanding these stages is important, especially as some people get stuck in the intermediary stages. If the change process is to be successful, the intrapreneur needs to help his/her colleagues through the different stages.

At whatever level intrapreneurs occur in the organization, possibly their key roles are to formulate the integrating vision, identify and assemble a coalition of supporters, then guide and co-ordinate the change process, allowing 'subordinates' to implement the strategy by transforming their own areas of responsibility in a way that is appropriate for them, provided it is consistent with the vision. Certainly the intrapreneur should not specify detailed guidelines for change or attempt to dictate the change process. Rather he/she should facilitate the change process by providing encouragement, support and resources, as discussed in Chapter 8. However, as Yukl (2002) has suggested, the successful implementation of change involves the intrapreneur in two overlapping sets of actions. These are 'political and organizational actions' and 'people-oriented actions'.

The former set of actions, relating to organizational politics, involves the following components.

- **Determining who can oppose and facilitate change in the organization, and deciding how they should be treated.** Should efforts be made to convert the sceptics or should they be isolated and/or removed? Should they be involved in the change process or kept separate from it? There are no hard-and-fast rules and every situation is different, but the issue has to be addressed before the start of any major change process.

- Building a broad coalition to support the change. Successful change involves co-operative effort with the power to facilitate action. Therefore it is essential to build a coalition of supporters both within and outside the organization.

- Filling key positions with competent change agents. These should be people who are committed to the vision and have the ability not only to communicate it effectively but to support it with their actions. Wherever possible, those in key positions whom it is not possible to win over should be removed, as their behaviour can quickly change from passive to active resistance. Also, removing such people signals the seriousness of the intent.

- Using task forces to guide implementation. These are extremely useful to guide the change process. They should be led by someone who understands and supports the new vision and has the skills to manage conflict and involve people in creative problem-solving. The composition of each task force should be appropriate for its responsibility but, as far as possible, should be drawn from all parts of the organization or sub-unit, bringing together people from different functional units and backgrounds. This not only helps to embed the process but brings different perspectives to bear in the creative problem-solving process.

- Making dramatic, symbolic changes that affect the work in order to emphasize the intrapreneur's commitment to change.

- Beginning on a small scale in order to demonstrate success, learn from any mistakes that might be made and overcome any resistance that might stem from uncertainty. However, this is not always possible as frequently it is necessary to change, simultaneously, all interdependent parts of the system.

- Changing relevant parts of the organization structure. According to Beer (1988) structural changes intended to facilitate the change process are unlikely to be successful if imposed. As a consequence, he proposes a task force to analyse how work is performed, and to recommend any structural changes that are required to bring about the change. However, when structural change is resisted, it might be easier to create an informal structure and postpone any formal changes until people recognize that change is needed. Informal teams (temporary task forces) can be created to facilitate the transition, without the expectation that they will become permanent. At a later stage of the process, however, they can, and often do, become part of the formal structure.

- Monitoring the process of change both to learn from the experience and to ensure that the different aspects of the change process are being effectively co-ordinated.

In contrast, the latter actions focus on the people that are part of the change process. These have to be motivated, supported and guided, not least because major change is always stressful and even the most committed need to be supported if their enthusiasm and optimism is to be sustained. Also, as Machiavelli (1999) recognized, the supporters of the intrapreneur are vulnerable, so they need to be protected. Thus successful intrapreneurs undertake the following actions.

- Create a sense of urgency about the need for change. The intrapreneur needs to persuade people not only of the need for change but of the need to follow his/her vision. If people have little appreciation of the problems, he/she will need to help them understand the issues and recognize the implications of not changing. When change is gradual and there is not an obvious crisis, many people fail to recognize the emerging threats and/or opportunities. Hence the need to create a sense of urgency.

- **Prepare people to adjust to change.** Change is disruptive, as has been mentioned already, and the change process generates stress and trauma for most people, even those most enthusiastic and committed to it. However, people do find it easier to deal with the negative aspects of change if they expect them, are aware of what is likely to happen and are equipped with the techniques to deal with them. It is the responsibility of the intrapreneur to arrange for his/her colleagues to be briefed prior to the change process, preferably by someone who has been through a similar experience, and for support to be on hand in the form, for example, of stress counselling.

- **Help people deal with the pain of change.** It is often difficult for people to accept the loss of familiar things especially if the past is associated with failed policies and practices. Indeed, they may feel personally responsible, either wholly or in part, and as a consequence may need help to express their anger or sadness, either individually or collectively.

- **Provide opportunities for early successes.** This gives people confidence and, as mentioned above, helps convert the sceptics. Hence, whenever possible, it is advisable to break up the process into a series of short-term goals that are not too difficult to achieve. With self-confidence comes the willingness to strive for greater achievements and longer-term objectives.

- **Keep people informed about the process of change.** This includes informing people about the steps that have been initiated, the changes that have been made, the improvements that have been achieved and, importantly, any difficulties that have been encountered and what has been done to overcome them. This ensures that people realize that the change process is ongoing and, if coupled with celebrations of success, rewards them for their achievements, thereby helping to maintain their enthusiasm and motivation.

- **Empower people to innovate change.** As mentioned already, the intrapreneur should not dictate how change should take place, but should empower key supporters to implement it in their own way. Thus individuals and teams should be invested with the authority to make decisions and deal with problems, while the intrapreneur acts, as discussed previously, as a facilitator encouraging, supporting and resourcing the change agents, and guiding and co-ordinating the change process.

- **Demonstrate continued commitment to the change.** Although the intrapreneur may delegate responsibility for certain aspects of the change process, he/she must indicate through his/her actions continued commitment to the project. Any indication that he/she no longer regards the project as important could undermine the whole process. Thus he/she must not just talk about the importance of the project but must invest his/her own time, energy and effort in it and should, in particular, be seen to be helping overcome difficulties and/or resolving problems.

Institutionalizing change

In an era of rapid change it is essential that organizations learn not only to accept change but to initiate it. As the Burtons Group case study demonstrated, it is possible to do this—to create a culture where change is institutionalized within the organization. The Japanese have done it through the concept of 'Kaizen'—the notion of 'continuous improvement' and, as Hamel (2000b: 13) has recognized, 'organisational learning and knowledge management are first cousins to continuous improvement'. As a consequence there has emerged, in recent years, the notion of the learning organization. Clearly all organizations learn but, according to Jackson and Schuler (2001: 231), learning organizations are distinguished from the rest by the fact that 'they combine an ability to manage knowledge with an ability to change continuously so as to improve their effectiveness'. The key, then, to a culture of continuous improvement and change is the acquisition of new knowledge. This can be acquired either by discovering it or by imitating best practice (benchmarking), but according to Senge (1990), organizations as a whole can only really learn when the individual members of the organization are learning. Thus a culture of personal development and lifelong education must be embedded within the organization and time must be made available not just for the learning to take place but for reflection and analysis, something that is often extremely difficult to achieve in an era of downsizing and greater 'productivity' gains.

Senge also suggests that one of the major barriers to learning in organizations is the somewhat simplistic mental models that people hold, and argues that it is necessary to help them understand and change their assumptions about how things work. By so doing, he suggests, it is possible to help them increase their ability to learn and solve problems, recognizing that they are not powerless and that they can, both individually and collectively, change the organization. Linked to this, he argues, is the need to encourage people to adopt the principles and practices of systems thinking. Systems thinking acknowledges that problems may have multiple causes and solutions, and actions may have multiple outcomes, including unanticipated side-effects. Systems are linked to their environment and in an open system (one that interacts with its environment) a change in the environment can necessitate a change in the system, which in turn will result inevitably in changes elsewhere in the system as it re-adjusts to create an equilibrium state. Thus by seeing organizations as systems, and viewing them more holistically, people can see the ramifications of, and need for, change throughout the organization.

Importantly, organizational learning requires that when knowledge is acquired, it is disseminated throughout the organization. All too frequently, however, this is not the case. Knowledge is seen as power and, as Yukl (2002: 299) has recognized, 'secrecy is the enemy of learning'. Thus it is frequently necessary to develop formal procedures for translating learning into practice and to transfer learning from one part of the organization to another. This can be done through manuals, though these often become enshrined as doctrine, thereby stultifying further innovation, or cascaded through the organization through workshops, seminars and mentoring. Importantly, learning is seen not just as formal training but as 'learning from experience', in particular learning from mistakes and 'failure', as well as from experimentation. Thus, within the learning organization, learning and innovation are increased 'by encouraging experimentation, reflection, knowledge importation, information sharing, diffusion of knowledge, systems thinking, and improvement of mental models' (Yukl, 2002: 301).

However, according to Hamel (2000a) the twin concepts of the learning organization and continuous improvement are about getting better not about being different. Hence he regards them as outdated industrial-age concepts. In a non-linear world, he suggests, it is not knowledge that will create wealth but insight into opportunities for discontinuous innovation. While he admits that continuous improvement is better than no improvement, he contends that it is radical, non-linear innovation that is required and this can only be achieved if companies 'escape the shackles of precedent and imagine entirely novel solutions to customer needs' (2000a: 13). There is little doubt that he is correct in these latter two assertions, but it is not clear whether organizations should abandon, entirely, the concept of continuous improvement and its links with learning. Apart from the fact that many organizations have yet to embrace the concept with any conviction, in an era of very rapid change it is important that organizations are at the forefront of knowledge in its broadest sense. Additionally, the whole concept of the learning organization is about breaking with the past and creating the conditions in which innovation and change can flourish, not least by equipping employees with the requisite attitudes, knowledge and skills not only to embrace change but to initiate it. Indeed, this is the first question Hamel asks when determining whether an organization is ready, in his terms, for the 'age of revolution'

Table 12.2: Questions to help determine whether your company is ready for the 'age of revolution'

Have individuals been given the training and tools they need to become business concept innovators?

Do the metrics of your company focus as much on innovation and wealth creation as on optimization and wealth conservation?

Does your IT system support a corporate-wide electronic marketplace for innovation?

Has your organization committed itself to systematically redesigning its core management processes to make them more innovation-friendly?

Does the 'wheel of innovation' spin rapidly in your organization, or is it limited by the speed of quarterly or annual processes?

Do would-be entrepreneurs know how to design experiments around radical ideas?

Are there formal mechanisms for capturing and monitoring the learning from innovation experiments?

Does your organization get the very best talent behind the best new ideas, even when those ideas are at an early stage of development?

Is your organization explicitly managing a portfolio of ideas, a portfolio of experiments and a portfolio of ventures?

Is your organization flexible enough to design the right kind of institutional home for promising ventures?

Are you confident that your company is in charge of the transformation agenda in its industry?

Source: Hamel (2000a: 312)

and at least one further question relates to the conditions that might expect to be found in a successful learning organization (see Table 12.2).

However, whether or not the learning organization is central to the institutionalization of change within organizations, Hamel recognizes that the role of senior management will be required to change. Whereas, in the past, senior management has been required to develop strategies, in the new order its role will be to 'build an organisation that can continually spawn cool new business concepts, to design context rather than invent content' (Hamel, 2000b: 106) and to put in place rules that can create a deeply innovative organization. Central to this will be the engagement of what Hamel calls 'activists', but which sound reminiscently like intrapreneurs. According to Hamel (2000a: 204) activists are:

> ... the coolest people on the planet. They change big, complicated things with their bare hearts. They punch more than their weight. And when they fail, they fail nobly. To be an activist you need more than an agenda and a clever campaign, you need a set of values that will set you apart ...

(Hamel, 2000a: 204)

The values he suggests they espouse are honesty, compassion, humility, pragmatism and fearlessness. So, if you possess these qualities, if you have the courage to speak the truth and to challenge tradition, if you care about your colleagues and the organization for which you work, if you are prepared to work outside your comfort zone and are willing to put your job on the line, then you may well possess the qualities of the intrapreneur and be the one to lead the change in your organization. So 'chill out', your company (and your country) needs you!

A CASE EXAMPLE

Jack Welch: an 'activist' CEO

Jack Welch 'retired' on 7 September 2001 after 20 years as chairman and CEO of the General Electric Company (GE). Born in Salem in 1936, he studied chemical engineering at the Universities of Massachusetts and Illinois before joining the company in 1961 as a junior engineer at the Pittsfield plant in Massachusetts. After being there only a year, he resigned to join International Minerals and Chemicals in Skokie, Illinois. Reportedly he felt under-appreciated by his boss, stifled by the bureaucratic environment of GE and offended by the US$1000 pay rise he had received. Fortunately for GE, his line manager, Reuben Gutoff, persuaded him to stay, promising to prevent Welch from being entangled in GE bureaucracy and to create a small-company environment with big-company resources. Gutoff remained Welch's boss until the latter was elected the company's youngest vice-president in 1972, and undoubtedly the experience coloured Welch's views of how a business should be run, as

he spent much of his subsequent career, first as vice-chairman, then, from 1981 to 2001 as chairman and CEO, attempting to rid the company of the paralysis that often typifies large corporations, while harnessing its resources. He likened managing GE to running a grocery store. 'What's important at the grocery store is just as important in engines or medical systems', he is reported to have said, 'if the customer isn't satisfied, if the stuff is getting stale, if the shelf isn't right, or if the offerings aren't right, it's the same thing. You manage it like a small organization.' As a result, the company went from strength to strength under his leadership. By the time of his retirement it was the largest, and arguably the most successful, in the world. It operated in 100 countries worldwide and employed 313,000 people. Its total assets were US$495 billion and its revenue for 2001 was US$125.9 billion from its diverse services, technology and manufacturing businesses. More importantly, perhaps, the company had topped the *Financial Times*' league table as World's Most Respected Company in 1998, 1999 and 2000, and, among similar accolades, had received the *Fortune* nomination as America's Most Admired Company in 1998, 1999, 2000 and 2001.

How was all this achieved? Much has been written about how Welch removed levels from the organizational hierarchy, how he re-shaped the company through more than 600 acquisitions, how he astutely moved it into services, and how he pushed it into newly emerging markets overseas. However, first and foremost, he achieved it by making the company informal, by violating the chain of command, communicating across the organization and by treating people as if they worked for a demanding, high-profile entrepreneur rather than an anonymous large-company chief executive. Although he had to make redundant 100,000 employees in the early 1980s, he believes that every person counts and was reputed to know by sight the names and responsibilities of at least the top 1000 people at GE. During his time as chairman and CEO, he devoted 50 per cent of his time to people issues and according to him his greatest accomplishment was 'to find great people. An army of them. They are all better than most CEOs. They are big hitters, and they seem to thrive here.' They thrived because he invested in them. In 1995, he introduced the Six Sigma Program, which required the training of tens of thousands of employees; while through the company's annual Session C reviews he personally reviewed the performance of the top 3000 executives and kept under scrutiny the top 500, the purpose of these sessions being to identify future leaders, set stretching assignments, develop succession plans and decide which high-potential executives should be sent for leadership training. His emphasis on personal involvement spans the organization. Every one of his 15 direct reports (his three vice-chairmen and the heads of the company's 12 businesses) would receive a handwritten two-page evaluation of his performance at the year end, giving Welch the opportunity 'to reflect on each business'. Each business head then emulated his boss and their reports did the same. As a consequence, Welch's leadership style was continually reinforced throughout the organization.

Clearly, he had a great belief in people. He believed that 'the idea flow from the human spirit was absolutely unlimited' and that 'all you have to do is tap into that well'. To help him achieve this, he would set demanding performance targets and challenge his team to ensure that each of the company's businesses was number one or two in its global market. He is fiercely competitive but believes in rewarding effort, and skilfully used rewards to drive behaviour. However, he believes passionately in differentiation. 'You can't run these 12 businesses as if they were one institution', he is reported to have said. As a consequence, although GE might have had an overall 4 per cent target for salary increases, some salaries may have risen by 25 per cent and bonuses could have been between 20 and 70 per cent of base pay. Additionally, stock options, originally reserved for the most senior staff, were offered more broadly and, under Welch, some 27,000 employees received them; some 1200 employees, of which 800 were below the level of senior management, having received options worth over US$1 million. However, options were not handed out automatically each year and he insisted that in any one year 25 per cent of the employees should be getting them for the first time. What this meant 'is that everyone is getting the rewards,' he said, 'not just a few of us'. However, he did not just use fiscal rewards to motivate people. He would promote people from within the organization, often passing over more senior or experienced managers. Additionally, he would make unannounced visits each week to plants and offices, arrange 'last minute' luncheon appointments with managers several layers below him and send handwritten notes to people. On one occasion, when one manager reputedly confessed to him that his wife had threatened to throw him out of the house if he messed up on a presentation, Welch arranged for her to receive a dozen roses and a bottle of Dom Perignon together with a handwritten note saying, 'Your husband did a fantastic job today. We're sorry we put him and you through this for a couple of weeks.'

In his 1981 report to share owners, Welch outlined his vision for GE. He wanted General Electric to be perceived as:

> . . . a unique, high-spirited, entrepreneurial enterprise, a company known around the world for its unmatched level of excellence. We want General Electric to be the most profitable, highly diversified company on earth,

with world quality leadership in every one of its product lines.

Undoubtedly he did not achieve all this by himself. Rather, he gathered around him a remarkable team, possibly the most talent-rich management team in the world. Even so, it was Welch who led and managed GE to unprecedented prosperity and for his remarkable achievements, he was nominated in November 1999 as *Industryweek*'s CEO of the 1990s.

Case example exercise

Review the above case example and complete the following exercises.

1. Welch suggests that a large business should be managed like a small grocery store. Compare the way Welch ran GE with the way Michael Pritchard runs the Spar Foodliner at Treherbert (see Chapter 2). Identify any similarities. What can you learn about running a large organization from the way Pritchard runs his store?

2. Compare Welch with Ralph Halpern (see the Burton Group case example in this chapter). Identify any similarities and consider the extent to which they both meet Hamel's activist criteria.

3. Having studied the cases, how would you go about (re-)creating an entrepreneurial culture in any large organization in which you might be employed, either now or in the future?

Chapter Review

➡ Entrepreneurship is developmental while intrapreneurship is restorative, intended to counter stagnation in established organizations and regain their entrepreneurial drive.

➡ While most large organizations are realizing that they need to be more innovative and flexible than in the past, there are numerous obstacles to the development of an intrapreneurial culture. These include:
  – the inherent nature of large impersonal, hierarchical organizations
  – the need for short-run profits
  – the lack of entrepreneurial talents
  – inappropriate compensation methods.

➡ The theory of intrapreneurship development suggests that it is necessary to:
  – commit the organization
  – determine the corporate entrepreneurship model
  – develop an intrapreneurial culture
  – identify intrapreneurial talent
  – reward intrapreneurs
  – develop an identifiable system for administering and evaluating projects.

➡ Changing the culture of any organization is not easy as people oppose change. To change an organization it is necessary to overcome the barriers to change and to:
  – create a sense of urgency and need for change
  – prepare people to adjust to change
  – help people deal with the pain of change

– provide opportunities for early success

– keep people informed

– empower people to innovate

– demonstrate continued commitment to change.

➡ Change needs to be institutionalized and seen as a process for continuous improvement.

Quick Revision

(Answers at the end of this section)

1. Which of the following is not one of the barriers to intrapreneurship with the corporate culture (i.e. which is the odd one out)?
   (a) the inherent nature of large organizations
   (b) the need for short-run profits
   (c) the market
   (d) the lack of entrepreneurial talent
   (e) inappropriate compensation methods

2. Innovation is necessarily a bottom-up process that can only work when supported from the top. Is this:
   (a) true
   (b) false?

3. Is intrapreneurship in the public sector about:
   (a) growth and efficiency
   (b) showing courage and imagination
   (c) both?

4. According to the Lewin (1951) model of change, the change process involves freezing the organization, changing it and then unfreezing it. Is this:
   (a) true
   (b) false?

5. What, according to Yukl (2002), is the enemy of learning?
   (a) tradition
   (b) secrecy
   (c) learning

Answers to Quick Revision: 1–c; 2–a; 3–c; 4–b; 5–b

Learning Style Activities

➡ **Activist:** Think of an organization known to you that needs to be more intrapreneurial? What is its present state?

➡ **Reflector:** From your understanding of intrapreneurship, identify the type of organization that needs to be created and the barriers that are preventing the organization from achieving this.

➡ **Theorist:** Consider the theories of intrapreneurship and organizational change and how they may assist you in changing the organization so that it may become more intrapreneurial.

➡ **Pragmatist:** Develop and implement an action plan to change the organization, so that it becomes more intrapreneurial. Monitor the results.

Reading

Connor, D.R. (1995) *Managing at the Speed of Change: How Resilient Managers Succeed and Prosper Where Others Fail.* New York: Villard Books.

DeSarbo, W., I.C. MacMillan and D.L. Day (1987) Criteria for Corporate Venturing: Importance Assigned by Managers. *Journal of Business Venturing* **2** (4), 329–50.

Drucker, P.F. (1985) Innovation and Entrepreneurship: Practice and Principles. London: Pan Books.

Duncan, W.J. (1988) Intrapreneurship and the Reinvention of the Corporation. *Business Horizons* **31** (3), 16–21.

Halpern, R. (1987) *Creating Wealth for the People.* Cardiff: Cardiff Business School.

Hamel, G. (2000a) *Leading the Revolution.* Boston MA: Harvard Business School Press.

Hamel, G. (2000b) Reinvent your Company. *Fortune*, 12 June, 105–20.

Hisrich, R.D. and M.P. Peters (1992) *Entrepreneurship: Starting, Developing and Managing a New Enterprise.* Homewood IL: Irwin.

Jackson, S. and R. Schuler (2001) Turning Knowledge into Business Advantage, in Pickford, J. (ed.) *Mastering Management 2.0.* London: Prentice Hall.

Jacobs, T. (1999) Punctuated Equilibrium: The Burton Group, in Johnson, G. and K. Scholes, *Exploring Corporate Strategy.* Hemel Hempstead: Prentice Hall.

Jick, T.D. (1993) *Implementing Change.* Burr Ridge IL: Irwin.

Jones-Evans, D. (2000) Intrapreneurship, in Carter, S. and D. Jones-Evans (eds) *Enterprise and Small Business: Principles, Practice and Policy.* Harlow: Prentice Hall.

Kanter, R.M. (1983) *The Change Masters: Corporate Entrepreneurs at Work.* London: Unwin Paperbacks.

Kirby, D.A., P. Livett, P. and J. Rindl (1991) Developing an Enterprise Approach to Local Government: Innovative Methods of Service Delivery in the Public Sector in England. *Proceedings of the ENDEC World Conference on Entrepreneurship and Innovative Change.* Singapore: Nanyasng Technological University.

Lewin, K. (1951) *Field Theory in Social Science.* New York: Harper and Row.

Machiavelli, N. (1999) *The Prince.* Harmondsworth: Penguin Books.

Macrae, N. (1976) The Coming Entrepreneurial Revolution. *Economist*, Christmas edn.

Maurer, R. (1996) *Beyond the Wall of Resistance: Unconventional Strategies that Build Support for Change.* Austin TX: Bard Books.

Peters, T. (1987) *Thriving on Chaos: Handbook for a Management Revolution.* London: Pan Books Ltd.

Pinchot, G. (1985) *Intrapreneuring.* New York: Harper and Row.

Ross, J.E. and D. Unwalla (1986) Who is an Intrapreneur? *Personnel* **63** (12), 45–9.

Senge, P.M. (1990) *The Fifth Discipline: The Art and Practice of the Learning Organisation.* New York: Doubleday Currency.

Sigsworth, E.M. (1992) The Burton Group PLC, in Hast, A. (ed.) *International Directory of Company Histories: Volume V.* London: St James Press.

Sinetar, M. (1985) Entrepreneurs, Chaos and Creativity—Can Creative People Really Survive Large Company Structure? *Sloan Management Review* **26** (2), 57–62.

Still, C. (1989) Eliminating the Barriers to Making Public Enterprise, in Dash, J. and T. Richardson (eds) *Making Public Enterprise Enterprising.* Canberra: Australian National University.

Yukl, G. (2002) *Leadership in Organisations.* Upper Saddle River NJ: Prentice Hall Inc.

Index